BERKSHIRE COUNTY: A CULTURAL HISTORY

CHURCH AT TYRINGHAM

*Photograph by Clemens Kalischer*

# BERKSHIRE COUNTY

## A Cultural History

by  RICHARD  D.  BIRDSALL

NEW HAVEN

YALE UNIVERSITY PRESS

1959

*For Sophia Lyman Birdsall*

# PREFACE

*Ille terrarum mihi praeter omnes angulus ridet*
HORACE

TO THE PRESENT AGE, when the communications revolution has virtually obliterated space, the feeling of regional identity which existed in areas like Berkshire County, Massachusetts, in the early nineteenth century has taken on a certain quaintness and unreality. Further, the province as a cultural unit has often been neglected of late, the victim of the stronger loyalty of modern men, historians included, to the broad concept of the nation state. For historians concerned with more immediate economic and political considerations, cultural phenomena like the religious and educational traditions of a particular locality have seemed at once too vague and too insignificant to merit close attention.

On a cultural level, however, certain severely defined areas like Berkshire remained remarkably self-contained prior to the Civil War. Economically and politically, Berkshirites were acting very much like their neighbors in western Massachusetts in the century before 1861; but morally, intellectually, aesthetically, they considered themselves rather special— and in many ways they were. By acknowledging the cultural validity of such a distinctive region as Berkshire and by studying the results of the accent on distinctiveness, we may see American culture in the antebellum century for what it was —an agglomeration of cultural units from Berkshire and Cambridge in New England to Natchez and the Yazoo country in the South.

Preoccupied with such considerations, the cultural historian may, it is hoped, be excused if he assigns only a subordinate role to politics and economics. He cannot, of course, be ignorant of them, and his recognition of their influence on culture must be clearly implicit in his study. The "forms which subjective experience takes" are, after all, never totally divorced from their political and economic groundwork, and any cultural historian who lets himself forget that fact risks falling back into the genteel tradition of Culture with a capital *C*. Yet, for the most part, his concern with the "cultural creation" of which Will Durant speaks, justifies him in taking for granted the "social order." Indeed, the possibility of straining out the "embellishment of life" for separate emphasis is perhaps suggested in Durant's admirable definition of civilization as "social order promoting cultural creation. Four elements compose it: economic provision, political organization, moral traditions, and the pursuit of knowledge and the arts. It begins where chaos and insecurity end. For when fear is overcome, curiosity and constructiveness are free, and man passes by natural impulse toward the understanding and embellishment of life."

For guiding my own free curiosity with both encouragement and criticism I am particularly indebted to Henry Steele Commager, Samuel Rezneck, and George Haines, IV. I wish also to thank the Ford Foundation, whose generous support has made publication possible. Parts of Chapters 2, 9, and 10 have appeared in the *Boston Public Library Quarterly, The New England Quarterly,* and the *American Quarterly,* respectively. I am indebted to these journals for permission to use the material here. And finally, I should like to acknowledge a genuine debt to the staffs of the American Antiquarian Society, the Berkshire Athenaeum, and the Massachusetts Historical Society for their patience, and to my wife for her constructive impatience.

R. D. B.

*New London, Connecticut*
*January 1959*

# CONTENTS

Preface                                        vii

1. A Place by Itself                            1
2. A Wilderness into a Paradise                17
3. Heads Full of Divinity                      33
4. A Great Deal of Dissent                     75
5. Character Factories                        103
6. A Dishonor to Be Ignorant                  152
7. The Right to Scribble                      180
8. The Immaculate Profession                  214
9. New England Character                      259
10. The American Lake District                323
Sources                                       380
Index                                         393

A map of Berkshire County faces page 18. Adapted from David Dudley Field, *A History of the County of Berkshire, Massachusetts,* Pittsfield, 1829.

# ABBREVIATIONS

BA: Berkshire Athenaeum.

Beecher, *Star Papers:* Henry Ward Beecher, *Star Papers or Experiences of Art and Nature,* New York, 1855.

DC: Dwight Collection, in the possession of Henry W. Dwight of Stockbridge, Mass.

Dewey, *Autobiography: Autobiography and Letters of Orville Dewey,* ed. Mary E. Dewey, Boston, 1883.

Field, *History of Berkshire: A History of the County of Berkshire, Massachusetts by Gentlemen in the County,* ed. David Dudley Field, Pittsfield, 1829.

Hawthorne, *American Notebooks: The American Notebooks by Nathaniel Hawthorne,* ed. Randall Stewart, New Haven, Yale University Press, 1932.

Holland, *Western Massachusetts:* Josiah G. Holland, *History of Western Massachusetts,* 2 vols. Springfield, 1855.

Hopkins, *Works: The Works of Samuel Hopkins, with a Memoir of His Life and Character,* ed. Edwards A. Park, 3 vols. Boston, 1852.

Leland, *Writings: The Writings of the Late Elder John Leland Including Some Events in His Life, Written by Himself,* ed. L. F. Greene, New York, 1845.

*Life and Letters of Sedgwick: Life and Letters of Catharine Maria Sedgwick,* ed. Mary E. Dewey, New York, 1871.

MC: Minot Collection, Massachusetts Historical Society.

MHS: Massachusetts Historical Society.

NYPL: New York Public Library.

SGW: Samuel Gray Ward Collection, Houghton Library, Harvard.

Smith, *History of Pittsfield:* Joseph E. A. Smith, *The History of Pittsfield, Massachusetts,* 2 vols. Boston and Springfield, 1869–76.

SP: Sedgwick Papers, Massachusetts Historical Society.

TWW: Thomas Wren Ward Collection, Massachusetts Historical Society.

# Chapter 1. A PLACE BY ITSELF

TO GOVERNOR FRANCIS BERNARD, signing the act of incorporation in the spring of 1761, Berkshire may well have seemed just another county in Massachusetts—the westernmost and the wildest, but otherwise undistinguished. Certainly the governor had never traveled far enough west in his state to cross the boundary into the new county. From the point of view of political expediency such a trip was patently unnecessary; to satisfy idle curiosity, it was impractical and indeed unthinkable. Few motives other than missionary fervor or economic need could have goaded a man into making the five-day journey over the rocky, uneven road and across what then loomed as a formidable mountain barrier. The settlers who did manage to take their horses or their solid-wheeled farm carts over the barrier and build their cabins in the Berkshire wilderness found themselves inhabitants of an almost isolated region largely self-contained and geographically independent of both the Yankee and the Yorker. Dominated by neither, the county in its first century was to qualify in many ways as a discreet region.

As manageable units for historical research, regions have been variously defined in administrative, geographical, and cultural terms, and for Berkshire County between 1761 and 1861 all three definitions had a certain validity. As an administrative unit, Berkshire, like all the counties in Massachusetts, increased in importance during and after the Revolution, when the state government began to conceive of it as a useful instrument for the coercion of recalcitrant towns.[1] As a geographical entity, only the Cape and the

1. Oscar and Mary Flug Handlin, *Commonwealth: A Study of the Role of Government in the American Economy: Massachusetts 1774–1861* (New York, New York University Press, 1947), p. 101.

1

Island counties in New England surpassed Berkshire for unity and self-containment. But its real significance as a region seems to lie in its special cultural flavor, made possible in part by its geographical insularity—the predominance of a neo-Calvinist orthodox theology in the early years, the harboring of a notable native literature in its later years, and the prevalence of a marked, if changing, provincial feeling throughout its first century of growth.

"Unlike most counties," observed Mark Hopkins in 1844, "Berkshire, having a peculiar geological formation, is a place by itself, separated from the rest of the world by natural boundaries; it has also been a good deal secluded; and while we have been a New England people, our business intercourse has been with New York. Each of these circumstances has had its influence upon us, so that between us and our fellow-citizens of the eastern part of the State, there is a perceptible difference." [2]

Shut off from the Connecticut River and eastern Massachusetts by the Berkshire Barrier, and from the Dutch Hudson River settlements by the Taconic Mountains, the area indeed merited its Indian name *Housatonic* ("Beyond the Mountain Place"). Berkshire County proper consisted of a strip of land nineteen miles wide running the full fifty-mile width of Massachusetts from Connecticut on the south to Vermont on the north and extending westward to the New York border. The imposing Berkshire Barrier, a range of mountains stretching a distance of thirty miles between the Connecticut and the Housatonic Rivers, mutely proclaimed that nature had not intended this western region to be a part of Massachusetts. Although not impenetrable, the Barrier, with its Hoosac Mountain peaks rising as high as twenty-four hundred feet, presented a considerable obstacle to the would-be traveler, and as late as 1838 Hawthorne

    2. *The Berkshire Jubilee Celebrated at Pittsfield Massachusetts August 22 and 23, 1844,* ed. E. P. Little (Albany, 1845), p. 56.

remarked on the "terrible bare, bleak" mountain road. "Think," he exclaimed, "of riding in a stage coach through the clouds!" [3] Earlier, Timothy Dwight had noticed a valley in Egremont "of rich soil and verdure . . . In this retired spot stood a few humble dwellings, which appeared, as if every storm, both of the natural and the political world would, pass over them without disturbing their peaceful inhabitants. No spot has presented to my eye more forcibly the idea of being sequestered from intrusion and bustle. It was a valley of Switzerland." [4]

Even after 1842, when the new Western Railroad was making regular trips over the Barrier, a psychological barrier between east and west remained. Berkshire natives liked to regard themselves as living in a place apart, and for many years easterners continued to think of the county as a remote frontier. After 1842 the Massachusetts Medical Society met only with great reluctance in Berkshire, and Harvard authorities found it an ideal spot for the rustication of an unruly student.[5] Emerson, when writing to his friend Samuel Ward, a littérateur and gentleman farmer in Lenox, whimsically called him "a prisoner in Berkshire" and spoke of his occasional trips to Boston as "escapes." [6]

From the west Berkshire was only slightly more accessible than from the east. The Taconics formed a western mountain wall higher than the Berkshire Barrier but only five miles thick at their base and pierced by passes at an altitude of nine hundred feet. Between the two mountain ridges stretched Berkshire County proper, consisting geographically of two parts. Then, as now, the northern area, drained by the

3. Hawthorne, *American Notebooks* (Yale University Press, 1932), p. 32.
4. *Travels in New-England and New-York* (4 vols. New Haven, 1821–22), *4*, 11.
5. Seth Webb to Henry D. Sedgwick, October 22, 1842; SP.
6. August 23, 1847; SGW.

impetuous, north-flowing Hoosic River, could boast the most rugged terrain in the county—the "rude, rough, rocky, stumpy, ferny" heights where Hawthorne [7] walked; and the towns of Williamstown, Adams, and Cheshire lay tucked into narrow valleys under the protecting shadow of Mount Greylock.

Extending southward were the wider and smoother valleys of southern Berkshire, drained by the sluggish and meandering Housatonic. This river, wrote Henry Ward Beecher during a summer spent in Lenox, "winds, in great circuits, all through the valley, carrying willows and alders with it wherever it goes. The horizon, on every side, is piled and terraced with mountains. Abrupt and isolated mountains bolt up here and there over the whole stretch of plain, covered with evergreens." [8] From Mount Greylock in the north to October and Monument Mountains in the southern section, the remnants of a medial mountain range dominated the scene. In valleys between these scattered mountains, Stockbridge, Lenox, and Pittsfield were gradually to spread out—each nearly encircled by hills.

Given its remote, frontier position, Berkshire County ought to have become, in Frederick Jackson Turner's scheme of history, a liberal if not a radical community. In actuality, old rejected ideas were being driven west along with the new, unwelcome ones, and in Berkshire the Turner thesis was, in certain fields, turned inside out. Jonathan Edwards would probably have preferred Boston to the Stockbridge Mission Station of which he assumed the direction in 1751, but Bostonians could tolerate his orthodox ideas no more willingly than did the Northampton Arminians who were putting him out. He turned westward, therefore, and planted his rigid theology in Berkshire—in a soil so fertile that his

7. Hawthorne, *American Notebooks,* p. 43.
8. Beecher, *Star Papers,* p. 178.

doctrine flourished for forty years from its first sowing, and the conservatism bred of that orthodoxy for many decades more.

Cut off from the "free and catholick air" of Cambridge and the other seaboard towns by nearly one hundred and fifty miles of rugged, back-country terrain, Berkshirites were to remain for almost a hundred years more or less resistant to the innovating ideas of Boston Unitarianism and the impacts of Irish immigration and a dynamic economic life. Even in 1810, after four turnpike companies had completed roads into the county, Timothy Dwight's description of Egremont held true for most of the Berkshire hill towns. With the world of real experience seldom extending in any direction by more than a twenty-mile radius, the eighteenth-century Berkshire farmer became conservative from ignorance as much as from conviction.

Nor did the fact that farming provided an almost universal means of subsistence encourage a broader outlook. Though only in the northern hill towns were farmers obliged to engage in a constant struggle for mere survival, everywhere in Berkshire the annual crop was of the greatest economic importance and needed to be tended with traditional, time-proven methods. Nature would not tolerate a farmer inclined to sportive experiments; and not until the nineteenth century with the arrival of such gentleman farmers as Elkanah Watson and Thomas Melvill did an innovating spirit smile on Berkshire agriculture. Even then, the plain dirt farmer reacted to any proposed change in methods, however manifest the improvement, with an ingrained resistance.

To the native conservatism, fostered by isolation and by the absence of any broad margins of wealth and leisure, the Edwardsean heritage added a religious set of mind which itself tended to encourage a fundamentally conservative outlook. If, as at least one critic has suggested, a conservative can be defined as one who believes in original sin, then Edwards, by making that doctrine essential to his analysis of the human condition, actively discouraged any generally liberal position. Having once concluded that social problems were only the outward expression of man's inner sinfulness, and that solutions could be effected solely by internal reform, the Berkshire intellectual was skeptical regarding the outcome of liberal programs of social readjustment. The main problem was to be solved not by intelligence but by appeals to conscience, and new ideas and institutions were greeted with suspicion unless they promised a contribution to moral reform.

In the basic orientation of Berkshire provincialism, then, faith was emphasized over reason and tradition over experimentation, and Berkshirites, preoccupied with satisfying minimum human requirements, had no desire to risk everything in the pursuit of some liberal Utopia. They deserved a place among proverbial plain-living, high-thinking New Englanders, only granting the identification of high thinking with moral tone rather than with intellectual caliber. Berkshire schools, far from being emporiums of intellect, were self-acknowledged "character factories." Still, if the tradition was narrow, it ran deep, and if it failed to produce any intellectual movements of startling originality, it did produce men of integrity and moral force. Supreme Court Justice Stephen J. Field and the Reverend Mark Hopkins were only two of the county's most eminent sons who made their mark in the American scene through strength of character rather than creative thinking. Mark Hopkins may have contributed nothing to the history of American philosophy, but he constantly demonstrated an ability "to see things together."

Such rural strength must have stemmed in part from that sense of identity and solidity which belongs to any individual living in a traditional society. But it must also have come from the broadly human perspective encouraged in rural intellectual life both by the lack of specialization and by the high degree of concreteness and low level of abstraction inescapable in a society like the Berkshire villages, where the few inhabitants met one another frequently and face to face. Certainly the simplicity of life and of social problems in Berkshire was such that positive personalities could readily develop.

Against the background of rural conservatism, Berkshire's often radical political life stood out as something of a paradox. Such radicalism was, of course, a fairly widespread phenomenon on the American frontier, but it did not penetrate deeply enough into the placid, traditional cultural life to cause much ferment. The Reverend Thomas Allen, greatest of the Berkshire political liberals, almost invariably took a traditional stand in matters of theology and church polity; and seeing no evidence to challenge the conservative view of human nature, he freely admitted "that every man by nature has the seeds of tyranny deeply implanted within him, so that nothing short of Omnipotence can eradicate them." [9] His liberalism was thus inclined to be a purely pragmatic affair rather lacking in theoretical analysis. Like nearly all Berkshire's radical political leaders, he seems to have arrived at his conclusions after listening to the discontented mutterings of poor hill-town farmers and as a result of memorizing Paine, Locke, and Jefferson. Falling back on faith and feeling, he made little attempt at a rational dissection of his beliefs. Indeed, experience and not reason was the primary root of radicalism almost everywhere in Berkshire, and the major Republican organ, the Pittsfield *Sun,* was more notable for the fervor of its sentiments than for the enlightenment of its political message. Probably the sole exception to this unintellectual approach was William Jarvis, the county's only real political philosopher and spokesman for Jeffersonian

9. "Petition of the town of Pittsfield to the General Assembly Met at Watertown, May 29, 1776," Massachusetts Archives 181.50, quoted in Smith, *History of Pittsfield, 1,* 352.

democracy. And Jefferson himself found fault with Jarvis when the latter revealed in his book, *The Republican,* a too conservative estimate of the position of the judiciary in government.

As for the Berkshire yeoman, he could on occasion be as politically radical as some of his leaders. In 1786 and 1787 he opened his arms to the men involved in Shays' rebellion. And later, if he happened to be a member of a minority sect, he fought the good fight for religious freedom with the Baptist John Leland as his hero. But in neither case did his action stem from other than *ad hoc* considerations. Shays' men were simply giving effective expression to economic grievances which he shared, and Elder John Leland was merely articulating for him his indignation at being taxed to support a church to which he did not belong. Even Leland, for all his Jeffersonianism in matters of religious freedom and judicial reform, never accepted Jefferson's faith in education. "That righteous Abel possessed . . . true piety, is certain," he proclaimed, "and who can imagine that schools, academies and colleges, were in existence in the days of Abel." [10] Such an emphasis on the heart over the head prevented Leland from ever developing into a coherent liberal. With his haphazard, often quixotic, ideas of reforming the status quo, he revealed both the narrowness and the inconsistencies typical of many later agrarian radicals. Oliver Wendell Holmes may well have been thinking of these unintellectual radicals of a subsequent decade in Berkshire when he described the virtuous rural citizen as "temperate in material things, and in things intellectual, totally abstinent." [11]

10. Leland, *Writings,* p. 492.

11. "Love of Nature," lyceum lecture reported in the *Commonwealth,* January 1, 1852, quoted in Eleanor M. Tilton, *Amiable Autocrat: A Biography of Dr. Oliver Wendell Holmes* (New York, Henry Schuman, 1947), p. 207.

Political radicalism in the lives of most Berkshirites, then, was merely a surface phenomenon, like a ripple or swirling eddy on the usually sluggish Housatonic. Beneath their political fervor they harbored an iron resistance to cultural change—a resistance which became one of the signs of a genuine, if rudimentary, provincialism within the county. Nowhere in America did provincialism develop in the strikingly definitive manner of such European regions as the Provence or Andalusia. Endowed with the natural American desire to move onward and upward, every farmer was at heart more a small-time entrepreneur than a soil-loving peasant, and the Berkshirite could never become, even in Massachusetts, the conversation piece which the Yorkshireman became in England. In fact, the term regionalism for the American urban mind eventually came to mean not a significant social force but a sentimental cult. The old home town emerged as a good place to come *from*, and the boys who loved it enough to stay there were assumed to be failures —swamp Yankees or mountain folk.

No wonder that amid sentimental maunderings about the old home town the authentic cultural identity of regions like Berkshire County became lost in indiscriminate wordiness. After all, provincialism by definition requires a standard of comparison, an outside point of reference. In Berkshire the seeds of provincialism may have been sown in isolation, but the actual flowering occurred only as the trend toward integration with Massachusetts and with the nation as a whole began to be reflected in a concurrent trend toward cultural cosmopolitanism. Only when improved roads encouraged both immigration and emigration, and when capital and goods began to travel back and forth with some frequency over the county borders, did conflicts develop in which Berkshirites felt obliged to take a stand and through which their provincialism became recognizable as such.

Their consciousness of being different could only evolve fully when forces reaching out to them from Boston and from New York City gave them something to be different from.

Intrinsic in Berkshire provincialism, however, was that indefinable sense of place which is the very flavor of local history. As a recent native of Berkshire has remarked, "no hills amid which people have lived long can be considered merely as geography, nor even chiefly as geography. They color the life which goes on in their valleys and on their slopes, and that life in turn colors them." [12] Certainly during the entire first century of Berkshire's existence as a county, the surrounding hills and valleys served as far more than a scenic backdrop for the human drama. Often they were woven into the fabric of the culture, and throughout the period the literary and epistolary output overflowed with enthusiastic comments on the countryside. When, in a letter from Lenox in 1839, Fanny Kemble described the natural beauties which lay all around her, she was speaking the thoughts of countless visitors and natives. To her eyes the Berkshires presented

> a landscape that combines every variety of beauty,— valleys, in the hollow of which lie small lakes, glittering like sapphires; uplands, clothed with grain-fields and orchards, and studded with farm-houses, each the centre of its own free domain; hills, clothed from base to brow with every variety of forest tree; and woods, some wild, tangled, and all but impenetrable, others clear of under-brush, shady, moss-carpeted and sun-chequered; noble masses of granite rock, great slabs of marble . . . clear mountain brooks and a full, free-flowing, sparkling river; —all this, under a cloud varied sky, such as generally

12. Walter Pritchard Eaton, introduction to *The Berkshire Hills*, Federal Writers Project, W.P.A., for Massachusetts (New York, Funk and Wagnalls, 1939), p. xi.

canopies mountain districts, the sunset glories of which
are often magnificent.[13]

That Berkshire culture owed much to its hills is convincingly
attested to by the many occasions on which they become the
subject matter for literature. Early in the nineteenth century
they inspired Bryant's "Monument Mountain." Later, Melville was to dedicate *Pierre* "To Greylock's Most Excellent
Majesty."

And Henry Ward Beecher summed up Berkshire's beauty
with a flourish when he wrote: "From Salisbury to Williamstown, and then to Bennington in Vermont, there stretches
a county of valleys, lakes and mountains, that is yet to be
as celebrated as the lake-district of England and the hill-
country of Palestine." [14] For the natives of Berkshire, Beecher
was by no means overstating the facts. Their love for their
hills and valleys gave them a feeling of solidarity and separateness which has carried over even into the twentieth
century. The simpler Berkshire folk, whom neither time nor
ability permitted to write encomiums, expressed their pride
through their Berkshire Agricultural Society and more particularly in such organizations as the Laurel Hill Society
which, when founded in 1853, became the first village improvement society in America. "We mean to work," said
society members, "till every street shall be graded, every
side-walk shaded, every noxious weed eradicated, every water-
course laid and perfected, and every nook and corner beau-
tified,—in short, till Art combined with Nature shall have
rendered our town the most beautiful and attractive spot in
our ancient commonwealth." [15] As the nineteenth century

13. Frances Anne Kemble, *Records of Later Life* (3 vols. London,
1882), *1*, 259.
14. Beecher, *Star Papers*, p. 181.
15. "Statement of the Annual Meeting of the Laurel Hill Association,
1855," quoted in H. M. Plunkett, "The Evolution of Beautiful Stockbridge," *New England Magazine*, new ser. 25 (1901–02), 210.

advanced and communities became more settled and prosperous, town dwellers increasingly found leisure time to
devote to civic development, and when Fanny Kemble returned to Lenox in June 1876 she found it "not so much
altered as improved. Sidewalks and small patches of grass
or turf are tidily kept and trimmed, the trees have grown
and spread till the place is quite embowered in them, and
all round the village in every direction handsome country
houses are growing up on the hillsides. It is a very charming
place." [16]

Eventually, in the course of the county's history, Mount
Greylock and the Pittsfield Elm became symbols for the
Berkshirites' pride of place, just as the Westminster Catechism had become a symbol of their conservative theology.
By the turn of the century they were well on their way to
provincialism, with all the virtues and faults which the term
implies. In their determined opposition to Boston, in their
firm attachment to institutions and ways which they considered unique, in their rustic, unpolished manner, they
could simultaneously stifle desirable growth in some directions and actively encourage creativity in other fields. Even
Mark Hopkins admitted that isolation did not necessarily
assure perfection. "Seclusion is not always connected with
innocence and simplicity. On the contrary there may often
be found in such situations, ignorance, and narrowness, and
inveterate prejudice." [17] Certainly would-be reformers from
the outside must have found Berkshire provincialism mad-
deningly narrow-minded at times, but the alternative to
provincialism in Massachusetts would have been centralization around the capital, and thus probably slow death at
the extremities. By holding aloof and refusing either to take
advice or to accept complete integration, Berkshirites may
have set their educational system back twenty-five years, but

16. *Further Records* (2 vols. London, 1890), *1*, 306.
17. *The Berkshire Jubilee,* p. 56.

they also managed to publish newspapers of spirit and freshness and, in their creative writing, to bypass Boston's slavish
imitation of the English in the pursuit of a genuinely native
literature.

But even during the years when Berkshire provincials
were at their most outspoken, their cherished separateness
was gradually beginning to disappear. The population was
increasing, a diversified economy was developing, and by the
1840's the railroads were carrying the more ambitious young
men of the county off to Boston and New York. Berkshirites,
in spite of themselves, were being integrated with the rest
of the population of Massachusetts, not to mention New
England and the nation; and the identity of their county as
an independent and inimitable region was fading. The full
realization of the threatening engulfment must have come
to them rather abruptly in the early 1840's—probably
brought home by the penetration of the railroad from the
east in 1842—and their intellectual leaders responded with
an effort to restore artificially the spontaneous phenomenon
which was dying.

The result was a kind of "second provincialism," spawned
at a jubilee in 1844 and destined for a longevity which
would very likely have surprised its sires. As it turned out, the
very industrialism which was destroying Berkshire as a self-
contained region was causing various emigrant sons to desire its preservation, and from their feelings of sentiment
and nostalgia this second provincialism derived its real power.
They wanted to find in the Berkshire of the 1840's and 50's
the Berkshire of their youth—a region of pure morals, un-
contaminated by the city's commercial values, and of creative
rural culture, untroubled by either industrialism or the social
ferment of Jacksonian democracy. Like most city-dwelling
Americans of the era who were faced with a perplexing
social scene in which the slavery question, economic insecurity, and Roman Catholicism all posed threats, they

wanted to rediscover the solid and changeless values associated in their minds with rural simplicity and to regain the old sense of belonging.

The second Berkshire provincialism came thus as a conservative movement in a period of strain and represented an aspect of that powerful mythology growing up around the more general conception of a New England character. Within the county it flowered almost by accident into a golden age of artistic production. The Jubilee may not have restored a lost integrity, but the enthusiasms engendered there did achieve for Berkshire a reputation as an American Arcadia, and for a time it served as a kind of rural salon to which writers like Beecher, Holmes, Melville, and Hawthorne came to work. Their presence made the county a culturally important region for some fifteen years longer, but by the early 1860's they had all returned to Boston or New York, and the dying gasps of regionalism were becoming unmistakable. Sentimentality could not breathe life into a ghost.

In the last analysis, of course, provincialism in Berkshire during the first hundred years was simply a repeated pattern woven into the highly colored fabric of the county's history, and to attempt to employ it as an exclusive organizing principle would be to tell a story as narrow, and possibly as bigoted, as the provincialism itself occasionally proved to be. Berkshirites were not always recalcitrant, nor always conscious of being different. Looked at in broad outline, Berkshire history was marked by the same shifting emphases— from religious to secular—which were generally apparent throughout the country. For this reason, events taking place in the county between 1761 and 1861 may be divided, with a minimum of artificiality, into three periods, one of them leading into the next and all of them revealing not only the pervasive provincial traits but the representative ones as well.

In the early years, when religion comprised the very core of cultural life, a listing of the most respected and productive figures in the county reads like a virtual roll call of the creators of the "New Divinity": Jonathan Edwards, Samuel Hopkins, Stephen West. Then, in the first decade of the nineteenth century, came the splitting of the Pittsfield Church by party politics, the establishment of the Berkshire Agricultural Society, and the founding of Lenox Academy; and vital energies, flowing into more practical and secular channels, produced the Berkshire Medical Institution, the Berkshire Gymnasium, the Berkshire Law Library, and the Pittsfield *Sun*. In the late eighteenth century, Berkshire's proudest architectural monument had been the Bulfinch church in Pittsfield. In the early nineteenth, Isaac Damon's County Court House and the Lenox Academy building ranked as the most important architectural additions, and the leading figures of the community were the scientist and educator Chester Dewey, the editor Phineas Allen, the gentleman farmer Elkanah Watson, and the lawyer-politicians Ezekiel Bacon, Theodore Sedgwick, Jr., and William Jarvis.

At last, with the arrival of William Cullen Bryant in Great Barrington in 1816 and the publication of Catharine Sedgwick's *A New England Tale* in 1822, the literary fruition began. Coming thus near the end of Berkshire's first century of development, writers could find inspiration in the county's heritage; and Berkshire culture was to reach its fullest and most self-conscious expression in the satiric editorials of Asa Greene, the rustic imagery of David Hitchcock, and several of Melville's short stories—all concerning themselves, as did Bryant's poetic genius and Miss Sedgwick's homely enthusiasms, in varying degrees with the Berkshire scene. Perhaps the most significant inner tension to develop in the native Berkshire literary culture during these years was that between the homespun tradition of Hitchcock and Greene on the one hand and the proper, respectable, "refined" work of Cathar-

ine Sedgwick's later phase on the other. Hardly had Hitchcock and Greene finished instilling the earthy coarseness of
the Berkshire loam into their simple prose and verse when
Miss Sedgwick set to work writing tracts like *Live and Let
Live* and *Home* by means of which she hoped to civilize and
standardize her uncouth fellow countrymen.

After 1861 there can be little doubt that Berkshire sub-
stantially lost its distinctiveness as a region. With the disappearance of effective geographical insularity, the small-town,
middle-class citizen gradually replaced both the farmer and
the country aristocrat, and provincial values gave way to
acquisitive ones of peculiarly bourgeois stamp, more universal than regional. Berkshire County, in short, had become
culturally indistinguishable not only from the rest of Massachusetts but even from New England as a whole.

## Chapter 2. A WILDERNESS INTO A PARADISE

WHILE the middle reaches of the Connecticut and Hudson rivers had been permanently and securely settled by the end of the seventeenth century, the Housatonic Valley remained for another seventy-five years almost a *terra incognita,* where remnants of the Mohican tribe found refuge. No wonder that the Reverend Benjamin Wadsworth, en route to an Indian conference in Albany in 1694, found his encampment worth a notation in his diary: "Thrô this place runs a very curious river, the same (which some say) runs thrô Stradford; and it has, on each side, several parcels of pleasant, fertile, intervale land. . . . Ye greatest part of our road, this day, was a hideous howling wilderness. . . ." [1] The hostility of the Indians and their French allies, the near impassability of the Berkshire Barrier, and the machinations of the fur-trading Yorkers were destined to leave it a howling wilderness, at least from the white man's viewpoint, for forty years longer. Yet settlement, when it did occur, came fairly rapidly, and by 1800 civilization had triumphed over insecurity and chaos, and men were proceeding, in Durant's phrase, to the "understanding and embellishment of life."

In the early years of the 1700's, when settlers from the east first began to fight their way over the rugged Barrier, the Berkshire area became a combination of military frontier, mission station, and small-town settlements. Although Dutch fur traders had been operating in the Housatonic Valley since 1700, the first real settlers were Yankees from the western Massachusetts towns of Westfield and Northampton. In 1722

1. "Wadsworth's Journal" [record of a trip from Boston to Albany made in Aug. 1694], *Collections of the Massachusetts Historical Society,* 4th ser. (1852), *1,* 103 f.

the Massachusetts General Court granted a petition signed
by Joseph Parsons along with sixty of his Westfield brethren,
and another signed by Thomas Nash and 115 Northampton
emigrants, for two townships seven miles square in the
Housatonic Valley. With the grant went the usual requirement that they must settle in a compact, regular, and defensi-
ble way, and must reserve one lot for their minister, one for
support of the church, and one for their schoolhouse. On an
April day in 1724 Chief Konkapot and twenty other Indians
signed a deed selling their land to the state "for £460, three
barrels of cider and thirty quarts of rum." [2]

To Matthew Noble of Westfield went the distinction of
becoming the first true settler in the valley. He moved to the
Southern Housatonic Township in 1725, and enough hardy
souls followed his example so that the area was incorporated
as the town of Sheffield by 1733. At first, however, settlement
lagged. With the outbreak of war in 1754, the risks of settling
in central Berkshire discouraged most would-be emigrants
from the east. So formidable did William Williams consider
the insecurities of the region, in fact, that he constructed his
home in Pontoosuc with heavy wooden ramparts and walls
of four-inch white ash planks, and named it, significantly,
Fort Anson.[3] No one could have told him then that the events
of the next five years were to make his Berkshire castle obso-

2. *A History of the County of Berkshire, Massachusetts,* ed. David
Dudley Field (Pittsfield, Samuel W. Bush, 1829), pp. 165–70. The first
county history of its type to be written in Massachusetts, and a work
of real merit, it illustrates nicely Kant's dictum that history is based in
geography. Professor Chester Dewey of Williams College wrote most
of Part I, "A General View of the County" which includes an account
of the geology, climate, flora, and fauna, as well as a general history
with a good deal of material on social life. Part II consists of a history
of each town, usually written by the local pastor. The history is
significant not only as a pioneering work in New England county history but also as an expression of that Berkshire County local spirit
which was rooted in geographical features.

3. Smith, *History of Pittsfield, 1,* 106.

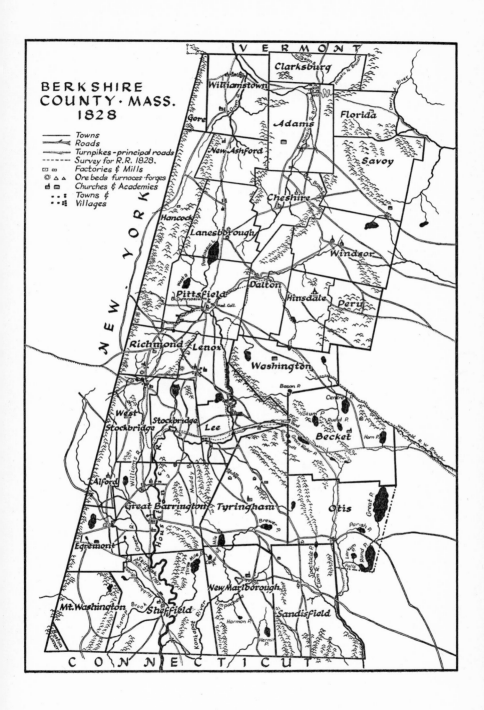

BERKSHIRE
COUNTY · MASS.
1828

Towns
Roads
Turnpikes - principal roads
Survey for R.R. 1828.
Factories & Mills
Ore beds furnaces forges
Churches & Academies
Towns &
Villages

VERMONT

Clarksburg

Williamstown

Gore

Adams

Florida

New Ashford

Savoy

Cheshire

Hancock

Lanesborough

Windsor

NEW YORK

Pittsfield

Dalton

Hinsdale

Peru

Richmond

Lenox

Washington

Bason P.

Centre

Yokum P.

Rudd P.

West Stockbridge

Stockbridge

Lee

Becket

Horn P.

Alford

Great Barrington

Tyringham

Otis

Brewer P.

Parish P.

Egremont

New Marlborough

Mt. Washington

Sheffield

Sandisfield

Harmon P.

Hermit P.

CONNECTICUT

lete. The victory of the British at Quebec in 1759 brought to an end the Indian threat in western Massachusetts, and Colonel Williams could soon write to his brother-in-law extolling the advantages of moving to Berkshire:

> Since my removal to this place, I challenge any man in the government, that has not had half the Fateague, to compare with me for Health or freedom from pain. All my Doctors Bill has been a gallopot or two of Unguent for the Itch. . . . No man or woman of but common Understanding, that ever came and got settled among us wished themselves back. The air suited them, they felt frisk, and alert, or . . . something indeard their Scituation to them; this with regard to the women. The men perceived soon the difference of the soil, and put what you would upon it, it would yeald beyond what they were acquainted with . . .[4]

By 1761 settlers had begun to stream up the Housatonic Valley and across the Barrier; and the western part of Hampshire County had been set off as the new county of Berkshire.

Between 1761 and 1790, in the brief span of one generation, thousands of peace-loving and ambitious newcomers succeeded in transforming the area from a frontier of the Old West to a settled agricultural countryside. In 1761 Berkshire County could claim only three towns and four plantations, with a total population of about 700 families.[5] By 1790 the population had increased to 30,000, and twenty-five of the thirty-one Berkshire towns had been incorporated. Such a rapid growth in one generation would indicate that the French and Indian threat to the western frontier had been sufficient to cause some build-up of population pressure in

4. William Williams to Nathaniel Dickinson, March 28, 1767; Williams Collection, BA (3 vols. typescript), 2, 260.

5. *Extracts from the Itineraries and Other Miscellanies of Ezra Stiles 1755–1794*, ed. Franklin B. Dexter (New Haven, 1916), p. 140.

the older settled areas. Not since the settling of the Connecticut Valley more than a century earlier had any significant
new acreage of desirable farm land been made so easily available to New Englanders; and with the Scots-Irish immigration
of the early 1700's, crowded conditions—already made acute
by the Puritans' prodigious natural increase—had become
intensified. Because no notable progress in agricultural tech-
niques had occurred to relieve population pressures, and because prices for even the less desirable land had become pro-
hibitive, men jumped at the chance to move to the frontier as
soon as they could safely do so.

   And from the land speculators came a further impetus to
settlement. Following the military victories over the French
in 1759, the Massachusetts General Court glimpsed a possible
source of revenue in the western frontier, and within the next
three years ten townships were auctioned off, seven of them
in Berkshire.[6] For the most part, ownership passed into the
hands of a few small groups of eastern Massachusetts and
Connecticut Valley magnates who hoped to make a profit
in reselling the land to settlers. Such men found effective if
unconscious allies in the soldiers of Sir William Pepperell
coming home to eastern Massachusetts after the Crown Point
Campaign—soldiers who talked enthusiastically of the well-
watered, heavily wooded slopes and fertile intervales they
had seen. Many of them substantiated their testimonials by
themselves emigrating to Berkshire. A few of the proprietors
followed their example, but a good number remained in the
east; and only by petitioning the legislature could settlers in
Tyringham, New Marlborough, and Pittsfield try to force
delinquent nonresident proprietors to fulfill their responsibilities to the towns.[7] In fact, the settlers' opposition to these
eastern absentee proprietors contributed to Berkshire's later

   6. *The Acts and Resolves, Public and Private, of the Province of
Massachusetts Bay* (21 vols. Boston, 1869–1922), *17*, 148 f.
   7. Ibid., *4*, 435, 664.

spirit of provincial independence with reference to Boston and all its works.[8]

Before 1761 the majority of Berkshire settlers who had braved the wilderness had come over the Barrier from Massachusetts, but at the turn of the nineteenth century these first families of the county—Nobles, Williamses, Dwights, Joneses, Allens, and Woodbridges originating in Westfield and Northampton and Deerfield—found themselves outnumbered by their new neighbors from Connecticut. During the generation after 1761 Massachusetts, Rhode Island, and New York all contributed segments of their populations to the flow of immigration, but none gave so generously as Connecticut. From that colony came not only the largest number of settlers but also most of Berkshire's later leaders, both civil and religious. Twenty-eight of the first thirty-six settled clergy were Yale men. Many of Berkshire's "mountain gods"—the Sedgwicks, the Ashleys, the Fields, the Sergeants, and the Hopkinses—had their origins in Connecticut. They and their less prominent neighbors found the southern door to Berkshire open through the Housatonic Valley and emigrated from their native colony by the hundreds.[9] To this predominantly Connecticut immigration and to the Yale education of her clergy, Berkshire cound trace, at least in part, the solid orthodoxy of her Congregational churches.

Then, in the last decade or two of the eighteenth century,

8. For a full discussion of the position of the proprietors see Roy H. Akagi, *The Town Proprietors of the New England Colonies* (Philadelphia, 1924); cf. Massachusetts Archives, 116, 117, for petitions of Berkshire settlers that lands of nonresident proprietors be taxed to support the Gospel.

9. Rising Lake Morrow, *Connecticut Influences in Western Massachusetts and Vermont* (New Haven, 1936), pp. 2–6; John Warner Barber, *Historical Collections, being a general collection of interesting facts, traditions, biographical sketches, anecdotes &c. relating to the history and antiquities of every town in Massachusetts* (Worcester, 1839), pp. 77 ff.

an increasing number of Massachusetts families traveled from Cape Cod and the seaboard counties through the barren uplands of Worcester County, past the well-settled Connecticut Valley, and on to Berkshire.[10] The greater proportion of them came seeking richer economic opportunities, but a few came as conscious dissenters from the old established religious order in search of intellectual freedom. One of these, John Bacon, disgusted by the liberal theology of his parishioners, left his pastorate at the Old South Church in 1775 to settle in Stockbridge, there to become, both on the Berkshire Bench and in the United States House of Representatives, a democratic champion of the simple but pious back-country farmer.

Most of the Rhode Islanders emigrating to Berkshire came for both religious and economic reasons; and traveling in fairly large groups, they generally chose the healthful air and well-drained fields of the then popular hill country. With his congregation of Baptists of the Six Principles, the Elder Peter Werden made the first settlement of Cheshire on the windswept summit of Stafford's Hill. Later a small group of Regular Baptists took refuge in the valley of Cheshire, and another settled the mountain town of Hancock,[11] and in Adams a group of Rhode Island Quakers found not only peace but ample water power and hence economic opportunities.

Meanwhile, the influx of Yorkers drifting eastward into the county had almost ceased. Before the middle of the eighteenth century, several Dutch farmers had brought their families over the Taconics into the fertile valleys, among them the Van Deusen and Burghardt families, who had moved to Berkshire in 1735 and subsequently ranked among the wealthiest landholders in western Massachusetts. Having settled mostly in Great Barrington, these Dutch immigrants— some of the first to resent the religious theology of Parson Hopkins—were destined in 1764 to help establish St. James

10. Holland, *Western Massachusetts,* 2, 463–619.
11. John Leland, *Some Events in the Life of John Leland Written by Himself* (Pittsfield, 1838), p. 40.

Church, the first Episcopal Church in western Massachusetts.[12]

Emigration out of Berkshire among the first generation of settlers was not large; but some did move on westward, and a few people, particularly in the hill towns, found conditions too severe and returned to their former homes. Yet even though they faced difficulties and discomforts, the pride of being the first settlers of the place provided motive enough to keep at least some of the new Berkshirites from moving on.

> We have not only had to endure the scoffs, flouts, and reproaches of the part of the people we moved from among [*wrote one of the founders of Cheshire, Joseph Bennet*], but we had the sympathy of sorrow and affection, on the other part add to this our coming such a long and tedious journey through so many difficulties that attended it, into a wild wilderness country and there set down without either friend or neighbor anigh us and to undergo all hardships that befell us, bear them we must for we have nowhere to go for relief. Thus by our own hardships, frugality and industry we were the first that brought forward this place.[13]

Indeed, a number of the new settlers considered Berkshire an ideal home, probably because, like that famous French traveler, La Rochefoucauld-Liancourt, they saw in the valley region "a continued tract of beautiful country, fine land, well cultivated . . . and a most excellent soil." Of Stockbridge, Liancourt had written in detail:

> Stockbridge is one of the richest townships in the state of Massachusetts. All its land is cultivated, except a very small portion, which will soon in its turn receive

12. Louis H. Von Sahler, "Isaac Van Deusen and Van Deusen Manor: An Outline," *New York Genealogical and Biographical Record, 28* (1898), 233.

13. Joseph Bennet to [?], June 1, 1773; Cheshire Church Records, typescript in BA.

culture like the rest. No timber is here preserved beyond
what is requisite for fuel. This township is for the most
part situated in a valley, but extends also upon some hills
of no great elevation. The soil is excellent and almost all
laid down in meadow. The cattle, butter, cheese, and
such other productions as are not consumed on the spot,
are generally sent to New York. Sometimes the certainty
of obtaining a higher price at Boston induces the farmer
to give a preference to the latter place, with which however the communication is difficult, because of the distance, and of the mountainous country that is to be
traversed. In such cases, all the other articles, except the
cattle, are sent down to New York by the North-River
which passes within twenty miles of Stockbridge, and
transported from New-York to Boston by sea.

There are likewise some forges and cast-iron-works in
this township: but the high rate of workmen's wages,
and the scantiness of the mine which begins to be exhausted, have for some years past caused a considerable
diminution of their labours. The easy circumstances enjoyed by the inhabitants render workmen scarce, and
high in their demands. The wages at present paid to
them are from thirteen to fifteen dollars per month. The
price of wheat is two dollars the bushel, of Indian corn,
one dollar; of oats, two shillings. A pair of oxen cost
from ninety to a hundred and ten dollars. Land bears the
price of from fifteen to twenty dollars the acre, in farm-
lots.[14]

Some Berkshire farmers, however—and particularly those
of the second and third generations and those living in the
hill towns—found little to praise in the county; and between

14. Duke de La Rochefoucauld-Liancourt, *Travels through the United
States of North America, the Country of the Iroquois and Upper Canada
in the years 1795, 1796, and 1797* (2 vols. London, 1799), 2, 212–14.

1790 and 1830, they emigrated in significant numbers to New York or Vermont.

In 1790 Jared Boughton of Stockbridge and his five brothers moved to central New York, and fifteen years later, Henry Brewster left a succinct account of his "deliverance" from Berkshire:

> I married at the age of twenty-three years, and unfortunately bought a farm and settled upon it, in one of the poorest mountain towns of the county of Berkshire. Unable to sell it, I was obliged to cultivate the ungenial soil of the Berkshire mountains for ten of the best years of my life.
>
> The day of deliverance came, however:—in 1805, I met with a large handbill sent out by James Wadsworth, Esq., of "Big Tree," proposing to exchange each alternate range of lots of land in "West Pulteney township," for improved farms in the county of Berkshire.[15]

Meanwhile, at the turn of the century, the 30,000 people living in Berkshire exhibited a remarkable homogeneity in racial stock and social background, the Dutch being the only notable exception. Not only did they share a common English racial heritage, but their characters and customs reflected several generations of similar cultural backgrounds in New England. Only in the 1830's, with the growth of industry and the beginnings of railroads, did the Irish come to Berkshire, and not until 1854 did Berkshire's first Catholic church, St. Joseph's, appear in Pittsfield.[16]

Superimposed upon this racial unity was a pattern of social classes probably less rigid than that generally known in the towns of the Connecticut Valley, where the aristocracy had been socially established for a century before the Revolution.

15. Orasmus Turner, *History of the Pioneer Settlement of Phelps' and Gorham's Purchase and Morris' Reserve* (Rochester, 1851), pp. 504–6.
16. Dewey, *Autobiography*, p. 23; *Life and Letters of Sedgwick*, p. 19.

Just as the Connecticut Valley dwellers had their "river gods," Berkshirites did have their "mountain gods" in the persons of Sedgwicks, Dwights, Ashleys, and Williamses, but this local aristocracy of resident proprietors found very little time to establish itself in positions of respect and power before the Revolution broke in upon it. Because much of the settlement of Berkshire came during and after the Revolutionary period, farmers and artisans appeared who had not been trained in a traditional reverence for the Dwights and the Sedgwicks. They were men who cast their votes at the town meetings for John Bacon, Barnabas Bidwell, and Thompson Skinner—all leaders of Berkshire's Jeffersonian party. The old aristocracy was losing its monopoly of political offices, and political liberalism had even broken the ranks of the clergy, with Parson Allen, Parson Judson, and Elder John Leland, all strong Jeffersonians.

Class distinctions continued to be honored, however, if only in the breach, and members of the landed aristocracy cherished their position well into the 1800's. In her recollections, Catharine Sedgwick was to recall the inability of her father, the staunch Federalist Theodore, to adjust to the new atmosphere: "He was born too soon to relish the freedoms of democracy, and I have seen his brow lower when a free-and-easy mechanic came to the *front* door, and upon one occasion I remember his turning off the "east steps" (I am *sure* not kicking but the demonstration was unequivocal) a grown-up lad who kept his hat on after being told to take it off." [17] And from Stockbridge, William Williams had written to Henry Sedgwick in 1805: "The tenants of the ancient demesne are all well,—so are the neighboring gypsies." [18] However light-hearted the jest, it was nonetheless a telltale if muted indication of the basic social thought of the mountain gods.

Still, a look at the social picture of the eastern seaboard cit-

17. *Life and Letters of Sedgwick,* p. 49 f.
18. Jan. 21, 1805; SP.

ies after the Revolution would have easily convinced either the Sedgwicks or the Williamses that their own positions were relatively secure. The inflationary pressures of the Revolutionary War, which in the eastern cities had destroyed much of the old gentry and had at once created a new rich class and increased the propertyless proletariat in the space of a single decade, produced no such cataclysmic effects on the simple agrarian economy of Berkshire. Changes did come, but only slowly over a thirty-year period, and never emphatically enough to alter the inherited social structure. In Boston, where time had not yet mellowed the newly wealthy citizens into an aristocracy, the social gap in the 1790's was relatively narrow and the economic gap wide. In Berkshire the opposite situation prevailed, and the social structure remained a basically conservative relic of the past—a reflection of the uncomplicated, almost precapitalistic agrarian economy of the Old West. It heard little from idealists active in the cause of human rights or from spokesmen for restless artisans.

Like the social structure, the economic underpinnings in Berkshire responded only gradually to the changes taking place farther east. The evolution from primitive frontier agriculture to a comparatively advanced state of industrialization occurred so slowly that the line between the old economic self-sufficiency and the emerging economic integration with Boston and New York is as hard to draw as the line between the old, spontaneous provincialism and the beginnings of the second, more artificial provincial phase. The parallel can hardly be called accidental, since the Berkshire economy inevitably played a part in the evolving provincialism. It could be argued, after all, that economic considerations eventually made geographical isolation both impractical and impossible.

By 1790 the agricultural phase of the Berkshire economy had crystallized, with the result that the picture of a largely self-sufficient region was as complete as it would ever become. With reference to the simple agricultural standards then current, the land was filled nearly to capacity; population density had increased from four to thirty-five persons per square mile between 1761 and 1790. The building of the turnpikes, the advent of sound money, and the appearance of established entrepreneurs had reduced the hitherto rather confused frontier conditions to a relatively organized system. In fact, a visitor would probably have been struck by the over-all similarity of economic activities in all the Berkshire towns. Whether the townspeople depended for support primarily on a constant flow of water power, as in Pittsfield, Adams, and Lee; on large and fertile plains, as in Sheffield and Stockbridge; or on a few meagerly productive "vertical" farms and considerable resources of lumber and potash, as in the hill towns, they almost always had a gristmill and a tannery and at least one sawmill. Over a third of the towns could boast, in addition, a small marble quarry and either a simple iron forge or a more advanced type of furnace. Whatever their other pursuits, however, 95 per cent of all the people devoted most of their time to agriculture.[19]

At no subsequent period in its history would the description of the economy of one Berkshire town have sufficed so adequately to describe every other town as well. In Pittsfield, as everywhere else, farming methods could hardly have been any more conservative. Few farmers did anything in the way of manuring or crop rotation to preserve the fertility of the soil, in spite of a few reprints of essays by Arthur Young in the *Berkshire Chronicle,* which must have shown them how deficient they were in improved agricultural procedure. They cultivated small kitchen gardens for their sweet corn, cucumbers, and peas, and reserved their cleared land for staple crops, just as their fathers had done. Their livestock would include a horse or two, oxen, cows, sheep, and swine—the swine being a "coarse, long-legged, large-boned, slab-sided, flab-eared,

19. Holland, *Western Massachusetts, 2,* 463 ff.

sharp-nosed generation, better fitted for sub-soiling than to fill a pork barrel." [20]

In what little spare time was left him from his planting or harvesting, the farmer usually found it necessary to double as a small-scale manufacturer largely for his own consumption. His wife produced whatever woolen cloth the family needed, sometimes even a modest surplus for sale, and took it to one of the four local clothier shops for fulling and dyeing. He might himself run his own leather tannery and, if he were opulent enough to own a large iron kettle, might also maintain his own potash works. In fact, the only major industry which he left entirely to outsiders was the manufacture of iron—an activity centered around the five iron forges then in operation in Pittsfield. Even the most enterprising and successful proprietors of one of these forges never hired more than six or seven men at any one time, and would himself often carry the daily output of a hundred or so pounds of wrought iron to the local store, to sell or barter.

Because the production of iron, like that of leather and woolens, often proved more than sufficient for local demand, all but the smallest towns had a local storekeeper who served also as an entrepreneur—and occasionally as a tavernkeeper as well.[21] He would arrange to export the surpluses forty miles overland to Hudson or Albany, New York, and thence down the river to New York City, and would either collect money or import such items as tea, rum, and sugar in return. Timothy Edwards of Stockbridge became just such a storekeeper-entrepreneur, holding virtually the only type of position in the county with any real money-making potential; but like his counterparts in other Berkshire towns, he never managed to approach the wealth of the old landed families who condemned a life of trade. The means of agricultural and industrial production in the Berkshire economy remained too primitive and inefficient, and the means of transportation to

20. Smith, *History of Pittsfield*, 2, 35.
21. Ibid., pp. 44–48.

outside markets too costly, to allow any entrepreneur to become more than simply well-to-do.

No wonder that Berkshire yeomen, seeking survival in
such a subsistence-level economy, emerged as political radicals and gave financial support to cultural activities, if they
gave at all, very reluctantly. They balked at paying school assessments, though spending twice the amount on roads; they
thought the yearly $1.50 subscription rate for the county
newspaper, the *Western Star,* excessive; and on occasion they
even wrangled rather impiously over the support required
by their leading cultural figures, the preachers of the gospel.

Not until the transition to a truly diversified economy in
the years after 1820 did Berkshire find men of means adequate enough to endow an academy or a library, to give solid
financial help to foreign missions as well as to their local
churches, and to patronize literature in a limited way. In
1801 the Englishman Arthur Scholfield set up his wool-
carding machine at Pittsfield; in 1802 Zenas Crane established his paper factory at Dalton; and in 1807 the agricultural publicist and gentleman farmer Elkanah Watson moved
to Pittsfield and began his campaign for scientific agriculture.
The influence of these men, and others like them, was to help
in bringing noticeable changes in the over-all economy by
1820, and a booming though small-scale industrialism by
1850.[22]

Not only did Watson organize the Berkshire Agricultural
Society as the first effective instrument in America for introducing the new farming to the old farmer, but he recognized
the importance of manufacturing as the source of real wealth
and repeatedly urged Berkshirites to turn to factory production. Berkshire, he felt sure, was "destined to become . . . a
respectable manufacturing county, in all those branches
where the excessive dearness of labor can in some measure

22. Pittsfield *Sun,* Nov. 2, 1801; *Berkshire Courier,* Dec. 9, 1841, Horatio Byington's speech before the Berkshire Agricultural Society.

be obviated by the powerful application of machinery." [23]
In the 1820's both Scholfield and Crane had begun to solve
the problem of a labor shortage in Berkshire by the extensive
use of machinery that Watson advocated, and had made their
ventures pay so handsomely that they had attracted local capital into their enterprises. And by the 1840's Watson's earlier
predictions of a highly prosperous future in Berkshire were
being borne out. In that decade the textile manufacturing
town of Adams doubled its population, the railroad was solv-
ing the problem of markets and supplies of raw materials,
and enough wealth had accrued from industrial ventures to
bring in capital, even from New York. Pittsfield, Lee, and
Great Barrington had become pre-eminent in industry along
with Adams; and Stockbridge and Sheffield had developed a
thriving commercial agriculture. Only the hill towns, with
their scarcity of resources, were suffering.

In spite of a significant investment by New Yorkers, the
majority of Berkshire industries of the 1840's and 50's were
locally owned, and to that extent Berkshire was still for Berkshirites. A former laborer, Charles Plunkett, owned one sizable Hinsdale textile factory and part of another, an affluence
for which he expressed his gratitude by building a public
library in the town; the local Quakers owned much of the
Adams textile industry; and Theodore Pomeroy, a scion of
one of Pittsfield's oldest families and Berkshire's leading in-
dustrialist, owned extensive interests in textiles and wagon
manufactures.

The Berkshire economic outlook, in short, had become as
radiantly healthy as Watson could have wished, and as early
as the 1830's America's distinguished visitors Tocqueville
and Beaumont had found good reason to be impressed by the
general prosperity.[24] Even in the depression of 1837 Cathar-

23. Elkanah Watson, "Speech before the Berkshire Agricultural Society," quoted in Smith, *History of Pittsfield*, 2, 335.

24. George W. Pierson, *Tocqueville and Beaumont in America* (New
York, 1938), p. 350.

ine Sedgwick was able to contrast the well-being of her county with the tragic scenes in New York City,[25] and still later, in the débacle of 1857, Edward Newton wrote with pride [26] that the Berkshire Bank remained one of the few in the state that was not in the least embarrassed.

Looking back over the changes which had come to Berkshire during his lifetime, William Allen, the former Pittsfield pastor, sat down in the 1850's to write a fitting and predictably provincial conclusion to a half-century of growth within the county:

> A wilderness has been changed into a paradise. A magnificent temple of science stands at the northern gate,—fit companion of its near associate, a towering mountain height,—in which presides a very learned and much honored son of Berkshire. In the central Pontoosuc is a large and prosperous Institution for the culture of the female mind and heart,—with a multitude of other schools of learning scattered over the whole region. Everywhere are the meeting-houses of stone, and brick, and wood with their spires pointing high upwards to the skies. The marble of Berkshire shines out resplendently in the magnificent structures of our cities, and in the wide-scattered, humble memorials of the dead. Its lime is boundless, and its iron is everywhere doing its mighty work or smoothing the way of the swift traveller. Its immense production of paper creates a repository of intellect for the whole country. Its flocks are associated with the finest of cloths. Improvement is everywhere making its rapid advances.[27]

25. Pittsfield *Sun,* June 22, 1837.
26. To Nathaniel Appleton, Oct. 24, 1857; Appleton Papers, MHS.
27. *Wunnissoo, or the Vale of Hoosatunnuk, a Poem with Notes* (Boston and New York, 1856), pp. 197–98.

# Chapter 3. HEADS FULL OF DIVINITY

WHETHER the historian, in viewing Berkshire religious life, accepts Mrs. Trollope's remark that all the bigotry in America was concentrated upon the Berkshire hills [1] or Mark Hopkins' more charitable characterization of the county as a sanctuary of "deep and pervading reverence," [2] he cannot look long at Berkshire history in the eighteenth and early nineteenth centuries without being struck by the dominance of religion—a dominance so great as to be remarkable even in religion-saturated New England.

Such was the vitality of religious thought and institutions in this period of Berkshire history that clergymen could dictate either directly or through the use of social pressure to almost every citizen and could color the conduct of the most worldly activities. Lawyers were chagrined to see a number of civil cases being settled out of court under the arbitration of church pastors or with church members as jurists.[3] In the Stockbridge Republican Library many of the books were such as any orthodox Berkshire cleric might have chosen for his own library.[4] Even in the pages of the *Western Star,* with its rationalist editor Loring Andrews, religious argument not infrequently pushed aside the "more important" political matters during the 1790's.[5] From common school through Williams College, young Berkshirites grew accustomed to finding the Westminster Catechism emphasized to the neglect

1. *The Berkshire Hills,* Federal Writers Project, p. 116.
2. *Miscellaneous Essays and Discourses* (Boston, 1847), p. 394.
3. Church Records of Williamstown, Stockbridge, and Sheffield; typescript in BA.
4. Records of the Berkshire Republican Library; Bernard Hoffman Collection, NYPL.
5. *Western Star,* January 4, 1791.

of merely secular knowledge.⁶ Sermons comprised three-
quarters of Berkshire's literary output, and only in the middle years of the Jeffersonian administration did political pamphlets begin to offer real competition to theological tracts in
the Stockbridge and Pittsfield printing presses.

The nature of Berkshire religiosity can be traced in part
to the county's first cultural institution, the Stockbridge Mission. During the twenty-five years after the incorporation of
Sheffield in 1733 Berkshire remained a frontier area always
subject to attack by the French and Indians, and always looking for protection to the secular arm of Fort Massachusetts
and the spiritual force of the Mission. The Fort had been
erected on the Mohawk Trail in Williamstown in 1744 to
guard both the Housatonic settlements and those in central
Massachusetts from attacks by the Canadian Mohawk Indians.
The Mission had been established some ten years earlier to
civilize and convert first the friendly Mohicans and eventually the hostile Mohawks.

In 1745, when the French and the Indians captured and
burned Fort Massachusetts, the Housatonic Valley was left
helpless in the face of any Indian attack. The Reverend Samuel Hopkins, then minister of the Northern Housatonic
Township, was reading the psalm to a small gathering one
Sunday afternoon when the terrifying assault on a neighboring town occurred. "All were put into the utmost consterna-
tion—men, women, and children crying, 'What shall we do?'
—not a gun to defend us, not a fort to flee to, and few guns
and little ammunition in the place. . . . Women, children,
and squaws presently flocked in upon us from Stockbridge,
half-naked, and frightened almost to death; and fresh news
came, that the enemy were on the Plains this side Stockbridge,

6. Sherman M. Smith, *The Relation of the State to Religious Education in Massachusetts* (Syracuse, 1926), p. 132. As late as 1861 Williams
College was unique in still using the Westminster Catechism as a text in
the "Saturday morning" class.

shooting, and killing, and scalping people as they fled. . . . Two men are killed and scalped, two children killed, and one of them scalped . . ." [7] Thoroughly alarmed, the frontier settlers continually dispatched desperate petitions to the general court begging for more adequate defense, and certainly the frontier defenses were far from reassuring at the time. Letters and reports of Captain Ephraim Williams toward the middle of the century reflect the constant problems connected with enlisting soldiers, procuring supplies, and maintaining proper intelligence and communication which beset the commander of the western Massachusetts frontier.[8]

But whatever the inadequacies of the soldiery, the Stockbridge Mission owed the comparative security of its existence to their protection. Quite appropriately, in view of Berkshire's significant religious and theological contributions later in the eighteenth century, this Mission represented the first real cultural venture of the area—the first attempt to progress beyond the basic necessities of securing food and shelter and providing defenses against the Indians. The Mission was conceived at a meeting of clergy and gentry including Jonathan Edwards, the Reverend Stephen Williams, and the "river gods" Israel Williams and Colonel John Stoddard at the latter's home in Northampton, and came into active being in 1735 when its first and greatest missionary, John Sergeant, left his tutorship at Yale and traveled the difficult road to Stockbridge. While gaining some support from the contributions of Bostonians to the Commissioners of Indian Affairs, the Mission received the greater portion of its support from the Society for the Propagation of the Gospel in England and Scotland and from the Reverend Isaac Hollis of London.[9]

Both Indians and whites were vitally concerned for the

7. Hopkins, *Works*, Memoir 1, pp. 41–42.
8. William Williams' Papers, Vols. *1, 2*; Hawley Papers, NYPL.
9. A nephew of Thomas Hollis, benefactor of Harvard College.

success of the Mission, most of the Indians having been persuaded by the argument of their leader Konkapot "that since
my remembrance, there were ten Indians where there is now
one: But the Christians greatly increase and multiply, and
spread over the land; let us therefore leave our former courses
and become Christians." [10] The interest of white men in the
Mission stemmed from both religious and worldly motives,
for besides saving the souls of heathen, they felt that in the
conversion of hostile Indians the Mission might well prove
more valuable than five regiments of soldiers on the frontier.
Indeed, so important did secular authorities consider the venture that Governor Belcher and the Provincial Council attended Sergeant's consecration as missionary at Deerfield, and
the Province appropriated funds for building a meeting
house at Stockbridge in 1739.[11]

In its early success the Mission owed much to Sergeant's
genius in winning the respect and love of the Indians and to
the basic soundness of his plans for their education and Chris-
tianization. He proposed to help the friendly Mohicans of
the Housatonic Valley by establishing boarding schools for
the children, where they might learn English and various
useful arts, and by converting the adults to Christianity
through instruction and sermons in their own language. In
1743, Sergeant wrote to Dr. Colman in Boston:

> What I propose therefore in general is to take such a
> *Method* in the Education of Our *Indian Children,* as
> shall in the most effectual Manner change their whole
> Habit of thinking and acting; and raise them, as far as

10. Reverend Nathaniel Appleton, *Gospel Ministers Must Be Fit for
the Master's Use . . . Sermon at the Ordination of Mr. John Sergeant*
(Boston, 1735), p. v.

11. Samuel Hopkins, *Historical Memoirs Relating to the Housatun-
nuk Indians* (Boston, 1753), p. 72. This Samuel Hopkins was minister
of the church in Springfield and uncle of the Samuel Hopkins of Great
Barrington.

possible, into the Condition of a civil industrious and polish'd People; while at the same Time the Principles of Vertue and Piety shall be carefully instilled into their Minds in a Way, that will make the most lasting Impression; and withal to introduce the *English Language* among them instead of their own imperfect and barbarous *Dialect*. And to accomplish this *Design,* I propose to procure an Accommodation of about 200 Acres of *Land* in this Place (which may be had without any cost of the *Indian Proprietors*) and to erect an House on it, such as shall be thought convenient for a Beginning; and in it to maintain a Number of *Children and Youth* (not under *ten,* nor above *twenty* Years of Age;) and to have them under the Direction, Care and Tuition of *two Masters,* one to take the Oversight of them in their Hours of *Labour,* and the other in their Hours of *Study;* and to have their Time so *divided* between Study and Labour as to make one the *Diversion* of the other, that as little Time as possible may be lost in Idleness.[12]

Although hoping to keep the Mission set apart as completely as possible from the white settlers, and especially from the rum-selling Dutch fur traders, he did ask that Colonel Stoddard choose four model families who might come to live in Stockbridge as a general civilizing influence. Ironically enough, it was the head of one of these families, the conniving and unscrupulous Ephraim Williams,[13] who by his ceaseless plotting to take over Indian lands was destined at last to be instrumental in undermining all that Sergeant was trying to do.

In spite of the machinations of Williams and the Dutch rum-sellers, Sergeant's achievements were impressive. Begin-

12. *A Letter from the Reverend Mr. Sergeant of Stockbridge to Dr. Colman of Boston* (Boston, 1743), p. 4.
13. The father of Col. Ephraim Williams, founder of Williams College.

ning with only fifty Indians, he had managed to effect the
conversion of two hundred and eighteen by the time of his
death in 1749. Fifty-five pupils attended the school run by his
assistant Timothy Woodbridge, while his Sunday congregation numbered forty-two regular communicants.[14] And not
only did Sergeant preach to the Indians in their own tongue
but he even translated Dr. Watts' *First Catechism* and several
prayers from the Anglican Liturgy.[15]

In the final analysis, however, the latitudinarian theology [16]
of this pioneer of all the missionaries to the Stockbridge Indians placed him in distinct opposition to the main theological current of Berkshire, and it remained for his successor,
Jonathan Edwards, to sound the dominant note. With his

14. Hopkins, *Memoirs,* p. iii.
15. Ibid., p. 144. That the Mission generally suffered from a shortage
of funds seems evident from the debts totaling £700 owed by Sergeant's
estate at his death. Sergeant himself was fully aware of the hindering
effect of sectarian spirit on missionary enterprise. His friend Benjamin
Colman wrote the Bishop of London to ask why the Society for the
Propagation of the Gospel should support Anglican missionaries in
Boston, Braintree, and Salem, where the inhabitants could easily support their own clergy. It would appear, he observed, that the Society
preferred to convert Congregationalists and Presbyterians in the towns
of eastern Massachusetts to the Church of England rather "than those
poor perishing *Heathen [in Stockbridge]* to the Christian Faith" (Hopkins, *Memoirs,* p. 70). Even the Boston Anglican, Caner, had to admit
that the Stockbridge Mission was a bona fide attempt to convert the
heathen, but he pointed out that most of its support came from England
and Scotland and that the colonists' main efforts were directed toward
defeating the Church of England. Cf. Reverend Henry Caner to the
Archbishop of Canterbury, Dec. 23, 1762, *Historical Collections Relating
to the American Colonial Church,* ed. William S. Perry (5 vols. Hartford,
1873), *3, 483–86.*
16. In the midst of the turmoil of the Great Awakening, Sergeant
preached to the Hampshire Association of Ministers meeting at Springfield, *The Causes and Danger of Delusions in the Affairs of Religion*
(Boston, 1743) and suggested that, since charity was more important to
Christianity than controversy, both sides forgive and forget.

distant and contemplative personality, Edwards was to be far less successful than Sergeant in converting and educating the Indians, but he was always an able champion of Indian rights. With extraordinary cruelty and selfishness, the Williams and Hawley clans had ousted him from Northampton,[17] and even in Stockbridge he found only relative peace.

Williams had, in fact, at first opposed Edwards' coming to Stockbridge but had later changed his mind. "I am sorry," he wrote,[18] "that a head so full of Divinity should be so empty of politics—but I want him to come . . . not because he would do good . . . but because his coming would raise the value of my land." He was soon to discover in Edwards, however, a man by no means devoid of practical abilities. In spite of being outnumbered and of losing his own appointee and deputy Joseph Dwight to the enemy when the latter married Abigail Williams, Edwards did not hesitate to carry on the fight against the grasping Williams faction with his pen. The absolute integrity of his dispatches to the Commissioners for Indian Affairs carried more weight than anything Ephraim Williams or Joseph Dwight could say. Yet so much of Edwards' energy was absorbed by the negative work of holding off the Williamses that he was able to contribute little to the forward progress of the Mission, and when Joseph and Abigail Dwight put to improper use the money sent by Isaac Hollis for the Indian School and permitted the children to grow up in filth and ignorance, Edwards could do little more than report their perfidy to the Boston Commissioners.

Between the time of Edwards' departure in 1758 to become president of Princeton and the spring of 1785 when the Stockbridge Indians were moved to New Stockbridge in central

17. Perry Miller, *Jonathan Edwards* (New York, 1949), pp. 224–27. Also cf. Jonathan Edwards to Joseph Hawley, Nov. 18, 1754; Hawley Papers.

18. To the Reverend Jonathan Ashley, May 2, 1751, SP.

New York, interested whites were to travel to Berkshire in
increasing numbers to assist in making a travesty of the word
"mission." The new missionary, the Reverend Stephen West;
the teacher of the school, John Sergeant, Jr.; and the Reverend Samuel Hopkins of Great Barrington did what they could
to defend the Indians, but they found the odds against them.
Every year of the 1760's saw more white settlers coming into
Berkshire, and by 1767 Samuel Hopkins felt moved to write:
"The Indians are truly in a deplorable state. And unless their
present connexions with the English can be broken, and some
laws be made to prevent their getting into debt and alienat-
ing their lands, and a good schoolmaster can be introduced
(there is none now) there is little hope that any good will be
done among them, by all the money that is laid out upon
them. . . . They are most of them drunkards . . . they are
consequently idle and of course poor, and many almost
starved, which leads them . . . to live on those who have
something and even to steal." [19]

After various futile attempts to protect the Indians by
legislation, the Commissioners at last managed to push a bill
through the legislature in 1773 which prohibited loans to or
judgments against any Stockbridge Indian in excess of 35s.[20]
But not much impressed by the act, Governor Hutchinson
sourly reported to the Lords of Trade that it, "like all former
laws, will probably be evaded and prove ineffectual." [21] The
steady demoralization of the Indians in Stockbridge became
all too evident when Stephen West sent letters to the Commissioners which included reports of idleness, drunkenness,
and even murder.[22] Eventually, the Mission's location in a
rich-soiled valley, inspiring ever greater pressures from greedy
settlers, proved its undoing; and the undertaking, which had

19. To Andrew Eliot, Mar. 30, 1767; SP.
20. *Acts and Resolves*, 5.238.
21. Ibid., 5.281 n.
22. Smith, *History of Pittsfield, 1*, 99–106.

emerged under John Sergeant as one of the most sensible and successful efforts ever made to help the Indians in New England, ended in failure. But in another, quite unintended sense the Mission proved of real significance, for it brought Jonathan Edwards to Stockbridge and thereby made Berkshire the greatest center of eighteenth-century Calvinist orthodoxy in New England.

Any understanding of the peculiarly conservative tone of the Congregational Church in Berkshire must take into account the occasional religious upheavals which had been going on east of the Barrier for over a century. From the time of Governor Winthrop, various ruling oligarchies of Calvinist clergy and elders had made efforts to impose a highly authoritative doctrine on their congregations—efforts which obviously coincided not at all with the Protestant insistence on the rights of individual conscience.[23] When they failed to establish their authority, as happened more than once in the eighteenth century, those of unbending orthodox convictions frequently moved to a new township on the frontier rather than submit any longer to worldly tendencies they found insupportable. Thus it was that John Bacon left Boston to settle in Stockbridge and Ephraim Judson moved from Taunton to Sheffield, when each had failed to carry his congregation with him in his strict Calvinist preaching.[24] Indeed, the ready reception which Edwards found for his extreme Calvinist views would suggest that Bacon and Judson were not the only ones who looked upon their new home as a wilderness Zion, a refuge of religious purity uncon-

23. This thesis is developed by Robert A. East, "Puritanism and New Settlement," *New England Quarterly, 17* (1944), 255–64.

24. Hamilton A. Hill, *History of the Old South Church* (2 vols. Boston, 1890), 2, 163; Franklin B. Dexter, *Biographical Sketches of the Graduates of Yale College* (6 vols. New York and New Haven, 1885–1912), 3, 28. It is interesting to note that both of these rigidly Calvinist clerics became Jeffersonians in politics in Berkshire.

taminated by Boston sophistications and heresies. When liberal Bostonians spoke scornfully of these frontiersmen who were reviving their own castoff ideas, Berkshirites could claim self-righteously and with some truth that theirs was the only home of true orthodoxy.

Certainly the orthodox Calvinist clergy found Berkshire County a well-favored spot, blessed as it was with a relatively small, "floating" population and a safe remoteness from the distractions and corruptions of the seaport cities.[25] While trade and industry, together with an almost steady flow of European contacts, might incline Boston Puritans toward Arminianism or even Unitarianism, Berkshirites continued to subordinate such pursuits to farming, of all occupations perhaps the most favorable to so decidedly supernatural a religion as Calvinism. The rugged face of nature on the Berkshire frontier, moreover, might well have helped to turn the undecided toward that stern belief. Always a fighting faith, Calvinism has all too often degenerated when opposition has been removed, and the tensed will remained a major asset on the frontier well after it had become a somewhat inadequate attitude in the easier life of seaboard cities. In such an atmosphere an anthropomorphic, socially centered religion might conceivably have seemed inadequate, and the more inclusive system of Calvinism might have appeared the truer distillation of common experience.

Far more important, however, as factors in keeping Berkshirites true to the Calvinist faith of their fathers were the general intellectual conservatism of the farmers and that disinterested enthusiasm of the orthodox clergy which led them to accept calls to the low-paid Berkshire pastorates scorned by more liberal theologians. After graduating from

25. Thomas Allen, *An Historical Sketch of the County of Berkshire and the Town of Pittsfield* (Boston, 1808), p. 2. Allen did not recollect a single vicious person among the sixty original families settling in Pittsfield.

Yale in 1741, for example, the Reverend Samuel Hopkins took over the Great Barrington pastorate at a salary of £35 a year while a friend and classmate was receiving £130 yearly at Southampton. In a very real sense the early Berkshire clergy were missionaries; and because most of the eastern clergy of more liberal persuasion preferred the amenities of civilized society and accordingly lacked missionary fervor, Berkshire fell to the Calvinists by default.

Unquestionably, the strongly religious character of early Berkshire culture owed much to the presence of these able and long-tenured clergymen who belonged to the first generation of settlers. Side by side with Edwards stood two others who eventually earned a place among New England's foremost theologians, notably Samuel Hopkins and Stephen West. Hopkins in a sense deserved more than Edwards to be called the father of the Berkshire tradition of orthodox theology, since he had himself refused the offer to become the presiding missionary at Stockbridge and had urged the Commissioners to appoint instead his friend and former mentor Jonathan Edwards.[26] Later, after Edwards had left for Princeton, Hopkins further bolstered the local orthodoxy by converting the newly arrived Stephen West from Arminianism to the "true Gospel doctrine." [27] West was shortly followed to the county by Thomas Allen, future leader of the Berkshire constitutionalists and a crusader for Jeffersonian democracy, and by Elder John Leland, one of the Baptists' most eloquent apostles of religious freedom. All of these clergymen attained an authority among their townsmen quite comparable to that of the Old Testament patriarchs, and like the patriarchs, they gained in stature with the years. Parson Allen wrote and preached in Pittsfield for forty-six

26. Electa F. Jones, *Stockbridge Past and Present* (Springfield, 1854), p. 163.

27. Alvan Hyde, *Sketches of the Life and Ministry and Writings of the Reverend Stephen West* (Stockbridge, 1819), p. 7.

years (1764–1810); Stephen West, in Stockbridge for fifty-seven (1759–1816).

Thus it was that Berkshire became the seedbed of the New England theology, that school of theological thought created by Jonathan Edwards and developed over the next century by his followers in southwestern New England. To maintain that Berkshire became Calvinist simply by accident—that Edwards, Hopkins, and West merely happened to settle there and found themselves able to dominate their fellow clerics—would be to ignore too many implications. It would not, indeed, seem too unreasonable to suggest that the agricultural way of life in Berkshire created a temper of mind receptive to the austerities of neo-Calvinism. If, as Guignebert has suggested, the "soft" ethics of the New Testament—the emphasis on God's love and forgiveness—were a product of the city, and if rural folk (the *pagani*) did indeed prefer the Old Testament ethic, then the Berkshire farmer might well have inclined to that Christian stoicism so notable in the Calvinist temper. Austerity and patience might be expected to be the dominant characteristics of men called upon for sustained effort and faced with a roughly predictable future. Unlike city dwellers, they were less likely to encounter either the sudden reversals of the precarious bourgeois existence or the uncertainties dictated by quixotic human nature.[28]

Those who called the revival of Calvinist theology the "Berkshire Divinity" did so with good reason.[29] Edwards wrote his major theological works at his hexagonal desk in

28. Charles Guignebert, *Christianity Past and Present* (New York, 1927), p. 175; Pitirim Sorokin and Carle C. Zimmerman, *Principles of Rural-Urban Sociology* (New York, 1929), pp. 424–27.

29. The Reverend Joseph Bellamy of Bethlehem, Connecticut (thirty miles south of Berkshire) was the only major figure in the creation of the new theology who did not live in Berkshire. Frank H. Foster, *A Genetic History of the New England Theology* (Chicago, 1907), pp. 107 ff.

Stockbridge; Hopkins contributed his *Sin, An Advantage to the Universe* while holding the Great Barrington pastorate; and Stephen West wrote his *Essay on Moral Agency* in the early years of his Stockbridge pastorate. From the time of Hopkins' arrival in Great Barrington in 1743 until West published his final work, *On the Atonement,* in 1815, Berkshire County was the scene of creative theological thought which had an importance far transcending that of eighteenth-century Berkshire; those works emanating from the county were an essential element in the formation of the conservative tradition in American religious thought, and the emotionally charged Calvinist neo-orthodoxy which they represented was by 1800 already known as Hopkinsian theology.[30]

Throughout New England in the generation following the Great Awakening of 1740, newly enlightened clergymen were attempting to revitalize the old orthodox Puritanism. The doctrines of original Calvinism, they realized, must be reclothed so as to carry conviction to the hearts as well as to the minds of those New Englanders they hoped to teach. The Great Awakening, in short, must be institutionalized by welding the existing emotionalism to correct doctrinal beliefs. A theological ballast must be created as a defense against creeping Arminianism and in defiance of its insidious teachings.

The Arminians were seeking, in effect, to purge Calvinism of its extreme supernatural emphasis and to humanize it in keeping with the modern temper. They minimized the importance of theology as being less practical than ethics; and

30. Foster, *Genetic History*, pp. 3–11. The term "Hopkinsian theology" was first used in the late eighteenth century when theological controversy was becoming a three-way struggle. The reactionary Hopkinsians and the liberals (Arminians) gained at the expense of the old Calvinists, who were squeezed into a middle ground. While Hopkins laid the basis for his system before 1769 when he left Berkshire, he published his most famous work, *System of Doctrines,* in 1793 at his Newport, Rhode Island, pastorate.

Edwards, who devoted most of his theological lifetime to
defending Puritanism against them, observed wryly: "It is
one great reason why speculative points are thought to be of
so little importance, that the modern religion consists so
little in respect to the divine Being and almost wholly in
benevolence to men." Believing in a universe acceptable to
human moral ideas, the Arminians rejected the absolute
sovereign God of the Calvinists and held man's efforts to be
a necessary part of the process of salvation.

Edwards saw the churches of eastern Massachusetts and
even some in the Connecticut Valley being riddled by these
subversive doctrines. The people of Northampton, under the
religious dominance of "Pope" Solomon Stoddard and the
social dominance of the "river gods," were finding the
humanistic and liberal doctrines of Arminianism increasingly
attractive. Stoddard, indeed, went even beyond the Half-
Way Covenant in allowing full communion to all citizens
not openly profane, and thus changed the church from a
fellowship of saints to a school for saints and sinners. Almost
everywhere, as settlements grew older, the people's Calvinism
underwent a change—known in Boston as "mellowing" but
in Berkshire as corruption. Churchgoers might still be re-
peating the old phrases of the Westminster Confession, but
Edwards felt that they were all at heart becoming Arminians
incapable of understanding the orthodox meanings.

To the purveyors of the new orthodoxy, the real issue between the Arminians and the Calvinists centered on the basic
question of whether Christianity was a religion of salvation
by grace or salvation by merit. Hopkins and West, as well as
Edwards, saw the simple Arminian definition of virtue in
terms of a respectable moral life as a fundamental denial of
the Gospel. Because Arminianism invited the "finite to accept itself with all its deficiencies as adequate," Edwardseans
could not but regard the belief as sinful.[31] Edwards himself

31. Miller, *Jonathan Edwards*, p. 124.

viewed sin not as a disconnected series of wrong choices
made by a free will but rather as a depravity affecting the
human race as such. Sin in his eyes was a failure to experience
the divine glory and a willingness to rest in that ignorance.
In pointing out the gulf which separates man from God,
he deplored "how vastly the generality of mankind fall below
their duty, with respect to the love of God; yea, how far they
are from coming half-way to that height of love which is
agreeable to the rule of right." [32] Human merit, he maintained, was insufficient to accomplish the salvation of man
from his natural sinful state to a state of virtue. In the grace
of God lay man's only hope.

Here was a basic attitude toward the relations of man and
God which reached to the heart of Calvinism—an attitude
which Hopkins and Edwards discussed together over and
over again. Both West and Hopkins were to follow Edwards
in reaffirming the Calvinist doctrine of the sovereignty of
God and the considerable chasm between God and man; and
Hopkins—or "Old Benevolence" as Edwards' daughters af-
fectionately called him—was always to be identified in the
New England mind with the famous test question: "Are you
willing to be damned for the glory of God?" Over a period
of thirty years the three theologians created a new and distinct body of doctrine which influenced Calvinist thinking
throughout New England, but it would be useless to deny
that at times their writings tended to degenerate into a tour
de force of logic. Arguing logically from his premises of God's
sovereignty and holiness, Hopkins ended by believing and
asking others to believe that sin was a positive advantage to
the world. And Stephen West went so far as to assert in answering the Universalists: "we may proceed to mention some
things which give reason to suppose that the very ends of
atonement may be more perfectly answered without the
universal salvation of sinners, than by it: And, that the

32. Ibid., p. 180.

eternal destruction of some part of the human race, will be-
stow a lustre on this doctrine, which it would want without
it." [33]

In a sense, Edwards, Hopkins, and West had created a
religion for angels—a coherent, highly complex theological
system at once too intellectual and too coldly logical for the
common man—and it remained for their epigoni in Berkshire to restate their doctrine in more comprehensible terms.
As revised by Jacob Catlin and Thomas Allen, the intellectual currency of the Edwardsean theology suffered a
considerable debasement. Arguments became simplified, distinctions became blurred, and second-generation ministers
turned away from the abstract speculations of their predecessors to talk in phrases of homely realism. Yet if they ob-
fuscated many of the issues and retreated noticeably from
Edwards' uncompromising positions, still they succeeded in
supplying scattered religious insights into life's paradoxes
and provided a down-to-earth emotional appeal for questioning congregations.

In restating the case for orthodoxy, Catlin left behind the
exalted level of Edwards in favor of homely illustrations and
strangely empirical arguments. He defended the doctrine of
divine sovereignty as a motive to morality by pointing out
"that piety and morality flourish most in the towns where

33. *The Scripture Doctrine of the Atonement, Proposed to Careful
Examination* (New Haven, 1785), p. 148. That West was ruthless in tearing down any premature optimisms that might be based on salvation
through wishful thinking is evident from this story of a parishioner:
"on Sabbath morning his hopes were bright; but when Dr. West had
named his text, laid out his heads, and proceeded some way in the
discussion of them, he began to tremble. At the close of the morning
service his hope was wavering and unsteady, hardly able to bear him up.
In the afternoon it failed him altogether,—as the application drew on
his hope was nowhere; it had quite deserted him." Albert Hopkins,
"Historical Discourse," *Proceedings of the Centennial . . . of the Berkshire Association of Congregational Ministers* (Boston, 1864), p. 26.

this doctrine is clearly preached." [34] Later in his career he indulged in arguments which were still more specific:

> Those who discard and scorn the moral government of Jehovah are fond of chance gaming. . . . could people convince themselves that chance orders events, and not the heart-searching God, this would relieve their consciences in every vile and abominable gratification. . . . The secret desire of the heart is to get free from a sense of Duty, and the divine law and government. . . . The wicked exert themselves . . . to build up the system of chance, instead of divine Providence. This, perhaps, is what principally engages mankind in card-playing, chance-games, and lotteries of every kind.[35]

The same pragmatic type of argument appeared in his major work when he was discussing the doctrine of depravity: "The Universal sinfulness of infants which is manifested in their first moral actions, proves incontestibly," he insisted, "that there is in them a native, and original propensity of the mind to evil. . . . the sad necessity of an abundant use of the rod of correction, is a conclusive evidence of original corruption of nature." [36]

Meanwhile, Thomas Allen was seeking to establish in Berkshire a socially inclusive Christianity, a religion of the heart which was as meaningful to the common man as to the self-appointed élite. While Stephen West was busy in Stockbridge drawing on the preachings and writings of Edwards and Hopkins to give authoritative shape to the reaffirmed orthodoxy, Allen was maintaining from his Pittsfield pulpit that "democracy is the essence of the Gospel." [37]

34. Jacob Catlin, *Sermons on Important Subjects* (Hartford, 1797), p. 204.

35. Ibid., p. 502.

36. Catlin, *A Compendium of the System of Divine Truth* (Hartford, 1818), p. 107.

37. *Berkshire Reporter,* Aug. 22, 1807.

Perhaps, in an age swinging away from eighteenth-century reliance on reason toward a religion of feeling and action, such relaxations of Edwards' stringent doctrines were inevitable, whatever the price in theological confusion, if Calvinism was to be brought within human reach. Certainly the revisions (and even surrenders) made by Catlin and Allen produced practical results. Their acceptance of activism helped to provide an important theological basis for the missionary movement which had many of its roots in Berkshire; and their liberalized interpretation of the doctrine of election can be seen partly as cause and partly as effect in the major Berkshire revivals during the second Great Awakening. In its final crystallization, Berkshire orthodoxy emerged as a conservative attitude of mind, inclined toward faith rather than reason, insisting on the supernatural elements of religion and on a transcendent God, and pessimistic in its view of human nature.

If Calvinism dominated the Berkshire religious atmosphere, however, it by no means enjoyed an exclusive reign. While in most towns probably three-fourths of the churchgoing people adhered to the respectable and established Congregational Church, the other fourth often participated in the activities of some dissenting society. Thus a lively party spirit often associated itself with the prevailing religious fervor and served to intensify the popular concern with religion. Berkshire, in short, frequently served as a spiritual battleground where the soul lost to the orthodox Congregational Church became fair game for the Baptists and Quakers from Rhode Island, or for the small band of Episcopalians drifting east from New York, or even for Mother Ann Lee's Shaker Missionaries.

Yet in spite of the comparatively large numbers of dissenters in Berkshire, the social strength of the established church was such that only rarely did anyone openly criticize it even on theological grounds, and the criticisms which did come were scattered and diverse. A Baptist pastor from Hancock named Clark Rogers objected to the unnecessary and undemocratic complexities of the orthodox theology, and said so in a pamphlet entitled *The Husbandman's Aim to Refute the Clergy;* and Israel Dewey, a wealthy Great Barrington Episcopalian with an aristocratic bias, had earlier taken strong exception to the all-inclusiveness of Hopkins' preachings on sin. Dewey and his cohorts did, in fact, finally force Hopkins to leave Berkshire in 1769 by effecting successive salary cuts. Later, the poet David Hitchcock, always an outspoken critic of social abuses, made a more generalized charge to the effect that orthodox doctrines were failing to inculcate morality. A man like Loring Andrews, who valued his public standing, dared do no more than insert a thin stream of guarded criticism in the pages of his *Western Star* lest he lose precious subscribers and loyal Federalist allies who also happened to be staunch Calvinists.

Apparently it was precisely this same immense social power of the established church which prevented the liberal, optimistic Unitarian temper from flaring up against Edwardsean orthodoxy. Here was a potentially explosive schism within the established church which in Berkshire spluttered but never went off. Apparently the liberals did not dare to speak out—or at least not with bold public pronouncements. So great was the strength of the new emotional orthodoxy that Unitarianism scarcely appeared in Berkshire until the 1840's, and those few men who nourished Unitarian convictions kept silent. Theodore Sedgwick, a Justice of the Massachusetts Supreme Court and the leading citizen of Stockbridge, called Channing to his deathbed in 1813 to confess his liberal theology; yet throughout his lifetime he had remained on the best of terms with "the little doctor" Stephen West, and very few Berkshirites would have supposed him a heretic.[38]

Orville Dewey, a famous Unitarian minister of New Bed-

38. *Life and Letters of Sedgwick,* p. 94. During the summer of 1838 Dr. Follen held Unitarian services in the Sedgwicks' house.

ford and New York City, was to recall many years after leaving Sheffield the submerged Unitarianism in his old home:

> I heard, in those days, a great deal of dissent expressed
> from the popular theology, besides my uncle's. I heard
> it often from my father and his friends. . . . I very well
> remember my father's coming home from the General
> Court, of which he was a member, and expressing the
> warmest admiration of the preaching of Channing. The
> feeling, however, of hostility to the Orthodox faith, in
> his time, was limited to a few; but somebody in New
> York, who was acquainted with it . . . sent up some in-
> fidel books. One of them was lying about in our house,
> and I remember seeing my mother one day take it and
> put it in the fire. It was a pretty resolute act for one of
> the gentlest beings I ever knew, and decisively showed
> where she stood.[39]

Dewey, in fact, hazarded a guess that half the Congregational Church members had liberal tendencies, but if they did, they never tried indulging them openly. Sheffield parish had only one church and one society and boasted a thoroughly orthodox history until the 1820's. Indeed, the Unitarian controversy which overtook eastern Massachusetts during the first quarter of the century hardly touched Berkshire, and not until 1890 did certain citizens of Pittsfield at last build the first Unitarian church in the county.[40]

Among the handful of Unitarian defectors from orthodoxy in the first half of the nineteenth century, Henry Dwight Sedgwick and his sister Catharine emerged as two of the most courageous. For Catharine, spending most of her life in Lenox and Stockbridge, the social risk of explicit liberalism

39. Dewey, *Autobiography*, pp. 38–39.
40. There were, however, three small congregations of that less so-
phisticated heresy, Universalism (the doctrine that all will eventually
be saved), in Berkshire in the 1840's.

was great. Friends plied her with orthodox tracts and assured her of their prayers; [41] but undismayed, she would often spend her Sundays at home with her Bible in preference to enduring the "unedifying" sermons of Stockbridge's "rustic parson," David Dudley Field. A thoroughgoing moralist, she felt convinced that the orthodox were simply seeking an easy route to heaven in place of the long and stony path of daily virtue.[42]

Yet even as Miss Sedgwick was expressing her objections, the orthodox church in Berkshire was continuing to extend its effective domain over county religious affairs through the Berkshire Association of Congregational Ministers. Founded in 1763 by parsons West and Hopkins, the Association took on a variety of duties: the licensing of Congregational clergy, the arrangements for ecclesiastical councils, the disciplining of wayward ministers, and, in the 1820's, the preparation of a county history.[43] Such an association of ministers represented,

41. Elizabeth Sedgwick Pomeroy to Robert Sedgwick, Oct. 1827; SP.

42. C. M. Sedgwick to Mrs. Henry Dwight Sedgwick, May 29, 1812; SP. Within the Sedgwick family the controversy proceeded with far more restraint and charity than prevailed in most pulpits. Catharine had to admit that the greater enthusiasm and energy of her orthodox acquaintances raised doubts in her mind about the Unitarians—"the indifference of the Unitarians seems to me to indicate a want of zeal. . . . While those of the orthodox faith are traversing sea and land, forsaking brethren and sisters, and houses and lands, and penetrating the untrodden wilderness, those of a 'purer and more rational faith' seem neither to lift their hands or breathe their prayers for its propagation" (letter to Mrs. Channing, Feb. 19, 1821; SP). Writing thus in the same year in which she joined the Unitarian Church, Miss Sedgwick had the perspicacity to recognize the salient weakness of Unitarianism in its lack of emotional vitality.

43. Like the rectors and vicars of rural England, many of the clergy of the Berkshire Association were interested in local history; at their meeting in Stockbridge, June 13, 1826, they voted:

"1st. That we will adopt measures to secure the writing, and as soon of course, a step away from the Congregational principle which allowed complete autonomy to each church and a step toward the integrated ecclesiastical polity of Presbyterianism. Certainly Congregationalism in Berkshire was more Presbyterianized in both polity and theology than in the other more liberally oriented Massachusetts counties, partly because the Berkshirites' emphasis on correct doctrine gave them a hard core around which to organize, and partly because the very survival of that doctrine required a closing of ranks against the liberals. If the members of the Berkshire Association, cohesive and single-minded as they were, never achieved any great success in their desire to Calvinize Boston, they did manage to make Berkshire the spiritual center of the Massachusetts Association of Congregational Ministers organized at Northampton in 1802. Even then, however, they could hardly have prided themselves on a complete victory, since four of the twelve Massachusetts districts had declined to become members of the orthodox-dominated state association.

While the years before 1763 had witnessed occasional informal gatherings of Berkshire clergy at irregular intervals, the Association as such was born only when Hopkins and West chose to father it, with a view to maintaining the orthodoxy which they had helped create.[44] Most of the Con-

as circumstances shall permit, the printing and circulation, of a History of the County; which shall embrace an account of every thing important in it, whether natural or artificial, civil, literary, or religious;—more particularly, which shall embrace an account of the settlement of the several Towns; the formation of Parishes and Churches; the settlement, dismission and death of Ministers; revival of religion, and sketches of the lives of eminent men.

"2nd. That Rev. Mr. Field be requested to collect and prepare the materials for said history."

These resolves are quoted in the introduction to Field, *History of Berkshire*.

44. Albert Hopkins, "Historical Discourse," *Proceedings of the Cen-*

gregational clerics in Berkshire felt a compelling need to talk
about their theological problems and to establish wherever
possible a body of uniform doctrine on debatable points.[45]
Especially in its precocious infancy, the Association was
superbly equipped for maintaining and transmitting the
new orthodoxy, with new pastors quickly falling under the
influence of Hopkins and West and with all the clergy com-
pellingly encouraged to form close personal relationships. A
dominant and magnetic personality, Dr. West inevitably
tended to mold such men as Alvan Hyde and Jacob Catlin
in his own orthodox image, and to these disciples fell the
leadership of Berkshire orthodoxy in the first quarter of
the nineteenth century.[46]

Before the turn of the century, the Berkshire Association had derived its strength entirely from the strength of
its member clergy in their own parishes. The people of Berkshire had early given proof of their eagerness for religion
and of their almost compulsive need to look to their ministers
for leadership, and even before the prospective church members had formally organized themselves, they would usually

*tennial,* pp. 21–22. The conflict between the Congregational principle
and the Presbyterian idea of Associations extended back through many
decades of New England history. The classic instance had come when
Cotton Mather, vigorously opposed by John Wise, tried to establish
a central authority to bolster a threatened orthodoxy. As Wise no doubt
recognized, the very principle of orthodoxy which implies authority
must necessarily be inimical to the ecclesiastical anarchy of pure Congregationalism.

45. The Association anticipated the Sabbath School Movement by a
decade in 1801 when it published *A Plan for the More Effectual Religious Instruction of Children and Youth* (Stockbridge, 1801), excerpts
in Pittsfield *Sun,* Dec. 23, 1800. This advised all the clergy to gather the
young people together for special instruction in the Westminster
Shorter Catechism and also recommended that clergy and serious people
try to persuade all school teachers to make use of the catechism or the
Bible daily.

46. Hopkins, *Proceedings of the Centennial,* p. 28.

have invited various young divines to preach for them on a trial basis.[47] Each preacher would be paid a salary either by the week or by the month, and so critical was the choice that very often a successful candidate might preach for several months before the suspense eased and he received the official call. With preaching jobs abounding, however, he need never have worried about finding eventual employment, and his decision to accept or reject a call might frequently hinge on rather personal and worldly considerations. Indeed, before the Reverend Alvan Hyde settled into his forty-five-year pastorate at Lee, he gave considerable thought to the healthfulness of the climate, the sufficiency of the salary, the guarantee of firewood, and the general character of the congregation as compared to West Stockbridge and Canaan, to which he had also received calls.

Like Hyde, most eighteenth-century Berkshire pastors accepted posts with the knowledge that they would spend their lives in filling them, and if ministerial power was not absolute, at least personal influence was profound under such a long-term system. Colonel Mark Hopkins once remarked that he could easily distinguish between a Lee Christian—solemn, taciturn, and rather dour like Hyde himself—and a Lenox Christian, always seeking to emulate Pastor Shepard's joviality,[48] and he might have characterized many another town just as succinctly. By the early nineteenth century, however, clergy and congregations were growing restless, tenures were becoming shorter, and men like hard-bitten old Parson Hyde

47. Great Barrington, while not incorporated until 1761 had boasted an organized church society of thirteen loyal members as early as 1742; Lanesboro, incorporated in 1765, had begun its church in 1764 with eight participating members; Lenox, incorporated in 1767, had formed a church by 1769; Lee, incorporated in 1777, had a church of thirty members by 1780; and Pittsfield, incorporated in 1761, formed a church of eight members in 1764. Cf. Church Records for these towns (typescripts in BA).

48. Hopkins, *Proceedings of the Centennial*, pp. 30–31.

were fighting in vain against the fading away of a system and of an era. "I have noticed with pain," wrote Hyde to a friend, "the dismission of ministers in your vicinity and in other parts of the country. . . . Are you aware that errors and delusions are creeping into the church?" [49] But neither Hyde nor any of the other old-time clergy could prevent the change from coming to Berkshire, and by 1840 the average tenure of a Congregational pastor was only twelve years, with his influence in the community dwindling accordingly.[50] Indeed, the change to a more or less peripatetic clergy appeared in tangible form in Stockbridge in 1838 with the building of a parsonage. Before this, the pastor had owned his own home.

Men of Hyde's generation had good reason to feel bitter when they remembered those eighteenth-century Berkshire clerics who had emerged from the heavy responsibilities of town leadership knowing as much about politics as about religion. With the solitary exception of a Lanesboro Tory named Daniel Collins, all of the Berkshire clerics had favored the Revolution; and Samuel Hopkins, not content with passive agreement, had become the actual leader of the Great Barrington Whigs of the late 1760's in opposition to the wealthy and largely Episcopalian Tory faction. Pittsfield's fighting parson, Thomas Allen, once a rifleman at the battle of Bennington, had assumed political leadership of all Berkshire in the period 1775–80.[51]

Not surprisingly, deep-seated religious principles had more than once influenced a cleric's political views. When Stephen West, for example, had delivered his funeral sermon at the execution of John Bly and Charles Rose for "burglary" (requisitioning supplies for Shays' men), he had expounded that Pauline doctrine of obedience to the powers that be which was so integral a part of his orthodoxy. "There are,"

49. *Memoir of the Reverend Alvan Hyde D.D.* (Boston, 1835), p. 138.
50. Holland, *Western Massachusetts*, 2, 463–619.
51. Smith, *History of Pittsfield*, 1, 340 ff.

he had declared, "particular occurrences which . . . turn
our attention to the nature and importance of civil government, and lead us to prize and revere it as a divine institution," and he had gone on to defend capital punishment as
being justified both by Mosaic law (the most excellent civil
government ever known on earth) and by the good of society.[52] Indeed the reminiscences of one parishioner would indicate that his liking for order extended even to his manners:
"His knock at the 'east door' was as recognizable as his
voice, that opened to him, he came in, and taking off his hat,
saluted each member of the family, down to the youngest,
with the exact ceremony, and something of the grace of a
French courtier; he then walked up to the table between
the two front windows, deposited his three-cornered beaver,
put his gloves in his hat, and his silver-headed cane in the
corner. . . . Then the dear little gentleman sat down, and
compressed the geniality of his nature into the social hour
that followed." [53]

Actually, few eighteenth-century Berkshire clerics had
been called upon to consider the merits of capital punishment in specific local instances, but all of them had maintained a tireless vigil over the manners and morals of their
communities and had occasionally proved stern discipli-
narians. And if pastoral authority had understandably tended
to vary with the strength of character of the individual cleric
and with the prestige enjoyed by the church, still such mis-
demeanors as frolicking, drinking, swearing, and fornication
had often brought church censure or even excommunication
upon the offender. By the 1820's, however, church discipline
was becoming limited mainly to admonitions for Sabbath-
breaking, and the keeper of the Stockbridge church records

52. Stephen West, *A Sermon Preached in Lenox, December 6th 1787
at the Execution of John Bly, and Charles Rose for Crimes of Burglary*
(Pittsfield, 1787), p. 7.

53. *Life and Letters of Sedgwick*, p. 61.

seldom recorded any proceeding more eventful than Thomas
Brown's confession on September 21, 1820, "that one sabbath morning I took a quantity of wool from the dip. This
was a violation of the fourth commandment and I am sincerely sorry."

Yet back in the 1770's and 80's, when moral discipline
remained closely linked to the larger issue of church authority and when the new orthodoxy was beginning its fight for
survival, church members did well to remember the example
of Mrs. Fisk and to mind both their manners and their
morals. No disciplinary case in all of the county's church history excited so much attention or stirred up so bitter a
controversy as the Fisk affair of 1779. In that year a Mrs.
Deane of the Stockbridge Church had married John Fisk, a
former captain in the Revolutionary army, who stood accused of the use of profane language. Mrs. Deane thus
brought excommunication upon herself. Indignant over
what she considered a gross injustice, she appealed her sen-
tence, and so inflammatory did the controversy become that
when the last words had finally been spoken, Berkshire
emerged, in the eyes of many, as the last stronghold of Puritan orthodoxy in New England.

In October 1779 Stephen West and John Bacon stood before the ecclesiastical council prepared to speak in defense
of the Stockbridge Church, and the Reverend Joseph Huntington traveled to Berkshire from his Connecticut parish to
plead the injustice of Mrs. Fisk's penalty. Neither Mrs. Fisk
nor the cause of liberal Congregationalism could have found
a better advocate. Flinging a challenge at both accusers and
council members, he posed question after question. Who
could name the crimes of this immoral man? How immoral
must a man be to become ineligible for marriage to a church
member? Admitted that sin intermixes itself with all we do,
what censurable error had Mrs. Fisk committed? Could anyone quote a biblical authority or a precedent in church his-

tory which might in any way justify the action of the Stockbridge Church? [54]

Having thus dealt with the immediate aspects of the case,
Huntington proceeded to a bitter attack on Berkshire orthodoxy—an attack which eloquently summarized the position of the liberal opposition. "It will do those who are rulers
in the house of God no harm," he declared, "to understand a
little of human nature." [55] Marriage, after all, is a union between a man and a woman and not between spiritual ideas.
The Puritans were exhibiting a sinful presumption in considering marriage as an institution for angels—and even
worse, in daring to judge the inner man, as they had done
with Fisk. By "over intense application to abstruse points and
curious unprofitable speculations," Huntington charged that
West had brought himself into a state of partial delirium
and had consequently carried church discipline to unscrip-
tural severities.

Leaning heavily on Edwardsean teachings and on the
Puritan tradition, West in his turn rationally argued that
in a world divided between the antithetical interests of Christ
and Satan, no middle ground can exist. He went on to speak
of "mongrel marriages" which allow the corruption of the
world to spread into the church. Would not the Reverend
Joseph Huntington's shockingly liberal view encourage young
bucks and debauchees to improve this hint into a liberty of
general indulgence? Granted that the Stockbridge Church
had imposed an unreasonable restraint upon the Fisks, are
not all Christian demands necessarily unreasonable?

In the end Mrs. Fisk, remaining in a state of excommunication, emigrated to Vermont. Despite the eloquence of the
actors, this dramatization of theological conflict brought

54. Joseph Huntington, *A Plea before the Ecclesiastical Council at
Stockbridge in the Cause of Mrs. Fisk by a Gentleman of Connecticut*
(Boston, 1782), pp. 16–18.

55. Ibid., pp. 30 ff.

no true solutions. Within Berkshire, however, the case had accomplished Dr. West's deepest purpose. It had produced a galvanic effect on the local orthodoxy and had welded Berkshire clerics together more closely than ever in their defense of the Edwardsean system.

Still, by the time Catlin and Hyde assumed leadership,[56] Berkshire orthodoxy was more on the defensive than it had been a generation earlier, and when the county's parsons came together at Windsor on October 15, 1816, for their semiannual meeting, they confessed to such doubts as West and Hopkins would never have admitted: "in what sense are militant saints in a state of probation?" they asked themselves that October, and the following February at Dalton they debated "How far can our churches hold communion with churches of other denominations?" Yet if, under the theologically uncertain leadership of the new generation, the severity of doctrinal controls abated, change came only very slowly and after several bitter rear guard actions. In 1788 a citizen of Lee named Jesse Bradley unhappily discovered just how far such men as Hyde were willing to go in their jealous defense of orthodoxy. In common with other heretics, Bradley had found the doctrine of universal salvation a logical corollary of Calvinism, and with more courage than most of his fellow-doubters he said so. The result was electrifying. Parson Hyde, realizing that Bradley's rebellion would bring into question the relationship between the orthodox church and other sects within the county, quickly sought the additional authority of an ecclesiastical council. The council in turn saw here an opportunity of reasserting, by compelling example, the principle of Congregational monopoly; and after declaring that Hyde's church might not

56. A direct line of influence can be traced through the orthodox leadership from Edwards to Hyde. Samuel Hopkins was the pupil and biographer of Jonathan Edwards; West, the pupil and biographer of Hopkins; and Hyde, the pupil and biographer of West.

dismiss a member and recommend him to a church with
which it was not in fellowship, they condemned Bradley
to the spiritual and social loneliness of excommunication—
a fate virtually equivalent to social ostracism in Lee in the
1790's.[57]

Such a case, however, could not silence for long the growing challenges from outside the church—challenges voiced
from within the county by mounting numbers of articulate
dissenters and from without by eastern liberals—and Association members felt increasingly compelled to band together
in a spontaneous spirit of friendliness allowing of "no attack
of motives, no invectives, no lashing hypercriticism, no personalities." [58] As the sense of insecurity deepened, the Association attempted to exercise its authority more rigidly. Even
early in the new century, no prospective cleric could have
hoped to receive a license without first being tested upon
the correctness of his views, and by 1832, when Professor
Mark Hopkins of Williams College was applying for membership, the prerequisites included two years' study of theology with one of the members of the Association or two
years' study and a certification from a theological school.[59]
Once installed, the properly qualified cleric could expect to
receive from the Association as much loyalty as he gave to it,
and he could preach the astringent doctrines of divine grace
confident in the powerful backing of Association members.
With the independence of the clerical profession thus guaranteed, and with the resultant long tenures, the letter if not
the spirit of the new orthodoxy was kept very much alive.

Members found the Association at times benevolent and at

57. *A Narrative of two Excommunications upon Jesse Bradley,* Stockbridge, 1796.
58. Hopkins, *Proceedings of the Centennial,* p. 40 (quoted from a letter of Chester Dewey).
59. *Early Letters of Mark Hopkins,* ed. Susan S. Hopkins (New York,
1929), p. 272.

times severe, but always unbending in support of orthodoxy. When the Reverend Samuel Monson found himself accused by a parishioner of passion, violence, and a disposition for worldly gain, he hastily appealed to the Association and was reassured that "nothing of censurable nature is supported by evidence more than those common frailties and imperfections that often adhere to wise and pious characters." [60] Yet two years later a West Stockbridge cleric named John Camp stood before the Association damningly accused of leaning toward liberal theological beliefs and was only restored to grace after a confession of error, an abject apology, and a promise of future restraint. [61]

With the coming of the nineteenth century, Berkshire clerics seeking to maintain the vitality of their orthodox church could no longer depend on the absolute authority of the past, and they felt obliged eventually to look more realistically to the current revivalist enthusiasms. All over New England they saw periodic revivals continually renewing the emotional fire of parishioners, and following the second Great Awakening at the turn of the century they could hardly have failed to realize that revivalism was assuming a major

60. *Western Star,* Sept. 18, 1792.

61. Ibid., Oct. 28, 1794. Parson Camp had preached a sermon in which he indiscreetly expressed his belief that even unregenerate men can do things which are acceptable to God. What was worse, an appendix to the published sermon represented the Berkshire Association as maintaining that a sinner who painstakingly attends to the state of his soul and to the will of God is no more likely to be saved than a sinner who is careless and openly vicious. The Association met on Oct. 14, 1794, to consider the case, and so highly did they value an appearance of unity that they published a description of the entire proceedings in the *Western Star,* concluding: "since our disunion has become a matter of public notoriety, to the great wounding of the cause of Christ, we feel it important to publish the above statement of our difficulties and settlement."

role in the life of the churches. Usually coming after several years of religious indifference, such New England revivals would often snowball until they had become social phenomena in which an entire town population might be drawn together in the experience of spiritual rebirth. Here was just the kind of emotional spirituality that Berkshire clerics needed to spark the religious imagination of congregations fast losing interest in abstract theological speculation. Here was a way of acknowledging the inability of human nature to live continuously on the supernatural heights demanded by their theology and of admitting the inevitable ebb and flow of human affairs. If kept within properly conservative limits, they saw no reason why revivals might not be encouraged.

Actually, Berkshire clerics need not have worried that emotionalism would get out of hand. Having never lapsed into an Arminian, moralistic religion, the congregations of the county had seldom indulged in those emotional extremities common to some towns in New York State and central Massachusetts, and Berkshire revivalism remained, for the most part, rather reserved. In fact, the Reverend Samuel Shepard of Lenox, who led the great revival of 1799, reported later that he had witnessed no outcries, visions, or wild enthusiasms of those awakened,[62] and both Shepard and Hyde took pride in the uniformity and purity of doctrine professed by awakened members of their churches.[63] Later, when Professor Chester Dewey was leading a major revival among Williams College students in the spring of 1812, he preached at length on the importance of consolidating their religion in definite articles of faith. "Fixed principles," he said, "are just as important in religion as in politics." [64] In much the same

62. Samuel Shepard, "The Revival of Religion in Lenox," *Connecticut Evangelical Magazine* (Oct. 1801), p. 146.

63. *Memoir of the Rev. Alvan Hyde*, p. 362.

64. Chester Dewey, *A Sermon Occasioned by the Present Religious Attention in Williams College* (Stockbridge, 1812), p. 10.

way, every Berkshire cleric struggled to provide sufficient theological ballast to keep the newly awakened on an unwavering course.

Always a ready spokesman, Alvan Hyde expressed the thoughts of most of his Berkshire colleagues when he came to the defense of conservative revivals but deplored the use of machinery "which quickly wears itself out . . ." [65] Mark Hopkins was almost equally cautious and suspicious of novelty, and when he witnessed the famous Troy cleric, the Reverend Nathaniel Beman, using the "anxious seat" during a revival in Williamstown, he admitted that he considered it effective and wisely done—but only because of Beman's genius. "Don't infer," he hastened to add, "that I am in favor of the new measures. . . . they could do harm. . . . ministers in general had better go in the old way." [66] Like Hyde, Hopkins dreaded the disease of sensationalism and feared any itinerant preacher who might spread the contagion. As Hyde was to put it later, "foreign aid, at such times, is often very dangerous . . . the plan of sending out evangelists as revival men, where there are settled pastors . . . will distract and rend the churches. Nothing should be allowed to weaken the bond between pastor and congregation; the only aid the pastor needs for revivals is a faithful, praying Congregation." [67]

In the final reckoning the success of the Berkshire churches in channeling the enthusiasm of the early nineteenth-century revivals went back in part to the solidarity of the clergy in the Berkshire Association and in part to the residue of enthusiastic religion which had always remained a characteristic of Berkshire religion since the days of Edwards. With a theology which emphasized the doctrines of depravity and grace, Berkshire religious leaders could never completely

65. *Memoir of the Rev. Alvan Hyde,* p. 356.
66. *Early Letters of Mark Hopkins,* p. 258.
67. *Memoir of the Rev. Alvan Hyde,* p. 141.

subside into pure moralism, and Berkshire's Methodist evangelists were to find to their disappointment that revivalism
in Berkshire would remain almost universally conservative,
with most of the fruits falling to the orthodox churches.[68]

Once the emotional drive of revivalism had been un-
leashed, religious activism came easily to Berkshire orthodoxy. In the hustle of the Jeffersonian era, public opinion
was already dictating that no man could deserve the name of
Christian who did not actively serve his God, and the orthodox churches had simply to align themselves with the activist
spirit of the nation to avoid the embarrassing consequences
of traveling any further down the dead-end street of their
own theological speculations.

Coming as one important result of the new activism, the
missionary movement, both at home and abroad, received
essential contributions from the people of Berkshire. Because
the County lay near the edge of the territory of compact settlement and harbored a number of well-organized churches,
it became a natural area from which efforts might be
launched to carry the Gospel into the thinly populated regions of central New York, and even to northeastern Berkshire where no regular clergy had settled. With such purposes
in mind, Berkshirites met on February 21, 1798, with their
neighbors from Columbia, County, New York, to organize
the first home mission society in the country. While the Berkshire Association of Congregational Ministers certainly constituted an indispensable element in the missionary project,
orthodox clerics by no means dominated the new society. The
majority of members, in fact, were laymen, and meetings
were generally held either in a schoolhouse or in a private
home. Besides the Reverend Jacob Catlin and the Reverend

68. Lorenzo Dow, *Biography and Miscellany*, Norwich, Conn., 1834;
*Memoirs of Life and Travels of Billy Hibbard*, New York, 1825.

Alvan Hyde, those who held offices in the society were such men as Barnabas Bidwell and David Rosseter, lawyers; John Hotchkin, preceptor of Lenox Academy; Timothy Edwards, Stockbridge storekeeper; and William Walker, Judge of Probate.

In an address to the Berkshire public the society clearly and conscientiously stated its principles—principles which included a considerably greater emphasis on works and a notably milder emphasis on grace than would have been considered permissible by most Berkshirites of the previous generation: "Friends and Fellow Mortals, We are all travelling, in rapid procession to the eternal world. On this narrow, and busy stage, we are forming characters, which will be established forever; and which will introduce us shortly, to realms of glory, or regions of woe. Eternity will be to us, joyful or sorrowful, according to the part we act in this life respecting the kingdom of Jesus Christ. . . . from this weighty consideration, may be urged the importance of missionary exertions." [69] Incorporated in 1816 and supported by a yearly income of $1,000, the Missionary Society continued to thrive for a generation and came to an end only when most of the work in its area of operations had been completed. Knowing that the missions on the far frontiers were being watched over by the American Home Mission Society, the Berkshire Society finally disbanded in 1858 and left the income from its trust fund to any destitute Congregational Church in the county.

Only eight years after the birth of the Home Mission

[69]. *Address of the Congregational Missionary Society of Berkshire and Columbia to the Churches and Congregations of Berkshire,* Stockbridge, 1805. The details of missionary activity often reached a wide audience through the Reverend Jedidiah Morse's journal of Orthodoxy, the *Panoplist.* In 1808, for example, there was a report of the Reverend Samuel Shepard's nine-day mission in northern Berkshire: he traveled 80 miles, preached thirteen sermons, visited ten families and two schools, and received $3.63 for the society. *Panoplist, 3* (1808), 514.

Society a young Connecticut boy named Samuel J. Mills came to Williams to prepare himself for foreign missionary work and, with the major revival of 1805 just over, found the school a fertile spot in which to plant his own religious fervor. He had soon organized a series of open-air prayer meetings, at one of which—the famous Haystack Meeting— he propounded his plans for world evangelism.[70] A few years later he and three of his fellow students at Andover Seminary presented a petition to the General Association of Massachusetts Congregational Churches which led in 1812 to the formation of the American Board for Foreign Missions.[71]

Meanwhile, the austerities of neopuritanism were finding their fullest expression in the multitude of Moral Societies, Bible and Tract Societies, and Sabbath School Unions springing up all over the county. Even before the organization of the central county society on June 11, 1815 (The Berkshire Society for Promoting Good Morals), Lenox, Stockbridge, and Sheffield had formed societies of their own for the encouragement of morals. The morality inculcated by these societies remained, for the most part, simple, formal, and individual; and if a Marxist should choose to see in their paternalistic regulation of the manners and morals of servants a bourgeois plan to keep the lower orders respectful,

70. Two years later, he and four of his friends formed a secret society of "the Brethren," whose membership lay open only to those planning to become foreign missionaries. Cf. Byram Green to Albert Hopkins, Aug. 22, 1845 (MS letter in Williams College Library), quoted in Leverett W. Spring, *History of Williams College* (Boston, 1917), p. 79.

71. During his years at Williams, Mills exercised a great influence over Edwin Wells Dwight of Stockbridge, and Dwight himself eventually took over the direction of a school in Cornwall, Connecticut, which trained youth from primitive societies to become missionaries. Dwight's biography of his prize pupil, Henry Obookiah, published in 1818, had a great influence on missionary endeavor in the Sandwich Islands, from which Obookiah had come and to which his early death prevented him from returning.

he could hardly think that their fundamental aim. Their essential emphasis was fixed rather on the danger of sabbath-breaking, swearing, and dancing—all well-intrenched folkways—and they avoided the large and often ambiguous questions of social and economic morality. They wanted, in short, a maximum of righteousness for a minimum of sacrifice. Religious leaders had long since recognized the declining role being played by religion in daily life, and in an unconscious effort to regain lost ground, they were clinging to a superficial insistence upon outward moral conformity. To enforce that conformity, the societies depended largely on moral suasion or, in the case of Sunday travelers, on a brief "arrest," and only once in Stockbridge in 1815 did they ever go so far as to fine as well as arrest an offender.[72]

During these years, Berkshirites proved themselves quite willing to walk along the road that led from the Puritanism of Jonathan Edwards to its degradation into Victorian respectability, and as piety continued to pass toward moralism, such additional groups were organized as the Berkshire Education Society (1818), intended to raise funds for the ministerial education of pious but indigent young men; the Berkshire Bible Society, which urged its members to "shake the drowsy poppies from our brows" and provide the destitute with Bibles;[73] and the Berkshire Sabbath School Union.[74]

72. Dwight, *Travels, 4,* 12; *Extracts from Reports Made to the Berkshire Society for Promoting Good Morals* (Pittsfield, 1815), pp. 6–15.

73. J. E. A. Smith, ed., *History of Berkshire County* (2 vols. J. B. Beers, New York, 1885), *1,* 436. From 1840 to 1844 all the active officers of the American Bible Society came from Berkshire.

74. Of these societies, the Pittsfield branch of the Sabbath School Union probably enjoyed the greatest success. In 1818 they could boast 167 pupils and 21 teachers, with sessions from 9:00 to 10:30 and 12:00 to 1:30 each Sunday. They emphasized rote learning and proudly reported that forty of their pupils had learned the whole of the shorter Westminster Catechism and that a total of 18,959 verses of the Bible had been memorized.

Inevitably, a profound change in religious thought accompanied the new activism—a change in which Alvan Hyde and John Leland found much to criticize. Barriers between the sects were breaking down,[75] parish divisions were fading, and the random conglomeration of ideas that passed for theology among the missionary societies and revivalists moved Hyde to declare: "I see much human frailty and imperfection in all these movements—much display—much which tends to evil, and will unavoidably issue in it, if God do not prevent. Many are burying truth, as fast as the Jews did before the advent of Christ, while they are full of zeal. Important distinctions are overlooked; and it is probable, that it will not be long, before it will be necessary to have another president Edwards raised up to make a mighty effort to rescue the truth, as it is in Jesus, from the mass of rubbish gathering around it." [76]

The Baptist John Leland spoke impatiently of the weighty machinery established in the societies; money and not grace, he said, was making the wheels turn. The societies were offering men a way of commuting their real religious duties (lives of sacrifice and virtue) into a cash payment; and they might as well retranslate the Bible accordingly. Let Matthew 10:7 —"And as ye go, preach, saying, the Kingdom of heaven is at hand"—be rendered so as to read: "And as ye go, preach to the people, your money is essential to the salvations of sinners, and, therefore, form into societies and use all devisable means to collect money for the Lord's treasury; for the millenium is at hand." [77] In short, Leland felt that the new societies were converting Christianity into a religion of merit in which good works in the form of contributions were replacing inner grace as the requirement for salvation.

---

75. *Berkshire Star,* July 31, 1817. Heman Willard wrote: "it is the glory of the Bible Associations that they stand upon a lofty eminence on which all classes and denominations of Christians may meet."

76. *Memoir of the Rev. Alvan Hyde,* p. 87.

77. Leland, *Writings,* p. 492.

By midcentury Berkshire religious thought had become so various as to make any generalizations impossible. In Lenox, then a particularly literary town, the Reverend Henry Neill was proving himself as much a literary critic as a theologian, and could discuss aesthetic theory and the ideas of Goethe with the most learned of his parishioners. South of Lenox, in Sheffield, the noted Unitarian clergyman Orville Dewey had returned to the family farm in 1848 to write his "Lectures on the Problem of Human Destiny" for delivery at the Lowell Institute in 1851,[78] using sources—the rational Christianity of Channing and German romanticism (especially Herder's *Philosophy of History and Humanity*)—which were far removed from the native Berkshire theological tradition.

During these same heterogeneous years a very un-Edwardsean theory of religious education was evolving, and as early as 1834 the Reverend John Yeomans had ventured to express an idea which Horace Bushnell developed more fully twelve years later in his *Christian Nurture*. "Who could foretell," asked Yeomans, "the effects of a thorough combination of science with religion, through the process of education? . . . It would be teaching religion diligently to our children; obeying a divine command, which is made the condition of a divine and gracious promise. It would be training up our children in the nurture and admonition of the Lord. . . . We exceed not the truth when we say that education may give universal prevalence to true religion." [79] Under the pastorate of John Todd (1842–72), Pittsfield was to become a center for the implementation of the Christian nurture theology, with Todd himself producing such religio-educational works as *The Young Man, Student's Manual,* and *The Daughter at School*. And if those seemed too unimaginative, Berkshire youth could always turn to Catharine Sedgwick's

78. Dewey, *Autobiography*, p. 108.
79. *A Sermon . . . on the Day of the General Election* (Boston, 1834), p. 24.

moralistic novels. Both Parson Todd and Miss Sedgwick emphasized manners as much as morals; their books aimed not only at making people Christians but also at making them ladies and gentlemen—aims which earlier Berkshirites would have found none too compatible.

Out of the midcentury babble of tongues in the County, any search for a single voice at once related to the Berkshire religious tradition and echoing some real significance for the future might well have led to Mark Hopkins, that most famous of Williams College presidents. While neither a systematizer nor a profound thinker, Hopkins earned for himself a place in the list of Americans from Edwards to William James who have concerned themselves with the psychology of religion. Born in Stockbridge in 1802, Hopkins had studied first in the district school and later at Lenox Academy, Williams College, and the Berkshire Medical Institute. Having received his medical degree in 1829, he had moved to New York City to practice his profession for nearly two years, and even after his return to Williams as an instructor, he had never been able to shake off the effects of his medical training. The problem of the relation of mind and body continued to fascinate him and eventually contributed to his rejection of philosophy and natural religion.

Hopkins turned away impatiently from the eighteenth-century attempts to prove the truth of Christianity through external evidence. For him the only real evidences must be internal. "My recitation with Seniors," he wrote to his brother, "was in Paley's *Natural Theology.* . . . I have undertaken to show that Paley's argument does not amount to much and to substitute a better in its place." [80] He shrewdly realized that even though Paley's books were widely used in the schools, they could hardly succeed in converting readers to orthodox religion. Because Paley used only external arguments, he could establish only natural re-

80. *Early Letters of Mark Hopkins,* p. 239.

ligion, and his books would consequently tend to limit thought to the framework and terms of natural religion. Hopkins, on the other hand, emphasized the internal evidences of Christianity and man's intuition as valid means of arriving at faith. The real arguments for Christianity, he felt, must be not the miracles but the transcendent character of Christ; not Old Testament prophecies but the perfect adaptation of Christianity to the human spirit.

When he talked about the problems of conversion, Hopkins sounded more like a country doctor than a learned theologian. His Lowell Institute Lecture of 1844, *The Evidences of Christianity,* contained the core of his religious thinking. With wry humor he admitted the fallacy of the idea that the "infidelity that springs from the heart" could be eliminated by a simple educational process or "a course of lectures on the evidences of Christianity." [81] He knew that man's heart would prevent a proper examination of the evidence: "the truth almost never has a fair chance with such a being as man, when the reception of it involves self-denial, or the recognition of duties to which he is indisposed." [82]

In his summary condemnation of infidelity, he seemed to anticipate the pragmatic tone of William James. An infidel, he pointed out, has nothing positive in his belief, and therefore nothing can be objected to. As for infidelity, "We can say that it is a state of mind from which no good can possibly come, either to the individual or the community. . . . It can be made to appear, from the very laws of the mind, that great achievements, powerful exertions, self-denying labors and sacrifices must spring from a vigorous faith." [83]

A century earlier Samuel Hopkins had insisted that a Christian hold orthodox beliefs on all the major points of

81. *Evidences of Christianity. Lectures before the Lowell Institute, January, 1844* (Boston, 1846), p. 334.

82. Ibid., p. 21.

83. Ibid., pp. 333–34.

Calvinism; now in the 1840's his grandnephew Mark was content simply to convert people to Christianity. In his rejection of the niceties of theological speculation, Mark by no means intended to minimize the importance of religion; but such a vague and unobtrusive theology did fit more easily into minds that were increasingly occupied with secular affairs. Under the old Berkshire orthodoxy, best symbolized by Stephen West and his extreme Edwardsean theology, religion had claimed an undisputed position at the center of men's lives, with all other activities merely subordinate. Now it had become only one activity among many, and Berkshire was belatedly following the rest of the country into more secular outlooks and pursuits.

# Chapter 4. A GREAT DEAL OF DISSENT

IN THE Massachusetts Constitutional Convention of 1820, when the relations of the established church with the civil government were being debated, a practical-minded Berkshire physician, Henry Halsey Childs, was to emerge as a leader of the liberal wing favoring equality of all religious sects before the law. While Berkshire, in the early 1800's, remained a stronghold of theological conservatism, an ever-expanding group of realistic Congregationalists had appeared who, along with the small but active dissenting sects, were highly critical of any tie between church and state. The controversy thus joined over church-state relations had been clouding the religious atmosphere in Berkshire for forty years and had taught Dr. Childs, by repeated example, the hopeless inexpediency of retaining those laws which would establish the Congregational Church. However conservative his basic intellectual position, he was among the first to concede to the pressure of events and to adopt a liberal viewpoint on this one vital political issue. "A standing army," he said, would be needed to enforce the "principle that the government has the right to compel the support of public worship." [1]

At first, when only a handful of people, few of them wealthy, had settled in the County and when most towns were finding difficulty in supporting even one church, the people had good reason for setting up a system whereby religious taxes could be levied in town meeting. But even as early as the mid-eighteenth century, citizens of Great Barrington experienced stirrings of the restless desire for religious freedom. To some of Samuel Hopkins' recalcitrant flock in these early

1. *Journal of the Debates and Proceedings in the Convention of Delegates Chosen to Revise the Constitution of Massachusetts, Reported for the Boston Daily Advertiser* (Boston, 1821), p. 165.

years, and particularly to the often wealthy Dutch settlers
among them, such an unbending morality and rigid Calvinistic theology as the new parson preached soon became intol-
erable. A few had protested the forced payment of church
taxes, a few more had demanded that they be allowed to
attend services in Dutch, and finally Hopkins had felt moved
to declare once and for all that "whoever does not like my
doctrine can pull up stakes and be gone." [2]

Instead, the rebellious members chose to defy his ulti-
matum and to invite the Reverend Thomas Davies, a missionary of the Society for the Propagation of the Gospel, to
come to Great Barrington to lead them in Episcopalian worship. These dissenting Dutchmen, together with several
Yorkers, formed St. James Episcopal Church in 1764 and, by
petitioning the legislature, managed to obtain the legal right
to share in the town's religious tax money. For the Congregational Church, the results were catastrophic. Hopkins, having lost one-third of his church membership and a part of his
salary, and finding that he could remain in Great Barrington
only by becoming a part-time farmer, soon moved on to
Newport; [3] and without him the church disintegrated. The
Congregationalists found no other minister, and the next
twenty-five years took their toll on the unused meetinghouse
—"the windows were broken, the door had fallen down, and
the floor had long been occupied by sheep." [4]

To the pessimistic conservatives who looked back on the
Great Barrington incident as the inevitable outcome of dis-
sension, an occurrence in Becket in 1798 came as a telling
refutation. In that small Berkshire hill town, where no majority sect and thus no town support of the Gospel had even
existed between 1788 and 1798, sixty citizens banded together in February to form a Congregational Church Society

2. Great Barrington Church Records, p. 388; BA.
3. Hopkins, "Memoir of Samuel Hopkins," *Works,* p. 52.
4. Ibid., pp. 55–56.

and penned a hardheaded preamble to their covenant: "We the subscribers . . . having found, by several years experience, the great difficulty of settling and supporting a minister, in the usual way of taxation, or even to supply the pulpit, by reason of the great number of ana-baptists and Methodists, who have appeared in opposition to taxation and have carried their vote . . . and to avoid contention with our neighbors of different denominations agree to support the church [*by voluntary contributions*]." [5] While neither large nor wealthy, the little Congregational group of Becket did persevere until they had built a meetinghouse and settled a minister; and the membership thereafter enjoyed a gradual but uninterrupted growth. Here was one town at least to which liberals could point as proof that the luxury of religious freedom did not always endanger the Gospel ministry.

The Massachusetts courts might continue to interpret the State Constitution so as to perpetuate the ties between church and state, but the ties were dissolving nonetheless. In Berkshire, where the 1770's and 80's had witnessed an unprecedented flood of new settlers, the populations of a few towns had begun to exhibit a religious diversity comparable to that of the seaports. When no one sect could any longer muster a majority of votes in town meeting, the separation of church and state was becoming, as it had in Boston and the larger eastern towns, a practical necessity.

Yet the large and wealthy town of Pittsfield, even with its numbers of outspoken dissenters, was to find religious freedom peculiarly elusive. With the steady growth in population, the original Congregational meetinghouse, built in 1762, had become too small by 1790, and a committee had met to estimate and apportion the cost of building a new one. As far as possible, they had decided to allow each citizen to pay his share either in materials or in labor. Stephen Fowler, for example, would supply the ridgepole; Colonel

5. Joseph L. Mills, *The Church's Retrospect* (Pittsfield, 1816), p. 16 n.

Oliver Post, fifty feet of oak posts; Zebulon Stiles, a fifty-foot
sill. But £700 still remained to be collected through taxes on
polls, personal property, and faculties. As soon as the town
—a parish for religious purposes—began pursuing its legal
right to tax polls and estates for the support of the Gospel,
the dissenters rebelliously broke ranks.[6] Although only forty
men, or one-tenth of the taxpayers, numbered themselves
among the dissenters, they could rally a strength out of all
proportion to their meager numbers; and Baptists, Methodists, Episcopalians, and Shakers all forgot their differences
in desperate cooperation against the Congregationalists.

The Pittsfield Baptist Church had begun in 1772 under
the leadership of Valentine Rathbun. A clothier by trade and
a man with very little formal education, Rathbun was one of
the most radical political leaders in Pittsfield during the
Revolution. So successful were his efforts at organizing the
Baptists that by 1790 a town meeting had to admit the presence of twenty-one bona fide Baptists on the list of taxpayers.
As for the Shakers, several apostate Baptists formed their entire strength in Pittsfield. On her tour from Harvard, Massachusetts, to Watervliet, New York, in 1780, Mother Ann Lee
had stopped in Pittsfield long enough to convert several Baptists (even including Elder Rathbun for six months) to
Shakerism by capitalizing on a revival then in progress. Having only been introduced to Pittsfield as recently as 1788, the
Methodist Church comprised the weakest group of dissenters,
but their numbers had increased so rapidly that, under the
leadership of the persuasive Lorenzo Dow, they erected their
own meetinghouse. The Episcopalians could count only six
Pittsfield taxpayers as members, but because four of these

6. The heaviest assessment on real estate was £10 10s 2d on Charles
Goodrich, who owned over a thousand acres; the largest assessment on
personal property was £7 on Colonel Danforth; and the largest on
faculty was £1 4s 9d on the lawyer-storekeeper John C. Williams. The
final cost of the building was £2,188, its estimated cost £1,100—thus the
necessity for two levies on the taxable polls. Cf. Smith, *History of Pittsfield, 1,* 434–38.

were men of wealth, the little group lent a tone of respectability to the dissenters' ranks; and it was they—opposing the
established church rather from policy than from principle—
who spearheaded the campaign for religious freedom.

At a town meeting in August of 1790, the dissenters presented a formal statement of their opposition to the new
meetinghouse. Signed by the Baptist Rathbun, the Episcopalian Van Schaack, and eight other opposition leaders, the
statement persuasively protested the general tax as a subordination of one sect to another in direct violation of the
Massachusetts Constitution. Further: "As the subscribers to
this paper are freeholders and inhabitants of the town aforesaid, differing in religious sentiments with those for whose
use the said place of worship is building, they do in this public manner disclaim any right or pretention to the same,
under the idea that it cannot . . . be considered as a town
building . . . and that as we, in our several stations, contribute a share of our property voluntarily to the support of
the gospel, according to our religious professions, we do
claim it as our right to be exempted from any assessments." [7]
When the protest failed to bring results, Van Schaack began
to devise a double-barreled campaign to gain tax exemption
for the dissenters. He would appeal to public opinion by carrying on an intensive campaign in the press, and at the same
time, he would take his case into the courts.

As a Federalist and a close friend of Loring Andrews and
Theodore Sedgwick, Van Schaack found quick support for
his plan of publicizing his views in Berkshire's leading newspaper, the *Western Star* of Stockbridge. On December 27,
1791, an article, enigmatically signed "T.Z." stated the case
for the dissenters:

> If the parishioners of the less numerous societies of
> Christians produce . . . in open town meeting reason
> able evidence of their belonging to a protestant persua-

7. Ibid., p. 457.

> sion, and contribute to the support of their own mode of
> worship . . . ought they after this is done to be bur-
> thened by those of another persuasion, because they have
> the majority of votes in the town meeting. . . . Is one
> sect of Christians competent to judge for another what
> is suitable provision for the institution of publick wor-
> ship of God and what sum is necessary to support the
> teacher of another persuasion? . . . Will our Constitu-
> tion admit that a majority in a town is to govern in reli-
> gious as well as civil matters? [8]

A series of six articles followed, all signed simply "A Berkshire Farmer," and all probably originating with Andrews
and Van Schaack. Indignantly accusing the courts of inter-
preting Article III of the Declaration of Rights so as to vio-
late minority rights, the writers argued that in Pittsfield
as elsewhere the majority was tyrannizing over a relatively
helpless minority when, after all, "no majority has the right
to impose taxation for their own benefit on the minority;
contrary doctrines tend directly to establish an alarming
aristocracy." [9]

The same article of February 7, 1792, pointed out that the
religious liberty then enjoyed in Boston had not driven civil
society into chaos. Berkshire's own history, in fact, could provide several examples of the healthy survival of religious sects
without any support from the town. "The Congregational
Society of West Stockbridge lately built a new meeting house.

8. *Western Star*, Dec. 27, 1791. Before this article appeared, Van
Schaack had written to Theodore Sedgwick asking whether he felt
that "the subject is too daringly or too sparingly handled" (Henry Van
Schaack to Theodore Sedgwick, Pittsfield, December 10, 1791; SP).
Realizing that the Congregational Church had always been a great bulwark to Federalism, Van Schaack feared that Sedgwick might in this
case favor expediency over justice. His fears, however, were groundless,
for equally outspoken articles continued to appear.

9. *Western Star*, Feb. 7, 1792.

Were those of other persuasions compelled to contribute towards the expense? They were not. The Congregationalists being a great majority in that town did not exact money from others, which, under similar circumstances they would not readily pay themselves." In Stockbridge itself, the article continued, the Congregationalists had built a church in 1783 without levying a religious tax; in Great Barrington and Lanesboro, the Episcopalians had built their own churches with no expense to the town; and in Hancock the Shakers had borne the entire expense for their new meetinghouse. A month earlier, the *Western Star* (January 3, 1792) had published a letter from a Stockbridge Baptist testifying to the absence of dispute in Stockbridge. "I now inform you," read the letter, "that the Baptists here support their mode of worship unmolested. The prevailing sect with us are the congregationalists . . . those gentlemen have as yet not discovered the justice or policy to burden people of other persuasions for building their Meeting House or supporting their Minister." [10]

An able mind and the leading Federalist political manager in Berkshire, Henry Van Schaack was not a person to be ignored, but even as he was preparing to take his briefs

10. The following list of names clarifies the motives of some delinquents in payment of the religious tax. "Names of Persons who wish to be added to the list of exemptions from the Minister's Tax:

| | |
|---|---|
| Robert Francis | — pleads conveniency. |
| Dyer Fitch | — rather a Baptist in sentiment |
| Seth James | — a Baptist as much as anything, and now supports Mr. Rathbun on Sundays. |
| Seth Dickinson | — can't pay his debts. |
| Caleb Wadhams | — cannot attend on Mr. Allen, because he thinks it not right to support a minister by a tax. |
| Israel Miner | — thinks he ought not to pay his rates to him, and is a Shaker as much as anything." |

Cf. Smith, *History of Pittsfield, 1,* 460.

against the assessors to court, the town meeting stood firmly
behind the religious tax—voting to indemnify the assessors
should Van Schaack win his case. Having heard Judge Paine
laugh his case out of the court of common pleas, Van Schaack
imperturbably gathered together his evidence and carried it
to the Supreme Court. He had already been assured by his
friend Dr. Parker of Boston that the higher court, with its
reputation at stake, could not afford to allow their personal
prejudices to override justice,[11] and just as Parker had pre-
dicted, the Supreme Court decided in Van Schaack's favor at
its October session in 1793. The Pittsfield Congregationalists
paid the costs of the suit, and the dissenters received an exemption from religious taxes upon presentation of certificates from their various pastors.[12] Yet Van Schaack could not
help knowing that his victory remained incomplete, and in
a letter to Judge Dana he described both his sense of triumph
and his disappointment that complete religious freedom had
still to be attained:

> It is, I think, about two years ago, in an intemperate
> desultory conversation (at Mr. Egleston's dinner table)
> that I had the extreme mortification to hear from you,
> sir, "that I must pay somewhere" meaning that I must
> pay somewhere towards the support of public worship.
> . . . But as the question—whether a town vote to build
> a place of public worship; for the sole use of one persua-
> sion, is compulsory on other Christian denominations to
> contribute towards a building in that predicament, has
> been solemnly determined by the court a day or two ago
> I feel I can resume the subject. I was insulted that you
> could imply that I was one of those who shift allegiance

11. Simon Parker to Henry Van Schaack, Jan. 17, 1792; Ballard Collection, BA.

12. Due recognition of the dissenters' victory came when the citizens
of Pittsfield met in 1794 and voted to raise £125 for religious purposes,
of which £15 would go to the dissenters.

to keep from paying,—I have always felt religious institutions as having powerful effects in the community to instill piety, to promote morality—it is grating to my feelings to be driven by a spirit of persecution to produce certificates of where I worshiped and where I paid in a government which secures the individuals who compose it.[13]

Six years later, Van Schaack was to see this same limited victory for the dissenters made a part of the state law. No longer able to ignore the dissatisfactions of dissenters in all corners of the state, Massachusetts lawmakers at last reluctantly passed an act providing that the town treasurer could exempt from taxation any dissenter with a certificate signed by his minister and a committee of two—hardly a revolutionary reform and one which the courts would effectively minimize by limiting application to incorporated societies.[14]

During the same years when sectarian rivalry was inspiring a conscientious battle for religious freedom, political and social schisms within the established church itself were beginning to work, albeit without conscious aim, toward the same end. With the continuance of the established church depending largely on the unity and vitality of the parish, such political schisms could obviously be nearly as effective as religious schism in promoting the separation of church and state. As the post-Revolutionary period advanced, the old-time concept of the territorial parish, where all persons living in a town automatically became church members, was gradually to break down and a new concept known as the poll parish was to develop—a voluntary association of people with no necessary relation to any given area.

13. Oct. 7, 1793; Ballard Collection.
14. Edward Buck, *Massachusetts Ecclesiastical Law* (Boston, 1866), p. 41.

As long as a single political party had dominated the country, the maintenance of a church establishment had presented few difficulties. Indeed, any clergyman could then have confidently preached on the text, "Fear God and honor the King." But even before the turn of the century, the classic alliance between the Congregational Church and the Federalist party had become rather looser in Berkshire than in parts of eastern Massachusetts, and when, in the winter of 1786–87, Squire Sedgwick's home was ransacked and Shays' men were roaming the countryside with green cockades of hemlock sprigs tucked jauntily in their caps,[15] many a Berkshire farmer was far less eager to support the government than was his pastor. In Egremont Shays' supporters entered the home of the Reverend Eliphalet Steele, boldly insulted him, and stole his watch, and when the breech between Steele and his flock failed to heal, he was dismissed, not to be replaced for twenty-six years afterward.[16] In Alford, Shays' Rebellion brought on a rift between pastor Joseph Avery and his parishioners and led to his immediate dismissal,[17] and a similar situation in Becket prompted the Reverend Zadock Hunn to depart hurriedly in 1788.

With such startling examples before them, many orthodox clerics in Berkshire carefully avoided too close a commitment to the Federalist party, and some adopted a studied oblivion to politics. Reporting on Stockbridge affairs to Theodore Sedgwick, then in the United States Senate, that stalwart leader of Berkshire orthodoxy Stephen West explained the general viewpoint:

> In our narrow circle, things go on pretty much in the old train. We now and then have a little specimen of the spirit of North and South end. Perhaps a little of

15. Ezekiel Bacon to Henry Van Schaack, Oct. 20, 1845; Ballard Collection.

16. Egremont Church Records, BA, p. 162.

17. Holland, *Western Massachusetts, 2,* 470.

party spirit is sometimes necessary as a stimulus to proper exertion. It may, however, I presume, sometimes rise so high as to act with too great a force. But, if there be small squabbles amongst little folks, they are only miniatures, I suppose, of those amongst their betters. The affairs and business of the world have, all along been one great squabble; and, they who have had the greatest hand in it, have sometimes come off by the wall. The Great Court of our nation I look upon to be the best court that is. How far it may be free from intrigue, I know not; and therefore suppose it proper to quit the subject.[18]

Ten years later, in his Fast Day Sermon, West turned to an unrestrained criticism of the Federalists for their prophecies of doom upon Jefferson's election. Submit gracefully, he advised, to whatever government may be in power, and always pray for the success of the new government. "We all ought to feel," he emphasized, "the danger there is of being too deeply involved in political strife and controversy. . . . Little reason have we to expect that anyone, whose mind is deeply engaged on political subjects will pay that attention to the things of religion, which is essential to his becoming a Christian . . ." [19] Catlin of New Marlborough and Shepard of Lenox joined West in warning their congregations to keep away from political quarreling; and in 1815 the Reverend Ebenezer Jennings of Dalton himself experienced the dangers of political dabbling when the democrats of his parish withdrew their support of him, following his remark from the pulpit: "If all democrats were not horsethieves, then all horsethieves were democrats." [20]

18. Dec. 3, 1791; SP.
19. Stephen West, *A Sermon delivered on the Public Fast, April 9th, 1801* (Stockbridge, 1801), pp. 22–25.
20. Pittsfield *Sun,* June 15, 1815.

As often as not Berkshire Congregationalists had the good sense not to insist that their political leaders hold orthodox doctrine; and thus it was that one Mr. Perkins, a theological liberal who represented the town of Becket in the Massachusetts legislative session of 1829, could report: "In the County of Berkshire, where I suppose there is not one Society that the gentlemen would call liberal, and where the great body of the people may be termed Orthodox, there is no exclusion on account of religious sentiment, as the history of their elections shows. In the town I have the honour to represent, nearly all are of the denomination which is so terrific to the gentlemen; perhaps I (their representative) am in a single minority." [21] Apparently the orthodox never intended to form a political bloc, partly perhaps because of their otherworldliness but partly too because of the increasing number of democrats appearing among the people even while the clergy remained conservative.

As the clerical sphere of influence grew more limited and congregations grew more boldly self-assertive, isolated instances of social and political unrest began bobbing up within various churches in the county. One of these cases—the Tyringham controversy of 1808–09—was destined to deal a severe blow to the established church. In 1808 the Tyringham townspeople, motivated by an unrevealed but probably personal animus, decided to dismiss their pastor, Joseph Avery, after nineteen years of service. Outraged by such treatment and finding his salary in arrears, Avery took revenge by suing for recovery. The Supreme Court under Chief Justice Parsons quite predictably awarded the decision to Avery, thus confirming for all Massachusetts the principle that a minister held his tenure for life unless terminated by mutual agreement.[22]

21. "A Reply to a Letter in the Christian Examiner," *Spirit of the Pilgrims* (Boston, 1830), *3*, 643.
22. 33 Massachusetts 165 (Pickering), 1808.

But the established church was not to triumph in Tyring-ham as it had thus triumphed in the courts, for those who had opposed Avery soon found a legal method of defying his victory. They simply presented certificates to escape taxation and left his friends to support him as best they might. Out of the extremity which faced the loyal orthodox congregation was to come a remarkably liberal and forward-looking plan, when, on June 15, 1809, they met to incor-porate a society of voluntary membership, known as the Fund Society, for permanent support of the Gospel. Quite distinct from the parish and empowered to hold property up to four thousand dollars, the Society was to meet once a year for the purpose of voting the interest from its property to the minister [23]—an enlightened method of Gospel support which was to spread to nearly every section of the state within the next few decades.

Meanwhile, as Jeffersonian Democracy infiltrated New England, the contest for religious liberty was becoming in-creasingly a political issue, and internal church rebellions were developing a familiar pattern of revolt against those individual pastors who seemed to symbolize church estab-lishment. Jeffersonians, in those days, could number only a handful of really articulate members among the Congrega-tional clergy—indeed only Thomas Allen of Pittsfield and Ephraim Judson of Sheffield in Berkshire, and in all the rest of Massachusetts only Bradford of Rowley and Bentley of Salem.

With dissenters quickly lining up on the side of Republi-can Congregationalists and Federalists holding fast to their supposed alliance with the official Congregational Church, religious freedom became a convenient point of departure for the inevitable controversy. Defenders of the establish-ment chanted in monotonous unison the usual accusations. Their atheistic Jacobin opponents, they charged, were plot-

23. Holland, *Western Massachusetts*, 2, 600.

ting, in the name of religious freedom, to do away with all religion and to lead America into chaos and terror. To such charges Parson Thomas Allen replied in 1808 with a fiercely liberal election sermon before the General Court in Boston. "Pious rulers," he declared—revealing a thoroughgoing change of heart since the meetinghouse controversy of the 1790's—"will be opposed to state establishment of religion, and to the imposition of creeds. They will leave religion, where Christ and his Apostles left it, to be propagated by the force of argument and persuasion, and not by the authority of civil government." [24] Rejoicing in the continuing strength of religious institutions, he noted with approval that "the ministers of Jesus Christ are not held in such high veneration and awe, nor considered such infallible oracles of truth, as they were formerly. It will be well, if the people will search for the truth with their own eyes, and if they look upon their teachers only as their helpers." [25]

While Allen was delivering this keynote address for the religious policy of the Republicans, John Bacon of Stockbridge, the leading Jeffersonian of southern Berkshire, took action. As president of the Senate, he proposed to the legislature a Worship bill, which would allow voluntary religious association. Such a law, he knew, would quickly destroy the parish as an effective unit and would render any church establishment completely impracticable. With their customary cries of atheism and Jacobinism, the Federalists voted down the bill; but as William Bentley observed in his diary, they could do nothing to stop the increase of sects which must soon make the law a necessity.

Meanwhile, at home in Berkshire, a major schism had

24. Thomas Allen, *A Sermon Preached before his Excellency James Sullivan, Esquire, Governor . . . on the Day of the General Election May 25, 1808* (Boston, 1808), p. 11.
25. Ibid., p. 14.

once again arisen in the Pittsfield Congregational Church.
Seventeen years earlier the meetinghouse controversy had
pitted the orthodox church members against the dissenters;
now, in 1807, a new argument was breaking out, this time
between Federalists and Republicans within the Congregational Church. Just as Stephen West had foreseen, men could
not become too much absorbed in politics without placing
their religious life in jeopardy.

During that five-year period between 1775 and 1780, when
the civil authority of Massachusetts had been excluded from
Berkshire and when Thomas Allen had emerged as the political leader of central Berkshire, some Federalist tempers had
already started to simmer. Always an ardent patriot, Allen
had fought Tories with real vigor and enthusiasm—especially the notorious Pittsfield Tory, Woodbridge Little.
But once the Constitution had taken effect, he began to grow
suspicious of Federalist intentions and opposed every Hamil-
tonian measure with steady persistence. By the time of the
Revolution the clergy's prerogative to discuss politics was
enjoying popular acceptance, and Allen did not hesitate to
capitalize on the privilege quite as extensively as did his more
numerous Federalist colleagues: "I may see occasion . . ."
he said, "to speak of the duties of rulers to the people, and
of the people to their rulers. When I believe I have a call in
divine providence to speak on those subjects, I shall not shun
to declare the whole counsel of God. The word of God is not
bound." [26]

Only with the election of Jefferson in 1800 did the rift
between Allen and the Federalists in his congregation as-
sume dangerous proportions. Led by Allen's old enemy,
Woodbridge Little, these Federalists, including most of
Pittsfield's citizens, addressed a formal Remonstrance to Al-

26. William Allen, *Account of the Separation of the Church and
Town of Pittsfield* (Pittsfield, 1809), p. 7.

len in March 1807, in which they arraigned him on several
charges. He had, they complained, inserted Jeffersonian arguments into his funeral sermon for his son the year before;
he had written a vicious article in his nephew's newspaper,
the Pittsfield *Sun,* on the death of Hamilton; he had delivered a toast on March 4 advocating "No compromise with
Federalists; no concurrence with neuters"; he had proclaimed that "the essence of Christianity is democracy." [27]
Allen replied to the charges with a straightforward question.
What, he asked, did the Federalists want from him? Pecuni-
ary satisfaction? A confession? A promise with regard to
future preaching?

The aggrieved members, he charged, had chosen a strange
and highly irregular way of expressing their dissatisfaction.
Why had they not come to him in private to discuss the issue, as the Bible and Congregational Church discipline required them to do? Frustrated by Allen's recalcitrance, the
Federalists turned to the Berkshire Association for advice,
only to be disappointed once again. Afraid to weaken pastoral authority by an outright opposition to Allen, the Association, although strongly Federalist, chose to equivocate
and to hand down a meaningless statement. The controversy
went on and the flames burned higher, fanned by the extreme
pronouncements of the two party organs, the Federalist
*Berkshire Reporter* and the Republican Pittsfield *Sun.*

Then, in the winter of 1808–09, Woodbridge Little, along
with 108 of his supporters, took conclusive action by presenting to the state legislature an application for the incorporation of a new parish to be called the Union Congrega-

27. *A Concise and Simple Narrative of the Controversy between
Thomas Allen and . . . Union Parish* (Pittsfield, 1809), pp. 9–11. Verifi-
cation of the charges against Allen would be difficult, as he wrote out his
sermons in his own variation of Weston's shorthand, and he sometimes
inserted extemporaneous remarks.

tional Parish of Pittsfield. The legislature speedily granted the application and legally incorporated the parish, and only the alertness of Timothy Childs, then a Republican senator from Pittsfield, prevented it from obtaining a share of church property.[28] On October 25, 1809, in spite of last-minute conciliatory efforts by the Pittsfield lawyers, John C. Williams, Federalist, and Ezekiel Bacon, Republican, the Union Parish ordained Parson Thomas Punderson as its minister, and the split was consummated. Less than a year later Parson Allen died, leaving his son William to succeed to his pastorate and to endure for seven more years the existence of two Congregational churches in Pittsfield. In 1817, with the general diminution of party spirit, they did at last reunite under Parson Heman Humphrey, but not before Pittsfield citizens had experienced deeply the effects of allowing political issues to penetrate the spiritual life of the town and had come to see the wisdom of cutting all ties between church and state. With the establishment of the Union Church as a poll parish in Pittsfield, the old concept of the church and town as coterminous had obviously become an anachronism.

As for the townspeople of Stockbridge, they had long since recognized the practical necessity for some degree of religious freedom, but not until 1818 were they to realize just how seriously the decline of the established church had affected the prestige of the presiding cleric. In that year, old Dr. West found himself formally accused of intemperate drinking by a young upstart assistant called Ephraim Swift, and although the accusation was never established, he was nevertheless dismissed from a pastorate which he had held for fifty-six years. A year later he died; and his fate, along with Allen's, came to symbolize for Berkshire political leaders, and particularly for those of the Jeffersonian party, the fading respect due the pastor as leader of his parish and the grow-

28. Allen, *Account of the Separation,* p. 22.

ing impossibility of maintaining the parish system amid the
increasing number of social and political cleavages within the
congregations.

Berkshire dissenters must have been watching the internal upheavals with interest and approval, and they themselves grew ever more importunate in their insistence on
the separation of church and state. As for Van Schaack, once
he had attained his immediate goal and had witnessed the
increasing identification of Jeffersonian ideals with the cause
of religious freedom, he found his enthusiasm sharply moderated by his Federalism. The new generation of dissenters,
therefore, turned instead to Elder John Leland, who had
come to Cheshire at the age of thirty-eight after a residence
of fourteen years in the Shenandoah Valley of Virginia and
who was destined to lend a peculiar dignity to the quarrel
with his philosophical speculations and trenchant summaries
of the principles involved. Having attained great prominence
among the small farmers as a Baptist preacher and a political leader, he had given important assistance to his friend
and hero Thomas Jefferson in the arduous task of disestab-
lishing the church in Virginia and had then returned to
his native Massachusetts, where the fight against ecclesiastical
pretensions was still going on. In Berkshire, and particularly
in Pittsfield, he discovered the perfect arena for his quarrel
with church establishments—an arena where some of the
leading Congregationalists stood ready to join the campaign
for religious freedom.

The Federalists might consider the Harvard-trained,
wealthy, and orthodox Thomas Allen a traitor to his class,
but from the Baptist Leland, poor and self-educated, they expected Jeffersonianism. Perhaps sensing his potential
strength, the conservatives soon brought into question the
purity of his attachment to religious liberty. Was the spirit
of Roger Williams truly working in him, they asked, or was it

rather the desire to make Thomas Jefferson president. Why shouldn't a Republican preach separation of church and state, when he knew Federalism to be ingrained in nearly every Berkshire cleric? But try as they might, the orthodox Congregationalists could never halt or even diminish Leland's tremendous influence. In Massachusetts, as in Virginia, his sermons, full of folk humor and sententious biblical phraseology, and his impressive patriarchal bearing, made him the natural political and religious leader of the middle and lower-class farmers.

To get their ears he had to resort to very eccentric anecdotes and illustrations; in which he managed to convey some religious instruction. What was at first a necessity became at last a habit; and his pulpit stories, and his odd, but impressive manner of telling them, soon attracted large congregations, and made him famous as a preacher throughout the State. He was a very sedate man, and his grave countenance never relaxed or changed expression when he was relating anecdotes that melted his audience into tears, or half convulsed them with suppressed laughter. . . . His pulpit shook with the thunder of his rough and ready eloquence. Never did a mesmerist so shape and control the will of a subject as he did the mind of his whole congregation and parish. The influence of his opinion and eloquence reached far out beyond the limits of the town, and impressed thousands. Cheshire, to a man, followed his lead, and followed his convictions long after he ceased to lead or live. For several generations they were born and they died Democrats of the Jeffersonian school . . .[29]

29. *Elihu Buritt: A Memorial Volume,* ed. Charles Northend (London, 1880), pp. 274 f.

His oratorical strength lay in his remarkable ability to dramatize current issues to his people—such issues, for example, as the election of Jefferson: "Pardon me, my hearers, if I am overwarm. I lived in Virginia fourteen years. The beneficent influence of my hero was too generally felt to leave me a stoic. What may we not expect, under the auspices of heaven, while Jefferson presides, with Madison in state by his side. Now the greatest orbit in America is occupied by its brightest orb; but, sirs, expect to see religious bigots like cashiered officers, and displaced statesmen, growl and gnaw at their galling bonds, and, like a yelping mastiff, bark at the moon whose rising they cannot prevent." [30]

All politics (and histrionics) aside, Leland rested his argument for religious freedom on two major premises: the inalienable rights of conscience and the impurity and worldliness of a religion connected in any way with the state. His unshakable belief in the rights of conscience came partly, no doubt, from his own individualism, which was so extreme as to border on anarchism. Even at the age of twenty-two he had irrevocably concluded that common sense directed every man to be his own theologian and philosopher. Had he not himself discovered that no two state constitutions were alike? "What, said I, do great men differ? . . . If so they cannot all be right, but they may all be wrong, and therefore, Jack Nips for himself." [31] Written during his first year in Berkshire, Leland's *History of Jack Nips* spread his doctrine of self-reliance through the county and beyond. Uniformity, he had concluded, could be neither possible nor desirable when history so clearly proved all attempts at standardization to be disastrous.

30. Leland, *Writings,* p. 255. Leland's most colorful activity was the supervision of the making of the mammoth cheese. Molded in a cider press and measuring thirteen feet across, the cheese was delivered to Jefferson in Washington by Leland himself.
31. Ibid., pp. 76–77.

Later Leland was to probe more deeply into his belief in the rights of conscience and was to find additional supporting evidence in the fact of the separability of life into various spheres. When man obviously cannot be predominantly classified as either a political or a religious or an economic entity, why, he asked, need his political, religious, and economic affairs encroach upon one another at all? Religion and politics lie in different departments: "religion is a matter between God and individuals: religious opinions of men not being the objects of civil government." [32] In forming any civil government, argued Leland, the people enter into a compact, but they do not simultaneously surrender their consciences. "There are rights which individuals possess, so inalienable in their nature that they cannot be surrendered. . . . If a creed of faith, established by law, was ever so short and ever so true; if I believed the whole of it with all my heart, should I subscribe to it before a magistrate, in order to get indulgence, preferment, or even protection, I should be guilty of a species of idolatry, by acknowledging a power, that the head of the church, Jesus Christ, has never appointed. . . . Most state constitutions require a religious test, to qualify an officer of the state. All the good such tests do, is to keep from office the best of men. Villains make no scruple of any test." [33]

This latter-day Roger Williams was championing the separation of church and state for the good of religion as well as of the individual. Only deism, a religion of this world, he felt, could exist logically as an established religion. Otherworldly by definition, any supernatural religion could only suffer from a connection, however remote, with the state. Religion was not, like education, a proper subject for legis-

32. Ibid., p. 181. The title of this particular piece is typical of Leland: "The Rights of Conscience Inalienable and therefore Religious opinions not cognizable by Law: or, the high-flying Churchman Stript of his legal robe Appears a Yahoo."
33. Ibid., p. 106 n.

lation, for religion originated in heaven and education among men. Whenever religious laws had tried to prevent error, to effect uniformity, or to support the Gospel, they had inevitably failed of their purposes, because they were attempting to reduce religion to a "level with the principles of state policy." [34] Leland granted that an Episcopal Church might stoop to use the secular arm, but a Gospel church, he maintained, could never do so, simply because its only discipline lay in dismissal from the fellowship. If a pure Christian Church would but prove to the world its ability to stand alone without state aid, then the deists would lose one of their major arguments.

In affirming the ruinous effects of politics on religion, Leland did not fail to see the equally deleterious influence which religion might have on politics. "Sycophants and hypocrites will take any oath to obtain office; but honest men will not . . . the best men are kept from office, and the people are deprived of their worth. Even the criteria for church membership by which the test oaths determine a Christian are highly fallible." How could anyone rationally deny the utter impossibility of the old Puritan ideal of the holy state when it is obvious and inevitable that "no body politic can form a Christian government and administer the same without breaking the rules of pure Christianity." [35]

In the Berkshire area, Leland delivered most of his speeches and orations in Pittsfield, Cheshire, Lanesboro, and Adams, and in the church on Stafford's Hill. "He would enter the old church and go singing up the aisle, his white hair flowing back, and carry his bible in a bag suspended on his arm." [36] In later years, he reached a still wider audience through the medium of the Pittsfield *Sun,* in which twenty-four of his articles appeared between 1822 and 1841. Beyond

34. Ibid., p. 251.
35. Ibid., pp. 253 f.
36. William Browne, "Pathways of the Past," p. 57; typescript in BA.

the bounds of Berkshire his influence spread through his published pamphlets, the numerous sermons preached on his extensive missionary tours, and his dominant position in the Shaftesbury Association—an organization of Baptist churches in Berkshire, southern Vermont, and eastern New York.

Leland remained, in fact, always as much a man of action as a man of words, and when the chance came, early in his Berkshire career, to represent Cheshire in the state legislature, he accepted the assignment with characteristic enthusiasm. A true successor to John Bacon, he traveled to Boston in 1811 to deliver Berkshire's demand for the abolition of the parish system, and lost no time in presenting to the legislators a petition requesting that all sects be exempted from supporting religious teachers. "The petitioners," he declared, "pray for the right of going to heaven in that way which they believe is most direct." [37] As he had expected, he soon found himself called upon to defend his petition against the attacks of outraged conservatives, and with the delight of a born controversialist he delivered a neat and persuasive summary of twenty years of pamphleteering. But even such a speech, with all its rhetorical power, could not convince the legislature, and summarily rejecting Leland's petition it passed instead the very limited Religious Freedom Act,[38] which merely granted tax exemption to anyone with a certificate of membership in a dissenting society, whether incorporated or not.[39]

Once the 1811 legislature had adjourned and Leland had

37. Leland, *Writings,* p. 355.

38. Berkshire's democratic editor, Phineas Allen, hailed the act with premature enthusiasm, imagining that it brought full religious freedom. Pittsfield *Sun,* June 22, 1811.

39. The Supreme Court of Massachusetts had ruled in 1810 in Barnes v. Falmouth that a dissenting society must be incorporated before its minister could be recognized. Cf. Jacob Meyer, *Church and State in Massachusetts 1740–1833* (Cleveland, 1930), p. 96.

returned to speech-making and sermon-writing in Berkshire, the cause of statewide religious freedom was to lie quiescent until the Constitutional Convention of 1820 revived the controversy. In the intervening years Berkshirites watched with acute interest as the smoldering Unitarian controversy broke out into actual schism. Within Berkshire the small number of Unitarians had never become active dissenters or even very articulate critics, and consequently had never emerged as a distinct sect; but elsewhere in the state, where their ranks were larger, they had begun to cause general alarm among the orthodox. Now, with eastern orthodoxy seriously challenged, even the more conservative among Berkshire Congregationalists felt compelled by feelings of loyalty and sympathy to support whatever forces opposed the Unitarians. Eighty-six orthodox churches in eastern Massachusetts had lost all their church buildings and all their property to those Unitarians who could muster a majority in their town meetings, and such events brought Congregationalists even in far-removed Berkshire to an abrupt realization of the material disadvantages which could occur under the parish system. Thus, when the Unitarians eventually aligned themselves with the social and political conservatives of Massachusetts and spoke out in favor of the parish system, orthodox Berkshire Congregationalists had little choice but to join hands with the dissenters in pursuing the liberal social policy of religious freedom.

When the Constitutional Convention met in Boston on November 15, 1820, Berkshire again provided an effective spokesman for religious freedom, this time in the person of Dr. Henry Halsey Childs of Pittsfield. Infuriated by the Unitarian controversy and determined to continue the fight begun by Bacon and Leland, Dr. Childs arrived in Boston in an uncompromising mood and proposed a motion that would replace Article III and would guarantee the principle of voluntary association with and voluntary separation from any religious society. The motion was a long and inclusive one, providing further that a man might pass from one society to another simply by filing a written notice with the clerk of the society; that only the religious society and not the parish could levy a religious tax; and that the equality of sects before the law, so flagrantly violated since the beginning of the commonwealth in 1780, should thereafter be respected.[40]

Yet even with the new and powerful support engendered by the Unitarian schism, Dr. Childs fought a losing battle against the immovable conservative opposition and failed to gain acceptance even for a revised and less inclusive version of his amendment.[41] Caleb Hyde of Lenox fared little better. In a final desperate effort to attain the desired reforms, Hyde ventured one of the most radical proposals of the Convention by proclaiming the right of every individual to worship God according to the dictates of his conscience, the right of all religious societies, incorporated or unincorporated, to elect their own teachers, and the necessity for abolishing any legal provision for the support of public worship. The conservative Convention refused even to print such a proposal, and in the end they passed an innocuous amendment which left the religious establishment virtually unchanged. Pittsfield citizens must have regarded the final amendment as quite inadequate, and they quickly voiced their disgust by voting it down 185 to 8. Throughout the state men who had hoped for a real reformation voted with those who opposed all change, and easily succeeded in defeating it.

Particularly in Berkshire, however, not even such a total defeat could silence the insistent voices clamoring for religious freedom, and within the year Berkshirites produced still another leader for their cause, this time William C. Jarvis, a Pittsfield lawyer and the County's most articulate

40. *Journal of the . . . Convention,* p. 159.
41. Ibid., p. 252.

political philosopher. In 1821, having already published his
major book, *The Republican*, he followed Bacon, Leland,
and Childs to Boston to represent the Berkshire liberals in
the House of Representatives. There, in addition to leadership of the "country party," [42] he presented for consideration
an act containing his town's cherished beliefs that no person
should be taxed by a society of which he was not a member
and that any person might separate from a society simply by
filing a statement with the town clerk. "The growth of
piety," he maintained, "is not to be coerced; religion is too
delicate, refined, and spiritual in its nature, to be promoted
by harsh expedients. It requires a gentle culture and its precepts must be gently instilled into the mind; they cannot be
forced upon the heart." [43]

But moral aspects aside, Jarvis the lawyer knew well that
he could draw upon the Constitution as an ally of religious
freedom. Convinced that the Constitution gave to every
individual the right to pay his tax to the preacher of his own
denomination, he felt that if doubts continued to exist over
Constitutional interpretation, then "it is the duty of the
legislature (not the courts) to make the path of the law plain
before the feet of the people . . ." [44] Like Bacon, Leland,
and Childs before him, Jarvis failed to get his bill through
the legislature, but like them he was keeping the issue

42. William Minot to Henry D. Sedgwick, February 5, 1822; MS in
MC: "There is a strong country party in our General Court headed by
W. C. Jarvis who propose to abolish all direct taxation and exact all
the support of the Commonwealth from the seaports—by duties on
auctioneers, licenses, Insurance Companies, etc. A Bill for this purpose
has been under debate for several days but it is ascertained by the
divisions which have taken place that it will not pass. It however indi-
cates the hostility of the country to the town."

43. William Charles Jarvis, *Speech in Favor of Religious Freedom in
the Massachusetts Legislature* (Boston, 1823), p. 11.

44. Ibid., p. 10.

stridently alive and was adding one more effective protest to the growing chorus of dissatisfaction that was to bring complete religious liberty to Massachusetts ten years later in the form of the Eleventh Amendment.

When the Amendment finally came, some Berkshirites, along with Alvan Hyde, still persisted in viewing religious freedom as an aspect of decline and an effort to tear down the pillars of society. Most of them, however, could feel only relief that justice had at last been done, and even so orthodox a clergyman as the Reverend John Yeomans felt moved to congratulate the legislature on the new religious freedom, and to echo all that his dissenting colleagues in Berkshire had been saying for half a century.

Later in the decade Mark Hopkins—always a faithful recorder of the day's events—was to regard the victory in the fight for religious freedom as an important victory for civil liberties. If not curtailed, he felt that the state might well have come to control property and life and perhaps even conscience,[45] and he saw in the very separation of church and state a recognition of the fact that government and law could not and should not attempt to determine morals. Government, he maintained, "can have no power to produce moral or social reformations. . . . Here religion comes in, society must be impregnated with virtue, else the government and the society tend downwards." [46]

Hopkins might well have gone on to point out that the churches in Berkshire had paved the way for, if not actually produced, a virtual revolution. The pattern of events had led most of the orthodox to join dissenters in a liberal cause, and the rigid Calvinist John Bacon had joined with his more radically oriented Baptist colleague John Leland to supply a bold and enlightened leadership for the cause of the sep-

45. M. Hopkins, *Miscellaneous Essays,* p. 344.
46. Ibid., pp. 342 f.

aration of church and state. Only in the later stages of the movement, with the decline of church power, had leadership passed into the hands of laymen—simply another indication that civil affairs were steadily pulling away from the influence of the churches. A long-standing alliance was ending in divorce by mutual consent.

# Chapter 5. CHARACTER FACTORIES

UPON spending a day in Great Barrington in 1839, that great apostle of free public education Horace Mann looked at the common school there with dismay and later deplored the failure of the citizens to make adequate provision for primary education. "To make an impression on Berkshire in regard to schools," he declared, "is like attempting to batter down Gibraltar with one's fist." [1] The county could still take pride in its private institutions for education. Lenox Academy, Pittsfield's Young Ladies' Institute, Williams College, and the Berkshire Medical Institution all enjoyed a widespread respect. But responsible citizens had to admit the justice of Mann's remark about public schools, and however strongly they might resent such impertinence from an outsider, they could hardly dismiss it simply as the petulance of a reformer.

Five years later even Mark Hopkins had to concede that Berkshire's seclusion had indeed rendered her unduly tardy and inefficient in the movement to revive the common schools.[2] The clerk of courts for the county, Charles Sedgwick, less charitably blamed the people's parsimony for the poor common schools and wryly noted that "the same people who have paid voluntary taxes of five, ten, and twenty dollars a day to pay my salary and send representatives to Congress . . . will wrangle till the sun goes down, to settle whether they shall pay the school teachers six or eight cents a head for their own benefit and the benefit of their children." [3] Horace Mann, himself a Unitarian, may well have

1. Diary for Aug. 19, 1839, in Mary Mann, *Life of Horace Mann* (Boston, 1865), p. 116.
2. M. Hopkins, *Miscellaneous Essays,* p. 400.
3. *Letters of Charles Sedgwick* (New York, 1863), p. 134.

suspected, without ever explicitly saying so, that the pervasive religious orthodoxy in Berkshire had created a spirit of obscurantism inimical to rational education.[4]

Explanations were many, but solutions remained few, and Berkshire common schools continued to develop very slowly and in general to lag far behind the church in receiving adequate support. A Massachusetts law of 1647 had required that each town of fifty families have a common school and each town of one hundred families a grammar or secondary school, but the law was not enforced very diligently. Although few Berkshire towns ever paid even minor fines for the neglect of education, many of them fell far short of the legal requirements. The citizens of Great Barrington had been employing the services of a minister for over twenty years when they at last invited a roving schoolmaster to hold sessions in various homes in 1763. Eight years later they paid a fine of almost £4 rather than vote any more money for education.[5]

Meanwhile, only three other towns in the county had actually tried to give their children a proper education. Sheffield, one of the oldest and largest towns of eighteenth-century Berkshire, had established three common schools as early as 1740 and managed to keep them in session nearly eight months of every year until the Revolution.[6] Twenty-one years later Pittsfield celebrated the event of its incorporation by building its first schoolhouse; and in 1763 the evidently prosperous citizens voted £36 for the construction of three district schools, each to be about twenty feet square with four windows.[7] Stockbridge citizens could point to the existence of the mission school for Indians as far back as

4. Mann, *Life of Horace Mann,* p. 155.

5. Charles J. Taylor, *History of Great Barrington, Massachusetts* (Great Barrington, 1882), p. 307.

6. Holland, *Western Massachusetts, 2,* 583.

7. Ibid., *1,* 497.

1739, but they would have had to admit that government funds had supported it and that the first town grant for a common school did not come until 1760.[8] Four years later they followed the example of their Pittsfield neighbors and decided to divide their town into two districts and to build two schoolhouses.

With the coming of Revolutionary hard times and the chaotic repercussions of Shays' Rebellion, many of the common schools in Berkshire suffered either neglect or abandonment, and in 1781 Great Barrington actually voted to sell the local school and to use the proceeds for building a dog pound. During the six-year period between 1775 and 1781, while the county had been running its own civil affairs, Berkshirites had, in fact, come to abuse as well as enjoy their independence. When a suspicious grand jury at last came to investigate conditions within the county in 1781, the town of Pittsfield self-righteously instructed its selectmen "to inform the grand jurymen that it was not deficient in maintaining schools either summer or winter"—a patent falsehood at a time when the town was openly voting "to raise no money for schooling." [9]

Because no Berkshire towns, and indeed few towns in all of rural Massachusetts, were meeting the educational requirements in the fourteen-year period after 1775, the state legislature finally gave legal recognition to the impossible gulf between theory and practice by passing the Education Act of 1789. Printed in the *Berkshire Chronicle* for December 21, 1789, the new act moderated previous requirements by legalizing the already widespread practice of dividing the towns into districts and by providing that towns of fifty families need hire a common schoolteacher only six months of the year. To Horace Mann this system of districting was

8. Ibid., 2, 591.
9. J. E. A. Smith, *The Public School System of the Town of Pittsfield 1761–1880* (Pittsfield, 1880), p. 9.

a major evil of Massachusetts education, bringing as it did
a multiplication of substandard schools, and he must have
foreseen that the rugged hills and numerous separate valleys
beyond the Barrier would lead to even more extensive districting than in eastern Massachusetts. By 1828 Berkshire's
thirty towns had indeed created 225 school districts.[10]

Between 1789 and the 1820's the common school apparently enjoyed neither a prominent place in the Berkshire
public mind nor a sizable share of town appropriations. The
citizens of Lee, like those of many another Berkshire town,
could resort unashamedly to educational penny-pinching—a
habit of economy frankly attested to in the minutes of a
1797 town meeting:

> Voted to raise $300 for the support of the Gospel.
> Voted to raise $200 to defray town debts.
> Voted to raise $200 to support schools.
> Voted to reconsider the last vote and in the room thereof
> to raise $150.
> Voted to raise $500 to repair highways.

At least one Berkshire citizen, however, found the school
situation so disgraceful that he penned an irate letter to
Loring Andrews, which eventually found its way into the
columns of the *Western Star:*

> Ye inhabitants of civilizations, attend to the following
> subject. Do not one of you filching misers think to
> screen yourselves from the following censure. . . . Not
> one will you see but such as are groaning under and
> complaining of their circumstances of education. . . .
> But let one plainhearted man advance and tell them,
> that he can put them in an immediate way to surmount
> this curse, they will shrink . . . your offspring grow
> up, somewhat like mechanical monuments, they neither
> know God nor man . . . their conversation may be

10. Field, *History of Berkshire,* p. 163.

compared to the lonely heath, whistled by the wind
. . . they are totally devoid of any delicate feeling.[11]

The shortcomings of primary educational facilities may
well have tended to become self-perpetuating, and parents
who had survived an unschooled childhood may have come
to regard any kind of formal learning as an unnecessary ex-
penditure for their children. Certainly the turn of the century brought no improvements. Virtually no Berkshire child
was spending an adequate amount of time in the local schoolhouse, and very few were receiving the advantages of intelligent and qualified instruction. Writing for the *Berkshire
Reporter* in 1807, a critic signing himself "Gulielmus" bitterly criticized the prevalent policy of knowingly hiring a
poor teacher simply to save money, and observed acidly that
"something resembling a school is established in almost every
vicinity, and the boy is sent perhaps two days in a week." [12]
Many years after his departure from Berkshire, Ezekiel
Bacon could look back to the Spartan scene of his boyhood
education with very little nostalgia. "The school houses . . .
were then little better than small barns, fitted up with coarse
backless benches, on which uneasy and restless urchins sat in
both mental and bodily torture." [13]

With the rapid improvements in Berkshire secondary
education during the early 1800's, with the rise of academies,
and with the increasing demands of Jeffersonians for an education that would promote enlightened patriotism, the inadequacy of the common schools at last began to attract attention.[14] Perhaps sensing a new popular interest in educa-

11. *Western Star,* Jan. 2, 1797.

12. Gulielmus, in *Berkshire Reporter,* Dec. 26, 1807.

13. Ezekiel Bacon, *Recollections of Fifty Years Since* (Utica, 1843),
p. 7.

14. Jarvis, *The Republican,* p. 112: "children ought not only to be
instructed in the social, moral, and religious duties of life; but patriotism
should be presented to their young and glowing minds, as one of the
most exalted duties towards the public."

tion, the Dalton political leader Henry Hubbard, along with Edward Newton and Catharine Sedgwick, inaugurated the Berkshire School Convention, an annual meeting for educational reform, but they found the job confronting them discouragingly complicated by years of inattention. The trend to the decentralization of education had continued ever since the legalization of school districts in 1789, and subsequently the districts had gained the power to tax (1800), had been incorporated (1817), and had received permission to appoint prudential committeemen to govern school property (1827). Then, in the year 1827, came both the high tide of local democracy in education and—with the establishment of supervisory town committees for schools by Hubbard and his colleagues—the turning point toward uniformity. Although these new committees at first possessed no power beyond the making of annual reports, they were to gain new powers rapidly.

In Berkshire the new trend to uniformity found early expression on the county level. Meeting at Lenox on November 7, 1826, the first convention of the Berkshire School Committees formally advocated the use of standard textbooks in all schools and named Colburn's *Arithmetic*, Willard's *Geography*, Goodrich's *History of the United States*, Murray's *Grammar*, and Leavitt's *Easy Lessons* (reading) as prescribed texts.[15] Further, the convention recommended the adoption of the monitorial system then used in the cities and the institution of annual teachers' conventions.

But the Gibraltar of Berkshire provincialism in education was not destined to be shattered by any dynamic reform movement from within. Having made their recommendations, the committees quietly adjourned with the thought that "uniformity and system are good, but peace and cordiality in school districts are better." Whenever a citizen tried to object to the expense of public education, they

15. Smith, *Public School System of Pittsfield*, p. 15.

soothed him with expressions of nationalistic feeling. An unimproved mind, they suggested, must necessarily result in a loss of energy to the republic—"Hence the obligation of the rich, to support free schools, and to educate our children at the expense of the town." [16]

At the two annual conventions which followed, Henry Hubbard pushed the patriotic emphasis to the extreme. "The education of a state or nation," he argued, "in order to be its cement, should beget a common character, common principles, and common sentiments . . ." [17] How could education act as a social cement in a state where citizens paid $163,929 yearly for public schools and $158,809 yearly for private instruction? [18] Hubbard went so far as to visualize public education as essential to the national welfare, and in appealing to the sentiments of those before him, he asked: "Is the separation of the rich and poor for the purposes of education, in accordance with the spirit of American liberty? . . . Pride, selfishness, the vanity of wealth, and the sighs of poverty, are lost in the common pursuit of knowledge. However exalted in after life, or however humbled, who can forget his schoolfellow?" [19] To the well-to-do, he held out the common schools as a sound insurance policy—a means of so enlightening the lower classes that they would never rise in rebellion.

Although Hubbard and the Berkshire County School Society continued to fight for improvements throughout the 1820's and 30's, their efforts to establish uniformity and to raise standards actually gained very little ground. Herman Melville still found much to criticize in the system even as late as the fall of 1837. After teaching a term at the Sykes' dis-

16. *Berkshire American,* Dec. 14, 1826.
17. Ibid., Mar. 5, 1828.
18. *The Quarterly Register of the American Education Society,* ed. William Russell (1830), 2, 230.
19. *Berkshire American,* Sept. 12, 1827.

trict school in Pittsfield, Melville wrote a disillusioned testi-
monial to his cousin: "Orators may declaim concerning the
universally diffused blessings of education in our Country,
and Essayists may exhaust their magazine of adjectives in
extolling our system of common school instruction,—but
when reduced to practice, the high and sanguine hopes excited by its imposing appearance in theory—are a little
dashed. . . . My school is situated about five miles from the
village. . . . My scholars are about thirty in number, of all
ages, sizes, ranks, characters, and education; some of them
who have attained ages of eighteen can not do a sum in addition." [20]

Very likely Melville did not exaggerate, for Berkshirites
did not see in public education economic or spiritual values
sufficient to justify a rise in taxes. He might also have complained with good reason of the alarming degree of pupils'
absences, of broken windows in many of the school buildings, of the traditional lack of uniformity in textbooks still
prevailing in spite of committee recommendations, and of
the immense problems involved in procuring good teachers.[21] Many towns found their teaching problem still further
aggravated by the extreme degree of subdivision—an evil
which was leading the 2,153 citizens of Williamstown to support thirteen public schools and the 3,703 inhabitants of
Adams to support seventeen.

Whatever the inadequacies of their schools, however, Berkshirites wanted no interference from outsiders, and when
Horace Mann became secretary of the newly formed Massachusetts Board of Education in 1837, they eyed his activities
with apprehension. Realizing that he vigorously opposed the

20. To Peter Gansevoort, Dec. 31, 1837; Gansevoort-Lansing Collection; NYPL.

21. "Abstracts of Massachusetts School Reports," *Annual Reports of
the Board of Education of the State of Massachusetts* (Boston, 1838–
48); Stockbridge, *Weekly Visitor*, Sept. 16, 1841.

district systems, private schools, and orthodox religion—all of which had a firm foothold in the county—they foresaw trouble. Edward Newton, for one, was convinced that Mann intended to foist his own Unitarianism on the public schools, and he speedily resigned his post as Berkshire's only representative on the state Board of Education. For his part, Mann continued to harbor a low opinion of Berkshire schools— Pittsfield he described in his diary as the town "which in the geography of common schools lies in the arctic regions, above the line (hitherto) of perpetual congelation . . ." And, still critical, he wrote of Richmond as "a border town of this state, and so far as their interest in schools is concerned, they are on the borders, at least of civilization, if not a little on the other side. When will Berkshire arise from her degradation?" [22]

The interferences which Berkshirites had anticipated began in 1838, when Mann succeeded in passing an act which recommended the consolidation of district schools in such a way that each would have a minimum of forty pupils. A year later their sense of grievance neared explosion with the reformer's stinging critique of the common school libraries in his report of 1839 and with his opposition to Packard's Select Library for Common Schools on the ground that the books listed taught sectarian doctrines (i.e. Calvinism).[23]

Not until 1844, however, did Berkshire's resentments at last find coherent expression. In that year Edward Newton, then a Pittsfield banker, wrote a letter to the Episcopal periodical *Christian Witness and Church Advocate* (published February 23) in which he fired his first unrestrained blast in the famous Common School Controversy. He approvingly cited Daniel Webster's argument in the Girard case to the effect that morality and religion were inseparable

22. Mann, *Life of Horace Mann*, p. 162.
23. S. M. Smith, *Religious Education*, p. 146. This list was prepared by F. A. Packard of the American Sunday School Union.

and that, by seeking to lop off the branches of sectarianism, Girard had laid the axe to the root of Christianity itself. "Can any one tell," asked Newton, "wherein the system of Mr. Girard, and the present system of our 'Board of Education,' or rather of its Secretary, differs?" [24] Rather angrily, Mann replied that the constitution required "principles of piety" to be taught in the schools, but expressly prohibited the teaching of the "tenets of any particular sect of Christians." [25] Since all sects were supporting the common schools, he maintained that their teachings must offend none; the schools must teach only the doctrines forming the least common denominator among the various sects.

With ill-concealed impatience, Newton again took up the argument. Mann, he said, was going too far; he was attempting to purge education of all the basic doctrines of Christianity and to admit only his own natural religion as suitable to be taught in the schools.[26] To combat this secularization, Newton suggested an alliance of all orthodox Christians—Congregationalists, Presbyterians, Episcopalians, and Baptists—which might restore the Westminster Catechism and biblical exegesis to their former and rightful place in public education.[27] These doctrines, Newton insisted, might not be acceptable to everyone but would certainly be welcomed by all Christians of orthodox belief and thus by a vast majority. Surely this alternative must appear preferable to Mann's system of excluding all doctrines offensive to any group. Not only did Newton echo that distrust of Mann's policy then widely felt in Berkshire, but he voiced the Berkshirites' bitter resentment at the interference by a Boston

24. *The Common School Controversy,* comp. Horace Mann, Edward A. Newton, et al. (Boston, 1844), p. 3.

25. Ibid., p. 9. For a discussion of the prophetic note in Newton's ideas (his foresight of the conflict of Catholicism and public schools), cf. Lawrence A. Cremin, *The American Common School* (New York, 1951), pp. 145–50.

26. Ibid., pp. 21–24.

27. Ibid., p. 23.

bureaucracy in what they regarded as their local affair: "I contend *that now it [the Board of Education] is wholly useless and burdensome as a state institution,* irrespective of the objections to it in a religious view. We do not need this central, all-absorbing power; it is anti-republican in all its bearings, well adapted, perhaps, to Prussia, and other European despotisms, but not wanted here. All that we require is, wise general laws, dependent for their execution on the virtue and interest of the people, leaving to the various sects the matter of watching against the improper encroachments of each other, experience having shown that they will be abundantly vigilant." [28] Eventually Mann was to win the Common School Controversy, but his very victory was to prove that there had been some truth in Newton's prediction. Mann's system, he had warned, would mean progress for secularism and bureaucracy and a loss for religion and local independence. Still, there could be no doubt that Mann's victory also meant a definite upgrading of educational standards.

The controversy, lasting as it had for eleven years, could hardly have been pleasant for any of the major figures involved, and certainly Mann had encountered one of the least attractive facets of Berkshire provincialism. He may have suspected with considerable justification that the county's stubborn resistance to school reform was at bottom economic, even though carried forward under the respectable aegis of a religious opposition to Unitarianism. Had he probed still deeper, he might well have discovered still another not-very-savory motive among Berkshire conservatives, namely their vague fears as to the social effects of public education. Even Catharine Sedgwick, who had been Mann's most effective supporter, had given hints of such a fear when she wrote:

> But while I should wish the humblest stimulated to the
> cultivation and enjoyment of their intellectual faculties
> I would have them feel that a dutiful performance gives

28. Ibid., p. 24.

dignity to the lowliest office—that a domestic may find
exercise for mind and heart in the prescribed duties of
her station and that their intellectual faculties do not
run to waste because they are not devoted to what is
esteemed their highest exercise. I have seen many persons disturbed with longings for something out of their
condition when they would have been made happy by
a right appreciation of what was within it. I do not
mean by this that I would discourage a taste for letters
in working men and women. Books are sure and unfailing friends and like all friends there [*sic*] value is more
fully realized in the shady than in the sunny places of
life. . . . I would carefully avoid affording our domes-
tics incentives to be authors instead of giving to their
own calling the dignity and worth of which it is suscep-
tible.[29]

The real stimulus to school reforms, then, had necessarily
come not from Berkshire natives but from a Bostonian outsider, and the outsider had succeeded because he had instinctively based his case not on any rational ground of self-
interest but on an appeal to each citizen's sense of moral
responsibility. Among Berkshirites whose Puritan ancestors
had once founded schools in a virtual wilderness the feeling
of a responsibility to tradition was strong, and moral shame
could inspire them, as could nothing else, to vote the necessary school funds. Thus indirectly did the old church-
centered provincial education in moral training lead, at last,
into the new age of free public education. And thus would
Berkshire's past provincialism eventually prove to contain
the seeds of its own destruction. It was not long before universal public education began to turn the minds of youth to
practical and secular channels, thereby causing the most able

29. To Professor Potter, May 9, 1838; Cleavland Collection, New-
York Historical Society.

among them to find Calvinism spiritually inadequate and Berkshire horizons too confining.

During the 1760's and 70's, while Berkshire's population was registering the most rapid growth in its history, the traditional form of secondary education, the grammar school, had lapsed into a period of definite decline throughout Massachusetts. Developed originally by the early Puritans with the sole purpose of preparing youths for college, the typical grammar school emphasized such scholarly subjects as Greek, Latin, rhetoric, and mathematics—subjects which some Berkshire citizens considered highly impractical. Their thoughts were preoccupied with the difficulties of providing simple necessities, and they needed their teen-age sons at home. Grammar schools, they knew, eventually led many of their students into the ranks of the clergy, and Berkshirites could procure a learned clergy from the older settlements much more cheaply than they could train their own young men for the ministry.

In all of Berkshire only Sheffield could claim the distinction of supporting an established grammar school for an extended period. Built in 1750, the brick building there kept its doors open to students until the early nineteenth century, except for the few Revolutionary years. It could boast only a single teacher but usually employed a thoroughly competent one, and in the 1790's drew students from all of southern Berkshire.[30] Much more typical of the county was Pittsfield, where one citizen found educational opportunities on the secondary level so hopeless that he complained publicly in the columns of the *Sun:* "I am told the laws of the land compel every township to maintain at least one Grammar School. A stranger, contemplating a settlement in Pittsfield inquired in vain into the reputation of the Grammar School. To our

30. *Western Star,* Dec. 5, 1796; Dewey, *Autobiography,* p. 22. Out-of-town students paid the tuition fee and boarded with Sheffield families.

shame be it told, there is no such thing in existence! On inquiry, it seems that it has been with infinite difficulty a Grammar School has ever been supported here. It is really astonishing that a place so rich—so beautifully situated . . . as
Pittsfield, should lie under such a heavy reproach." [31] In Pittsfield, and in a few other Berkshire towns, failure to support a
grammar school stemmed in some degree from the absence
of civic spirit and from the presence of private schools, but
most towns simply lacked the desire to provide anything beyond a none-too-adequate common school education for their
children.

The first half of the nineteenth century saw a predominance of private and semiprivate enterprise in Berkshire education, with academies and private schools filling the fifty-
year gap between the almost nonexistent grammar schools of
the seventeenth and eighteenth-century tradition and the
public high schools which gained strength in the last half
of the nineteenth century. Perhaps these private institutions
owed their success to Berkshire's prevailing conception of
education in terms of the individual; apparently the idea of
a universal education permeating the whole society simply
did not exist and hence the low state of the common schools.
The private school could thrive because it required only the
support of the education-conscious few and not of the entire
taxpaying population—a population which still regarded
such schooling as a special luxury.

Generally, these private institutions owed their existence
to the efforts of either one man or a small group of public-
spirited citizens. The best of Berkshire's academies, Lenox
Academy, came into being in 1803, when twenty-five of the
county's leading men petitioned the legislature for permission to avail themselves of the benefits of the Academy Act of
1789, which offered half a township on the Maine frontier to
every academy with a fund of $3,000. Signers of the petition

31. Pittsfield *Sun,* Aug. 5, 1813.

included, among others, Azariah Egleston, an Episcopalian and a Republican businessman, who had been subsidizing a small grammar school in Lenox since 1792; the Reverend Samuel Shepard of the local Congregational Church; William Walker, Judge of Probate; and the town doctor, Eldad Lewis.[32]

Inspired partly by the success of the Lenox undertaking and partly by a recognition of serious need, a few other citizens eventually made similar efforts. A Pittsfield manufacturer of guns and carriages, Lemuel Pomeroy, bought the old Army Cantonment Ground in Pittsfield in 1827 and erected there three handsome brick buildings to be known as the Berkshire Gymnasium. Then he managed to persuade his son-in-law, Chester Dewey—a professor at Williams College and Berkshire's foremost scientist—to become the first head of the new school. Meanwhile, in North Adams, two doctors attending the wealthy farmer Nathan Drury in his terminal illness were demonstrating equal or even greater persuasive talents by encouraging the old man to leave $3,000 for a new school to be appropriately christened Drury Academy. Of all the private schools in Berkshire, however, none could surpass the general excellence of Mrs. Charles Sedgwick's School for Girls at Lenox. Motivated to some extent by enlightened public spirit but chiefly by a realization that her husband's meager salary as clerk of courts was inadequate for raising a family, the ever practical Mrs. Sedgwick conceived the idea of taking girls into her own home for instruction, and she soon achieved a statewide reputation.

As the number of academies in the state began to increase, the legislature hastened to step in with laws of control and regulation. Fearing that too much subdivision might produce the same weakening effect on the academy level as had already occurred in the common schools, the legislators did all

32. *One Hundredth Anniversary of the Founding of Lenox Academy* (Pittsfield, 1905), p. 12.

that they could to prevent the founding of too many academies by refusing state aid to any academy not serving an area of 30,000 people and not already supported by local subscription in the amount of $3,000.[33] Under this restriction, one academy should have been sufficient to serve all of Berkshire, or at least so Egleston and his colleagues thought when they originally named their school in Lenox the Berkshire Academy.[34] The following year, they must have foreseen future developments and consequently rechristened it the Lenox Academy. Within the next twenty-five years, two academies were incorporated in Pittsfield, one in Williamstown, and one in Stockbridge, all of them still serving as regional schools and drawing their students from several towns.

In the 1830's and 40's, however, with the establishment of larger numbers of academies, the regional conception started to fade. Some of the new academies, such as those at Egremont and Hinsdale, began as little more than expressions of local pride, and they foundered within a few years simply from lack of funds and a shortage of students. Only the larger and wealthier towns, like Williamstown and those in the Housatonic Valley, could support really successful academies. Unlike the substandard district schools, the marginal academies could not rely on any town funds and had to compete for students on the "open market," and most of them inevitably perished. Certainly, this elimination of the weaker academies contributed largely to the maintenance of the reputation for genuine distinction which the word "Academy" enjoyed.

For their support, the academies looked to the income from their subscription funds and to tuition fees, and five of the more fortunate ones—Lenox, Sheffield, Drury (North

33. *One Hundredth Anniversary of . . . Lenox Academy,* pp. 19–20.
34. Report of the Meeting of the Trustees of Lenox Academy, Apr. 20, 1803; Ballard Collection.

Adams), Lee, and Hinsdale—received land grants from the
legislature of half a township in Maine. Until the 1820's,
tuition at Lenox Academy remained fixed at a fairly typical
figure of $2.25 per quarter; then, under a new system after
midcentury, the quarterly tuition varied according to the
course taken (primary, $3; higher English, $4; languages and
mathematics, $5). For most young scholars, however, pay-
ment of tuition by no means comprised the only outlay associated with attending an academy. If they came from out of
town, they must board with a private family at a cost of $1.25
to $1.50 per week in 1803 and $1.50 to $2.50 in 1850. Un-
doubtedly many Berkshire families found the financial strain
of sending a son to the academy burdensome, but few ever
regretted the sacrifices they made. The Berkshire academies
made education a real spiritual adventure.

To the trustees of the academy, usually a fairly representative group of civic leaders, went the responsibility for hiring
a teacher. Had it gone instead to the town meeting which
elected public school boards, the clerical influence might
have loomed less large. Of the sixteen original trustees of
Lenox Academy, Samuel Shepard, Jacob Catlin, Ephraim
Judson, and Thomas Allen were all clergymen; and until
1871, a clergyman always served as president of the board of
trustees. When those men who were Lenox trustees in 1810
gathered in Wilson's Coffee House for their annual meeting,
they debated at length before deciding upon a list of qualifications they considered necessary in a teacher. Finally, they
agreed that he must (1) manifest a real veneration for the
Christian religion, (2) accept both state and federal constitutions (3) be of good moral character, (4) be capable of instructing in learned languages and sciences, and (5) be a man
of prudence and discretion.[35] Obviously, in the hierarchy
of values of Berkshire education Christianity, patriotism, and
morality came before scholarly competence. Such a hier-

35. Minutes of Trustees' meeting, May 22, 1810; Ballard Collection.

archy merely reflected the formula of conservative educators
the world over—a formula written into both the sermons of
Arnold of Rugby and the records of the Lenox Academy trus-
tees. Most of the Berkshire academies, of course, ended by
hiring teachers of known orthodox beliefs. Hotchkin of
Lenox had studied two years at that stronghold of orthodoxy,
the Andover Theological Seminary; Chester Dewey of the
Berkshire Gymnasium had studied theology with Stephen
West and was a member of the Berkshire Association; and
Jared Curtis of Stockbridge Academy professed orthodox
Congregationalism and later left Stockbridge to become a
cleric.[36]

Once hired, the teacher could usually expect little interference from the trustees. In fact, when Levi Glezen came
to Lenox as the first teacher at the Academy, he must have
been generally gratified at the free hand granted him. Not
only did the trustees empower him to hire his own assistant,
to collect all students' fees, and to make minor repairs on
the Academy building, but they guaranteed him a net salary
of $550 at the end of the year.[37] Mathew Buckham, principal
of Lenox Academy in the 1850's, remarked: "To say a word
of praise for the old Academy is like praising the old Stage
Coach. But even so it shall not lack the world of praise from
me. It had this great advantage over the High School—that
it gave a great opportunity to a teacher of exceptional personal gifts and power of influence. . . . the High School
teacher has not the same opportunity. He is an employee in
an organization which prescribes to him his work, calls him
to account for accomplishing certain specific things, and
rather discourages any spontaneity or initiative in him." [38]

At Lenox, as at most of the Berkshire academies, the character of a teacher with so broad an authority naturally deter-

36. Field, *History of Berkshire*, pp. 238–396.
37. Minutes of Trustees' meeting, May 21, 1807; Ballard Collection.
38. *One Hundredth Anniversary of . . . Lenox Academy*, pp. 59–60.

mined the character of the school. Boys who had attended the Lenox Academy during its first twenty years remembered their alma mater in terms of the odd mannerisms and near-sightedness of the excellent grammarian, Levi Glezen. With Glezen's successor, John Hotchkin, school emphasis turned from grammar to classical languages. "There is more of mental discipline," Hotchkin often said, "in Andrew's and Stoddard's Latin Grammar than in all the mathematics extant." [39] And his students remembered for a lifetime his painstaking thoroughness and his famous dictum, "Whatever you get, get it got."

When, after twenty-four years, Josiah Lyman succeeded Hotchkin at Lenox, the conservative and classical education gave way to a more scientific approach. A brilliant mathematician and a professional mechanic, Lyman had graduated from Williams College in 1838 and had come to Lenox eager to pursue his specialized studies. Under his direction, the Academy purchased a Herschelian telescope and made extensive additions to the natural history cabinets; [40] and his scientific lectures and demonstrations equaled those offered in some colleges.

At other academies in Berkshire the same tendency prevailed for the school to reflect the character and interests of its teacher. As long as Chester Dewey presided over the Berkshire Gymnasium,[41] it too enjoyed a scientific emphasis. In-

39. Ibid., pp. 23, 66.
40. Ibid., p. 26; Pittsfield *Sun,* Aug. 31, 1848.
41. The Berkshire Gymnasium, patterned on the gymnasia of Europe and influenced by the famous Round Hill School of Northampton, differed somewhat from other Berkshire academies; the students lived in dormitories and greater emphasis was placed on science and physical education. Its director, Chester Dewey, described its aims: "It is conducted on the general plan of the gymnasia of Europe, and it is designed to enable the pupil to obtain a more complete education in a shorter time, by employing more teachers and more hours in study; and by various exercises for the body, to give strength and firmness to

clining toward the newer scientific curriculum, Dewey, and
of course most of his students, believed the path of the human race to lie onward and upward—a view strangely inconsistent with his orthodox religion.[42] Meanwhile, three blocks
away, the Pittsfield Female Academy underwent a minor
revolution in 1835 when the Reverend Eliakin Phelps, so do-
cile that he would hold the hands of an unruly pupil and
weep while rebuking her, was succeeded by the irascible Mr.
Jonathan Hyde, a stern Philadelphian, who emphasized those
essential female accomplishments, penmanship, music, and
dancing.

Although a part of the curricula offered by the academies
remained identical with that of the old grammar school,
everywhere new studies were appearing and were continually
increasing in number and scope. Students of the classics
might still concentrate on Caesar, Cicero, Virgil, and the
Greek Testament, but the practical studies, which Franklin
and Rush had recommended in the eighteenth century as
more proper to American education, were infiltrating all the
Berkshire academies.[43] Often called "people's colleges," the
academies represented the most dynamic and least tradition-
bound branch of American education in the first half of the
nineteenth century; and because they were responsible only

the constitution and electricity and energy to the mind; and by particular watchfulness and attention to morals and manners and religious
duties, to form the pupils to a high and noble character" (Field, *History
of Berkshire,* p. 164).

42. Chester Dewey, *Introductory Lecture Delivered to the Medical
Class of the Berkshire Medical Institution,* August 5, 1847 (Pittsfield,
1847), p. 7. Dewey regarded the American telegraph as an instrument
of moral, intellectual, and commercial good and as "the unrivalled
discovery of the ages."

43. Cf. Benjamin Rush, *Thoughts upon the Mode of Education
Proper in a Republic* (Philadelphia, 1786), p. 31: "let our youth be
instructed in all the means of promoting national prosperity and independence, whether they relate to improvements in agriculture, manufactures, or inland navigation."

to the local trustees, they could experiment with whatever new course they pleased and could adapt the curriculum to student needs. In Berkshire, where fewer than 10 per cent of academy graduates intended to go on to college, most students naturally hoped to find courses to prepare them for "the great and real business of living." Texts like Davies' *Surveying* and Preston's *Bookkeeping* eventually came to supplement the old geometries and algebras; courses in French, history, geology, and chemistry appeared on school lists; and by the 1840's, Morse's time-tested *Universal Geography* had disappeared in favor of the more specialized texts like Hitchcock's *Geology,* Hale's *History of the United States,* and Burritt's *Geography of the Heavens.*

As the years went on, many of the Berkshire academies began to encourage the diffusion of scientific knowledge. Realizing how many of their graduates would one day become tillers of the soil, they introduced Johnston's *Agricultural Chemistry*—a synthesis of the work of Liebig and Humphrey Davy in the form of popular lectures by a Scot chemist and country gentleman. In chemistry itself, they made available Benjamin's Silliman's excellent text, *Elements of Chemistry,* which, once published in 1847, went through forty editions in nine years. Exponents of natural science found Hitchcock's *Geology* a particularly congenial work, since they wholeheartedly agreed with his attempt to present his topic in "proper historical and religious relations." [44] Where textbooks seemed inadequate, a few schools supplied apparatus for experiments, mineralogical cabinets, and special lectures—all of which tended to make the sciences rather more exciting to the student mind than the classics. In the summer of 1820 Lenox Academy even invited Amos Eaton, the fa-

44. In Hitchcock's *Geology* the frontispiece shows a paleontological chart of the animal kingdom with a crown and cross placed upon man and a respectable blank in his line of descent labeled "unknown," to separate him from lower forms of life.

mous popularizer of science and later head of Rensselaer
Institute, to deliver a five-week series of lectures; and Dr.
Mark Hopkins once came to the Stockbridge Academy to
lecture on human anatomy.[45]

History, English literature, and moral science, along with
the natural sciences, were gaining ground in the academies.
History texts such as Samuel Goodrich's *Peter Parley's History,* the more advanced *History of the United States* by
Salma Hale, and Shurtleff's *Governmental Instructor* came
to be considered good improving material for reading practice and for instilling patriotism. Occasionally, students studying Cowper's *Task* and Pope's *Essay on Man* must have found
the aesthetic effect rather thoroughly lost in grammatical
analysis, but most of them did have the more inspiring experience of using Cleveland's *Compendium of English Literature* with its wide selection, which included Junius, Locke,
and More, as well as Milton and Shakespeare. The only modern language pursued beyond the elementary stage was
French, with which students became acquainted in the pages
of Racine, Voltaire's *Charles XII,* and Guizot's *History of
Europe.*[46] Not until the 1850's did daily vocal music become
a fixture in the academies, and only in two of Berkshire's private schools—The Young Ladies' Institute of Pittsfield and
the Reid-Hoffman School at Stockbridge—could students
take courses in instrumental music. As the academies continued to expand their programs and to maintain the excellence
of their instruction in the sciences, many citizens began to
urge that colleges introduce new studies into their curricula.
Only after ancient history had been taught in the academies

45. Ethel M. McAllister, *Amos Eaton Scientist and Educator* (Philadelphia, 1941), p. 198; Sarah C. Sedgwick and Christina S. Marquand,
*Stockbridge, 1739–1939, A Chronicle* (Great Barrington, 1939), p. 190.
46. Berkshire Gymnasium catalogs, 1828, 1830, 1837; Pittsfield Young
Ladies' Institute catalogs, 1843–62; Lenox Academy catalogs, 1840,
1842; NYPL and American Antiquarian Society.

for a generation did it appear among the entrance requirements of a college (i.e., Harvard, 1847).[47]

Strangely enough, moral science texts in the Berkshire academies presented something of an anomaly in an area where the religious background of both students and teachers reflected an almost exclusive Calvinistic tone. Far from indoctrinating or even introducing Calvinism, the texts adopted a rather apologetic attitude and admitted little more than that Christianity was not an unreasonable religion. Paley's *Natural Theology* cited not only the human eye but the ingenious mechanism of the snake's fangs for dispensing venom as evidence that an invisible intelligence created nature. Butler's *Analogy* likewise argued against atheism by assuming a correspondence between the natural and supernatural worlds. In his *The Improvement of the Mind* the great hymn-writer Isaac Watts combined Lockean psychology with Christian apologetics and practical hints on how to study; and when President Francis Wayland of Brown University wrote *Moral Science,* he included rational appeals to the conscience by insisting that, whatever might be the case in the next world, sin could cause real personal and social suffering in the here and now. He exposed the irrationality as well as the wrongness of sin and emphasized not just the virtues of a Christian but the duties of the citizen of a republic.

Hotchkin or Dewey or any other Berkshire preceptor might work Calvinist doctrine into his morning prayers or his personal talks with his students, but as long as moral science texts left the subject of religion quite free of any sectarian doctrine, the student inevitably emerged with a strong impression that morality loomed far larger in importance than doctrine—a conviction which more and more Berkshirites were translating into everyday life. Throughout the academy

47. Elmer E. Brown, *The Making of Our Middle Schools* (New York, 1903), p. 232.

program the emphasis on personal morality predominated. In fact, Mrs. Sedgwick's concise description of her school as a "character factory" might have been made with equal aptness and sincerity by any of the academy teachers. All of them regarded moral training as even more important than mental training and could not conscientiously turn out intellectual but irresponsible graduates. In their moralistic enthusiasm, some were even calling education the source of true piety.

At this sacrilege John Leland rebelled; speaking in the accents of the old Berkshire religious tradition, he preached a fiery sermon on the text "School Academies and Colleges are the inexhaustible fountains of true piety, morality and literature." Purity, he reminded the erring Berkshirites, meant the dedication of the heart to God, and the righteous Abel had possessed this true piety without benefit of school or academy. "True piety proceeds from a fountain, distinct from schools of learning. That true piety in the heart is the gift of God, all confess, who possess it. . . . But why should true piety and literature be classed in the same grade, when they are radically different in their natures? The greatest scholar, is often at the greatest distance from true piety. . . . Science informs the mind in things of this life—piety gives knowledge of, and prepares the soul for the life to come. And as well may cold iron and hot be welded together, as piety and literature." [48] Leland was shrewdly putting his finger on a basic change which had overtaken men's minds in the century since Edwards, the scholar-saint. Not only in Berkshire but everywhere in New England a profound secularization had occurred; and men's lives had become so separated into various distinct realms that the old Calvinist concept of an organic unity of politics, art, economics, and education subordinate to religion no longer remained possible. Leland may have been right in thus carefully distinguishing between piety and literature, but overemphasis on this distinction was

48. Leland, *Writings,* p. 409.

to lead his spiritual heirs into the obscurantism of fundamentalism.

Exhibiting wisdom in handling religion, few of the academy teachers asserted that they taught true piety, but they presented the case for religion on rational grounds without emphasizing any creed and without insisting dogmatically upon the supernatural. They seldom tried to cross the line which separated Christian education from indoctrination. Neither secular nor sectarian, the academies handled the difficult problems of religious education well. In fact, this self-restraint in the teaching of religion made many Berkshirites feel that Horace Mann, and not the orthodox Christians, had acted the part of the aggressor in the Common School Controversy. The problem of religion would, they were sure, have been handled just as sensibly by the public schools as by the academies, had Mann only been willing to let the subject rest. Certainly the course in moral science at the academies presented a widely acceptable metaphysical framework for students possessed of different sectarian backgrounds but of a common mid-nineteenth century American set of mind—practical, moral, and optimistic. Eschewing sentimentality, the moral science dealt in a briskly impersonal way with the difficulties of adolescent adjustment to an adult world and with the central educational problems of motivation and character formation.[49]

Because the larger academies hoped to attract students from Boston, New York, and Philadelphia, their brochures included enthusiastic descriptions of Berkshire's attractions and advantages and could truthfully expand upon the wholesomeness of student life. An Academy catalog for 1840 pointed out with pride that: "Lenox Academy is pleasantly situated in a central part of the beautiful and retired village

49. That the effort to provide something in this area is necessary even in public, secular, mass education would be confirmed by the rise of guidance courses in the mid-twentieth century.

of Lenox, Massachusetts. Professor Silliman, in speaking of
Lenox, says that it has a fine mountain air, and is surrounded
by equally fine mountain scenery, and that it is one of the
finest inland villages. The moral atmosphere of the place is
also salubrious and will challenge a comparison in this respect, with the most favored New England villages. The avenues to temptation are comparatively few, and the character
and habits of the people eminently virtuous and intellectual." [50] William Cullen Bryant, always a loyal son of the
Berkshire hills, thought enough of Lenox Academy to insert
an enthusiastic paragraph in the New York *Evening Post,*
later reprinted in the *Massachusetts Eagle.* The school, he
wrote, deserves admiration because "it has been 'known' only
by its fruits" and never by indulging in the modern and vulgar habit of "puffing." He pessimistically concluded, however, that "a school that is not puffed now-a-days is in danger
of being utterly forgotten." [51]

Undoubtedly, girls' schools found the attractions of Berkshire's rural atmosphere and moral tone highly favorable. A
pioneer in this field was the Pittsfield Female Academy, established in 1807. Thirty-five years later the Reverend J. W.
Tyler founded the Pittsfield Young Ladies Institute in the
buildings of the old Berkshire Gymnasium, and by 1853 it
was enrolling 264 pupils from six states. When the Reverend
J. H. Agnew bought the school in 1853, he changed the
name to Maplewood Institute and might have developed it
into one of the leading women's colleges had not two serious
typhoid epidemics in the 1860's caused its ruin. In the same
period Mrs. Sedgwick's School for Girls was offering the special advantage of readings by Fanny Kemble during her summers at Lenox in addition to occasional lectures and readings
by the principal's sister-in-law and Berkshire's leading author,

50. Lenox Academy catalog, 1840; NYPL.
51. Lenox, *Massachusetts Eagle,* May 4, 1844.

Catharine Sedgwick. So high and well-merited a reputation did the school eventually attain that Emerson chose to send his daughter Ellen there.

Because the Berkshire academies, with the single exception of the Berkshire Gymnasium, had no dormitories, students boarded in private homes and consequently enjoyed close relations with the townspeople. The towns always took considerable pride in their academies, and town and gown never drew closer than on the occasions of the annual exhibitions. On the last Wednesday in August 1830, a vistor to Lenox would have seen a large and varied throng gathering into a loose formation before the academy building. The day being a full holiday for both Lenox and several nearby towns, the triumphant academic procession was large, with students, parents, friends, teachers, and trustees all marching, to the rhythm of the Lenox band, to the Church on the Hill. There trustees and distinguished visitors sat on the stage, students and parents on the main floor, and the band in the choir loft, and except for the two-hour lunchtime intermission, the exercises continued throughout the day.[52]

After a prayer by Samuel Shepard, the local pastor and president of the trustees, the long-practiced student declamations began. In 1830 young Alexander Hyde of Lee opened the program with a verbal flourish: "Be not deceived, my countrymen," he resoundingly cautioned. "Believe not these venal hirelings when they would cajole you by their subtleties into submission."—and so on to the end of Josiah Quincy's "Spirit of the American Revolution." Forty other declamations, essays, and disputations followed, with a musical interlude after every fifth recitation. A few of the young orators were one day to become famous. In the class of 1830, at Lenox, William L. Yancey learned something of the elo-

52. *One Hundredth Anniversary of . . . Lenox Academy,* p. 24; Stockbridge, *Berkshire Herald,* Jan. 12, 1832.

quence which he later used with such effect in Alabama.[53]
Quite appropriately, he chose for his exhibition-day performance an extract from one of Hayne's speeches answering
Webster. Much less in character was Henry Shaw's earnest
delivery of Webster's "The Eloquence of John Adams," in
which few of his patient listeners could have discerned any
of the folksy humor later to distinguish the Josh Billings of
the *Farmers' Allminax*. The titles of the original essays offered a much more accurate reflection of the student mind.
"Reflections on America," "The Indians," "The Folly of
Passion Contrasted with the Guidance of Reason," "Personal
Effort," "The Twenty-Fifth Century—a Glance at the Future"—all suggested those primary values of patriotism and
personal self-reliance so much emphasized at the academies.
On one memorable occasion, the exhibition-day audience
heard Fanny Kemble deliver an original and rather lengthy
poem, unpoetically entitled, "Lines Addressed to the Young
Gentlemen Leaving the Academy at Lenox, Massachusetts."

> Life is before ye—and while now ye stand
> Eager to spring upon the promised land,
> Fair smiles the way, where yet your feet have trod
> But few light steps, upon a flowery sod. . . .[54]

Miss Kemble was here clearly expressing the fundamental
aim of the academy—preparation for life—and not even the
most unreceptive audience could have found her dull.

Like Fanny Kemble, Mark Hopkins found much to praise

53. That the fiery secessionist orator of the Alabama Resolutions was
educated in Berkshire was the result of the death of his father and his
mother's remarriage to the celebrated Troy divine, the Reverend
N. S. S. Beman. After graduating from Lenox in 1830 he entered the
sophomore class at Williams College in the fall; and his oratorical
ability was used by Williamstown politicians in the campaign of 1832.
Cf. Leverett W. Spring, *A History of Williams College* (New York,
1917), pp. 145–47.

54. Frances Anne Kemble, *Poems* (Boston, 1859), p. 222.

in Berkshire's educational facilities, but criticized what he considered a growing materialism. Recognizing the two great advantages of the academy education to be thoroughness and moral training, he happily saw in his own county a region "where these unfounded and dangerous opinions of the sufficiency of mere intellectual education have not taken deep root." [55] Still, he felt that the academies were beginning to concentrate too heavily on science and hoped that languages might one day receive more attention, and that the freshman year of college might eventually be given there—a hope already fulfilled at Lenox, where a certificate usually admitted the bearer to the sophomore class in college. Hopkins deplored the Yankee view of education as merely a means to gain wealth and to get ahead of one's fellows, and warned that if ever such a viewpoint should become universal, "all that now excites the enthusiasm and warm devotion of the highest order of minds would be gone." The true purpose of the academy, he concluded, was "to elevate the nature of man, to quicken and call forth all that is good within him; and since, in a government like ours, there will always be a continuity from the highest to the lowest, it is to do what we can to elevate the whole mass. It is to join the top of the water-spout to the cloud, so that the lowest drop may be taken up and float in the upper sky." [56]

Many critics of the academies, however, with an eye for economic factors, complained of their undemocratic nature. After all, how could the poor man afford to pay his son's tuition at the academy? What real chance had Hopkins' "lowest drop" of rising through the waterspout to the clouds? In 1824 the Massachusetts legislature had virtually abolished the law requiring grammar schools by revising it to apply only to towns of over 7,000 inhabitants, of which only five existed in the entire state. Within Berkshire the academies

55. M. Hopkins, *Miscellaneous Essays*, p. 230.
56. Ibid., pp. 216–17.

were doing the work of the old grammar school, and in most cases doing it better, but they did inevitably discriminate in favor of the well-to-do. At the time of the repeal of the grammar school law, when George Ticknor, J. G. Carter, and other educational authorities were attacking the aristocratic tendency of the academies, the city of Boston was already starting on a solution. Three years earlier the Boston English Classical School had been established as a free public high school—the secondary school of the future.[57] But not until twenty years later did this type of institution begin to take root in Berkshire.

Evidently the social make-up of Berkshire—together with the large number of villages nearly equal in size, the universality of farming, and the proud spirit of individualism—operated to the advantage of private and semiprivate schools and academies and tended to discourage community ventures in free public education, whether on the common or secondary level. Pittsfield and Sheffield had established high schools by the mid-1840's, but towns with adequate academies adopted the high school system only slowly and reluctantly. Closed during the Civil War, Lenox Academy reopened in 1866 as the town high school. A few of the academies, among them Drury Academy in Adams, eventually developed into quasi high schools, with much of their support coming from the town and almost the entire tuition fee being remitted to town students. In a town like Adams, with its large population and flourishing textile and shoe mills, such a system proved to be quite workable.

In 1844, four years after the demise of the Berkshire Gymnasium, the first real public high school in the county appeared in Pittsfield, with the Reverend John Todd, a minister who was at heart a schoolmaster, as chairman of the board. Never very receptive to educational innovations, the

57. Emit D. Grizell, *American Secondary Education* (New York, 1937), p. 39.

townspeople accepted it with only tentative approval and sat
back to see what might happen. At the end of the first year
Parson Todd could report a total attendance of sixty-six boys
and forty-six girls and an average daily attendance of seventy-
three, with three-fourths of the absences attributable to sickness. Among the courses offered, reading and spelling had
the greatest popularity, closely followed by arithmetic, writing, English grammar, geography, and Latin. Neither Greek
nor history nor the newer vocational studies attracted more
than a small percentage of students.

Even with its first successful year behind it, the school remained on the defensive, and to Todd fell the responsibility
of presenting its case in the Pittsfield town meeting. Unless
the townspeople would agree to another yearly allotment of
$500, the new school could not survive. With true advertising
instinct, Todd secured a choice spot in the Pittsfield papers
and published a school report which could not fail to appeal
to any reader's self-interest and sense of economy. How, he
asked, could any citizen regard the new public school as anything but a necessity, when without its help in supplying
teachers the district schools must wither? And how could
anyone in Berkshire fail to recognize his great good fortune
in being able to maintain a high school for the small yearly
sum of ten dollars per pupil, when the figure often ran as
high as forty dollars in the cities? [58]

Todd's campaign succeeded, and the new high school continued to function; but even in 1850, when Jonathan Tenney
became principal, difficulties were still arising. More than
any other single man, Tenney shaped the Pittsfield high
school, and as secretary of the Berkshire Teachers' Association he also made his influence felt in nearly every other
public school in the county. Like Horace Mann, he advised
the establishment of Teachers' Institutes and encouraged
parents to take an interest in their local schools; and because

58. Pittsfield *Sun,* Apr. 10, 1845.

Berkshirites regarded him as one of themselves, they often
accepted his suggestions with much better grace than they
had ever accepted Mann's freely given advice. After receiving
his M.A. from Dartmouth in 1846 and serving for four years
as preceptor of Pembroke Academy, Tenney went on to become one of the leading figures in New England education.[59]

At Pittsfield he encountered one financial crisis after another. His own meager salary obliged him to take on additional work as the Berkshire representative of the American
Mutual Life Insurance Company. At the same time, a shortage of school funds forced him to adopt the monitorial system of which he thoroughly disapproved. By employing one
of the older students as a teacher, however, he did find that
he could save enough to make necessary repairs on the school
building.[60] Realizing that the city high schools were then
offering a multiplicity of courses, Tenney insisted that his
school take care not to spread its limited resources too thin.
To the chairman of the Pittsfield School Board, Dr. Root, he
wrote: "In my opinion it may not be best for us to make
much of the modern languages,—of painting,—or of drawing
even, beyond map and line drawing . . . before our first
year is ended. I would have no instruction in instrumental
music at present. If we could have vocal music twice weekly,
I would like it much, if a good teacher residing in the village
can be obtained. I feel that we must *lay the foundation* in
the fundamental branches of knowledge, or perhaps, better,
that we get the roots well started from *good seed* . . . before
we attend to the branches." [61] Under Tenney the new high

59. Henry Barnard thought so much of Tenney's abilities that he
once asked him to become his partner in editing the *American Journal
of Education;* but feeling that the financial risk was too great, Tenney
refused. After four years at Pittsfield, he left to become School Commissioner of New Hampshire.

60. Jonathan Tenney to Dr. Oliver Root, Apr. 16, 1851; Tenney Collection, American Antiquarian Society.

61. Ibid.

school thus retained one of the great virtues of the academies —thoroughness.

The story of higher education in Berkshire centers in only two towns—first in Williamstown, where Williams College began its existence in 1793, and then in Pittsfield, where the Berkshire Medical Institution enjoyed a brief but illustrious forty-four years. Without those two sound institutions the county could hardly have asserted her cultural independence of Boston and New York as she did in the early nineteenth century. Berkshire-trained college men and physicians did much to save her from the fate of cultural colonialism.

When Williams College opened its doors on an October Wednesday in 1793, it became the second college to be established in Massachusetts. Almost thirty years earlier a group of leading citizens in the Connecticut Valley had petitioned the legislature for permission to establish Queens College at Hatfield, but the Harvard authorities had managed to exert so much last-minute pressure on Governor Bernard that he denied the request. The Harvard Overseers' Remonstrance fairly represented Boston opinion in expressing the fear that a new college in the west not only would injure Harvard but would be generally detrimental to educational standards.[62] Although some Harvard men felt no more amenable to the proposed founding of Williams a generation later, they could no longer muster enough influence to block the petition; after a year's delay, the legislature at last granted the charter, on June 22, 1792.

A man without formal education, Colonel Ephraim Williams had nourished such a taste for literature that he had carried eleven books on his last military campaign.[63] At his death in battle against the French and Indians on September

62. Josiah Quincy, *The History of Harvard University* (2 vols. Cambridge, 1840), 2, 464–75.
63. Spring, *A History of Williams College,* p. 15.

8, 1755, it was found that he had left a will requiring that his lands be sold to establish a free school in the area west of Fort Massachusetts, and he had stipulated only that the town must fall within the Massachusetts border and that it must be called Williamstown. In accordance with his demands, the executors duly sold his lands and lent the money out at interest; and when, in 1785, they could be sure that the West Township would fall within Massachusetts, they applied to the General Court for an act enabling them to carry out Williams' desires. Nine of Berkshire's leading citizens became trustees, and in 1788 they voted to erect a building. Within two years an impressive four-story brick building appeared in Williamstown, built at a cost of $11,700. Part of the money came from Williams' estate, part from a lottery granted by the legislature, and part from the money-raising efforts of the townspeople. For two years the new institution operated as a grammar school, with a lower department comparable to a common school, and then the trustees abruptly decided that they could best realize the true intentions of Ephraim Williams by converting the school to a college.

The *Western Star* of August 27, 1793, carried a formal announcement of the opening of the college. "The qualifications for admission," read the article, "will be the same with those required by the laws of Yale College." Williams, however, did make one exception to this rule in providing that applicants might substitute a knowledge of French for Greek. Whether the trustees were bidding for French-Canadian students or were simply expressing their enthusiasm for French, this exception was perhaps the only point on which Williams was more liberal than Yale.[64] Since all of the teach-

64. In 1798 French was dropped from the curriculum and a student resolution against the French was sent to President Adams. Parrington's view of Williams College in 1810 (the year in which Bryant entered the college) as far more liberal than Yale has very little factual basis. Cf. Vernon L. Parrington, *Main Currents in American Thought* (3 vols.

ers and seven of the trustees had graduated from Yale, they quite naturally tried to make Berkshire's new college a miniature reproduction of their alma mater. By 1796 La Rochefoucauld-Liancourt could comment, after traveling through Berkshire, that Williams was "said to be a tolerably good seminary." [65]

The parallel between Williams and Yale extended even to their presidents. Timothy Dwight himself could have stood no firmer in his defense of the Federalist party and the orthodox church than did Williams' first president, the Reverend Ebenezer Fitch. And although he declined the honor, Theodore Sedgwick, then the leader of Federalism in Berkshire, was offered the first chair of civil law and polity. Meanwhile, that purveyor of news and Federalism to all Berkshire, Loring Andrews, was rejoicing in the enlightened wisdom of President Fitch's politics:

> It is a fortunate circumstance that the seats of learning in the New England States are generally under the direction of men justly esteemed . . . for their attachment to the true interests of their country, to energetic government, order and peace. . . . on a late occasion, the Head [*Fitch*] of an infant Seminary in this Commonwealth delivered an address to the candidates for a first degree, which did honour to his head and heart . . . "above all (said he) beware of that demon Democracy, that spectre stalking from the Pandemonium of the Jacobins, tinged with the blood of at least a million, and threatening, in its progress, to overturn all order and government." [66]

New York, 1927–1930), 2, 240. In 1808 when the new eight-volume edition of Edwards' works was published, seven Williams students subscribed; a larger number than in all other New England colleges combined. Cf. Spring, *History of Williams College*, p. 63.

65. *Travels in the U.S.*, 2, 211.
66. *Western Star*, Oct. 6, 1795.

The Republican "spectre" happened to be enjoying considerable strength in Williamstown and nothern Berkshire during those years, and the partisan tone of the new college infuriated them. Republicans filled many a column in the Pittsfield *Sun* with vigorous censure of Williams for its narrow partisan spirit.[67] John Bacon's son, Ezekiel, then a student at the college, wrote to his father in Congress an angry description of Fitch's reaction to Jefferson's inaugural:

> It will however require something more than a wise and salutary management of our political and temporal concerns, to reconcile *one class* of our citizens to the general government while it is in the hands of its present keepers,—I mean the Clergy, amongst whom we hear of not a single one who relents from his enmity or renounces a single prejudice which he may have formed against the president. In this temper of mind, worked up to a pitch which it would seem sometimes forbad the free exercise of his reason the President of our College continues to stand. . . . Ever since commencement his invective against the general government and his hatred to all who are its friends and in short to every man and thing that is called Republican seems to have been increasing and forms in one shape or other as I am well informed the almost constant theme of instruction to his pupils.— In their compositions and discussions before him, they have full license to abuse by name Mr. Jefferson and all concerned with him in the administration, in terms more low and vulgar than the most vulgar of our newspapers, and when they have done Mr. Fitch sits ready to stamp their words with the weight of his opinion.[68]

At last, with Fitch's resignation in 1808, the political bickerings abated, only to be followed by a controversy which

67. Pittsfield *Sun,* Oct. 17, 1801.
68. Dec. 28, 1801; Gallatin Collection, New-York Historical Society.

threatened a catastrophe for Berkshire. By 1815 many ob-
servers were detecting signs of premature decrepitude in the
college, probably brought on by a severe lack of funds and a
student body which had dwindled from a high of 115 to fifty-
eight. Increasing numbers of dissatisfied citizens were suggesting that the school move to a more centrally located town
in Massachusetts, and finally the trustees felt obliged to appoint a committee to consider the idea. The committee duly
met and advised against removal, but their decision proved
useless in its effort to quiet the dissenting voices, some of
them coming from within the college itself. Not only did the
new president, Zephaniah Moore, think a new location ad-
visable, but even a group of students of the Philotechnian
Society cast a nearly unanimous vote in favor of removal.
Hopeful citizens of Northampton promised $12,500 should
the college be moved to their town. Stockbridge immediately
countered with an offer of $13,000, and until 1818 the disput-
ing forces swayed back and forth without reaching any final
decision. Then the Reverend Theophilus Packard, a power
in the Congregational Church, assumed firm leadership of
the removal faction and demanded that the college be moved
to Amherst. Berkshirites found themselves obliged to rally
all their forces in opposition.[69]

Meeting at Williamstown, a small but determined group
of Berkshire citizens drew up and published a manifesto in
the hope of persuading the public to their viewpoint. As long
as the college remained in Williamstown, they argued, it
would always draw considerable numbers of students away
from the expense and the "allurements to dissipation" associated with Harvard and Yale.[70] After all, the members of
the state legislature had never intended that Williams should
equal, either in splendor, numbers, or wealth, the venerable

69. Spring, *History of Williams College*, pp. 94–106.
70. *An Address of Citizens of Berkshire County . . . Meeting at
Williamstown* (1819), p. 7.

institution at Cambridge. On the contrary, they must have recognized Williamstown as a poor location for a great university but a perfect site for a small country institution where the expense of education might remain so low as to be accessible to all classes.[71] "We are of opinion," said the defenders of the Berkshire location, "that an institution, designed as Williams College was, to be rigidly economical in all its operations, and well shielded from anything like extravagance and dissipation, ought not to be placed in a larger town than Williamstown." Even granted that the legislature could rightfully revoke the charter, still "there is a strong implied contract, which lies at the foundation of all morals of legislation, and all confidence in the community that rights thus vested shall not be vacated without absolute necessity." [72]

When Henry Dwight of Stockbridge, counsel for those desiring to keep the college in Berkshire, argued the case before the legislature in 1820, he cited William Jarvis' persuasive observation that the people of Berkshire, excepting only the Congregational clergy, wholeheartedly approved of the Williamstown location.[73] Because Berkshirites were able to illustrate the truth of Jarvis' statement by their willingness to make great sacrifices, Dwight won his case before the legislature and saved the college for Berkshire. Under the leadership of Daniel Noble, Class of '96, citizens of the Williams-

71. Ibid., p. 10.

72. Ibid., p. 13. In contrast to the Dartmouth College Case, the state legislature had here granted Williams' original charter, and no attempt was made to claim for the Williams charter that sanctity which the Supreme Court had decided was attached to that of Dartmouth College (a charter granted by the British government).

73. Brief of Henry W. Dwight on removal of Williams College; DC. Used with the permission of Henry W. Dwight of Stockbridge, Massachusetts, the owner of the Dwight collection. The clergy favored removal partly in deference to Theophilus Packard and partly, one suspects, in the hope of moving the college away from Berkshire political radicalism.

town area had raised $18,186—more than enough to convince the legislators of their sincerity.

Strangely enough, in spite of the supposed support proffered by the Berkshire clergy to the removal faction, they were, in their practice of disinterested benevolence, actually engaging in an endeavor which helped the college in Williamstown. By forming a Berkshire branch of the American Education Society they contributed both to making the school financially solvent and to keeping it democratic. Formed in 1818 under the direction of the Reverend Heman Humphrey of Pittsfield, the Berkshire Education Society hoped to come to the "aid of indigent young men, of good talents and hopeful piety, in acquiring a learned and competent education for the gospel ministry." [74] Already, in the year of the new society's formation, twenty-three Williams students were receiving aid of something less than fifty dollars per year from various societies, the American Education Society included. Hoping to recruit new members at one dollar per year, the new society argued that the presence of a still larger number of pious students at the college would restrain the passions of those others more rowdily inclined. Besides providing a good supply of schoolteachers for the vacation months, these proposed charity scholars, coming as they would from the lower classes of society, would be uniquely qualified to become clergy to the poor. So successful was the new society in its project that it turned over $299 to the American Education Society in its first year and made larger per capita gifts to charity scholars than did any other branch of the society.[75]

While the Williams administration was coping with the crisis, faculty and students had been devoting their energies to educational matters and had begun the program which eventually gave the college something of a reputation in the

74. *Berkshire Star,* June 20, 1816.
75. Ibid.; Pittsfield *Sun,* June 10, 1818.

natural sciences. Quite appropriately, they added a globe and telescope and a sprig of laurel to the college seal in 1805 —symbols of the strides to be made in the sciences of botany and astronomy within the coming generation. For the development of science courses and the encouragement of student interest in them, two men, Chester Dewey and Albert Hopkins, deserved most of the credit.

Graduated from Williams in 1806 and converted to orthodoxy during the great revival of a year earlier, Chester Dewey had proceeded to Stockbridge almost immediately after his graduation to study theology with Berkshire's most distinguished divine, Stephen West. While there, he must have undergone a change of heart or at least of ambition, for in 1808 he left Stockbridge to accept a tutorial position at Williams and to study chemistry under Yale's Silliman during his vacations. Two years later he became a professor of mathematics and chemistry. His varied activities included preaching in Berkshire pulpits, organizing among Williams students in 1823 the first antislavery society in Massachusetts, compiling local meteorological data for the Smithsonian Institution, and carrying on a considerable correspondence with European scientists.[76] Lecturing with enthusiasm and wit, he was largely responsible for the students' tremendous interest in natural history, which reached its height in 1817. In that year the students themselves arranged for the printing of 500 copies of Amos Eaton's *A Manual of Botany,* when no publisher would take the risk.[77]

Albert Hopkins, younger brother of tutor Mark Hopkins, joined the faculty in 1826 and soon proved to be the man to fill the vacancy left by Chester Dewey's resignation the following year to become head of the Berkshire Gymnasium.[78]

76. Pittsfield *Sun,* Sept. 3, 1868; Spring, *History of Williams College,* p. 139.

77. H. H. Ballard, "Amos Eaton," *Collections of the Berkshire Historical and Scientific Society,* 2 (1892), 265.

78. Like Bancroft in going from Harvard to the Round Hill School

Under his able tutelage students of geology and astronomy discovered the fascinations of their surroundings. He led the first American geological field expedition to East Mountain during his years at Williams and later climbed Mount Greylock with his classes to view the magnificent glacial cirque, the Hopper.[79] For Williams' rapid advances in geological studies, however, he and Dewey had to share the credit with the Berkshire hills. All around Williamstown they rose in impressive formations, presenting the scientist with an almost irresistible incentive. When he was not climbing mountains and peering at the formations of Berkshire gneiss, Hopkins found time to go to Europe in 1834 to purchase astronomical instruments, and a year later the Hopkins astronomical observatory was begun on the campus, the second of its kind in America.[80] In his oration at the laying of the observatory cornerstone, he expressed an attitude toward the new sciences quite typical of Berkshire:

> Freedom from a narrow and selfish bias is to be secured not so much by particular precepts, as by the application of a system calculated to give to the mind expansion and enlargement . . . prepare yourself for action, action, the beginning, middle, and end of all that duty will require or society demand. . . . [*let us be*] observers of Nature, with a view to elicit truth, by habits of close attention, to improve our discriminating powers, to mature the judgment by careful balancing of possibilities

in 1823, Dewey was moved in part by the conviction that secondary education must be improved before the colleges could really advance.

79. Hopkins had once imposed upon himself a rule never to do anything for his own amusement. At Williams, however, he found an opportunity to combine amusement with utility in making steam engines and drawing plans for a unique steam vehicle to be driven by jets of steam pouring from the spokes of wheels. *Early Letters of Mark Hopkins*, pp. 248–49.

80. Grace G. Niles, "Albert Hopkins and Williamstown," *New England Magazine*, new ser. *31* (1904–05), 667.

—to wean ourselves from vitiating tastes and frivolous amusements; by furnishing the mind with an exhilarating and dignified object of pursuit.[81]

Hopkins' attitude toward science was, in short, unmistakably conservative. In his humanistic frame of reference the value of science study, like that of a study of the classics, lay first in mental discipline and moral training; and he could assign only a secondary importance to it as an exploration of the unknown, an aid to man's conquest of nature. Science had become generally, in that period of New England history, simply a method, and seldom a faith to conflict with religion; and indeed many of the leading New England scientists, from Chester Dewey in Berkshire to Edward Hitchcock in Amherst, were orthodox Calvinists.

Until 1848 science and teachers of science were enjoying an almost unique prestige at Williams. Then, with the arrival of Professor Arthur Perry, the study of political economy began to overtake the sciences in popularity. Twenty years before, every faculty member had shunned the teaching of the political economy course, in which the deadly Say's and Ely's *Premiums* had constituted the sole text, but Perry's inspired guidance made the course one of the strongest in the college curriculum.[82] An American apostle of the Manchester brand of economics, he did not shrink from indoctrinating his students with his own belief in free trade and laissez-faire.

By midcentury Williams College had become completely representative of Berkshire life. Its president, Mark Hopkins, himself a life-long Berkshirite, always emphasized moral training over the purely intellectual and regarded close student contact with good teachers as more important than extensive equipment or a large library—an opinion which eventually gave rise to the popular conception of the univer-

81. Ibid., p. 670.
82. *Early Letters of Mark Hopkins*, p. 173.

sity as a log with the student on one end and Mark Hopkins on the other.[83] Both his own writings and the curriculum of the college he directed reflected his conviction that thorough and logical cerebration was more important than research, and in his time German influence touched Williams only very slightly. Throughout most of Hopkins' presidency (1836–72), the college retained its traditional reputation as a school for able country boys who could not afford Yale or Harvard.

Fully as integral a part of the Berkshire scene as Williams was the once famous Berkshire Medical Institution, founded in 1823. Seven medical schools had already sprung up in New England, but none of them was closer to Berkshire than Castleton, Vermont. There, Dr. J. P. Batchelder was rather discontentedly teaching when he suggested to Berkshire's Dr. Henry Halsey Childs that the time had come to establish a medical school at Pittsfield. Responding with alacrity, Childs pressed the idea at a meeting of the Berkshire District Medical Society and received an appointment, along with Drs. Burbank and Collins, to petition the legislature for a charter and endowment.

Hoping to avoid the expected Harvard opposition, Childs hastily explained to the legislature that the proposed institution would offer no competition at all to Harvard, since it would expect to attract only students of small means, who were then having to go outside Massachusetts to find an inexpensive medical school.[84] Nothing that Childs could say,

83. In *Mark Hopkins and the Log* (New Haven, 1956), pp. 29–30, Frederick Rudolph demonstrates Hopkins' anti-intellectualism by quoting from his inaugural address: "I have no ambition to build up here what would be called a great institution. The wants of the community do not require it. But I do desire, and shall labor that this may be a *safe* college."

84. Henry Halsey Childs, "A Dissertation on the Progress of Medical Science—Read at the Annual Meeting, June 2, 1823," *Medical Dissertations, 4,* 1829), 59.

however, forestalled the inevitable opposition, coming partly from Harvard and partly from those conservatives who remembered Childs' offensive behavior in the 1820 Convention and had been awaiting their chance to embarrass Berkshire radicalism. Had William Jarvis failed in his skillful maneuvering as speaker of the House, the charter might never have been granted; and even his eloquence could neither persuade the legislature to vote an endowment nor dissuade them from requiring that the new school be affiliated with Williams as an encouragement to respectability.

The school soon established itself in the erstwhile Pittsfield Hotel—a former hostelry of democrats which had lost its *raison d'être* in the era of good feeling. Purchased for $3,000, the three-story building with its supplementary stables provided all the space the school could need, and after three years Pittsfield citizens managed to raise the total $3,000 to pay off the mortgage held by the trustees. Among the trustees were Levi Lincoln of Worcester, William Jarvis, Henry Brown and Henry H. Childs of Pittsfield, and Daniel Noble of Williamstown—all of them Jeffersonians against whom the eastern conservatives had many grievances.[85]

The new medical school had actually begun to function in September of 1822, four months before it received an official charter. The twenty-five students then in attendance appeared well pleased; and so enthusiastically did they talk of their year in Berkshire that eighty students registered for the following fall. Each student paid forty dollars per term for tuition and $1.75 per week for his room, meals, and laundry at the school dormitory. The faculty, though small, was of good quality. Dr. Childs taught the theory and practice of medicine; Dr. Batchelder, anatomy, surgery, and physiology; Dr. Asa Burbank, *materia medica;* and Professor Chester Dewey, chemistry, botany, and mineralogy. In addition, Dr.

85. Smith, *History of Pittsfield,* 2, 361–63.

Alfred Perry and Dr. William Tyler [86] taught obstetrics and gave special lectures. They had been chosen by the Berkshire District Society to act as part-time teachers and to maintain a close contact between the Institution and the Medical Society. Both sides gained strength from the relationship, and as the Medical School continued to enjoy a remarkable success, Berkshire physicians found themselves able to adopt a fairly firm attitude toward Cambridge. By 1830 the Berkshire school fulfilled the worst fears of the conservative Bostonians when it graduated twenty-four medical students to Harvard's twenty.[87]

86. William Tyler presents a fair example of the difficulties facing an indigent youth in Berkshire in pursuing a medical education before the days of the Berkshire Medical Institution: "18 years of age I labored on the farm with my Father as I have heretofore when not in school. . . . In November I left my father's house to teach school for the term of 4½ months in the Town of Half Moon. . . . While attending to my school, I studied Anatomy under the tuition of Dr. Silas Hamilton. . . . I buy a few Physical Books and return to my Father's in the Spring and labor with him through the Summer of my 19th year, but I have a great desire for literature and a liberal education. But I met with a repulse." "This Winter I keep school in Williamstown . . ." "1st of November 1800 begin school again in Half Moon where I continue my study of Physic what time I can gain." "1801 studied with Dr. Jarvis . . . about six months . . ." "The Fall of 1801 taught school in Cheshire one year for $120. Studied physic all leisure time." "1803, began study with Dr. Burbank . . . pursued it during the Summer . . ." "In the Fall went to New York and attended medical lectures at Columbia Medical School. My Winter studies were attended with a continual series of successes, and with the expense of $180. I have gained a considerable fund of useful knowledge or information. My next object is to get a Diploma or License to Practice Physic or in my profession." "Dec. 25, 1806, I have got license to practice Physic & Surgery, and the solicitation of my Father and friends to practice in Lanesborough." Dr. William H. Tyler, "Register," in "Berkshire Genealogical Notes," 2, typescript ed. Elmer I. Shepard, Williamstown, 1941.

87. Walter L. Burrage, *A History of the Massachusetts Medical Society 1781–1922* (Norwood, 1923), p. 334.

Heartened by the success of their school, members of the Berkshire Medical Society boldly began to seek still more independence. On December 7, 1830, Dr. Childs again presented a petition to the legislature, this time asking that they incorporate the Berkshire District Society as a separate organization with no ties to the state society. After all, Berkshire physicians, living at so great a distance from Boston, could not possibly benefit from the society library and entertainments, and their own society could boast the impressive total of sixty bona fide members.[88] Acting with foreseeable consistency, the legislature denied the petition; but two years later the Massachusetts Medical Society did make a concession to the importunate Berkshirites when they passed a bylaw providing that district societies might keep for their own use one-third of the money collected from dues. Not until 1837, however, did the Massachusetts Medical Society give the Berkshire Medical Institution itself full recognition, this in spite of the assurance written into the original charter that Berkshire graduates should enjoy equal rights with Harvard graduates. Finally, in 1837, the Massachusetts Society agreed to admit Berkshire graduates as fellows without requiring a special fee or examination. With the increasing number of concessions made by the state society, and with the penetration of Berkshire by the railroad in 1842, medical relations between Bostonians and Berkshirites became closer and friendlier, and Berkshire experienced a further triumph in 1852 when the Massachusetts Medical Society held its annual meeting in Pittsfield.[89]

88. Ibid., p. 82.

89. Burrage, *Massachusetts Medical Society,* p. 136. For a time Dr. Oliver Wendell Holmes was evidently toying with the idea of accepting Childs' twice-repeated offer of a professorship at Pittsfield (his usual vacation spot). Cf. H. H. Childs to O. W. Holmes, Jan. 18, 1840; Holmes Collection, Harvard University.

During the years of its brief life span (1823–67), the Berkshire Medical Institution not only graduated 1,138 well-trained doctors but made many impressive contributions within the community and the state. As a direct consequence of Dr. Childs' consuming interest in the subject, Berkshire became the first medical school to establish a professorship of pathology. Even in the 1820's Dr. Childs had recognized that medical science must virtually reach a standstill until doctors could succeed in replacing the old speculative pathology with a new theory at once empirical and systematic —a theory to which he hoped the new Berkshire professorship might contribute, but which, of course, was not fully realized until Pasteur came forward with his germ theory of disease.[90] Meanwhile, within the county, the Institution was providing a clinic for the needy and had opened, to both students and the general public, a natural history lyceum with an annual series of lectures, the first ones delivered by the geologist-cleric Edward Hitchcock.[91] More ambitious but less effective was the Institution's effort, under the constant prodding of one of its own recent graduates and Berkshire's leading satirist, Asa Greene, to raise the premedical educational requirements.

> A majority of physicians are extremely destitute of almost every kind of learning not immediately connected with their particular calling. The classics are to them a dead letter; history is a sealed book; polite literature is hardly treated with civility; and geography itself is shut

90. In the Pittsfield *Sun* of Apr. 5, 1868, Dr. Childs was quoted: "In the infancy of the natural sciences, and for many centuries they made but little progress. Shrouded in mystery and degraded by superstition and the sport of hypothesis, they added little to the advancement of medical science. Not till facts were made the basis of reasoning, and speculation abandoned for sound theory, do we chronicle the discovery of important truths."
91. Ibid., Sept. 18, 1823.

out of doors. Hundreds of Doctors, every year, receive diplomas which they cannot construe, to gain the universe; and are going about to parsons and lawyers and schoolmasters, to ask the meaning of the honors wherewith they are decorated. They know not whether Apollo, or Vulcan, or Bacchus, is the patron god of their profession. . . . While they are the disciples of Aesculapius, they are forgetful to become the votaries of Minerva. Students of Medicine have mostly, too little *preparatory* learning. It is, in many instances, scarcely three years from the time of laying aside the axe, to that of assuming the lancet.[92]

Quite early in its existence the Institution apparently led all the other medical schools in the country in suggesting and publicizing the ideas of a national medical convention. The idea received a cool reception among members of the Massachusetts Medical Society—an indication that, although sound, it was probably premature. With doctors from four states often practicing within its boundaries, Berkshire could recognize and appreciate the need for a national convention to standardize medical education and medical fees much more fully than could a self-sufficient area like Boston. The possibility of a sectional meeting had received some support among Boston doctors, but a national meeting was apparently beyond their powers to conceive.

All the time that the Berkshire Medical Institution was so capably manifesting its worth, however, it was continually facing financial crises and was never self-supporting and never out of debt. The long-suffering faculty always found themselves squeezed from both directions. While paying forced loans to trustees, they were having to accept part of their salaries in the form of I.O.U.'s from indigent students. In fact, when John Batchelder left the school, the trustees

92. Asa Greene, editorial in *Berkshire American,* Jan. 18, 1827.

owed him some $200, and he held over $400 in I.O.U.'s from former students. Eventually, such a shaky financial foundation seeemed doomed to give way. The collapse came finally in 1867, when the school, having no financial cushion and depending entirely on student fees to pay its bills, suffered a recession in enrollment. The buildings were sold to the town in 1871 for a new high school, the debts were paid, and the remaining $4,400 went as a gift to the local library, the Berkshire Athenaeum.[93]

Thereafter, Berkshire schools, with the exception of Williams College, became assimilated into the general state system. The elementary schools were upgraded in all departments and the school buildings improved; and all the academies—some better, some worse than the new public high schools—experienced a general standardization. The century of relative independence for Berkshire education was over—a century in which Bostonians and state government officials had paradoxically goaded Berkshirites into action on the elementary level and at the same time balked and delayed in approving charters for Williams and the Medical Institution. By 1860 Berkshire's educational system had improved to the point where it would have compared favorably with that in any Massachusetts county and had become one of the main solvents of provincialism. Reinforcing and cooperating with an expanding economic life, the schools had begun to bring Berkshirites into mental contact with other areas and to make young men of ambition think of choosing city life in preference to the limited possibilities within the mountain barriers.

93. Smith, *History of Pittsfield*, 2, 370–73.

# Chapter 6. A DISHONOR TO BE IGNORANT

IN OCTOBER 1823 Theodore Sedgwick, Jr. stood before a meeting of the Berkshire Agricultural Society to expound a theory strangely inconsistent with his father's aristocratic bias. "We must," he said, "so educate our people that every man shall have a just sense of his own value and importance as a citizen, with a good coat for a holiday and a Sunday, so that he shall consider it a dishonor to be ignorant . . ." [1] Other men in early nineteenth-century Berkshire—among them Timothy Edwards, Samuel Bush, and Elkanah Watson —nourished the same conviction, and it was through their various influences that three important channels of adult education were opened to Berkshire citizens: the town library, the lyceum lecture, and the county Agricultural Society.

Among educational institutions the library had come relatively early to Berkshire, and even in the first decade of the nineteenth century Orville Dewey could look back to a well-established village library:

> For books to read, the old Sheffield library was my main resource. It consisted of about two hundred volumes,— books of the good old fashion, well printed, well bound in calf, and well thumbed too. What a treasure was there for me! I thought the mine could never be exhausted. At least it contained all that I wanted then, and better reading, I think, than that which generally engages our youth nowadays,—the great English classics in prose and verse, Addison and Johnson and Milton and Shake-

1. *Address of Theodore Sedgwick Delivered before the Berkshire Agricultural Association October 2, 1823* (Pittsfield, 1823), p. 8.

speare, histories, travels, and a few novels. The most of these books I read, some of them over and over, often by torchlight, sitting on the floor . . . and to this library I owe more than to anything that helped me in my boyhood.[2]

By 1800 not only Sheffield but Stockbridge, Pittsfield, Lee, and Great Barrington had established libraries where citizens, "not professional but readers," could find Johnson, Pope, and Shakespeare. Not public in the modern sense, these early society libraries looked entirely to their membership for support. After buying a library share, each member would pay an annual assessment on it—a payment which contributed to the running expenses of the library and to the purchase of new books.

The original society library, the Philadelphia Library Company, had appeared in 1731, a creation of Benjamin Franklin's active mind. Eighteen years later the idea spread to New England with the founding of the Redwood Library in Newport and the appointment of Ezra Stiles as librarian. Soon similar society libraries were springing up all over Massachusetts, first in the eastern towns and then in the more remote western settlements. Salem was enjoying the advantages of a library by 1760; Andover, by 1770; Easthampton, by 1792; and Greenfield, by 1801. Only in the 1850's did the new type of tax-supported, free town libraries, begin to replace society libraries, although the original free town library appeared in Peterborough, New Hampshire, in 1838.[3]

The first mention of a library in Berkshire came in 1772, when Moses Ingersoll left a will which included his share in the North Parish public library valued at £1 10s. Then in 1794 the Reverend Alvan Hyde informed a correspondent

2. Dewey, *Autobiography*, pp. 28–29.
3. Arthur E. Bostwick, *The American Public Library* (New York, 1910), pp. 6–10; Edward Edwards, *Free Town Libraries* (New York, 1869), pp. 273–80.

that the society library of Lee had the only available copy in
Berkshire of Jones' *Treatise on the Trinity;* [4] and in 1796
Pittsfield apparently founded its own library, in which eighty
volumes had accumulated by 1800.[5] The treasurer of the
Pittsfield Library Society, Thomas Gold, published an announcement in an 1801 Pittsfield *Sun,* stating that any
member in arrears on his annual library tax must either pay
or forfeit his share.[6] These brief hints, along with Orville
Dewey's reminiscences, constitute all the known facts about
the libraries in Sheffield, Great Barrington, Lee, and Pittsfield and prove little beyond their mere existence. Only the
Stockbridge library left any detailed records which have
survived.[7]

Founded in 1794, the Berkshire Republican Library of
Stockbridge flourished until 1818. Since Stockbridge was
generally Federalist and since the names of Theodore Sedgwick, Henry Dwight, and Ephraim Williams appeared on
the list of original members, the word "Republican" in the
name would seem rather to have indicated the absence of
artificial qualifications for membership than to have defined
any political bias. The founding of the library would no
doubt have been impossible without the interest and cooperation of a fairly large group of citizens, but two men,
Timothy Edwards and Barnabas Bidwell, led the undertaking. Both college graduates, they occupied positions of
some importance in the county. Timothy Edwards, the eldest
son of the theologian, had graduated from Princeton in
1757 and in 1771 had returned to Stockbridge to open the
first general store in Berkshire. For the next forty years he

4. Hyde, *Memoir,* p. 35.
5. Smith, *History of Pittsfield,* 2, 641.
6. Pittsfield *Sun,* May 19, 1801.
7. Berkshire Republican Library MSS (including records of directors'
meetings, treasurers' reports, lists of books bought and sold, and membership lists) are in the Bernhard Hoffmann Collection, NYPL.

was to remain one of the town's leading citizens, first as judge of probate for a decade, then as a member of the Massachusetts Provincial Congress, and finally as a commissioner in the Massachusetts—New York boundary dispute. Barnabas Bidwell, also the son of a Berkshire clergyman, had become the leading author of his class at Yale and had seen his five-act blank verse play, *The Mercenary Match,* published during his senior year. After remaining at Yale for three years as a tutor, he turned to the study of law. Then, once settled in Stockbridge, his success as a lawyer led him into a political career, and he became treasurer of Berkshire County in 1791—a position from which he was ousted for embezzlement in 1810. Before his disgrace he had served two years as librarian of the Berkshire Republican Library and had resigned to represent the Republicans in Congress in 1805. He and Edwards, together with the Stockbridge farmer Jonathan Patten, became the first directors of the Berkshire Republican Library.

The beginnings of the Library will probably always remain obscure, but when the proprietors gathered at Pepoon's Inn for their annual meeting in the spring of 1795 they testified to the spectacular success of the new venture. The directors reported that they had examined the library books and had found all but one in good condition. The ruined book, they assured their listeners, had been duly paid for. Convinced that the Republican Library could not have been better named, they looked upon its year-old career with approval. "Probably," they said, "there has been more reading in the town since this library was introduced and in consequence of its introduction than there was in a considerable number of preceding years; and this reading has not been confined to any one class of citizens; or to a few individuals in each class; but has been very generally diffused among all ranks and denominations of people: So that its tendency must be such as cannot fail of affording satisfaction to every friend of social happiness and the advancing improvements of civil society." [8]

Certainly the proprietors attending this annual meeting had reason to be proud of the year's achievements. Although one Silas Whitney held four shares in the Library, most of the proprietors owned only one share. With the money resulting from the sale of 173 shares at three dollars per share, the directors had purchased the original stock of books and the necessary bookcase. Ordered from T. Allen's bookstore in New York City, the books were shipped up the Hudson River and then overland to Stockbridge. There, according to the original rulings, each book might be taken out for a month, and a member with one share might borrow two books at a time.[9] Such a system hardly encouraged cursory reading, unless one happened to be the librarian. To Dr. Horatio Jones went the distinction of becoming the first librarian, but evidently the job rotated freely thereafter, for the Library treasurer recorded almost annual charges of twenty-five cents for moving the books and case to the home of the new librarian.[10]

The job of librarian was never highly paid, but then neither was it very arduous. In return for a salary of thirteen dollars a year he had only to keep the library open every Saturday for the three hours just before sunset, and to check in all of the books on quarterly library days. Falling on the last Saturdays in June, September, December, and March, those special days were usually advertised in the *Western Star*. Eventually the jobs of librarian and secretary-treasurer became consolidated, and the librarian became responsible for handling money as well as books.

8. Annual Reports of Directors at the Meetings of the Proprietors of the Library; Hoffmann Collection.

9. Constitution of the Berkshire Republican Library, Dec. 15, 1789; Hoffmann Collection.

10. Treasurers' reports of the Berkshire Republican Library, 1795–1818; Hoffmann Collection.

Once the 173 shares had been sold and the original books bought, the Library depended for financial maintenance upon fines, biddings, and an annual twenty-five-cent tax on each share. Any borrower keeping his book beyond the allotted month paid seventeen cents a week if it was of Octavo size or larger, and twelve cents a week if it fell into the small-size category. If he damaged the book by turning down a leaf, leaving dirty fingermarks, dropping tallow, or spilling ink, he paid an eight-cent fine; if he tore a leaf or cracked the cover, he paid seventeen cents.[11] Whenever two proprietors wanted the same book at the same time, they made competing bids for it. Almost always, the total expenses of repairing and rebinding old books and buying new ones fell below the annual income, and only in 1798 and 1799 did the treasurer record a small deficit. The value of a share, estimated annually, reached a high of $2.67 and a low of $1.75, but usually remained fixed at about $2.00. Because the price of books stayed high during this period, any Stockbridge citizen holding a library share could congratulate himself on having made a good investment. By paying the price of one average book and joining this two-book-a-month club, he could avail himself of a library of almost three hundred volumes.

No complete catalog of the books in the Stockbridge Library has survived the years, but a few lists of books purchased and a single list of books sold at a Lenox auction in 1803 indicate the general nature of the collection. Certainly, these lists must suggest to the modern librarian a strange preponderance of serious titles and a lack of imaginative works of fiction and poetry. Theological works, while present, by no means dominated the shelves. They included Mosheim's *Ecclesiastical History,* Paley's *Horae Paulinae, Guide and Refuge,* and *Gospel Its Own Witness,* and Jacques Necker's *Of the Importance of Religious Opinions* in a

11. Bylaws of the Berkshire Republican Library, 1808; Hoffmann Collection.

translation by Mary Wollstonecraft. Titles of biography and travel apparently comprised a rather large group: [12] *Life of Baron Frederic Trenck,* Rousseau's *Confessions,* Boswell's *Johnson,* Marshall's *Washington,* Hayley's *Life of Cowper* and *Historical Memoirs of the Duke of Cumberland,* Smith's *Tours in America* and *Travels of Anacharsis in Greece,* Sir John Carr's *A Northern Summer or Travels Round the Baltic,* J. Moore's *Residence in France,* Jonathan Carver's *Travels through the Interior Parts of North America 1766–68.* The fairly numerous works of philosophy and history included: Hume's *Essays,* Adam Smith's *The Theory of Moral Sentiments,* Necker's *On Executive Authority,* Voltaire's *Works,* La Rochefoucauld's *Maxims,* Burke's *Works,* John Mason's *On Self-Knowledge,* Lord Kames' *Sketches of the History of Man,* Mary Wollstonecraft's *A Vindication of the Rights of Woman,* Hubbard's *History of the Indian Wars.* Among the usually unclassifiable lighter works, the lists record such titles as *Elegant Extracts*—"useful and entertaining passages in prose and poetry for the improvement of young persons"—*The Repository*—"a collection of fugitive pieces of Wit and Humor"—Fanny Burney's *Evelina* and *Cecilia,* Henry Brooke's *The Fool of Quality,* Father Duminil's *Alexis, or The Young Adventurer,* Macklin's *The Man of the World.*

12. Harry M. Lydenberg, "The Berkshire Republican Library at Stockbridge 1794–1818," *Proceedings of American Antiquarian Society,* *50* (Apr. 1940), 4–38. This is an excellent study of the library from the bibliographer's viewpoint. In Appendix A Lydenberg discusses other society libraries, and quotes the vote of the Royalston library, Mar. 7, 1787: "Voted that the money laid out for books being divided into ten equal parts, be laid out for books upon different subjects in the following proportion, viz.: three tenths parts for books in Divinity and Moral philosophy; three tenths for history and biography, two tenths for arts and sciences, one tenth for law and physic, one tenth for Poetry, Novels, and Miscellany." Lilley B. Casswell, *History of Royalston, Massachusetts* (1917), pp. 106–7.

In selecting their library, the directors evidently knew what they were about. Often of recent publication, the books exhibited not only a generally high quality but a remarkable catholicity, and some of the titles remain in print and are even read today. Although procured in various ways, most of them dated back to the original New York City purchase. Captain Henry Brown brought ten more works back with him after a trip to New Haven, and the Library occasionally purchased secondhand volumes from individual members, but probably additions from other sources were rare. Except in 1803, when they gained sixty-four dollars from a book auction, the annual income seldom exceeded forty dollars—hardly enough to afford a surplus after paying the librarian and rebinding worn books, at a cost of sixty-five cents apiece. The proprietors frequently discussed the problems of repairing and rebinding at their annual meetings, but they rarely felt that wear and tear had been excessive in view of "the avidity with which almost everyone appears to have used his share in the library." [13]

At a time when almost all Stockbridge citizens devoted long and strenuous hours to their day's work, the hours left for reading must have been few; and the Berkshire farmer who spent his winter evenings with Hume, Paley, or Adam Smith displayed a fortitude and a concern with enduring values somewhat rarer in the subsequent age of periodicals and newspapers. Just who belonged to the Berkshire Republican Library must remain unrevealed, but lists of dues for the period 1806–08 indicated 130, about 10 per cent, of the town population to be the average membership. The census listed thirty-five of the members as heads of families and fifteen as women, but gave no idea of the number of young

13. Annual Report of the Directors, Apr. 9, 1794. The wear and tear on one perennial favorite was such that the directors reported on Apr. 4, 1798, that "the two volumes of *Elegant Extracts* will soon be entirely ruined unless thoroughly repaired."

people included. Whatever their numbers, the latter received special consideration in 1826, when a group of Stockbridge citizens founded a juvenile library of 160 volumes.[14]

Among the members of the original Stockbridge Library were such college graduates as Jared Curtis of Williams, principal of the Stockbridge Academy; John Bacon of Princeton; Theodore Sedgwick of Yale; Dr. Erastus Sergeant of Yale; and Samuel Whelpley of Yale, a historian and the Baptist minister of West Stockbridge. A library which attracted both the town's leading families and its common citizens must have offered a considerable variety of reading matter; and no one, except perhaps Stephen West, owned a private library so complete that he saw no advantage in joining the society. Even Theodore Sedgwick, with a large library of his own, apparently found membership profitable.

The records have left the sudden death of the Berkshire Republican Library in 1822 a subject for surmise; but whatever the preceding events may have been, the *Berkshire Star* of May 30, 1822, carried the following notice of a local auction: "About 150 volumes of books belonging to the Stockbridge library will be sold at Public Vendue at Hick's Inn in Stockbridge, on Wednesday, the 29th of May instance at one o'clock P. M. The Books are such as have been selected for the use of the library and among them are many valuable works. There are many of them in good condition and all such books as would be useful, either in a public or private

14. Field, *History of Berkshire,* p. 270. With no catalog of this juvenile library extant, one can piece together bits of evidence as to the reading of Stockbridge youth. Catharine Sedgwick found these books memorable: Berquin's *Children's Friends,* four volumes translated from the French; *The Looking Glass,* "an eclectic that contained the most pathetic story of "Little Jack"; Mrs. Barbauld's *Economy of Human Life,* "unmeaning and tedious"; Howe's *Letters from the Dead to the Living* "had a mystification that excited my imagination." *Life and Letters of Sedgwick,* p. 67.

library. Two sets of Hunter's *Sacred Biography* will be sold: this valuable work ought to be in every town library." The Berkshire educator Chester Dewey attributed the decline of the society libraries in part to the appearance of new and less edifying reading material. "Many of these libraries," he wrote, "have indeed been divided among the proprietors, since the greater multiplication of books and especially of *periodical* works. The consequence is, that while there is more reading than formerly, there is far less reading of the substantial authors in the English language." [15] The customary cultural lag in Berkshire had enabled its citizens to maintain their literary taste in the face of the downward trend in reading matter until comparatively late and had thus paradoxically proved a real contributor to the strength of Berkshire culture.

The Stockbridge library by no means passed unmourned. In fact, during the following month two long letters appeared in the *Berkshire Star* containing "Reflections," "Meditation," and "Recommendations" of "Amicus" (very possibly C. M. Sedgwick)—letters which argued that the Berkshire Library ought to be restored if only for the educational values it afforded to children, women, and working men. "It is not thought unbecoming that girls who are destined to be mothers . . . should be competent to direct the youthful mind. Indeed there is nothing more striking, in the existing state of our society than the value which is put upon female education, unless it be that an opinion has got abroad, that even a laboring man may be the better for knowledge, more useful on that account to himself, to his neighbors—a better citizen—a better man." [16] And what better influence on the young mind than those books of unexceptionable moral value by Miss Edgeworth and Miss Moore? A good library

15. Field, *History of Berkshire*, p. 173.
16. *Berkshire Star,* June 20, 1822.

for the young, Amicus argued, would simply constitute a fair debt owed to our children and would, after all, cost only the equivalent of ten good merino sheep.

The great educational value to both youth and adults of the old society libraries of Berkshire was even more tellingly stated by the Reverend Edmund H. Sears in his recollections: [17]

> My memory reaches back very distinctly to the time when I was five years old, and I have some dreamy impressions of something anterior to that date. . . . My father was a man of sound judgment and very strong feeling. Though his early education was scanty, he became a man of considerable information, and had some taste for books. . . . About this time my father brought home from the library Pope's Works, in two volumes, and I was completely bewitched by the harmony of the numbers. . . . Afterward I began to read Pope's Homer myself, and became so familiar with its contents that I could repeat whole books from beginning to end.
>
> This rhyming propensity, early waked up within me by Pope, proved a benefit to me of a kind which I was then little aware of. . . . it gave me a command of the English language such as I could not have gained by being drilled, during these romantic years of boyhood, through all the Latin class-books in existence. . . . I do not think I could have had a more profitable exercise in the best classical school in New England. I was mastering the English tongue, and making it flexible as a medium of thought, without any disgusting associations of crabbed lessons and pedagogues.
>
> The most profitable works furnished me by the pub-

17. Born in Sandisfield in 1810, Sears later moved to eastern Massachusetts and Unitarianism and is remembered chiefly as the author of "It Came upon the Midnight Clear."

lic library—books of history, biography, and travels—
were read by me with increasing interest and excited
many high resolves and bright anticipations.[18]

Such strictures as those written by Amicus in the *Berkshire Star* must have pricked many a reader's conscience, for
Berkshire citizens were supporting less library activity in the
1820's and 30's in proportion to their numbers and their
wealth than had the generation before them. Not until ten
years after the juvenile library had appeared in Stockbridge
did the Young Men's Association of Pittsfield finally establish a membership library, and even in the 1840's the only
Pittsfield library open to the public was the circulating library operated by the Little and Werden Bookstores of Pittsfield and North Adams. Borrowers could rent books there at
six cents a week, but they might keep new volumes only three
days and could not lend a rented book outside of the immediate family.[19] Apart from the membership and rental libraries, several private and institutional libraries were
growing steadily. The law library in the Sedgwick family
included over 120 volumes in 1822 when Charles Sedgwick advertised it for sale.[20] The Williams College Library
harbored over 2,000 volumes, and the one at Lenox Academy
had 300 volumes in 1828.[21] By far the most significant of the special libraries, however, was the Berkshire
Law Library, which the members of the Berkshire Bar established at Lenox in September 1815. The first such collection in the state, it included books of statutes, reports, and
commentaries which came to be invaluable to members of
the Bar whenever they attended court sessions in Lenox. The

18. Chandler Robbins, "Memoir of Rev. Edmund Hamilton Sears,
D.D.," *Proceedings of the Massachusetts Historical Society, 18* (1880–81),
224–26.
19. *Massachusetts Eagle,* Mar. 2, 1843.
20. Pittsfield *Sun,* Dec. 19, 1822.
21. Field, *History of Berkshire,* pp. 168, 341.

idea soon attracted imitators in counties all over Massachusetts. Supported by a three-dollar initiation fee and small
fees accruing from legal business, it had 310 volumes by
1828 and had grown to 1,825 volumes by 1873.[22]

Only in the middle of the nineteenth century did the
movement toward town-supported public libraries begin to
spread through New England. The first Massachusetts town
library opened its doors to the citizens of Wayland in 1850,
and five years later Lenox became the first town in Berkshire
and the ninth in the state to set up a free public library.
The following year the town erected an octagonal brick
building to house its books, the majority of which had been
purchased five years before. At that time John Hotchkin,
retired preceptor of Lenox Academy, had persuaded the
town meeting to vote $300 for a town library, provided that
he could raise a like amount by subscription. The townspeople having agreed, he had then, with the aid of the
clerk of courts, Henry Taft, and four others, organized the
Lenox Library Association and had raised the promised
$300. Open only to members for the first four years, the li-
brary eventually offered its privileges to all the townspeople
in return for their assuming half the expense of its support.
Meanwhile, the Library Association continued to contribute
the other half and to exert a controlling influence, and during the 1850's and 60's it often became the beneficiary of
public lectures given by such noted summer residents as
Samuel G. Ward, Fanny Kemble, and Henry Ward
Beecher.[23]

In 1871 the Lenox Library became one of the first of
Berkshire cultural institutions to receive the largesse of a
wealthy New Yorker who summered in the county. Mrs.
Adeline Schermerhorn purchased the beautiful Lenox Court
House (vacant since 1868 when Pittsfield had become the

22. Ibid., p. 109; Pittsfield *Sun,* Dec. 24, 1873.
23. Pittsfield *Sun,* Dec. 24, 1873, and Sept. 1, 1904.

county seat) and conveyed the property to five trustees with the instruction that the building be named the "Charles Sedgwick Library and Reading Room" in memory of Berkshire's beloved clerk of courts from 1821–56. To guard against discord, Mrs. Schermerhorn further provided that no religious or political meetings be held in the assembly hall of the library building.[24] In 1874 a merger of the Charles Sedgwick Library and the Lenox Library Association was effected, and for some years Lenox possessed the best public library in Berkshire.[25]

Just before the citizens of Lenox had begun to enjoy the benefits of their first public library, some of their Pittsfield neighbors had organized the Pittsfield Library Association, destined to become the most highly developed society library in Berkshire history. With shares selling at the fairly high figure of five dollars each, the library had managed to accumulate 1,400 volumes by 1859, and the Reverend Heman Humphrey felt moved to write an eloquent letter to the *Sun,* extolling the Association and incidentally appealing for more funds.[26] James Beebe, a wealthy Bostonian reared in Pittsfield, obligingly responded with a check for $500—just the impetus needed to bring on a rush of new members, the purchase of additional books, and the leasing of better quarters for the library. Throughout the 1860's financial support came from the proceeds of concerts given at Maplewood Institute, from a course of lectures organized by the Association, and from the almost forced sale of shares. Finally, in 1867, the Association changed its name to the Pittsfield Athenaeum and six years later became a free public library.

Similarly, in several Berkshire towns, the founding of pub-

24. *Lenox Library Association* (Lenox, 1948), p. 2.
25. *Dedication Exercises of the Charles Sedgwick Library and Reading Room at Lenox, Massachusetts, January 9, 1874* (Pittsfield, 1874), pp. 19–24.
26. Pittsfield *Sun,* Jan. 27, 1857.

lic libraries came only as the joint result of town action and the generosity of one or two individual donors. Stockbridge citizens, for example, received compelling inspiration to found a library in 1862 when the wealthy New Yorker Nathan Jackson contributed $2,000 toward its support, and when a local business man, John Z. Goodrich, donated the building. By 1864 the library had 2,000 volumes, and opened its door daily to the public.[27]

The pattern of library donations was becoming familiar and almost traditional in the county. Many sons of Berkshire, having made their fortunes either in the big cities or within the county, found satisfaction in endowing libraries for their old home towns. The town of Hinsdale was enabled to erect a superb library when the heirs of Charles H. Plunkett provided a gift of $25,000. Charles' father, Patrick, had migrated from Ireland to Lenox in 1795 penniless, and his son had become wealthy in the Berkshire textile mills. In Lanesborough, one of the few towns managing to maintain a library without the help of a wealthy benefactor, citizens reserved the town dog-license money to support their modest public library.[28]

During these same years, the lyceum movement provided still another medium of adult education for the people of Berkshire. Organized in 1826 in Millbury, Massachusetts, by Josiah Holbrook, the lyceum came no doubt as the ultimate expression of the desire to popularize education—a drive which was also impelling the academy movement and the common school revival. Emerson, himself one of the great lyceum lecturers, once described the catholicity of this latest innovation: "My pulpit is the lyceum platform," he said. ". . . Here everything is admissible, and philosophy, ethics, divinity criticisms . . . all are permitted. And all may be

27. Ibid., Dec. 24, 1873.
28. Ibid.

combined in one speech; it is a panharmonicon—every note on the largest gamut, from the explosion of the cannon to the tinkling of a guitar." [29]

In Berkshire the lyceum movement had begun comparatively early. In fact, the Berkshire Medical Institution had organized a pioneer lyceum as early as 1823. Meeting in the chemical room of the Institution on Thursday evenings, audiences could usually expect to hear lectures on natural history, occasionally accompanied by demonstrations of chemical phenomena. Still, the program remained flexible enough so that an audience gathering in January of 1824 heard a discussion of Greek Independence. Voicing their righteous indignation against the Turk, they voted that "The destroyers of civilization and religion ought no longer to hold that land where civilization and religion first dawned on the human race. The abomination of desolation should be driven back to the exility and barrenness of those deserts whence it originated. Resolved that a committee, make a collection to aid Greece in establishing literary institutions." [30] Like Dickens' Mrs. Jellyby, Berkshirites evidently thought it more important to provide for their remote neighbors than to look after their own struggling schools and libraries.

Berkshire's first regular town lyceum appeared in Lenox in 1830, and within four years the county could boast ten lyceums and a greater lyceum attendance than either Franklin County with five lyceums or Bristol County with seven —both areas being comparable to Berkshire in wealth and population.[31] Through the 1850's enthusiastic responses to the lyceum programs continued. The popular Berkshire lyceum lecturer, Samuel Bush, editor of the Lenox *Journal*

29. *Journals of Ralph Waldo Emerson,* ed. Edward W. Emerson and Waldo E. Forbes (10 vols. Boston, 1911), 5, 280.

30. Pittsfield *Sun,* Jan. 1, 1824.

31. *Third Annual Report of the Board of Education of the State of Massachusetts* (Boston, 1839), p. 75.

*and Argus,* rather romantically attributed their success to the "vigorous yeomanry, whose quiet homes are in this beautiful valley . . ." and who, after the labors of summer, enjoy an opportunity "to cultivate and expand the undying mind. . . . in autumn with its solemn quiet and hours of leisure." Seeking a further explanation, he concluded that the lyceum flourished in Berkshire for the same reason as did Williams College and the academies: "We live far away from the great world and are not distracted by its allurements nor its follies—the book of God's works is spread out before us." [32]

No doubt the aims of the Berkshire lyceums exceeded their accomplishments; but after all, the great enthusiasm which lay at the heart of the lyceum movement required great expectations—a fact recognized by the Berkshirites themselves. When the Berkshire cleric Edwin Dwight delivered the introductory lecture at the Stockbridge lyceum, he chose as his subject "The Importance of Exalted Aims in the Improvement of the Mind." Quite justifiably, he felt that, lacking a high aim, such obstacles as sloth, love of riches, a prejudice against learning, or a complacency with knowledge already attained might well become insurmountable. The lyceum, then, must seek to bring about nothing less than the acquisition of all knowledge useful to man—in short, a knowledge of all the sciences. The aim might seem overly ambitious but need not be discouraging, for, said Dwight, everyone is an amateur in learning, and knowledge has never been the exclusive property of the expert. With such equalitarian sentiments, Dwight apparently hoped to inspire even in beginners a sort of democratic confidence which might overcome their traditional awe of learning. "Medicine, law, and theology," he argued, "are generally considered as distinct and independent departments of science which are to be intruded upon and invaded by none but those who are

32. *Massachusetts Eagle,* Oct. 16, 1834.

devoted professionally to the pursuit of them. But why is this? Has an individual no right or reason to know anything of facts and truth, deeply interesting to every man living, because it does not fall within his sphere to be a professor of them? If so, the same might be said of every other branch of knowledge and men must content themselves with absolute ignorance." [33]

Through the lyceum programs, Dwight maintained that the acquisition of knowledge could become enjoyable and that the dullest mind might be inspired with an interest in learning. Quite apart from the pleasure of acquiring useful knowledge and the advantages of sociability, however, the lyceum could supply the deeper enjoyment of self-improvement. Always striking a responsive chord in the American mind, this idea of self-improvement became the moral justification of the lyceum. "Here," said Samuel Bush about the Lenox Lyceum, "the social principle is developed in beautiful simplicity. Here the head and heart act conjointly and while the former is instructed in the truths of science and philosophy, the feelings of the latter are chastened and refined, and you go from these meetings disposed to be better neighbors, better men, and better Christians." [34]

Generally, during the 1830's, the lecturers in Berkshire lyceums were local figures—schoolteachers, clergy, and editors—and the topics remained noncontroversial. Samuel Bush, a favorite in Berkshire, usually chose romantic variations on the theme of the sublimity and delight of learning; and John Hotchkin almost invariably spoke on classical subjects or on the new science. "Last evening we had at the Lyceum," wrote Mrs. Charles Sedgwick to her daughter, "quite a splendid audience and a very capital lecture from Mr. Hotchkin attended with some experiments with the air

33. Edwin Dwight, "An Introductory Lecture for Opening the Lyceum at Stockbridge January 30, 1839," p. 31; DC.
34. *Massachusetts Eagle*, Oct. 16, 1834.

pump. You know Mr. Hotchkin has made a pathetic appeal
to the ladies for their assistance. I promised . . . a sketch
of Governor Winthrop . . . from that historical manuscript
of mine . . . will be read next time." [35]

So effectively did Mr. Fowler of Pittsfield lecture on
phrenology in the local lyceum in 1835 that even the skeptical Phineas Allen had to admit: "There is something in the
science of phrenology." [36] The Stockbridge lyceum learned
the facts of a rather more substantial science when Professor Perry of the Berkshire Medical Institution lectured on
the history of anatomical studies. Albert Hopkins reported
that the discourse seemed learned,[37] but complained that the
delivery was poor—a serious defect in an age which demanded as much eloquence of its lyceum lecturers as of its
politicians.

As early as 1839 a few lecturers had begun to use the platform for partisan purposes and to speak on such inflammatory topics as temperance, abolition, and the tariff. When
Dr. Peck of Sheffield spoke to the Great Barrington lyceum
on the unobjectionable subject, "A History of Rome with
a Biography of Julius Caesar," a writer in the *Berkshire
Courier* noted with relief: "These are the subjects best
adapted for a lyceum, and they should be strictly adhered to.
In our humble opinion nothing of a sectarian or partisan
character . . . should be allowed." The public, he argued,
attended the lyceums to become informed on matters of general interest, not to hear a temperance or abolition lecture,
which might act as a firebrand to destroy the lyceum.[38] He
may well have been thinking of such speeches as Henry D.
Sedgwick's fiery abolition address at the Stockbridge lyceum
—an address which had stirred up tempers and emotions to

35. Elizabeth Sedgwick to Catharine Sedgwick, Dec. 9, 1833; MC.
36. Pittsfield *Sun,* Mar. 5, 1835.
37. *Early Letters of Mark Hopkins,* p. 229.
38. *Berkshire Courier,* Jan. 10, 1839.

unlooked-for extremes.[39] With the arrival of the 1850's, a "great emotional machine" was indeed being unloosed in American society, and in spite of disapproving voices, Berkshire lyceum audiences heard more and more on controversial topics.

Much larger and better organized than before, the Berkshire lyceums of the 1850's often invited famous literary men to speak to them and offered to professors from Williams College a welcome opportunity for disseminating their views among the people of the county. In the later years of the decade Pittsfield generally saw a capacity crowd of 1,000 souls file into Burbank Hall for the weekly lyceum lecture. Any Berkshirite willing to pay his twenty-five-cent admission fee, might have heard Emerson discoursing on transcendental doctrines, President Mark Hopkins speaking on "Method," Herman Melville describing the south seas, the Reverend Henry Ward Beecher extolling the values of country life, Professor Chadbourne of Williams expounding on Iceland, Dr. J. G. Holland of Springfield talking about American social life, Professor Arthur Latham Perry preaching the gospel of free trade, or Horace Greeley giving his famous advice to young men.[40]

Phineas Allen, an ardent democrat and free trader, did what he could to keep Berkshirites away from the Greeley lecture. An editorial in the *Sun* of Dec. 13, 1860, stated quite flatly,

> In our advertising columns will be found notice of a lecture by Mr. Greeley of the *Tribune,* upon "America, west of the Mississippi." We think that the condition of America, including this side of the Mississippi, may have

39. Henry D. Sedgwick, *The Practicability of the Abolition of Slavery: A Lecture Delivered at the Lyceum in Stockbridge, Massachusetts, February, 1831,* New York, 1831.

40. Pittsfield *Sun,* Jan. 19, 1854; Aug. 9, 1855; Dec. 13, 1860.

preoccupied the attention of the citizens generally,—
and that the anticipated demands for the necessities of
life, on the part of the laborers who have been suffering
from the teachings of Mr. Greeley and his co-adjustors,
will make them careful in the outlay of even 25¢ for
the entertainment to which they are invited.[41]

As the lyceums continued to flourish, they encountered
still another criticism, this time from a group spearheaded
by Horace Mann. The modern lyceums, charged Mann,
were spreading themselves far too thin and were indulging
increasingly in an ineffective, episodic treatment of a hopelessly wide range of materials. They were trying so hard to
please that they were failing to instruct. Neither thorough
nor systematic, most of the lectures dealt merely with the
showy phases of a subject—hardly a sound educational approach. "A vagrant, wonder-hunting mind," said Mann, "is
incompatible with sound knowledge." The lyceums, he felt,
were accomplishing little more than keeping people from
vice in their hours of leisure.[42]

Although partly justified, Mann's criticisms failed to recognize the simple alternatives then possible—the lyceum
or nothing. Because he could think of education only in
terms of the public school education of children, he was
incapable of judging the lyceums with a fair and unbiased
eye. Years of single-minded devotion to public education had
developed in him a kind of all-or-nothing, reformer men-
tality, and he had come to begrudge every penny spent on
education which did not directly benefit the public school
system. Actually, the lyceum constitutions usually included
among their aims not only adult education but the improvement of the common schools.[43] While never regarding them-

41. Ibid., Dec. 13, 1860.
42. *Third Annual Report . . . of the Board of Education*, p. 77.
43. Carl Bode, *The American Lyceum* (New York, 1956), pp. 23–26.

selves as substitutes for the common schools, the lyceums did aid them indirectly by encouraging adults in educational interests. Frequently, a discussion period would follow the lecture, and from time to time an entire session was reserved for free discussion. During such times the lyceums were consciously promoting active mental participation among members of the audience. Like the libararies, they were providing much-needed resources for adult education.

Berkshire County could take pride in the high degree of excellence attained by her institutions for secondary and higher education, her libraries, and her lyceums, but it was the Berkshire Agricultural Society that was destined to become her most original contribution in the early nineteenth century. Indeed, the people of Berkshire revolutionized the very meaning of agricultural society. The eighteenth-century American agricultural societies were located in the cities, and their membership consisted mainly of agrarian aristocrats—those gentlemen of means and leisure who were often poultry and cattle fanciers with literary and philanthropic tendencies. These societies never achieved contact with the plain dirt farmer—the practical man who was unconsciously but diligently practicing the errors of his forefathers in tilling the soil. Partly from ignorance and pride and partly from a conservatism born of a fear of venturing and possibly losing his daily bread, the average farmer was not inclined to new departures. To the Berkshire Agricultural Society and to the many American societies patterned after it went the task and the glory of bringing the new farming methods to the old-time farmers.

To overcome the old prejudices and to popularize the new learning of Tull, Bakewell, Townshend, and Davy required not only energy but considerable tact and imagination—all qualities which the founder of the Berkshire Agricultural Society, Elkanah Watson, providentially possessed. Having won a modest fortune in land speculation,

Watson purchased the Pittsfield home of Henry Van Schaack in 1807 and settled down to the life of a country gentleman, Berkshire-style. Before long, however, he came to realize that his habits of activity put any real retirement out of the question: "to retreat was impossible,—to labor in person *was impossible*. To fill up the void in an active mind, led me first to conceive of an agricultural society on a plan different from all others." [44]

Watson had traveled widely in England and on the continent in the years 1779–84 and had observed the new agriculture at first hand; [45] and a special interest in Spanish merino sheep [46] inspired his first educational enterprise in Berkshire. Having bought a pair of these sheep, he decided to exhibit them to the public under the great elm tree in the Pittsfield public square, and there he was gratified to note the interest in this novel sight expressed both by the farmers and their wives. "It was by this lucky accident, I reasoned thus,—If two animals are capable of exciting so much attention, what would be the effect on a larger scale with larger animals? The farmers present responded to my remarks with approbation. —We became acquainted by this little incident; and from that moment, to the present, agricultural societies, cattle shows, and all in connection therewith have predominated in my mind, greatly to the injury of my private affairs." [47]

Watson lost little time in launching his project. At his invitation, several leading citizens from various parts of the

44. Elkanah Watson, *History of Agricultural Societies on the Modern Berkshire System* (Albany, 1820), p. 115.

45. *Men and Times of the Revolution or the Memoirs of Elkanah Watson*, ed. W. C. Watson (New York, 1856), pp. 76–239.

46. Watson was a friend of the agrarian aristocrats, Colonel David Humphreys and Chancellor Robert Livingstone, who had been mainly responsible for the introduction and culture of Spanish merino sheep in America.

47. E. Watson, *History of Agricultural Societies*, p. 116.

county met on January 30, 1808, at Captain Pepoon's tavern and there organized the Berkshire Agricultural Society. Their purposes, they decided, would be specifically to publicize merino sheep and generally to serve as a clearing house of agricultural information: "all the respectable farmers of the county . . . will bring to this common fund, like bees to the hive, their stock of experience, for the good of the whole." [48]

But for Watson's brilliant innovation, the agricultural fair, the noble scheme of the Society might have remained only a blueprint. The annual Berkshire Agricultural Society Fair breathed the first real signs of life into the Society, and saved it from becoming as moribund as the Massachusetts Agricultural Society, where gentlemen farmers contested rather languidly for annual premiums. Born partly of Watson's experience that autumn day in 1807 and partly of his memories of fairs seen on his European travels, the original Berkshire Agricultural Fair was held on October 2, 1810. So colorful and absorbing did Watson make the event that farmers scarcely knew they were being educated. After the exhibition of 383 sheep, twenty bulls, and fifteen yoke of oxen, and the awarding of seventy dollars in premiums, came the climactic grand procession, with its "sixty yoke of prime oxen, connected by chains, drawing a plow, held by two of the oldest men in the county,—a band of music;— the society carrying appropriate ensigns, and each member carrying a badge of wheat in his hat. . . . four marshalls on grey horses, headed by Sheriff Larned, conducted the procession, which extended about half a mile." [49]

An energetic egotist and a great showman, Watson gained yearly triumphs over New England reticence, fear of ridicule, and dislike of pageantry. He persuaded the members to wear the wheat badge in their hats; he succeeded in bringing the

48. Ibid., p. 117.
49. Ibid., p. 123.

women into active participation in the home manufacturing division and urged them to stand up to receive their premiums; and after an initial failure, he even had Berkshire orthodox clerics delivering prayers at the meetinghouse exercises. At the second and third Annual Fairs, Watson introduced not only the exhibition of home manufactures, but a ploughing match and an agricultural ode.

Occasionally, one of these annual odes would prove to be an important addition to Berkshire culture. In 1823, for example, the Great Barrington lawyer-poet, William Cullen Bryant, brilliantly caught the spirit of Berkshire's rites of autumn:

> Far back in ages
>    The plough with wreaths was crowned.
> The hands of kings and sages
>    Entwined the chaplet round;
>
>        .    .    .    .    .
>
> Honor waits, o'er all the earth,
>    Through endless generations,
> The art that calls her harvest forth,
>    And feeds th' expectant nations.

Set to music by one of the finest musical talents in early nineteenth-century America, Thomas Hastings of Albany, the ode, when sung in Bulfinch's Pittsfield Meeting House, comprised a high point in Berkshire cultural history—the art and the life of the people fused into an organic unity. A quarter of a century later Oliver Wendell Holmes struck an earthier note when he wrote one of his most famous and best loved odes: "Clear the brown path to meet his coulter's gleam."

Perhaps less relevant for the student of culture but equally effective educationally were the exhibitions of superior cattle and crops and the most exciting event of all, the ploughing match. In the heat of the contest, customary prejudices disappeared, and on one occasion the crowd cheered a Negro to victory.[50] At the height of its development, the Berkshire Agricultural Fair appealed not only to the farmer's self-interest and spirit of emulation but to the simple need for a good holiday.[51] Seldom was education combined with such sociability and genuine entertainment; and Theodore Sedgwick, Jr., a president of the Agricultural Society, summarized its attractions with fitting enthusiasm:

> Here, Sir, will be a fine sight, far superior to the lions, or rope-dancing, or a bull-baiting, or Master Hunter in the Circus.— Besides our shows bring money into the pocket, those take it out. . . . Who does not desire to see so rare a sight? Clean hands, are no longer necessary to indicate a gentleman; what a change! The poor pompous things, who have consumed industry's substance in the flame of the cannon's mouth are obliged to appear in our ranks; the hoe and the spade, promise to take the place of the torch. What a revolution! Sweet corn is better food than powder. . . . What is industry without a little excitement, stir, a fair, a fete, an agricultural show, or some such thing? What is man alone without society, a poor dull, mopish, ignorant selfish thing? [52]

Whoever the Society's president might be, his address always constituted an important part of the annual exercises in church. In fact, on such occasions it took on the aspect of a lyceum, with the president usually ranging broadly over both the agricultural and the social problems of Berkshire. Elkanah Watson took advantage of this public forum to urge that Berkshire become an American Yorkshire—specializing

50. Basil Hall, *Travels in North America in the Years 1827 and 1828* (2 vols. Philadelphia, 1829), 2, 54.

51. In a letter to Henry Dunham, Oct. 6, 1851, Jonathan Tenney describes a cattle show: "It was very quiet, for as soon as anyone began to make a disturbance, he was hurried off to the 'lock-up.' I believe they had seventeen in at one time" (Tenney Papers).

52. *Berkshire Star,* Sept. 23, 1824.

in woolgrowing, carding, weaving, and dyeing. Only thus, he maintained, could she withstand the challenge of the West. Thomas Melvill, Jr., conscientiously confining himself to strictly educational topics, delivered an excellent summary of some of Sir Humphrey Davy's ideas and of the best methods for ploughing and fertilizing. And in 1823 Theodore Sedgwick, Jr. improved the occasion by exhorting Berkshire yeomen to awaken to their own dignity—an anticipation of one of the main themes of the Grangers.

Like most benevolent societies and like many of Berkshire's educational institutions, the Berkshire Agricultural Society suffered some financial embarrassment, largely brought on by its own generosity in dispensing premiums. Prizes at the Annual Fair often equaled, and sometimes even exceeded, the year's income; and Watson, realizing the strength of men's self-interest, was constantly urging that the prizes be still further increased.

Still, the Massachusetts legislature unexpectedly appropriated $200 for the Society just five years later and a like amount in 1818. Annual membership dues and occasional gifts supplied additional support; and any member who regarded the yearly five-dollar fee as exorbitant could forget his complaint, when he recalled Watson's words of 1816: "Your measures . . . are considered by the American nation, not as localized, or identified with the immediate interests of Pittsfield,—or Berkshire,—or Massachusetts. No, gentlemen, I can say with pride and pleasure, the eyes of America are fixed on your patriotic course. For some weeks past, we find the public papers, from Maine to Georgia,—from the Atlantic, to the Mississippi; all teeming in the praises of your society, and holding it up to view, as worthy of general imitation." [53] Watson knew whereof he spoke, for by 1820 agricultural societies of the new Berkshire type had appeared in New Eng-

53. E. Watson, *History of Agriculture Societies,* pp. 138–39.

land and New York, and even as far south as Kentucky and North Carolina.

Not only the Berkshire Agricultural Society, but the academies, the Medical Institution, and Williams College as well concerned themselves primarily with the practical aspects of life—aspects which apparently remained uppermost in Berkshire minds. The Agricultural Society, of course, concentrated on the improvement of farming methods; the academies, on moral training; the medical school, on pathology and on professional ethics and standards; and Williams, on character building. Even the libraries seem to have given preference to moral, biographical, and historical works over such aesthetic and essentially "impractical" genres as fiction and poetry; and lyceum lecturers often chose scientific or social topics for discussion. In the final analysis, the lyceums, like the libraries and the agricultural society, offered Berkshirites an opportunity for self-improvement; and the knowledge they gained, far from being an end in itself, presented simply a means to a better life economically and spiritually. In their educational quest they rarely accepted counsel from the outside, and eventually Bostonians became as reluctant to give help as were Berkshirites to ask for it. Indeed, when Elkanah Watson requested funds from the state agricultural society, John Adams' answer was short and to the point: "You will get no aid from Boston; commerce, literature, and theology are all against *you;* nay medicine, history, and university and universal politics might be added." [54] For a time, at least, the people of Berkshire were to remain self-sufficient of necessity.

54. Ibid., p. 33.

# Chapter 7. THE RIGHT TO SCRIBBLE

IN THE SPRING following Shays' Rebellion, Barnabas Bidwell, then a young Yale tutor, came home to the small Berkshire town of Tyringham and found that "the majority of the populace has been disaffected to Governmental measures." Still, he did note with satisfaction that "Gentlemen of learning and the liberal professions, especially the Clergy, are universally for government." [1] A few such gentlemen of learning, driven by a kind of missionary fervor, saw in the establishment of a free Berkshire press one way of reeducating their less enlightened fellow townsmen in the "correct principles of government." The political damage wrought by Shays' Rebellion must be rectified and "the ignorant, uninformed, but well-meaning common people" must learn the enormity of opposing their government under the aegis of a demagogue. Not by accident were the first Berkshire newspapers solidly Federalist. Such men as Roger Storrs of the *Berkshire Chronicle* and Loring Andrews of the *Western Star* may have wanted to bring news and culture to rural Berkshire, but they wanted much more deeply to bring a revision of political views.

It was only in this post-Revolutionary era that a general production of the printed word became common in western Massachusetts, with Springfield in 1782, Northampton in 1786, Pittsfield in 1787, and Stockbridge in 1789 emerging as the first towns to boast printing presses and local newspapers. Fresh from a wholehearted participation in the Revolution and prompted by a growing patriotic concern with

1. *Proceedings of the American Antiquarian Society,* new ser. 4 (1885–87), 368–69, Letter from Barnabas Bidwell to David Daggett, Tyringham, June 16, 1787.

the conduct of American government in both domestic and foreign affairs, Berkshirites were developing an appetite for news.

Within Berkshire the history of the press, from its faltering beginning in 1787 until 1860, can be divided into two periods. Between 1787 and 1825 Berkshire journalism owed its stability and most of its influence to two publications— the *Western Star* of Stockbridge and the Pittsfield *Sun*. Published by printer-editors who dedicated themselves to their newspapers, they dominated the county so completely that the five other Berkshire newssheets of the period proved to be no more than ephemeral gestures. Only in the second period, after 1825, did the county witness a proliferation of newspapers spreading from Lee and Great Barrington in the south to North Adams and Williamstown in the north. In those later years Berkshire could boast four major newspapers published regularly plus some twenty others destined to survive for only a few months or years, some dying from lack of support, others fading out along with some particular cause —perhaps Whiggery or temperance—that had called them into being. Berkshire readers of such publications might at times be tempted to think back nostalgically to the higher literary standard and broader perspectives of the early local papers, but at least they could no longer complain of the absence of local news or of the extensive copying from Boston and New York papers.

The earliest of all Berkshire newspapers was E. Russell's *American Centinel*. Printed on sheets ten inches by eighteen inches, the first issue appeared on December 1, 1787, its bold motto being:

> Here you may range the world from pole to pole
> Increase your knowledge and delight your soul.[2]

2. Holland, *Western Massachuetts, 1,* 465. The simple wooden frame press designed by Adam Ramage dominated American printing in this period.

It evidently ceased publication with the third issue, and the next journalistic effort came less than a year later with the weekly publication by Roger Storrs of the *Berkshire Chronicle,* from May 8, 1788, to September 30, 1790. Like its predecessor, the *Chronicle* was published on a simple Ramage type press in a small gambrel roof cottage just west of the Pittsfield Meeting House, and similarly it died in infancy.

Then, late in 1789, Loring Andrews' *Western Star* appeared in Stockbridge [3] and with the first issue began to earn a reputation as one of the finest journals west of Boston. Always the humble servant, intelligence agent, and political mouthpiece of Theodore Sedgwick, that presiding genius of Berkshire Federalism, Andrews seldom strayed far from his favor. "Two posts have arrived my dear sir," he wrote to Sedgwick with concern in 1797, "by which I have received neither a paper nor a line from you. . . . May I yet indulge the hope that I have not given you offense? To a cooler judgment, and to a more deliberate reflection, it may appear that I have done amiss. . . . but you, sir, must determine—all rests with the decision which your goodness, wisdom and judgment shall prescribe." [4]

The next editor of the *Western Star,* Horatio Jones, was to encounter a somewhat more absorbing problem when, shortly before the election of 1800, the Reverend Thomas Allen persuaded his nephew Phineas to come to Pittsfield as printer-editor of a much needed Republican journal. Having served a year's apprenticeship in the printing office of the well-established *Hampshire Gazette* of Northampton and a year as a journeyman in Springfield,[5] the youthful Phineas could scarcely have found his uncle's proposal unattractive, and in

3. Judging from C. S. Brigham's survey of American newspapers, Andrews was the first newspaper editor to make use of this poetic name.
4. Feb. 20, 1797; SP. Andrews' courtship of Sedgwick's daughter Pamela was further reason for these obsequies.
5. Pittsfield *Sun,* May 10, 1868.

September of 1800 he established himself in Parson Allen's cottage where the old Ramage type press still stood ready for use.

This printing equipment had already produced three other papers, the *Centinel,* the *Chronicle,* and a small, abortive Federalist journal, the *Berkshire Gazette*—all of which had quickly perished. They had failed partly no doubt from lack of subscribers but largely because the political opinions of editors Russell, Storrs, and Merrill diverged sharply from Allen's own. Only with the arrival of Phineas Allen could the Pittsfield press completely equal the *Western Star* in the close harmony of ideas and aims between editor and patron. In the first issue of the *Sun,* dated September 16, Allen gave clear notice of courage and a singlemindedness careless of public opinion, when he expressed in phrases dear to his uncle's heart his determination that the newspaper "will be decidedly Republican." The motto which appeared near the top of the front page declared:

> Here all may scribble with unbounded sway
> If they will but do it in a decent way.

Apparently no printer-editor could hope to succeed in the Berkshire of the 1790's and 1800's without the wholehearted backing of a wealthy patron. Indeed all of the editors of failing newspapers, from E. Russell in 1787 to Cornelius Sturtevant of the *Political Atlas* in 1808, pointed to financial embarrassment as the immediate cause of their leaving the business.[6]

6. For a subscription to any of the Berkshire newspapers (all weeklies) in the years 1787–1825, the price remained two dollars. Usually one dollar went to the postrider for delivery; forty cents for paper; thirty cents for printing; and thirty cents for profit. Until 1801, when Zenas Crane established his paper mill at Dalton, Berkshire newsprint was extremely expensive, because it had to be transported over the mountains from Springfield. Milton W. Hamilton, *The Country Printer: New York State 1785–1830* (New York, 1936), p. 62.

The *Sun* and the *Western Star* each enjoyed a subscription of close to five hundred during most of the early period, and like the early academies, both sought to serve all the inhabitants of the County. Neither Pittsfield nor Stockbridge, each with a population under 2,500 at the turn of the century, could have begun to support its own press independent of outside interest. In fact, even when Berkshire, with its 34,000 people, was maintaining only two newspapers, financial problems always loomed large, and particularly the perennial difficulty of persuading delinquent subscribers to pay their bills. Thus, in 1804, Heman Willard's books showed 500 accounts of less than one dollar due from either subscribers or advertisers—accounts which he could not prudently turn over to the sheriff as long as he remained an editor dependent on public favor.[7] The postrider, Simon Hough, testified rather pathetically to the widespread nonpayment of debts when he wrote his annual New Year's appeal:

> To get my bread, my clothes and wood
> And do the publick some small good,
> I did set out a post to be
> And bring the Star each week to thee.
>
> .     .     .     .     .
>
> But since I'm poor, and want your aid,
> My hearty thanks I give,
> To all who take the Star, and pay,
> And help the poor post live.[8]

Because advertisers more often paid their debts, they very soon came to provide a larger share of the editor's income than did subscribers. Apparently they did not consider exorbitant the standard rate of forty cents per columnar inch

7. Both Williams and Andrews did eventually collect their bills through the sheriff, but only when they had decided to leave the county and had sold their papers.

8. *Western Star,* Apr. 16, 1793.

for the first three weeks and ten cents for each week thereafter.[9] Legal notices generally proved the most lucrative advertisements, but lost and found articles, the merchants' advertisements for calico and St. Croix Rum, and the farmers' publicizing of stud horses for hire also took up considerable space in the weekly issue. A further addition to the editor's income came from the printing and the selling of books and pamphlets and from the sale of lottery tickets and patent medicines.[10]

Even when an editor had paid his printing and paper bills and had hired a postrider to distribute his newspaper, he had still to count on a cash outlay for the collection of news. Soon after the establishment of the *Western Star,* Loring Andrews engaged a man to ride to Kinderhook once a week to bring back the New York newspapers from which he extracted so many of his own columns.[11] Meanwhile, the competing *Berkshire Chronicle,* specializing in the republication of Boston news, sent its envoy, Parker Fellows, on a weekly journey to Springfield, and an article which had appeared on Monday in a Boston paper might be expected to reappear in the *Berkshire Chronicle* of the following Thursday.[12] Because local news could be spread easily by word of mouth, editors were actually reflecting their readers' wishes in omitting from their columns all but the barest outline of local events—births, deaths, and serious accidents. The postrider would often gather these bits of information from clergymen on his weekly route and would then report them to his editor for inclusion in the following issue of the paper.

Undeniably the Berkshire press remained predominantly political in the years between 1787 and 1825, but editors Andrews and Allen always insisted upon some regard for

9. Ibid., Sept. 1, 1804.
10. Ibid., Dec. 3, 1803.
11. Ibid., Dec. 8, 1789.
12. *Berkshire Chronicle,* Apr. 22, 1790.

broader cultural functions. If the Stockbridge printing office represented the informal center of Berkshire Federalism, it served with equal effectiveness as a bookstore and reading room. While general stores might be expected to keep in stock such standard and much demanded works as Cullen's *Practice of Medicine,* Webster's spelling books, and Thomas' *Almanack,* they could not begin to compete with the exten-sive stocks lining the printers' shelves. In December 1791 Andrews could advertise seventy-five titles, twenty-five of which he listed as children's books and only three of which—*Robinson Crusoe, Fanny or the Happy Repentance,* and *Louisa*—were novels.[13] Six years later, disgruntled by Henry Brown's pilgrimage to New Haven to purchase books for the Stockbridge library, Andrews patriotically offered to sell to the Berkshire libraries any of the sixty-four books in his stock at as low a price as a New York, New Haven, or Boston book dealer would demand.[14] In 1807 a Pittsfield printing office advertised an impressive list of 117 titles, and only in the years after 1825 did the printers begin to lose the book selling business to the stores.

Because the printing of the newspaper required only two of the six available working days, these same early bookselling Berkshire printers found ample time for such publishing activities as printing catalogs for Williams College and Lenox Academy, not to mention commencement programs and fourth of July orations for the political parties; and in their occasional publication of books and pamphlets they found still another way of making a significant contribution to the literary and cultural life of the county. So busy were the Berkshire presses before 1820 that some 141 titles of Berkshire imprints during that early period appear in the library of the American Antiquarian Society, largest single collection of Berkshire imprints. Of these titles, Berkshire authors

13. *Western Star,* Dec. 3, 20, 1791.
14. Ibid., Mar. 13, 1797.

had themselves produced close to one-third, with funeral sermons, fourth of July orations, and the theological works of West and Catlin predominating. In 1808, for example, Cornelius Sturtevant found nearly one hundred subscribers in Berkshire for reprinting Dr. Stephen West's book on the Atonement—240 pages of good paper, well bound, for seventy-seven cents. Other titles, almost all reprints, ranged from Soame Jenyn's *Internal Evidences of the Christian Religion* (an Englishman's confutation of deism) to Joel Barlow's *Hasty Pudding* and Hubbard's *History of the Indian Wars.*[15] Because presses in the early 1800's were relatively inexpensive to buy and simple to operate, and because labor comprised the main expense, Berkshire publications, whether sermons or books, could compete with Boston and New York editions both in price and in quality.

Meanwhile, the early Berkshire newspapers were providing for county residents not only the desired contact with the outside world but a heretofore almost nonexistent contact with each other. Postriders for the *Western Star* often carried letters to towns without post offices; in fact, until the establishment of the Williamstown post office in 1797, postrider Simon Hough represented the only regular means of communication between central and northern Berkshire. In 1791 Stockbridge had become the site of Berkshire's first post office, but only after Loring Andrews had written to Theodore Sedgwick urging the advantages of "having a permanent channel of intelligence established" and had begged his patron to exert himself in Congress so that the projected post office between Springfield and Kinderhook might be located in Stockbridge.[16] Andrews conducted the new post office in his own printing office for several years.

Not by chance did Berkshire printing offices become centers of culture as well as of communications for the county.

15. Ibid., Jan. 4, 1791; Aug. 7, 1797; Feb. 26, 1803.
16. Feb. 8, 1791; SP.

A man of strong convictions and the most articulate of the printer-editors, Loring Andrews had never intended that his newspaper should be narrowly political. With characteristic straightforwardness he had outlined his position in the first issue of his *Western Star*. In his role as an editor conducting a free press, he regarded himself as a necessary contributor to the survival of the new government—a true patriot, performing the essential function of enlightening the people. "It is owing in great degree to the want of information," he maintained, "that the people are so often suspicious of their rulers, and entertain the idea that the interest of the peoples and the interest of the government is unconnected." Not only could the free press offer a sure defense against tyranny but it could provide the best possible means of keeping alive the spirit of the late glorious Revolution. His paper, he promised, not merely would contain simply useful private transactions and public transactions of general interest but would supply its readers with a week-to-week history of the world, at a time when Europe remained in a general ferment and when America was progressing to greatness.

He kept his promise; and in the hope of achieving complete effectiveness in his patriotic mission he went even further. "Whatever are my own sentiments, as an individual," he wrote, "as the Editor of a Paper, it ever has been, and ever shall be my aim, to give every political writer an opportunity to declare his opinions to the publick." Andrews' successor was to modify this high tone considerably eleven years later when a rival, Phineas Allen, arrived upon the scene with his unabashed declaration of Republicanism. Making few pretenses to political neutrality, Allen declared in his editorial credo: "As that great Luminary animates, warms and illumines the world, so it shall be our humble lot to imitate, so far as our little circle extends, those bright qualities of the celestial orb. It shall never be the object of this paper to darken, misinform, or mislead its readers. The Editor is determined it shall be conducted with Candor, Fairness, and Impartiality. At the same time it will be decidedly Republican." [17] With the advent of the Pittsfield *Sun* any pretense of political impartiality vanished from the Berkshire press.

Whatever their political beliefs, however, Berkshire editors consistently exhibited not only patriotism but a general rationalistic bias, which was characteristic of American printers but something of an anomaly in Calvinistic Berkshire. Not Jonathan Edwards and religious orthodoxy but Ben Franklin and the enlightenment became their source of spiritual inspiration, and in 1790 Andrews explicitly acknowledged this debt by publishing in his paper a series of five articles on Ben Franklin as America's model editor and citizen.

In the years of the 1790's, before the establishment of the *Sun* and before party spirit had become fully awakened in the county, the pages of the *Western Star* included such political discussions as were never again equaled in the Berkshire press either for their thoughtfulness or for their perspective.[18] Andrews himself contributed a number of editorials aimed at developing and publicizing agrarian Federalism, and later in the decade communications to the editor included an able defense of Washington's foreign policy by Elias Boudinot in letters to Theodore Sedgwick and two contributions by

17. From the prospectus in the first issue of the Pittsfield *Sun,* Sept. 16, 1800.

18. Even a cursory reading of those Berkshire papers printed between 1787 and 1825 would inevitably reveal the striking preponderance of political material. Scarcely a single issue devoted less than one half of its columnar space to articles in some way connected with politics, and a sampling of the *Western Star* for 1790 (one issue for each month) actually produced these results: United States political news (including the proceedings of Congress), 32.3 per cent; foreign intelligence, 17.2 per cent; documents and state papers, 7.4, per cent; political opinions and commentary, 10.5 per cent; literature, 9.4 per cent; advertisements, 21.4 per cent; nonpolitical editorials, 1.3 per cent. From the 10.5 percentage of 1790, political commentary was to climb to 16.9 in 1801 and 26.6 in 1810.

Sedgwick himself, one supporting Jay's Treaty and the other defending the constitutionality of the conduct of foreign affairs by the executive. As spokesmen for the opposition, John Bacon and Barnabas Bidwell wrote several heated letters to the editor arguing against the assumption of state debts, the establishment of a national bank, Jay's Treaty, and other controversial Federalist measures. Andrews might privately consider Bacon "a bitter enemy to the federal government. . . . and as d——d a Jacobin as ever met in any conclave of Sedition within the limits of United America," [19] but he deserved credit for seldom letting his personal prejudices prevent him from printing Bacon's communications, and he referred to him publicly only in restrained, formal terms. In fact, political argument seldom sank to the level of personalities in the years of the 1790's.

With the 1800's, however, came a Jeffersonian victory and the appearance of the Pittsfield *Sun,* and a rougher, freer style abruptly invaded the Berkshire press. Logical argument gave way in many columns to personal invective and doggerel verses, and the new freedom of speech introduced by Phineas Allen often bordered on license. While contributing occasional editorials to the columns of the *Sun,* his uncle, the Reverend Thomas Allen, remained the political philosopher and rarely stooped to a discussion of personalities. It was the relentless Phineas who led the Berkshire Republicans in outspoken denunciation of the opposition. Throughout this period the columns of the *Sun* and the *Western Star* and an occasional minor journal remained, next to the polls themselves, the principal battleground on which Berkshirites waged their political battles.

The Federalists, although a seemingly hopeless minority, did not intend to lose Berkshire by default. Shrewdly realizing the inadequacy of purely defensive operations, Theodore Sedgwick wrote: "I am perfectly satisfied that no party in

19. Loring Andrews to Theodore Sedgwick, Jan. 18, 1796; SP.

popular government can maintain its ground by acting merely on the defensive. The war must be carried into the enemy's camp by offensive operations. . . . I do not approve of the silence of the Federalists." [20] Actually, the Berkshire Federalists were far from silent, and by the early 1800's their political invective had become quite the equal of Allen's. The *Berkshire Reporter* of February 7, 1810, carried a typical Federalist blast: "It is painful and distressing to view a scene marked only by human deformity and corruption. Yet such is our fate as often as we turn our attention to the prostituted pages of the Pittsfield *Sun*."

Unlike the Republicans, the Federalists, in their journalistic attacks, frequently tended to translate politics into local terms and seemed to concentrate their remarks less often on Jefferson and Madison than on Allen and his Pittsfield *Sun* or the Republican embezzlers Bidwell and Skinner. Much of their verbal offensive limited itself to rather sterile and outdated abuse, with two notable exceptions. When Berkshirites organized the first Massachusetts chapter of the Washington Benevolent Society in Pittsfield in November 1811, the Federalist press immediately recognized the political potentialities of such an organization and furnished its readers with detailed reports on Society activities. For the large orthodox religious group within the county, the Federalists reserved their most effective political weapon—logical argument. "Democracy in politics," asserted the Stockbridge *Farmers' Herald*, "is an exact parallel to Arminianism in religion. Both . . . flatter and please the corrupt nature and propensities of man, and both are a grand perversion of the truth. Both rely strongly upon good works, but it is a very difficult task to discover them. . . . The one strikes at the root of vital piety, the other at the heart of political prosperity." [21] The Federalists had here discovered a profound inconsistency

20. Theodore Sedgwick to H. Bleecker, Jan. 23, 1812; SP.
21. *Farmers' Herald* (Stockbridge), July 30, 1808.

in the strange alliance of democracy with orthodox religion
—the former being rooted in the rational theology of Locke
and Jefferson and in confidence in human nature; the latter
in an emphasis on divine guidance. But, unfortunately for
the Federalists, orthodox Berkshirites of the early nineteenth
century were willing to disregard logic and consistency.
Whatever their intrinsic contradictions, democracy and orthodoxy, as typified by Thomas Allen and John Bacon, were
carrying the day in Berkshire; and politically the *Western
Star* could shine only dimly alongside the dominating rays of
the Pittsfield *Sun*.

Nothing in the Berkshire press during these years mirrored
local affairs so accurately and colorfully as did the advertisements. Occupying over one-fifth of the space in every issue,
these advertisements presented information useful and often
essential to Berkshire citizens in their economic and social
life. Farmers advertised their horses and storekeepers their
rum, and cuckolded husbands libeled their wives:

> Whereas my wife Azubah hath eloped from my bed and
> board, and saith our marriage covenant is broken, and
> shall not be mended:—and 2ndly, she does not believe
> in the resurrection of the body:—3rdly, she wishes that
> I was in h——l: 4th she will not obey me in things that
> are lawful and right, if she goes to h——l: 5th she has
> clandestinely taken provisions out of my house when I
> was busy in hay time—6th she upholds our children ig-
> norant and young, in taking things out of my house, to
> the damage of the family: 7th she wishes I would sell
> her, but she will pick her man: 8th she has taken in a
> man who keeps a fiddle. These are therefore to forbid all
> persons harbouring, trading or meddling with said Azu-
> bah, and to desire the grand jury to take cognisance of
> her behavior, as she is now in open rebellion, and does
> that which is next akin to the sin of witchcraft. And

whereas Christian Wood and Azubah Wood, my children, have ran away, I will give one penny reward to any
person who will return them and no charges paid. I also
forbid all persons dealing with said children.

(signed) Samuel Wood [22]

Meanwhile, in the years between 1800 and 1815, the all-
pervasive party spirit invaded even the literary columns, with
political doggerel appearing both in the "Rivulet" section
of the *Sun* and in the "Museum" of the *Western Star*. Recognizing, as Andrews did, the unusual knowledge of and interest in politics among Americans, he expressed a hope that
his readers would not neglect the arts. "It would be gratify-
ing . . ." he said, "if in seasons of dearth, with respect to
publick Intelligence, the pen of genius would exert itself, in
the formation of useful and instructive essays; a part of the
*Star* would be cheerfully devoted to give them a place." [23]
"But," stipulated Andrews, "poetry designed to meet the
public eye should be tolerable at least." [24] Like Andrews,
Phineas Allen feared that politics might crowd all else out
of his newspaper; and when one of his readers submitted a
biographical sketch of the poet Cowper, he took the opportunity to add an editorial preface: "From the beginning of
this paper, the editor, expecting a good number of his readers
would be of the sober and pious class, was determined to introduce subjects to gratify their taste as well as to correct
that of others . . ." [25]

Although never large, the production of newspaper essays
by Berkshirites certainly reached its peak in the 1790's, and
those appearing in the *Western Star* during this decade seem
to fall naturally into two categories—the first, typified by the
"Berkshire Sentimentalist," urbane, moralistic, allusive, and

22. *Western Star,* Aug. 12, 1794.
23. Ibid., Aug. 23, 1791.
24. Ibid., Dec. 14, 1790.
25. Pittsfield *Sun,* Feb. 10, 1801.

not very original, following the style of the English *Gentleman's Magazine;* the second, exemplified by the "Cordwainer" and the "Plough Jogger," self-consciously rustic and
concerned in a rather rambling way with the local scene. In
his series of essays for the *Star,* the "Berkshire Sentimentalist"
proposed to discuss everything from the values of local spirit
to the relative merits of wit, the nature of laws, and the best
form of government; and his essays generally digressed so extensively that they took on the aspect of a kind of political
stream of consciousness.

In affecting the sophistication of the English coffee house
literati, the "Sentimentalist" shared his style, if not necessarily his political beliefs, with a few other essayists, notable
among whom were the "Moralist," who covered several
inches in the *Western Star* with a self-righteous castigation of
gossiping,[26] and "Pious," who decried cant in the *Berkshire
Chronicle.*[27] As a reaction to these pretentious gentlemen appeared the "Cordwainer," alias "Ned the Nipper." Protest-
ing to be a simple homespun fellow without much education,
he nevertheless proposed to expose the highfalutin gentry
with his rustic wit: "Strange times these, my dear readers—
What would have been said in the reign of King George had
a paltry shoe-maker presumed to write in the newspapers?
. . . the world is getting strangely topsy-turvy— We poor
vulgar tradesmen and labourers, thanks to Mr. Paine and
General Washington! begin to hold up our heads and look
about us." [28]

After seeing three of his essays published in the *Western
Star,* Ned pronounced it "rare sport to write for the instruction of mankind, this being an author is a bewitching
thing." [29] "If I knew everything like Mr. Paine," he went on,

26. *Western Star,* Jan. 12, 1792.
27. *Berkshire Chronicle,* Sept. 16, 1790.
28. *Western Star,* Aug. 19, 1794.
29. Ibid., Sept. 9, 1794.

"I would only tell the world that which could do it some good." Other essayists preceded and followed him in the use of his earthy, rustic style—among them the "Plough Jogger" with his broad ridicule of Berkshire's legal system,[30] and "Dolly Distaff" with her outspoken animadversions against taverns and gaming; [31] and both foreshadowed in their handling of this style the really effective form of satire which Asa Greene was to develop in the 1820's.

At the same time a few Berkshire bards were pleased to see their poetry appearing in the columns of their local newspapers. Derived from such English poets as Cowper, Young, and Gray, most of the poetic effusions adopted a consistent tone of sentimental melancholy and, forgetting their native Berkshire hills, became preoccupied with such stylized natural phenomena as "groves" and "grottos," "dew-formed gems," "verdant shades," and "balmy breezes." One Berkshire "poetry-lover" submitted to editor Willard "the following original lines from the fertile imagination of a Berkshire female"—lines which he considered unexcelled in the county "for purity of language and delicacy of sentiment."

Poem—by Emily

Let that lov'd form attend me still,
Where e'er my pensive footsteps rove,
Reclining by the murmuring rill,
Or deeply musing in the grove.

．　　．　　．　　．　　．

O fortune grant my ardent prayers,
Let that lov'd youth be ever mine,
Who all those shining virtues shares,
That speak a soul that's half divine . . .[32]

30. *Berkshire Chronicle,* Aug. 12, 1790.
31. *Western Star,* Feb. 18, 1794; Feb. 25, 1795.
32. Ibid., July 14, 1804.

A more robust, less pretentious, and more truly native poetic inspiration found expression in the colorful "Poem on the Wolf-Hunt in Stockbridge," unfortunately anonymous:

> Last Thursday was a day of sport
> To drive the wolves from mountain fort
>
> .      .      .      .      .
>
> Five hundred men, or less or more,
> Set out the wood and hills t'explore;
> Colonels, Captains, Soldiers, all
> Were arm'd with powder, gun and ball,
>
> .      .      .      .      .
>
> They range through woods, and hills and dale,
> They climb up racks and sink in vales;
> They drag along through snow and frost,
> Some faint, some hungry, others lost.
> At length, much tir'd, they all agreed
> 'Twas best no further to proceed;
> That each for home should shape his course,
> For fear of meeting something worse;
> Then home they came, as wet as muck,
> All cry'd "The devil take the luck;"
> Convinc'd, with all their forces join'd
> That wolves were not to be Burgoyn'd.[33]

By the end of the 1790's the original productions of the local "pen of genius," for which Berkshire editors had pleaded, were dwindling noticeably. Local geniuses had begun to occupy themselves almost exclusively with political pamphleteering, and columns devoted to partisan politics were swelling every issue. In fact, by 1800, editors found themselves forced to resort to borrowing—either from popular books or from Boston and New York papers—if they hoped to provide their readers with any literary fare.

33. Ibid., Feb. 9, 1790.

Gradually, however, much of the space no longer reserved for local literary geniuses was being given over instead to a coverage of local news considerably more exhaustive than in earlier years. The newspapers were becoming a public forum for the discussion of county problems and particularly those arising over the controversial activities of the schools. At the same time the *Sun* and the *Star* were becoming so well established that their mentors were editorializing in increasingly confident tones and had abandoned the cautious air of tentative experiment. Gone were the desperate appeals to delinquent subscribers over unpaid bills. The editors of both papers could relax in a satisfied knowledge of long subscription lists—long enough, in fact, to tempt large numbers of newcomers into the field of Berkshire journalism after 1825.

"This country is not priest-ridden, but press-ridden" [34] wrote Longfellow while summering in Pittsfield in 1848; and whether or not he was thinking of his immediate surroundings, certainly the years between 1825 and 1860 did witness an astonishing multiplication of Berkshire newspapers. As a response to both the growth and the redistribution of population in the county, no less than twenty-five weekly journals appeared during these years.[35] With the Berkshire population

34. Henry Wadsworth Longfellow, *Kavanagh, A Tale* (Boston, 1849), p. 62.

35. Berkshire newspapers, 1825–60: Adams: *Berkshire American* (1826–28; 1830–32); the *Socialist* (1826–28); Adams *Gazette, and Farmers' and Mechanics' Magazine* (1832–33); *Berkshire Advocate* (1833); *Greylock Mirror* (1834); *Weekly Transcript* (1843 to present); *Greylock Sentinel* (1851–55); *Hoosac Valley News* (1857–90). Great Barrington: *Berkshire Courier* (1834 to present); *Independent Press* (1845–47); *Housatonic Mirror* (1846–47). Lee: *Berkshire Democrat* (1840); *Home Companion* (1841–?); *Central Berkshire Chronicle* (1842); *Valley Gleaner* (1857–84). Lenox: *Massachusetts Eagle* (1833–42, then moved to Pittsfield)—formerly *Journal and Argus* (1830–32); *Berkshire Journal* (1830); *Berkshire Star and County Republican* (1828–30), previously at Stockbridge as the *Western Star*; *Berkshire Herald* (1832–34). Pittsfield:

increasing from 36,000 to 55,000, with eleven of the hill towns losing some inhabitants to the manufacturing towns of the valleys, and with Pittsfield and Adams quadrupling in size, entrepreneurs in most growing urban areas immediately recognized the establishment of a press as an effective way of encouraging local spirit and of building the reputations of their towns as centers of industry and trade. One enthusiastic North Adams resident, carried away by the impressive success of local business enterprises, even threw down a bold challenge to his Pittsfield neighbors. "By the way," he wrote in an open letter in the Pittsfield *Sun,* "Adams is 'some pumpkins,' and the sooner you own up to it the better it will be for the *small towns.* We are surprised at our greatness; we have eight churches, where large numbers worship God according to the dictates of their own conscience, and many places where intoxicating drinks can be bought." [36]

Other Berkshirites, motivated less by self-interest and more by a crusading instinct, ventured into the newspaper business either to support one of the numerous reform movements of the period or to champion some political conviction. With the *Berkshire Courier* consistently extolling Henry Clay, Henry Strong found ample provocation for beginning his publication of the *Argus* to lend journalistic support to John Quincy Adams. Later T. D. Bonner's *New England Cataract* appeared and quickly earned a reputation as the most tactless and hard-hitting temperance journal in New England. In that same year came Jonathan Field's *Weekly Visitor,* dedicated almost equally to a defense of the Democratic party and

Pittsfield *Sun* (1800–1906); *Argus* (1827); *Massachusetts Eagle* (later *Berkshire County Eagle,* 1842 to present); *Berkshire County Whig* (1840–49); *Berkshire Agriculturist* (1847–58?); *Old Tip* (1840); *New England Cataract* (1844–47); *Star* (1846). Stockbridge: *Weekly Visitor* (1844–46). Williamstown: *American Advocate* (1827–31).

36. Pittsfield *Sun,* Jan. 27, 1859.

to the popularization of applied science, and soon afterward
the *Greylock Sentinel* was founded as an antislavery publication.

The mainstream of Berkshire journalism, however, lay not
in these relatively ephemeral publications but rather in those
four major newspapers whose publication continued throughout much of the nineteenth century. The *Berkshire Courier,*
begun in Great Barrington in 1834, and the *Weekly Transcript,* founded nine years later in Adams, soon took their
places in importance beside the Pittsfield *Sun* and the old
*Western Star,* now rechristened the *Massachusetts Eagle.* All
of these papers became subject to similar problems and popular pressures and developed along fundamentally parallel
lines, but each did manage to maintain its own distinctive
character both in tone and in content. Changes of editor
came only infrequently. Phineas Allen and his son edited the
Pittsfield *Sun* from 1800 until 1872; the Boston emigré J. D.
Cushing guided the career of the *Berkshire Courier* throughout its first twenty-five years; and Henry Chickering controlled the *Weekly Transcript* from 1844 to 1856. Only the
*Massachusetts Eagle* of Lenox and Pittsfield, with twelve different editors between 1825 and 1860, proved an exception.

Not surprisingly, the Pittsfield *Sun* retained its fiercely
Democratic political bias as long as the Allen family stayed
in control. No real criticism of that infallible party ever
appeared in its pages, and even in the 1850's its editors
opened its columns to a defense of the Kansas-Nebraska Act
and to occasional attacks on the abolitionists as wild ranters
—a stand which lost it the cherished sobriquet the "Berkshire
Bible." Yet the Allens did reserve considerable space for discussions on the less controversial subject of agricultural progress, devoting a column in nearly every issue to agricultural
intelligence. Quite regularly they would offer information on
such useful topics as oiling harness leather, Wisconsin dairy-
ing, or the sow's destruction of her young, subtly intermixed

with a little agrarian Democratic philosophizing; and readers could always expect a full coverage of the annual Berkshire Agricultural Society Fair.

Although endowed with a new name, the *Massachusetts Eagle* continued to fullfill its role as political counterweight to the *Sun*. Published for a time in Lenox, it was moved to its permanent home in Pittsfield in 1842 and ten years later again underwent a change in name, this time to the *Berkshire County Eagle*. Of its numerous editors, Charles Webster, Samuel Bush, Henry W. Taft, Samuel Brace, Charles Montague, and Henry Chickering attained the greatest local prominence and made the most significant contributions. In his answer of January 8, 1835, to an argumentative editorial in the *Sun,* Samuel Brace gave definitive expression to the paper's staunch political conservatism. He noted the unhappy consequences of populist movements in the Roman Empire and warned Berkshirites against "that spirit which begins to prevail in our own country, which labours to excite jealousy towards men of wealth; to break down the influence of the higher classes in society; and to quarrel with that distribution of property which seems to be the necessary result of human nature itself . . . called appropriately agrarianism." [37]

Because the *Massachusetts Eagle* adopted a less violent attitude toward politics than did the *Sun,* it generally reserved more space for other topics and concentrated particularly on an all-out bid for the favor of Berkshire's female population. No other paper in the county tried so hard to pursue a policy which might win the approval of the ladies—a policy which Charles Montague was to carry to its extreme in the 1840's. In the issue of November 12, 1840, he printed a song, with full piano accompaniment, containing a concise if not very original statement of his chivalric convictions:

37. *Massachusetts Eagle,* Jan. 8, 1835.

The lords of creation men we call
And they think they rule the whole
But they're much mistaken after all
For they're under woman's control.

While the editors of the *Sun* were discussing new fertilizers, the *Eagle* was publishing "Advice to Girls," "Pride in Dress a Fable for the Young," and "A Substitute for War," and occasionally it even devoted its entire first page to distaff interests. On November 17, 1848, for example, three articles— "Maternal Courage" (an essay), "Whispers to Wives" (practical advice on humoring husbands), and "The Stepmother" (a story by Louise Hunter)—completely filled page one.

Meanwhile, another Berkshire newspaper, Great Barrington's *Berkshire Courier,* had made its appearance in 1834, and soon it too came to offer a faithful reflection of the personal convictions of its editor. J. D. Cushing took an intense and abiding interest in the problems of religion and education, and he included in each issue of his paper a special religious department in which he published such essays as Lyman Beecher's "The Necessity of Revivals" and Webster's "Estimate of the Bible" along with a few locally written exhortations like "Go to Meeting," "One Sin May Destroy the Soul," and an interminable serialized tale by a Berkshire pastor's wife entitled "Lights and Shadows." Although admittedly Whig by political preference, the *Courier* actually exhibited less concern over politics than any other of Berkshire's major journals. Cushing's colleagues might give most of their energies to political editorializing, but he often chose instead to comment on local lectures and libraries. Of Henry Ward Beecher's sermon in the Great Barrington church, he wrote: "The sermons were splendid efforts . . . and many of our mammon-worshipping citizens must have felt with peculiar force the earnest and impressive truths presented." [38]

38. *Berkshire Courier,* Aug. 4, 1853.

Having been lured to Berkshire from Boston in 1827 with the hope of opening up new journalistic horizons, Cushing soon found the enthusiastic reports of Adams businessmen somewhat overdrawn. After the disappointing failure of his Adams *Republican* and a brief and not very rewarding connection with the *Berkshire Star,* however, he did at last find in the *Courier* an opportunity for the realization of some of his journalistic ambitions. Even though a comparative stranger in the county, he was shrewd enough to recognize the acute sensitivity of most Berkshirites to educational criticism, and he consistently showed tact and discretion in his fault-finding editorials. Applying the Boston yardstick to Berkshire schools, he inevitably found them lacking—a fact which he pointed out as gently as possible. Never castigating, but always trying to encourage growth, he wrote: "The fact that the interests of common school education are not cared for to a reasonable extent in this part of Massachusetts ought not to be allowed to rest as a dead statement in one number of a newspaper; it should be repeatedly brought before the public mind." [39] He went on to urge the establishment of a normal school in the county.

Later he published in the *Courier* a lengthy essay on "intellectual feasts," congratulating Lee's young people for their winter evening attendance at lyceum debates but deploring the indifference of Great Barrington townspeople to the fine course of lectures then being offered. "Think," he exclaimed, "of a beautiful moonlight evening, a capital lecture from one of our most learned Berkshire men in a village of 4,000 and only twenty-nine of them turning out to hear it." [40]

Still, Cushing did have the satisfaction of knowing that he had provided Great Barrington with an established press—a luxury which the considerably wealthier town of Adams did not enjoy until nine years later. After a failure of five pre-

39. Ibid., Dec. 2, 1852.
40. Ibid., Feb. 3, 1859.

vious publications in the town, the Adams *Weekly Transcript* finally began its successful career in 1843. Founded by John Briggs in October, it passed into the more efficient hands of Henry Chickering within six months, and he, with the help of Henry C. Dawes and later of H. A. Marsh, continued in the position of editor until 1855. In that year, Chickering sold the *Transcript* in order that he and Marsh might move to Pittsfield to publish the recently acquired *Berkshire County Eagle.*

During Chickering's journalistic reign in Adams, his temperance sentiments left their imprint on nearly every issue of the *Transcript.* He might follow the editors of the *Courier* and the *Eagle* in his leanings toward the political doctrines of the Whigs, but in state and county elections he would almost always support any temperance slate even though it required a temporary desertion of the Whig camp. In fact, the election for county commissioners in 1847 found him urging that regular party lines be abandoned altogether and that the issue be resolved into a simple choice between the "license" and "no license" candidates. Occasionally inclining to slight the factual coverage of local events, he gave a disproportionate amount of space to reprinting the morally edifying stories of T. S. Arthur, and even discovered in the annual Berkshire Fair of 1851 an excuse for launching out upon a coy discussion of his favorite topic: "Drunkenness at the Fair— The invisible *spirits* of evil which must have been gathering in considerable force in the vicinity of the Fair grounds on Wednesday last, became suddenly visible *with the aid of glasses,* on the following day." [41]

Probably more popular in Berkshire than Chickering's temperance tirades was his infectious enthusiasm for the new railroad. He greeted the opening of service on the Pittsfield-Adams Railroad in November of 1846 with an elation equal to that of any Adams merchant and five years later announced

41. *Weekly Transcript,* Oct. 9, 1851.

with satisfaction the breaking of ground for the Troy-Green-
field line.[42] Few journalistic contributions delighted him
more than did that poem submitted by a South Adams bard
which expounded the joys of a railroad trip to the Berkshire
Fair.

As the nineteenth century advanced, all the Berkshire editors enjoyed a new latitude in their selection of subject matter and found their reading public quite receptive to extended and often rather personal editorials. No longer
obliged to provide a verbatim reproduction of parts of the
Boston and New York papers, they could now impart to their
weekly editions more of their own individuality; and journalism became far more personalized than in the years before
1825. No editor could long remain unaware of the new power
he possessed. A few of them, like John Goodrich and, to a
lesser degree, Henry Dawes—both lawer-editors—capitalized
on their positions to further their political ambitions; others,
notably Samuel Brace, J. D. Cushing, and Henry Hubbard,
assumed civic leadership in the common school revival.
Newspapers had emerged as the harbingers of social change.
"It shall go like the wild and wandering air. . . ." read the
*Weekly Transcript* motto, "for life and its changes are impressed there."

Many of these second-generation Berkshire editors had prepared themselves for their active role in civic life by a formal
education, and a new division of labor in the printing office
freed them from many of the humdrum responsibilities
borne by earlier editors. Unlike their predecessors, nearly
all Berkshire editors after 1825 had received their educations
not by serving an apprenticeship as printers' devils but in
college classrooms. Samuel Brace had graduated from Yale,
Asa Greene and Henry Taft from Williams, and several others could boast membership in the Berkshire bar. Realizing

42. Not completed until 1874 with the finishing of the 4.7 mile
Hoosac Tunnel.

that Berkshire presses could not hope to compete with the large-scale production and superior technology of the cities, these editors willingly left the business of book publishing to city printers; and within their own offices, most of them were content to entrust much of the actual printing to assistants.

After 1830 only a few Berkshire editors had to face the acute economic problems so prevalent earlier in the century. The increase in population, along with the evolution toward commercial agriculture, brought an unprecedented demand for newspapers, and subscription lists grew larger with every year. Berkshirites were finding their weekly newspapers well worth the modest yearly subscription cost of $1.50 to be paid in advance or $2.50 to be paid at the end of the year, and even a few city dwellers joined the ranks of subscribers or advertisers. The *Weekly Transcript* availed itself of the services of the V. B. Palmer Company, with offices in Boston, New York, Baltimore, and Philadelphia, which offered both advertising space and subscriptions at the regular local rate. Quite probably an occasional Berkshire emigré did take advantage of this opportunity to maintain his home town associations, and a few nationally known patent medicine companies evidently found advertisements in the country press reasonably profitable. For the most part, however, both advertisers and subscribers were local Berkshirites.

In spite of his comparative freedom from economic worries, however, the editor's life had not become an easy one. With the great increase in the number of papers being published came a corresponding rise in the number of "exchanges" and a far more difficult problem of selection than any that had confronted earlier editors. Obliged to examine "hundreds of exchange papers every week," Henry Chickering soon came to regard his task of selection as incomparably more challenging than writing original articles. "A paper when completed," he felt, "should be one that the editor would be willing to read to his wife, his mother, his sister, or his daughter. . . . Every subscriber thinks the paper is printed for his special benefit . . . one wants stories, another abhors all this . . . something spicy comes out and the editor is a blackguard." [43]

Whatever their differences, all the major Berkshire newspapers after 1825 revealed the same significant tendency to emphasize local spirit through the inclusion of more local news, through editorials extolling the superiority of country newspapers over the monstrous city weeklies, or through enthusiastic reports on the beauties of Berkshire scenery. Even the literary columns reflected the growing local consciousness, particularly in those essays and sketches which sought to revive Indian legends of the Taconic region.

If, in the years before 1825, advertisements had offered a better clue to local history than had news items, the situation was reversed only very gradually during the second quarter of the century. In the 1830's the number of local items remained spotty, and only such momentous events as Fourth of July celebrations and Berkshire fairs received full and detailed coverage. Then, in the 1840's, editors began to increase regional emphasis and to print, in the first issue of each year, a sort of local almanac. As early as January 2, 1840, the *Massachusetts Eagle* added to its traditional list of national and state political officials a list of the faculties of Williams College, Lenox Academy, and the Pittsfield Female Academy and printed in full the new constitution of the Stockbridge Common School Society. Ten years later whole columns were being devoted to Berkshire news, and by 1859 the *Courier* regularly reserved two columns every week for a section headed "Western Massachusetts," and the *Sun* followed suit with a "Local Intelligence" division. One typical issue of the *Sun* would inform the reading public of the death of the fine horse Rattler, of Colonel Nathan Messer's early peas, of a railroad excursion from Troy to North Adams by

43. *Weekly Transcript,* Sept. 30, 1847.

a large number of stockholders, and of the fact that one hundred and thirty dogs were registered in Great Barrington.[44] Another would mention the installation of the Reverend Roswell Foster as pastor of the South Congregational Church, the meeting of the Berkshire North Association at which John E. Todd had been licensed to preach, and the number of depositors in the Lee, North Adams, and Pittsfield Savings Banks.[45]

As life in Berkshire became more varied and complex, editors discovered so much newsworthy material all around them that even Cushing's precious religious department in the *Courier* was crowded out. Most newspapers found it worth while to appoint agents in nearby Berkshire towns who would not only sell subscriptions and advertisements but gather news as well. In this field, at least, the city weeklies then being brought into the county by railroad could never compete with the local press.

Probably the strongest incentive to the growth of a spirit of fraternity among Berkshire editors came with the necessity for making common cause against these giant city weeklies, and particularly against the weekly editions of Henry Raymond's New York *Times* and Greeley's *Tribune*. These wealthy and powerful publications could offer every Berkshire subscriber more reading matter at a lower cost, but local editors determined that they could not and should not suffocate the Berkshire press. In the very year that the railroad reached Adams, Henry Dawes stated the case for the local newspapers:

> Let no farmer, and no other man relinquish the newspaper published in his own neighborhood, for the sake of taking some other, larger, cheaper, or more popular paper published abroad. The newspaper published in one's own county, is, as a general rule, more valuable

44. Pittsfield *Sun,* June 9, 1859.
45. Ibid., Feb. 3, 1859.

than any other, if it be for nothing but the advertisements; for even they are the thermometer of a business
place and often the key which opens the door to excellent bargains. It is of no little consequence to the farmer
to know what is going on in his own market town, the
competition in selling goods, and the competition in
buying produce; the changes in business operations; the
settlement of estates; sales of farms, stock, etc. We venture to say, there is no man who may not every year
much more than save the price of the subscription to
his neighboring newspaper, from the advertising columns alone; and on this ground ought to patronize their
own newspapers. This should be done also for weightier
reasons, one of which we will name: the mammoth
weekly sheets of the cities furnished at a price with
which no country printer can compete, for the reason,
because made up generally, from the matter once used
and paid for in the daily papers, are encroaching largely
upon the country newspapers, thus discouraging improvement, and gradually bringing the whole country
under the influence and in some sense the control, of
the leading cliques in the cities. Thus, a tone is given
to the morals, the politics and the habits of the country.
The people of this country get full enough of this influence through their own papers; and if they would not
complete the supremacy of the cities over the moral and
political destiny of the country, let them support the
country newspapers. Take the city papers if you can
afford it, and as many of them as you please; but first
see to it that your home paper is a regular visitor at your
fireside. Support them first and liberally, and they will
hardly fail to support your interest.[46]

46. Ibid., Sept. 17, 1846. Henry L. Dawes progressed from his Berkshire editorship eventually to the United States Senate, where he spon-
sored the Dawes Act of 1887 changing the land system of the Indian
Reservations.

Soon, in fact, the line between country and town parties in journalism became so sharply drawn that Berkshire editors consciously gave preference to country newspapers in their search for reprintable extracts. To justify such a policy, Cushing of the *Courier* pointed out that the country editor, faced with stringent space limitations, had developed the difficult art of condensation for which his prolific city colleagues saw no necessity. Consequently, as extracts from the New York and Boston papers which had so dominated the Berkshire press in 1800 decreased, more selections appeared from such papers as the Springfield *Gazette,* the Westfield (Massachusetts) *Messenger,* and the Stillwater (New York) *Gazette.*

Quick to sense the tendency of the cities to exert a moral domination over Berkshire, local editors led in the movement to inspire and consolidate local pride. "I wonder," read one letter in the *Courier,* "if our villagers are aware of the luxury of *a plunge* in Green River these sultry July days? . . . Pure as the crystal sands over which it flows—unfailing as the mountain foundation from which it springs . . . it is as Tonic as Old Neptune's 'wave bath' itself." [47]

At some time during these highly self-conscious years, nearly every one of the major papers published some form of the very popular Berkshire travel log. Even in 1834 the forward-looking *Massachusetts Eagle* had given space to the enthusiasms of a native calling himself "Peregrine": "Did you ever take this ride, and for miles and miles follow that beautiful little river as it wound among the mountains, and as you crossed it and recrossed it cause you to stand in a puzzle as to where it would next lead you? Now it winds and dances with its silver murmur among the hills, at home there —a child of the mountains. What beautiful rivers! What variety of scenery!" [48]

The ever practical Chickering was not long in recognizing

47. *Berkshire Courier,* Dec. 23, 1852.
48. *Massachusetts Eagle,* Sept. 11, 1834.

the potential profit in Berkshire's natural charms. Other newspapers might indulge in flights of pure sentiment, but he saw promise of a flourishing tourist trade. Of the famous Natural Bridge near North Adams he remarked: "If some little pains were taken to make it known abroad, it might become quite a place of resort to strangers. Certainly this and old Greylock and the Tunnel would be attractions of no small magnitude to call visitors from abroad and our citizens would reap no small benefit. . . . We throw out these remarks hoping that a public spirit may be engendered and something done." [49] The evolution of Berkshire into a fashionable vacation spot for weary New Yorkers had, in fact, already begun by the 1850's.

In these same chauvinistic issues, however, much of the literary fare offered to Berkshire readers did not originate with Berkshire authors. Usually moral and sentimental in tone, most of the selections came from the work of well-known contemporary writers. By the 1840's conscious preference was being given to American authors; Lydia Sigourney was replacing Mrs. Hemans, and Longfellow and Fitzgreene Halleck were crowding out the once popular Southey and Young.

Of all the literary contributions made by Berkshirites to their newspapers, few ever approached either in originality or in artistic caliber the satiric essays of Asa Greene printed in his own publication, the *Berkshire American*. Unlike the pillars of Berkshire journalism, the *American* and a few other short-lived journals addressed themselves to narrower audiences; and because their editors felt the sense of responsibility less acutely, they dared to be far more outspoken in their opinions than did the *Sun,* the *Eagle,* the *Courier,* or the *Transcript*. They had ventured little; they regarded their presses as experimental; and the prospect of losing their small investment was evidently of slight concern.

49. *Weekly Transcript,* Sept. 4, 1851.

Certainly the most highly personalized venture in the history of Berkshire journalism began in December of 1826 when Dr. Asa Greene established his *Berkshire American* in Pittsfield.[50] Born in the central Massachusetts village of Townsend, Greene had graduated from Williams in 1813, had received his M.D. degree from the Berkshire Medical Institute in 1827, and by 1829 had established himself as one of the most trenchant critics of Berkshire society of his generation. As long as the productions of his pen found their way into the editorial columns of the *Berkshire American,* this otherwise average publication retained an aura of distinction. In everything he wrote, whether intended for instruction or purely for amusement, his comic spirit shone through, and many a Berkshire reader must have welcomed his view of the press as a source of pleasure:

> Hail! faithful sheet of mingled black and white,
> My constant friend, companion, servant, guide,
> My morning's early visitant, and last
> Of hangers-on at waning hour of eve.
> Thou art my coffee's sweetener, and thou
> Unto the choice Havana's curling smoke
> Giv'st ten-fold fragrance: thou the gath'ring *blues*
> Driv'st far away, and ennui slips out
> When thou com'st in. Come often, then, my Jo,
> Of all my friends most welcome, at what hour
> So e'er thou show'st thy comely face, at morn,
> Or noon, or night, or intervening times.
> Impertinent, 'tis true, thou sometimes are,
> Intrusive never: and to thee, my friend,
> At any, every hour, I'll be "at home." [51]

At no time during his brief journalistic career in Berkshire, however, did Greene manage to attract more than 400 sub-

50. Two months later he moved the newspaper to North Adams.
51. *Berkshire American* (North Adams), Aug. 29, 1827.

scribers,[52] and he never succeeded in making his paper a financial success. The explanation for his failure lay partly, no doubt, in the increasing competition of the late 1820's, but much more decidedly in his often unflattering attacks on the County. Berkshirites either could not understand his wit or resented his insinuations about their shortcomings. Quite often satire has proved itself a poor vein for writers forced to depend on the general public for support, and not even Dr. Greene's obvious genius or his fresh journalistic approach could recommend him to an audience who felt both insulted and resentful. More than a few of Greene's contemporaries must have agreed with the Massachusetts journalist-historian Josiah G. Holland, who found his wit "queer to say the least." [53] Finally, in 1829, Greene gave up the hopeless fight and in 1830 left Berkshire to become editor of the *Evening Transcript* in New York. There, at a time when sentiment enjoyed more popularity than did satire, he wrote some of the best satiric novels to come out of America in the 1830's and 40's.

By the 1860's Berkshirites could look back over the history of their newspapers with justifiable pride. From its narrowly political beginnings late in the eighteenth century, the Berkshire press had expanded until not only politics, but religion, literature, social reform, agriculture, science, and innumerable local events received coverage in nearly every issue of the major publications. In fact, as an outlet for the works of local writers, it had, in the 1820's, climactically published the pieces of a poet and a novelist of national distinction. And if there was nothing especially revolutionary in their over-all journalistic tradition, still a few editors had had the courage individually to make creditable experiments. Many of them had consciously encouraged the development of local pride, and during the two decades before the Civil

52. Holland, *Western Massachusetts, I,* 471.
53. Ibid., p. 468.

War many had made their newspapers bulwarks of Berkshire independence against a threatening inundation by the New York weeklies.[54]

54. The influx of newspapers and periodicals into Berkshire would indicate the presence of readers of large and fairly catholic appetite. Stockbridge, a town of 1,941 persons in 1850, handled in its post office the following subscriptions: Berkshire publications: *Massachusetts Eagle,* 18; *Culturist and Gazette,* 14; Pittsfield *Sun,* 7; Barrington *Courier,* 6; *Greylock Sentinel,* 4. American publications: New York *Observer,* 17; Boston *Culturist,* 14; *Daily Tribune,* 10; *Home Missionary,* 10; *Missionary Herald,* 9; *Sailor's Magazine,* 9; *Youth's Companion,* 6. English publications: *Blackwoods,* 2; *Westminster Review,* 1; *Edinburgh Review,* 1. This is a selection of the most popular journals from the complete list printed in Electa F. Jones, *Stockbridge, Past and Present,* pp. 234–35.

## Chapter 8. THE IMMACULATE PROFESSION

WHEN the young Berkshire lawyer Henry Dwight Sedgwick declared "the proper season for reform" to be at hand,[1] he was expressing a widely felt impatience with the inherited system of courts and legal practice in post-Revolutionary times. The heritage had come from eastern Massachusetts and from England, and neither Sedgwick nor the more public-spirited of his colleagues could ignore its patent inadequacies for the special needs of their own rural community. The problem was hardly unique, for in Berkshire the legal history of much of inland and rural New England was going on in a microcosm. There, in the generations preceding and following the Revolution, the legal aristocracy was breaking down, the complexities of the common law were coming under bitter attack, and a respected democratic legal profession was beginning to emerge.

Berkshire legal history began in a spirit of quiet conformity when, in June 1761, the Massachusetts General Court passed a bill officially establishing courts in the newly incorporated county. Berkshirites, who until then had been carrying their legal business over the formidable hill barrier to Springfield, must have welcomed the naming of Great Barrington (the population center of the county) as shire town and the appearance among them of those regular county courts provided for in the Massachusetts Provincial Charter. The Court of Common Pleas, with its four justices, maintained a general jurisdiction in civil cases involving more than 40s; the Court of General Sessions, composed of the same four men and later of all the justices of the peace acting under a separate commission, controlled county prudential affairs and had a criminal jurisdiction wherever a punish-

1. To William Minot, Feb. 5, 1822; MC.

ment involved some penalty less severe than deprivation of life or limb or banishment; and finally, the Court of Probate provided a judge and registrar to probate wills and deeds. Meeting four times a year in all, the courts would sit twice in the Great Barrington meetinghouse and twice fifteen miles to the north in the great hall of Fort Anson in Pittsfield,[2] a rather impressive and expensive legal machinery for a county of only four small towns and six unincorporated plantations.

Paralleling many other Massachusetts counties, Berkshire possessed at this time its own local upper class, consisting of the larger landowners; but in Berkshire these newly arrived first families commanded at best a tenuous respect. Still, during the provincial era, Berkshirites looked to them instinctively for leadership; and with the composition of the bench remaining decidedly aristocratic, anyone chancing to have court business grew accustomed to encountering a Dwight, an Ashley, or a Williams on the bench. Men of college education and wide experience but with no particular legal training, these patriarchs of Berkshire's wealthy families dominated the bench until the Revolution. The presiding justice of the Court of Common Pleas was General Joseph Dwight, the son of a Hatfield "river god." Having graduated from Harvard in 1722, he had commanded the Massachusetts artillery at Louisbourg and then had settled into his comfortable legal career in Berkshire in 1751. Like others of what might be called the aristocracy, he helped to restrict control of Berkshire legal affairs to a small, select group by the simple means of holding two positions—the second one being judge of Probate.[3] His son Elijah, another exponent of pluralism, became both registrar of probate and clerk of courts; and

2. Smith, *History of Pittsfield, I,* 133.

3. Emory Washburn, *Sketches of the Judicial History of Massachusetts* (Worcester, 1840), p. 394. Marriage further compounded the legal aristocracy when Theodore Sedgwick married Pamela Dwight, daughter of the judge.

Mark Hopkins followed the same familiar pattern by filling simultaneously the posts of county treasurer and registrar of deeds.[4]

Scarcely less illustrious within the county than Dwight himself were his three associate justices: John Ashley (Yale, 1730), one of the original settlers of Sheffield and owner of 1,600 acres in southern Berkshire; Colonel William Williams (Harvard, 1729), Pittsfield's most prominent citizen; and Timothy Woodbridge, Berkshire agent for the Commissioners for Indian Affairs and the only noncollege man on the bench. Upon Dwight's death in 1765 Colonel Williams succeeded him both as chief justice and judge of probate, and the Dalton physician Dr. Perez Marsh (Harvard, 1748) stepped into the vacant associate justiceship. Like the rest, he possessed the necessary qualification for high legal office —he was to the manor born.

Less exclusively aristocratic than the judges, the gentlemen of the bar in colonial Berkshire divided themselves into two groups, one of which could hardly have termed its members gentlemen at all. They were, in fact, plough-joggers fortuitously turned attorneys, and what meager records they have left mark them as conspicuous if unconscious pioneers in Berkshire's legal evolution. Numbering among themselves such rank legal amateurs as Jabez Ward, William King, and Joseph Gilbert of Great Barrington, they appeared in court only to plead the cases of their friends and neighbors and then returned to their farm chores. In 1812 David Hitchcock was to look back on this group with a disapproval not unmixed with humor:

> Though *pettifogging* is in a great measure done away
> in New-England, we still remember the time, when,

4. This Mark Hopkins, a younger brother of the eminent theologian and Great Barrington pastor Samuel Hopkins, was the grandfather of Mark Hopkins, president of Williams College, and the grand uncle of Mark Hopkins, the railroad builder.

even in these States it prevailed to an alarming degree. It is true, there were some regular practitioners in law, but they were far from being plenty. Individuals, therefore, who contended, were, on this account obliged to plead before a justice of the peace in their own behalf; and were many times so ignorant of their causes, and so unintelligible in their harangues, as to reduce him to the necessity of deciding at random, or else not at all. In such cases, the party who won, instead of imputing his success to accident or chance, attributed it entirely to his own ingenuity; and not only so, but the audience who heard him, would flatter and encourage him in this vain imagination: He would be successively employed by others on similar occasions, till his name and popularity rose to such a degree, as to induce a belief that he was an all-prevailing advocate for the distribution of justice: This, however, injured none but employers, and approved attorneys who were neglected in consequence.[5]

The other group quite predictably consisted almost entirely of members of Berkshire's first families and simply represented the younger generation of those local aristocrats dominating the bench. Usually equipped with a college education and occasionally with additional training in Mark Hopkins' Great Barrington law office, they almost invariably remained conservative in their social views and proved themselves, during the Revolution, to be far less patriotic than their rustic counterparts. Their rigidly selective ranks included John Ashley, a pro-British "rescinder" in 1768; Woodbridge Little (Yale, 1760), the leader of Berkshire Toryism in the Revolution; Daniel Jones, a Pittsfield Tory who moved to New Hampshire upon the outbreak of violence; David Ingersoll (Yale, 1761), a Great Barrington land speculator whose Toryism led him to emigrate to

5. David Hitchcock, *The Social Monitor* (Stockbridge, 1812), p. 164 n.

England; and those two rather conservative patriots Colonel
Mark Hopkins and Theodore Sedgwick (Yale, 1765), the
latter being "fierce for moderation" during the Revolution.

Such was the procedure followed in the Berkshire courts
that a very decided advantage fell to professional attorneys
and to the judge who might occasionally step down from the
bench to play an attorney's role. Farmers who were arguing
cases without benefit of higher education must have been
baffled by the close adherence to inherited common law
forms and by the great strictness in pleading required of
them. This strictness evidently continued in force notwithstanding the legislative enactment of 1701 providing that "no
writ. . . . shall be abated . . . for any kind of circumstan-
tial errors or mistakes" so long as the intention be under-
standable.[6] At the September term of the courts in 1768
laymen and self-styled attorneys had good reason to be en-
raged at the numerous abatements of writs over legal technicalities of the common law. In one case of trespass—David
Wilmot, plaintiff, vs. James Gray, defendant—the court ordered an abatement of the writ and Gray recovered costs by
reason of the following errors:

> (1) Defendant was named James Gray, *Gentleman* and
> it should be *Esquire* as he had recently been made a
> major in the army.
> (2) Defendant was listed as living in Hartford and at the
> time of the writ he was residing in Albany.
> (3) Defendant asserted that Wilmot was a yeoman not a
> gentleman as he calls himself.

At the same session a writ was abated because the plaintiff
listed as his residence the county of *Dutchers* rather than
*Dutchess*.[7]

6. Henry W. Taft, "Judicial History of Berkshire," *Four Papers of
the Berkshire Historical and Scientific Society* (Pittsfield, 1886), p. 97.

7. Ibid., p. 98.

Finding in the common law a bulwark affording effective protection against any would-be levelers of their professional status—or of their property rights—Berkshire lawyers and judges may well have reveled in its technicalities. And alongside the growing popular resentment over this tendency of the law to become an occult science, another bitterly felt resentment was beginning to simmer. Many of the Berkshire farmers, overwhelmed with the financial burden of stocking and working their new farms, would fall behind on payment of promissory notes, whereupon the gentlemen creditors would press for recovery of debts and the courts would usually decide quite justly in favor of the gentry. According to one anonymous and unusually sympathetic Great Barrington lawyer, the plight of the Berkshire settler was indeed deplorable: "While you were thus honestly employed in cultivating your new farms, you were under a necessity of contracting debts. Innumerable lawsuits were soon commenced, heavy bills of cost were taxed upon you, larger, in many instances, than the original debt: and thus you came to be cruelly oppressed, even by the law which was designed to determine and secure the rights and properties of the people. From whence originated your violent prejudices against law." [8] The legal system was far too cumbrous and expensive for thinly populated Berkshire; and Pittsfield's parson, Thomas Allen, enthusiastic reader of Tom Paine, regarded the court system as an instrument of oppression. "We have," he said, "been ruled in this county for many years past with a rod of iron." [9]

As the wealthy continued to carry their complaints to court, "prejudices against law" grew still more violent. The year 1768 found William Whiting, gentleman, bringing suit

8. *An Address to the Inhabitants of Berkshire,* by "Impartial Reason" (Hartford, 1778), p. 7.

9. Thomas Allen, "Petition and Memorial of the Town of Pittsfield . . . May 29, 1776," Massachusetts Archives, 180.150.

against John Denmore, yeoman, for failure to work faithfully enough to be worthy of his three-pound monthly hire
in the plaintiff's potash works on Lebanon Mountain. And
in a later case, a Pittsfield gentleman, Charles Goodrich,
sued a Mountain Grant yeoman, H. Desmond, for the
amount of thirty pounds for having cut down certain of his
trees that exceeded one foot in diameter.[10] With decision
after decision going in favor of the gentlemen, no wonder
that the common people of the county came increasingly to
view the courts as executors for the wealthy.

Such resentments against the Court of Common Pleas
were, moreover, supplemented from time to time by a more
general aversion to that authority which the Court of General Sessions exercised in its administration of county affairs.
Decisions as to the building and repair of county roads and
bridges or the issuing of tavern licenses were by no means inspired by malice, but often they necessarily overrode a local
or class interest for a wider county benefit and thus could
arouse real discontent in a frontier society impatient of restraint.

Throughout Massachusetts in the 1770's this feeling of
animosity toward the courts was beginning to discourage all
respect for law among the middle and lower classes, and
eventually Berkshire yeomen found an unlooked-for support
in their opposition to the existing legal system. The royal
promulgation of the Coercive Acts (in retaliation for the Boston Tea Party), with their constriction of the Massachusetts
Provincial Charter and with the provision for putting county
judges under stricter royal control, had become known in
Massachusetts by August 1774 and quickly roused a group
of Pittsfield Whigs to action. Under their authoritative
leadership Berkshire became the first Massachusetts county

10. Records of the Berkshire Court of Common Pleas (1768), 2.21;
Berkshire County Court House, Pittsfield, Massachusetts.

to bring about a thorough and radical reform—a reform effected by the straightforward expedient of forcing the closing of the courts.

At a convention called at Pittsfield on August 15, two of the town's most respected and substantial citizens, Dr. Timothy Childs and John Strong, were chosen to draw up a petition "to the Honorable Court." This petition demanded that the courts should "immediately cease, and the people of this Province fall into a state of nature until our grievances are fully redressed." [11] Those grievances of which Childs and Strong were thinking were, of course, more grievances against British tyranny than against the local tyranny of the wealthy, but Berkshire yeomen were in no mood to quibble. When the justices arrived at Great Barrington to hold court on August 18, they found fifteen hundred unarmed but determined men who "filled the Court House, and the avenues to the seats of justice, so full that no passage could be found for the judges. . . . The sheriff commanded the people to make way for the court; but they gave him to understand that they knew no court, or any other establishment than the ancient laws and customs of the country; and to none other would they give way on any terms." [12]

Once popular pressure had forced the courts to close, Berkshire entered an interregnum period during which independence from inherited authority and inherited legal and judicial method became a leading theme. The county went even further than its neighbor Hampshire County in opposing both British rule and the rule of the Provincial Congress [13] in Boston. From 1774 to 1780 committees of patriots, later to be known as the Berkshire Constitutionalists,

11. Smith, *History of Pittsfield, 1,* 194.
12. Boston *Massachusetts Gazette and Newsletter,* Sept. 1, 1774.
13. I.e. the Massachusetts Convention.

governed the county, with the outspoken Parson Allen providing their political leadership.

On several occasions the town of Pittsfield had reason to address remonstrances to the General Court, and those addresses, written in the hand of Parson Allen, suggest the basic tenets held by the recalcitrant Berkshirites. If they had been led to declare their abhorrence of the present constitution of Massachusetts, their only motive, they said, had been an "invincible love of civil and religious liberty for ourselves and future posterity." As administered by the British, the Provincial Charter had become an instrument of deep corruption, and even as continued by the colonists, it was perpetuating in office the selfish and the parasitic.

Having declared the governor, lieutenant-governor, and council in abdication, members of the General Court had not only proceeded to follow the old oppressive charter but had exhibited an undignified penchant for nominating and then electing themselves to various government posts. Charles Goodrich of Pittsfield and William Whiting of Great Barrington, then delegates to the General Court, had actually presumed to return to Berkshire with commissions as justices of the peace. The unfortunate Goodrich, although a genuine patriot, was treated little better than a Tory by Pittsfield citizens who felt that this so-called "new" government bore far too close a resemblance to the old. The Constitutionalists of the western county were decidedly unprepared to tolerate government from above, whether administered by Englishmen or by Bostonians.[14] What the "westerners" wanted and what they tirelessly agitated for was a constitutional convention which would build a new and generally acceptable foundation under the government. With this in mind, the people of Lenox agreed "that the Happiness of the good people of the State of the Massachusetts Bay depends very much on a form and Constitution of government

14. Massachusetts Archives, 181.50.

without which we cannot subsist," [15] and then, in a slightly whimsical mood, they went on to vote unanimously that, lacking such a convention, they would ask to be incorporated into some other state (for example, New York) that could already boast a constitution. They were, in short, indulging unconsciously in a curious paradox by simultaneously exhibiting extreme provincialism—in their threatened political separation from Massachusetts—and extreme broadmindedness—in their concern over such great questions as the proper foundation of government and the methods for drafting and ratifying a constitution.[16]

Meanwhile, within Berkshire, in the absence of the regular courts, legal affairs were generally being handled by the Committee of Inspection and Safety in each town and occasionally by the local church. The Lanesboro Church, for example, took it upon itself to censure Nathaniel Williams for Toryism and later to settle a boundary controversy between Deacon Ebenezer Buck and Colonel Miles Powel; the Stockbridge Church excommunicated Huldah Deane for theft and lying; and the Cheshire Baptist Church excommunicated Nathan Nichols for passing counterfeit money.[17]

As to the benefits of the town committee judiciary, opinions varied. In 1775 Parson Allen reported to the General Court: "The people of the county, under the lenient and efficient rule of their several committees . . . had lived to-

15. Records of the Town of Lenox, 1.53 (Lenox Town Hall).

16. In their urgent concern over the great constitutional questions, Berkshirites were at one with the relatively conservative Essex Junto. Two studies have dealt with the Berkshire Constitutionalists in some detail: Robert J. Taylor, *Western Massachusetts in the Revolution* (Providence, 1954), and Robert E. Brown, *Middle Class Democracy and the Revolution in Massachusetts, 1691–1780* (Ithaca, Cornell University Press, 1955). Taylor's thesis that there was a real internal revolution, at least a revolution of social attitude, is opposed by Brown's denial of any great change.

17. Church Records of Lanesboro, Stockbridge, Cheshire; typescripts by R. H. Cooke in BA.

gether in the greatest love, peace, safety, liberty, happiness, and good order." [18] Even if Allen was overstating the case, the greater number of the people undoubtedly did favor the new order. In fact, Berkshire towns polled in 1778 voted by considerable majorities against a return either of the Court of Common Pleas or the Court of General Sessions. Such single-mindedness, however, could not silence the submerged anti-Constitutionalist minority, and local conservatives like wealthy Theodore Sedgwick complained indignantly. "In the confusion which was at once the cause and consequence of a dissolution of government [*wrote Sedgwick to Aaron Burr*], men's minds as well as actions became regardless of all legal restraint . . . the *people* were the fountain of all honour. The first thing they did was to withdraw all confidence from everyone who had ever any connexion with government. Lawyers were, almost universally, represented as pests of society. . . . Abilities were represented as dangerous, and learning as a crime, or rather, the certain forerunner of all political extravagances." [19] Thomas Allen could certainly never agree unreservedly with so acid an accusation, but by the following year even he was beginning to harbor doubts. "We always had a sense of the necessity of law," he wrote, "especially in times of war; we felt the want of a due exercise of it, and in many instances the sad effect of not enjoying it."

Even in the absence of any records pertaining to the committees' legal procedure, enough evidence survives to hint at a far greater leniency to debtors than the old Court of Common Pleas had shown. Always seeking the elusive goal of "substantial justice," the committees seldom enforced the letter of the law against any delinquent debtor who could

18. Smith, *History of Pittsfield, 1,* 338.
19. Aug. 7, 1776, Matthew L. Davis, *Memoirs of Aaron Burr* (2 vols. New York, 1836), *1,* 92–93; quoted in Lee Nathaniel Newcomer's *The Embattled Farmers* (New York, 1953), p. 99.

plead insuperable hardship. "Public interest" deserved first consideration, they felt, even though property rights might occasionally suffer.

Still, the citizens of Pittsfield must eventually have concluded that, whatever the good intentions of their committee, its very informality was leading to inequities, and in October 1778 Pittsfield established an official Town Court to be endowed with all the powers formerly held by the Court of General Sessions. The experienced Colonel William Williams became chief justice, with four associate justices to assist him, and a detailed list of costs was drawn up: summons for juror, 4s; writ of execution, 6s; travel, 1s per mile, jurors' and witnesses' attendance on trial, 18s per day. Except for a comparatively easygoing attitude toward debtors and for the fact that the town meeting elected the judges, the procedure of the new court differed very little from the regular courts of the Province.[20]

This return to traditional procedures would offer one indication that, whatever Berkshire conservatives might think, the Constitutionalists were hardly anarchists. Indeed, so strong was their desire for government that they at last settled for a state constitution which John Adams had steered rather farther to the right than they would themselves have chosen to go. But most of them voted for ratification, and throughout Berkshire popular interest and enthusiastic support ran noticeably higher than in most other sections of the state. In August 1780 Berkshirites completed their return to loyalty by restoring the regular courts.[21]

For the more radical farmers within Berkshire, however, the compromise agreed to by the constitutionalists was soon to prove a poor bargain. The constitution and the bill of rights, just though they then seemed, offered no effective

20. Smith, *History of Pittsfield, 1,* 379–84.
21. George H. Tucker, *Berkshire County, Its Shire Towns and Its Court Houses* (Pittsfield, 1918), p. 3.

means of combatting postwar economic distress; and throughout the early 1780's the ranks of discontented debtors swelled
continuously. As early as August 1780 the Revolutionary inflation was dropping off, farm prices were going down, and
creditors were trying to collect notes which had been written
during wartime prosperity and which few could pay. The
courts were crowded with creditors' suits. Nearly all of the
165 cases heard at Great Barrington in August 1781 involved
"gentlemen" vs. "yeomen," and executions in debt cases, already high in 1782 and 1783, reached a peak in 1784. Certainly by that time many Berkshirites were ready to concur
with the feelings of the Berkshire yeoman who called the
Court of Common Pleas "a Damned Pack of Rascalls." Sum-
moned to apologize, he complied by declaring, "I have called
you Damned Rascalls, and I ask your forgiveness, but you
really are so." [22]

When, in 1786 and 1787, Shays' Rebellion brought the
discontented into open revolt, they lost no time in singling
out for attack those courts which they had become accustomed to regarding as the immediate instruments of government power. "The organization of courts and the collection of debts," the Lenox novelist Catharine Sedgwick was to
recall fifty years later, "formed one of the principal grounds
of discontent. The party in favour of the state government,
and, of course, of the support of the laws, was commonly
called the court party." [23]

Thus, for the second time in thirteen years, grievances
against the courts in Berkshire found their ultimate expression in a show of force. The weapon of violence first used by

22. Records of the Supreme Judicial Court, Berkshire (1782), p. 291;
Suffolk County Court House. Quoted in L. N. Newcomer, *Embattled
Farmers*, p. 136.

23. Catharine Maria Sedgwick, *A New England Tale* (New York,
1822), p. 283 n.

Revolutionary patriots could prove equally effective in the hands of malcontents, and in August 1786, a mob of 800 assembled at Great Barrington to prevent the Court of Common Pleas from sitting. Confronted with threats of violence, the four justices agreed not to act under their commissions until the grievances should be redressed.

During the year's hiatus in court sessions, the disaffected group, becoming less violent and more constructive, met in a county convention at Lenox on November 8, 1786,[24] to pass eighteen resolutions, a large number of which dealt with legal reform and indicated the prevalent antipathy to current legal practices. Similar in purpose to the more famous convention held earlier in Hatfield and to the later Worcester gathering, this Berkshire convention stood firm in their determination to brook no compromise. They wanted a wholesale solution for every dissatisfaction and plunged unrestrainedly even into areas of social and political reform. They wanted to reduce the number of civil offices, to redistribute the tax load, and to move the General Court to a more convenient place than Boston.

As for legal reforms, the list of resolutions was long. The second called for

> an alteration to the practice in the Court of Common Pleas and General Quarter Sessions so far as to place those courts upon a foundation that is calculated to a speedy, judicious, and cheap management of the decisions of all causes in those courts conformable to the precepts of sound wisdom and economy which the critical depressed circumstances of the people dictates which we seriously believe cannot be effected short of a total change of these institutions . . . substitute in lieu thereof a new court combining in its Institution and

24. MS in DC.

Jurisdiction what ought in a free country to appertain to the [*town*] and at the same time to enlarge the jurisdiction of the Justice of the Peace.

The third resolution went on to maintain, at less length but with equal decisiveness, "that the present mode of instructing candidates for the lucrative and popular profession of the law and their admission and installment of attorneys through the medium and pleasure of the Bar and without the examination of the Judges in open court as to their qualifications is unreasonable, unconstitutional, and dangerous to society." In the fourth and fifth resolves, the radicals directed their criticism to the odious adherence to British common and statute laws in the determination of cases, as leading to ill-convenienced and peculiar uncertainties. The existing form of writs and processes and pleadings, they complained, was too prolix, intricate, and expensive for a free people. Finally, in their sixth and seventh resolves, they advocated the elimination of imprisonment for debt and the acceptance of personal property as legal tender for debts; and in the eleventh they suggested that deeds be registered in the respective towns rather than at the county probate court.

Such demands for reform represented a rather typical reaction of American back-country farmers, especially those of inland Massachusetts, to those courts and lawyers still tainted by Toryism.[25] Quite probably, however, the resentment felt against lawyers boiled up more heatedly and with less restraint in Berkshire than in most sections, simply because no particular prestige had yet attached itself either to the courts —only twenty years old at the onset of the Revolution—or to the law itself—undermined by occasional jurisdictional disputes with New York.

25. Charles Warren, *History of the American Bar* (Boston, 1911), pp. 212–14; James W. Hurst, *The Growth of American Law; The Law Makers* (Boston, 1950), p. 90.

After the suppression of Shays' Rebellion, when many of these demands brought no reform, the dissatisfied would-be reformers at last temporarily abandoned the struggle. Exhausted and annoyed by the long years of social ferment, some merely yearned for the peace and order offered by the proposed federal Constitution and others (more optimistic) hoped that they glimpsed some prospect for eventual reform within its framework. Such peacemakers as Lanesboro's Jonathan Smith found, in both groups, a receptive audience. To his fellow citizens Captain Smith addressed a plea:

> I am a plain man and get my living by the plough. I am not used to speak in public, but I beg your leave to say a few words to my brother plough joggers in this house. I have lived in a part of the country where I have known the worth of good government by the want of it. There was a black cloud that rose in the east last winter, and spread over the west. . . . It brought on a state of anarchy, and that leads to tyranny. . . . It is better to have one tyrant than so many at once. Now . . . when I saw this Constitution, I found that it was a cure for these disorders. It was just such a thing as we wanted. . . . I did not go to any lawyer and ask his opinion; we have no lawyer in our town, and we do well enough without. I formed my own opinion and was pleased with this Constitution. . . . But I don't think the worse of the Constitution because lawyers, and men of learning, and moneyed men, are fond of it. . . . Some men think that our liberty and property are not safe in the hands of moneyed men, and men of learning. I am not of that mind . . . these lawyers, these moneyed men, these men of learning, are all embarked in the same cause with us, and we must all swim or sink together; and shall we farmers, let us suppose a case now. . . . Suppose two or three of you have been at the pains to

break up a piece of rough land, and sow it with wheat;
would you let it lie waste, because you could not agree
what sort of a fence to make? Would it not be better to
put up a fence that did not please everyone's fancy,
rather than not fence it at all, or keep disputing about
it until wild beasts came and devoured it . . . now it is
the harvest—now is the time to reap the fruit of our
labor, and if we don't do it now, I am afraid that we
never shall have another opportunity.[26]

Having listened to such words as these and having already
fallen into a mood for compromise, the men of Lanesboro
cast their votes in favor of the federal Constitution. Only
seven of Berkshire's twenty-two towns, however, finally voted
for ratification.

Still, succeeding years were to prove the optimists largely
justified. With the completion of the jail and the county
court house in Lenox in 1792, the law was to gain noticeably
in outward dignity—a gain being registered more impor-
tantly, if less tangibly, in the foundations of prestige being
laid, year by year, in the public mind. For the Berkshire
bar, the decades following the establishment of the federal
Constitution were periods of growing stability. In spite of the
sharp competition for business among Berkshire lawyers,
their sense of their common interests was sufficient to compel them to take action for their mutual protection. Although an official Berkshire Bar Association did not appear
until 1871, an exclusive organization of local lawyers was
developing as early as 1792—an organization which successfully fulfilled all the basic functions of a bar association.
At first, the lawyers concentrated their cooperative efforts primarily on the enforcement of professional ethics, with a

26. *Journal of the Debates and Proceedings of the Massachusetts Constitutional Convention, held January 9, February 7, 1788, to Ratify the
Federal Constitution* (Boston, 1788), pp. 203–5.

view to protecting their own interests against rate-cutting and to protecting the public against pettifoggers. Then, during the September session of the court in 1792, they met to draw up a set of rules which would cover such matters as legal education, admission to the bar, and minimum fees. They agreed: "1st— That in the future we will not make any allowance for any term of time which an apprentice may have spent in any office out of this commonwealth. 2ndly— That we will not recommend to the Court any person for the oath of an attorney who shall not have had the usual Education at some college or university unless such person shall have studied as an apprentice (four to seven years) in the office of some attorney practising at the Bar of the Supreme Court." [27]

For the most part, aspiring lawyers in Berkshire met these educational requirements by apprenticing themselves to practicing attorneys—much as their clerical counterparts affiliated themselves with local clergymen. The local clerkships most sought after in the early 1800's were those with Theodore Sedgwick, Barnabas Bidwell, and Daniel Dewey, and in the 1830's those with Henry W. Dwight, Increase Sumner, and George J. Tucker. Of all these men, only Tucker attended the famous Litchfield Law School which Tapping Reeve had established twenty miles south of Berkshire; and not until 1842, when James D. Colt was admitted to the bar, could any Berkshire lawyer boast attendance at the Harvard Law School.[28] The most popular law school with Berkshirites was that of Judge Samuel Howe, begun at Northampton in 1823.

Such an extreme paucity of law school students on the Berkshire bar represented a trend by no means peculiar to this single county. Almost everywhere in New England, prospective lawyers were finding it cheaper and more con-

27. Rules of the Berkshire Bar, 1792; SP.
28. Smith, *History of Berkshire County, 1,* 330–57.

venient, if not more educational, to enter an attorney's office. In some offices the "education" might prove to consist largely of janitorial and secretarial chores, but certainly many lawyers took a sincere interest in their students. Even at its best, however, such an informal system of apprenticeship could never offer either the scope or the uniformity of a formal law school education.

Perhaps aware of the shortcomings in their legal preparation, Berkshire lawyers soon discovered a thoroughly effective means of supplementing their often meager legal knowledge. In the fall of 1815 a few of them became legal pioneers when they established at Lenox the Berkshire Law Library. Intended originally for the use of both bench and bar during court terms, the library soon proved an invaluable aid to legal education both for clerks and for practicing attorneys, and two of the most eminent leaders in American legal affairs may well have owed something of their legal knowledge to its convenient location only seven miles from their Stockbridge home. These were David Dudley Field, one day to become famous as the codifier of New York State law, and his brother, Stephen J. Field, destined to sit on the Supreme Court of the United States. Indeed, many of the learned justices of the Massachusetts Supreme Court had long since recognized the need for some such institution. "Books of law," they had remarked in 1804, "sometimes an extensive library, are indispensable requisites in discussing and deciding questions of law. . . . In many counties this opportunity [*to consult books*] cannot be had." [29]

Ironically enough, the new law library was to prove not only a step in the direction of professional competence but a significant contribution to the future democratization of the bar—two eventualities which many Berkshire lawyers

29. Frank Grinnell, "Constitutional History of the Supreme Judicial Court of Massachusetts from the Revolution to 1813," *Massachusetts Law Quarterly*, 2 (1917), 502.

had grown accustomed to regarding as mutually exclusive. The ambitious but indigent young men of the county suddenly found that, simply by paying a nominal fee, they might command the means to a basic legal education; and much to the credit of the library's founders, nothing was done to restrict this privilege.

As the years passed and cases grew increasingly varied, the law library became ever more indispensable. With the coming of the railroad and the beginnings of extensive manufacturing enterprises, the economic and social relations of the back country were to equal in their complexity those of the older seaboard cities; and side by side with the usual cases involving debt, trespass, and the disposal of ecclesiastical property appeared new problems with which local lawyers had had little or no experience. Even as early as the 1820's, they found themselves called upon to handle cases involving the collection of turnpike fees and vandalism to factories.

Long before such specialized legal problems had arisen, however—in fact, before the turn of the century—members of the bar faced the more fundamental problem of attempting to fix fees at a standard level in the hope of insuring fair competition. No lawyer, they decided, would thereafter take any case before the Court of Common Pleas where a sum of less than 12s was involved; he would insist on a standard retaining fee of 12s; and he would accept no less than 16s in arguing a case before the jury in the Court of Common Pleas or 24s in arguing before the Supreme Court. Finally, for the declaration in a real action, he would never charge the plaintiff less than 15s.[30] By asserting a rigid control over admissions to the bar, Berkshire lawyers managed to maintain these standards with considerable success and to eliminate those who sought to emulate the farmer-lawyers of the colonial era.

This is not to say, however, that the post-Revolutionary

30. Rules of the Berkshire Bar, 1792; SP.

Berkshire bar was becoming once again the exclusive domain of the wealthy. Granted that, unlike the Republican-
dominated bench, the bar would always remain more Federalist than Jeffersonian, still the Sedgwicks, the Dwights, and
the Fields soon accustomed themselves to sharing the alternating prestige and infamy of their profession with a Bidwell, a Bacon, or a Whiting. Indeed, even as early as 1793, the
wealthy conservative Henry Van Schaack was complaining
to Theodore Sedgwick: "It is a pity that this immaculate
profession should be subject to the admission to the Bar . . .
of the family of the wrongheads." [31]

Van Schaack was, of course, giving political overtones to
what remained essentially a question of professional standards. Along with many other conservatives, he viewed the
admission of Republicans to the bar as a potential threat to
the establishment of a highly respected and self-perpetuating
legal profession. Believing as they did in the fundamental
equality of men, might not Republicans eventually aim at
a leveling of legal standards to the point where public respect for the law and for lawyers would vanish? Conservatives
looked back with horror to the legal vacuum within Berkshire after the second closing of the courts and speedily
concluded that rampant radicalism could bring only lawless-
ness. Ultimately, this sense of apprehension spread to the
Massachusetts Supreme Court, whereupon the conservative
judges decreed that all would-be attorneys must thereafter
be examined and that only leaders of the county bars might
be eligible for appointment as examiners. Four years later
(in 1810), still fearing for the dignity of the legal profession,
they added new requirements for the admission of attorneys:
to the lower courts, five years' training, or three years' for college graduates; to the Supreme Court (as attorney), two years'
subsequent practice or (as counselor) four years' subsequent

31. Henry Van Schaack to Theodore Sedgwick, Jan. 13, 1793; SP.

practice.[32] Only at the time of the onrush of Jacksonian democracy would admission to the bar at last be placed on an
openly competitive basis—with no exclusive in-group empowered to pass judgment.

Meanwhile, in their intensive campaign to ensure professional standards, Berkshire lawyers may well have been losing
as much in popularity as they were gaining in dignity and
security. Political feelings had remained touchy within the
county ever since the days of Shays' Rebellion, and any group
in which both Federalist domination and special interest
had managed to survive could expect little support in so over-
whelmingly Republican an area as Berkshire.[33] That local
Baptist patriarch Elder John Leland stated the case for Berkshire Jeffersonians with bold precision. "Written standing
*laws*," he declared, "are the legitimate voice of the people.
Common law is the stretch of power of the judges. Bar rules
are the contrivance of lawyers." [34] Leland went on to warn
the people of Cheshire thunderingly against "the host of
lawyers who infest our land like the swarm of locusts in
Egypt and eat up everything green." [35] And even in the pages
of the traditionally Federalist Stockbridge *Western Star*,
lawyers fared little better. "We do not want so many lawyers
in Congress," wrote one anonymous critic, ". . . they live
at hearts ease all their days—men of pleasure that scarcely
bring in water to wash their own hands. . . . We can never
have things right in America until we change . . . and send
[*to Congress*] good, sensible men of our own cloth." [36]

A glance at the Berkshire bench after 1800 would have as-

32. Alfred Z. Reed, *Training for the Public Profession of the Law*
(New York, 1921), pp. 83–87.

33. By 1802 the Federalists held only six towns in Berkshire, four of
these small hill towns.

34. Leland, *Writings,* p. 733.

35. Ibid., "An Elective Judiciary," p. 292.

36. *Western Star,* Oct. 31, 1796.

sured any enthusiastic Republican of a satisfying quota of "good, sensible men of our own cloth." With the reconvening of the courts late in 1787 the flavor of aristocratic colonial days began to disappear. To Thompson J. Skinner went the office of presiding justice—an office which he held from 1795 until 1807. Neither a college graduate nor a lawyer, Skinner had settled in Williamstown in 1775 and had quickly become the champion of the common man in Berkshire politics. His colleague, John Bacon, who served on the Court of Common Pleas from 1789 to 1811, was atypical in being a Princeton graduate and a former cleric, but in his enthusiasm for the Jeffersonian party he rivaled even Skinner. Having moved to Stockbridge in 1775, he had risen to a position of popular political leadership in southern Berkshire quite comparable to that enjoyed by Skinner in the north. Meanwhile, another future associate justice, Nathaniel Bishop (1795–1811), had moved to Richmond in 1777, had become a prominent farmer and landowner, and eventually had been sent by the Republicans to the legislature. Only David Noble of Williamstown (1795–1803) could offer as qualifications both a college education and a law degree, and even though a member of the generally conservative Berkshire bar he espoused the anti-Federalist party.[37]

As they might have expected, members of this thoroughly Republican Berkshire bench enjoyed no more popularity with Federalists than did the bar with Jeffersonians. One conservative Berkshire lawyer, Ethan Stone, deposited an unequivocal expression of his sentiments on the steps of the

37. Editor Loring Andrews of the *Western Star* found such an anti-Federalist domination of the bench deplorable: "I wish to heaven," he wrote to Theodore Sedgwick on Nov. 20, 1794, "some influence could be made from one quarter or another with our *passive* Executive, to prevent either W——— or B——— from being appointed judges . . . Mr. Timothy Edwards would make an infinitely more respectable Judge than either of the Skinnerites—cannot some plot be laid at Head Quarters?" (MS in SP).

Lenox Court House in 1800, shortly before leaving the county to practice in Cincinnati:

## Berkshire Looking Glass

A shrewd anti-federal chief-justice presides
Whose name represents him a flayer of hides.
Next sits an old democrat stiff as a hog;
His opponents never yet have ringed him or yoked him,
Although while alive to tough Bacon they smoked him.
The next on the bench is a Phoenix on earth,
A republican Bishop, and such too by birth,
And what is still stranger a Noble we find,
Who is even proud of a plebian mind.[38]

By 1800 both the Court of Common Pleas and the Court of General Sessions had become almost entirely Republican; but now, although the new court personnel did faithfully reflect the dominant political views of the county, they decidedly lacked, for the most part, that legal knowledge necessary to the performance of their functions with authority and dispatch. It was the Federalists' turn to find fault, and the experienced Federalist lawyers did not hesitate to attack both the personnel of the bench and Republican alterations in the structure of the state's judicial machinery. The Court of Common Pleas, which had once enjoyed a modest degree of respect enabling Berkshirites to possess a certain amount of local autonomy in the law, now found that, under the inefficient control of relatively uneducated judges, its decisions were increasingly being regarded by litigants as merely a step on the way to the Massachusetts Supreme Court.[39]

Secure in the knowledge of such inefficiencies, the Federalists could restrict their differences with the plebian court to

38. DC.
39. Cf. Hurst, *Growth of American Law*, p. 96; Francis R. Aumann, *The Changing American Legal System: Some Selected Phases* (Columbus, Ohio, 1940), pp. 40–50.

the high ground of legal competence, and eventually they
rallied popular support behind them. In their dismay over
the loss of local court prestige and in their growing discontent
with fumbling and uncertain court decisions, Berkshirites
soon felt compelled to support the efforts of educated, conservative lawyers to reform the decentralized court system
which the legislature had created. Within Berkshire, the
"Country Lawyer of Otis" led the critical movement against
the Court of Common Pleas. In a series of ten closely reasoned articles appearing from time to time in the *Western
Star* of 1795, he stated his dissatisfactions simply and briefly.
The present system, he maintained, was unnecessarily slow
and expensive; and the appointment to the Court of Common Pleas of men without legal knowledge at a small salary
was actually decreasing local self-government. Indeed, he felt
that the much-needed reform could only be effected by establishing a circuit Court of Common Pleas with well-educated
judges and by giving the court final jurisdiction in all cases
involving less than fifty pounds.[40] With the establishment of
such a system in the three western counties, he estimated that
more than £10,000 a year might be saved and that three-
fourths of the business of the Supreme Court might be eliminated. No cases need then be carried over from one term to
the next, and some of the money saved might well be used to
give judges of the Court of Common Pleas a decent salary in
place of the paltry thirty pounds a year they were receiving.[41]

When, in 1811, the legislature reorganized the judiciary,
they made many of these proposed reforms realities. Most
important, the legislature did establish at that time a Circuit
Court of Common Pleas, to be replaced nine years later by a
State Court of Common Pleas, and the old Republican bench
of the early 1800's with its distinctive Berkshire character
was relegated to the archives of memory. Serving as chief jus-

40. *Western Star,* Apr. 14, 1795.
41. Ibid., Apr. 28, 1795.

tice from 1811 to 1814, Ezekiel Bacon, a Pittsfield Republican, became the only Berkshirite to gain a position on the new court.

In all of the Massachusetts counties this same centralizing tendency was beginning to overtake the Court of General Sessions, and eventually a parallel evolution came about. In Berkshire this lower court had originally included all local justices of the peace. By 1807, however, it had shrunk to a chief justice and three associate justices and had become, like the Court of Common Pleas, dominantly Republican. Finally, in 1828, it met an even severer fate than had that court, when the legislature decided to abolish it altogether and to entrust its civil and criminal jurisdictions to the county commissioners and the Massachusetts Supreme Court respectively.[42]

Again the process of court reorganization had erased county boundaries and had brought the assimilation of a local Berkshire court into the less colorful but more efficient state system. Still, Berkshirites continued to take an active interest in the functioning of the bench; and if they sent few justices to the state courts, the ones they did send made lasting contributions to Massachusetts legal history. Foremost was Theodore Sedgwick. A Federalist leader of national fame, he had published in the columns of the *Western Star* (June 4, 1800) what the Republicans called his "Political Last Will and Testament" and had retired from the United States Congress to Stockbridge to await the imminent ordeal threatening the Republic under Jefferson. A year later, however, he found his public career unexpectedly extended by an appointment to the Massachusetts Supreme Court. There he filled with distinction the office of judge, and by a quiet and skillful manipulation of political strings he managed to effect much-needed reforms.

42. G. J. Tucker, "The Courts of Berkshire a Hundred Years Ago," Pittsfield *Sun,* Sept. 27, 1900.

A quarter of a century later the eminent Chief Justice Lemuel Shaw recalled, in an address before the Berkshire bar, some of the deplorable practices which Judge Sedgwick had discovered in the Supreme Court of 1802. Faced with a three-year backlog of cases, he and the other judges found the press of business so great that they were often unable to arrive at an agreement in instructing the jury on points of law and thus were forced to transfer an undue share of responsibility to the jurists. The blame for this unreasonable overload of work fell not upon any negligence by the judges but upon the plethora of appeals coming in from the lower courts. A solution to the difficulties might have come about much earlier had the legislature seen the wisdom of adopting the *nisi prius* system, whereby a jury trial might be conducted under the direction of a single Supreme Court Justice, with all decisions subject to revision by the full Court. Instead, the well-meaning but nearsighted legislature of 1799 had thought to remedy the already serious inefficiency simply by enlarging the Court from five to seven and by requiring a quorum of three to attend all hearings.[43]

When Judge Sedgwick joined the Court three years later, he immediately recognized the harmfulness of such legislation and clandestinely set about trying to upgrade the courts. More than ten years in the national Congress had taught him the wisdom of proceeding without fanfare and of avoiding unnecessary antagonisms, and he at first confined his reforming zeal to a mildly critical correspondence. Feeling that the increased number of judges was leading to the same vulgarization of the bench which he had hotly criticized in Berkshire, he wrote a letter designed to sound out Harrison Gray Otis, then Speaker of the House. "The salaries of the judges," he ventured, "ought to be permanent . . . and

43. Lemuel Shaw, "Address . . . to the Berkshire Bar . . . May 1830," *American Jurist,* 5 (1831), 8–10.

competent . . . there will soon be two vacancies and it is an office which, of all others, ought not to go abegging." [44] Further experience on the court convinced him that salaries would become adequate only with a reduction in the number of judges and with the adoption of the *nisi prius* system. Once again he wrote to Otis:

> I remember that last summer I mentioned to you my opinion that the *nisi prius* system, for the purpose of discovering the truth *in issues,* was preferable to any mode which had ever been adopted. I had pleasure, then, in believing that your judgment concurred with mine. My experience since has, if possible, more firmly established the opinion which I then entertained. The nearer then you can approach to and the sooner you can arrive at this point, the more will your country be indebted to your services. Whenever this shall have been attained, five judges will be fully adequate to do the business of the state promptly and without delay. . . . I think that appeals and reviews, in trials of fact, are a grievance and that their evils will constantly increase. The rights of property would, in my opinion, be infinitely better secured, if questions of fact were never reviewed, but in the English method of new trial.[45]

Finally, on January 4, 1804, Sedgwick submitted to Otis a series of four bills in which he embodied all his carefully pondered ideas on judicial reform, and by 1806 most of them had become law. In that very year, however, Sedgwick's satisfaction turned to bitterness and he received the greatest disappointment of his public life when he saw himself passed over for the post of Chief Justice in favor of Theophilus Par-

44. Theodore Sedgwick to Harrison G. Otis, May 14, 1801; SP. Quoted in Grinnell, "Constitutional History," p. 498.
45. Stockbridge, Feb. 7, 1803; SP.

sons.[46] A greater legal mind than Sedgwick, Parsons enjoyed a brilliant success in his new post—a success based in part on those reforms which his colleague, Judge Sedgwick, had worked so hard to bring about.[47]

Meanwhile, back in Berkshire, the increasing social stability developing in the early years of the nineteenth century, along with a reasonable economic prosperity, was doing much to erase once explosive class feelings, and even when an occasional gentleman of the bench was known to have patrician antecedents and sympathies, he aroused none of that extreme feeling against the courts which had characterized the earlier years. Indeed the title of judge as it was applied to such men as the farmer-mechanic-surveyor-justice William Walker of Lenox, or to the mellowing patriarch Nathaniel Bishop, had become a title of affection as well as respect.

During the early nineteenth century the convening of the

46. H. G. Otis to Theodore Sedgwick, May 25, 1806; SP. Otis expressed his regret that Sedgwick was taking the appointment of Parsons as a personal insult and assured him that it was a popular decision with the bar. Feeling that Mr. Parsons was the greatest legal talent in the United States, Otis agreed with the bar but informed Sedgwick that he considered him next only to Parsons in qualifications for the position and begged him not to retire in protest over the appointment. That, he said, would be a calamity.

47. Cf. Frank G. Cook, "Theophilus Parsons," in William D. Lewis, ed., *Great American Lawyers* (8 vols. Philadelphia, 1907–09), 2, 86. Cook states that a major factor in causing Associate Justices Sewall and Parker to recommend Parsons over Sedgwick for the Chief Justiceship was their belief that true reforms could be effected only by bringing in a new man. Perhaps if Sedgwick had been less discreet in his work for reform, he would not have been considered as too conservative for the post. Cook, failing to recognize Sedgwick's efforts, heaps all the credit for expediting court business on Parsons. A thorough discussion of Sedgwick's position appears in Richard Welch's unpublished dissertation, "Theodore Sedgwick" (Harvard, 1952). His disappointment is obvious from a letter written in 1806: "My friends try in vain to soothe me. . . . They say I am reconciled . . . they lie like hell." S. C. Sedgwick and C. S. Marquand, *Stockbridge, 1739–1939*, p. 175.

courts in Berkshire came to be a busy and colorful occasion, to which every Berkshirite could look forward with confidence that the judges would be competent and that justice would, in the main, prevail. Young Henry Taft, one day to become Berkshire's clerk of courts, editorialized enthusiastically in the *Massachusetts Eagle:*

> Lenox is alive during the administration of Justice. The goddess has occupied her throne here for more than a week past, and our Village has abounded with Judges and Jurors, lawyers, and litigants, prosecutors and prosecuted. To us who live in the country, the occasion is quite imposing. It presents to us a vast variety of characters: young attornies in the bustle of new found business, and the older ones assuming more and more the dignified gravity of the bench; waiting jurymen chatting in little clusters by the wayside; worrying clients complaining of sleepless nights; witnesses of all orders and descriptions. . . . spectators trading horses in the street, and politicians smoking over government affairs in the bar room. Our boarding houses have their long tables lined on both sides with earnest applicants, and all expect more business, more calls, more conversation, and more cheerfulness. —Messages are sent, and errands done between one end of the county and the other; business accounts are settled, plans laid; caucuses, conventions and singing schools agreed upon; news-papers subscribed for and distant matters in general arranged for the ensuing Winter.[48]

Taft's satisfaction with Berkshire legal affairs was evidence that the county had indeed achieved progress, if not without pain. Berkshirites had come to recognize, first, the impracticable character of a sharp social and economic separation and of an intellectual barrier between the lawyers and the

48. *Massachusetts Eagle,* Sept. 25, 1834.

people; later, the inevitable confusion arising from a vulgarization of legal institutions into people's committees; and finally, the dangers inherent in a bench lacking a proper legal education. The first quarter of the nineteenth century at last brought some hope of solution when Berkshire became better integrated into the more efficient state system of courts and approached a workable fusion of professional competence and democratic selection in the make-up of her bar.

Throughout these legally eventful years, Berkshire lawyers may well have welcomed their well-filled calendars and crowded offices, particularly in view of the phenomenon they had witnessed in the 1820's. Within a decade, they had seen the number of cases brought before the Court of Common Pleas register a sharp decline, until the 1,484 actions entered in 1816 had shrunk to a mere 911 in 1826 and to 691 in 1828. Had they sought an explanation for such a falling-off of litigation, they might possibly have found it in the virtual disappearance of that sharp party spirit which had racked Berkshire from the 1790's until the conclusion of the War of 1812. Certainly the explanation could not have been economic when the expense of court cases had not increased; but Chester Dewey, ablest historian of early nineteenth-century Berkshire, suggested still another possibility. The decline in cases, he decided, could be attributed to a higher moral spirit then being inculcated by the "moral societies," Bible societies, and temperance groups.[49]

Yet just how much restraining effect a man's membership in a church or moral society might have on his love of litigation might well be brought into question. Writing in 1844, Charles Sedgwick remarked on both the pettiness and a certain stubborn grandeur innate in the picayune bickering which comprised a considerable element in the legal business:

49. Field, *History of Berkshire,* p. 110.

I do not think a verdict is always perfectly conclusive evidence that justice has been done. From what I have seen of law suits, I am inclined to think that Courts are often looked upon by the parties who resort to them as a kind provision of Providence to throw off the responsibility of doing justice from the only persons who know exactly what justice requires and place it where it is impossible to tell in nine cases out of ten precisely what ought to be done. The cause that I have been investigating for four days and nights has deeply impressed me with the dignity of human nature and the usefulness of the ordinary labors of the most honorable and learned profession that exists among men. Two respectable counsellors of the Berkshire Bar and two highly respectable practitioners in the court of chancery in New York one of whom was obliged to leave a sick child behind have given their unwearied attention to the merits of a dispute that has lasted for fourteen years between two pious and excellent church members about this one fact whether there ought or ought not to have been deducted from a farm sold in 1830 four acres on account of waste land. Four acres at $30 per acre!! This dispute had once been referr'd to some neighbors—once settled by the parties, once adjudicated upon in the Supreme Judicial Court and is now reviewed upon new discovered evidence in the Court of Chancery, one of the parties residing in New York and reviewed by a man who has acquired a considerable property by very hard labor. Does not that show an unconquerable love of justice? [50]

Meanwhile critics of the Berkshire bar were complaining that the law was too technical or that it was too expensive. "The rescuing of the law from the clouds of unintelligibility

50. To William Minot, Dec. 8, 1844; MC.

in which it is now enveloped," Andrews remarked, "is an object the people universally wish to see affected. . . . [*moreover*] when any set of men grow rich and powerful they cannot be too strongly guarded against in a Republican government." [51] In time, the clergy too felt moved to join the chorus, and the Reverend Heman Humphrey of Pittsfield noted with disapproval: "It has been estimated that in 1816, the *law tax* of this county including costs of suits and loss of time in attending courts, amounted to about $110,000." [52]

By the 1820's the complaints against lawyers in Berkshire had ripened into demands for specific reforms. William Cullen Bryant, then a Great Barrington lawyer, made a determined but abortive attempt to bring about a change in the bar's restrictive rule regarding the appointment of justices of the peace. According to the practice then prevalent, any lawyer wanting to become eligible for appointment as a justice of the peace must first become a counselor of the Supreme Court—the attainment of which position required the payment of a not inconsiderable fee. After himself resigning as the town's justice of the peace, Bryant, in letters to Captain Pope and Colonel McKay of Great Barrington and to his friend and counselor Theodore Sedgwick, Jr., of Stockbridge, urged that this unfair system be done away with in order that such a deserving man as his friend Charles Leavenworth might be eligible.[53]

Actually, Bryant's reforming zeal seemed mild in comparison with the ambitious scheme of a group of North Adams merchants and manufacturers who joined forces in 1821 to form the "Patriotic and Economical Society." A kind of better business bureau seeking to exercise some of the powers

51. *Western Star,* Feb. 23, 1790.

52. Heman Humphrey, *Sermon Preached before the County Educational Society at Lenox,* Pittsfield, 1818.

53. William Cullen Bryant to Theodore Sedgwick, Jr., June 11, 1825; SP.

of the old-time guild, this society hoped to take over the arbitration of local business disputes and thus to cut off the lawyers' life blood. In the preamble to their constitution, they stated: "A community in which a spirit of litigation prevails, cannot be prosperous and happy; and whereas such a spirit does prevail in this county, and is nurtured and kept alive for the mercenary purpose of enriching a few professional and unproductive men . . . a recourse to law for the collection of debts greatly adds to the embarrassment." [54] The society did enjoy a modest success, but they were never able to make their authority absolute, and members could still turn to the courts as a last resort.

In the period after the 1820's, with a more complete integration into the state legal system, Berkshire lawyers began to broaden their horizons of legal and judicial criticism and commentary. Either they wrote on issues of state and national import, as did William Jarvis, John Leland, Asa Greene, and Theodore Sedgwick, Jr., or they actually left the County to make their marks on the national scene in the rôles of law reformers, scholars, and justices, as did Henry Dwight Sedgwick, Theodore Sedgwick, II, David Dudley Field, and Stephen J. Field. Almost all of them concentrated on two controversial questions which were giving rise to heated arguments throughout the country. What, they asked, should be the position of the judiciary in the government? And what reforms should be introduced into current legal practice? The first question attained national prominence as soon as Jefferson reached the presidency; the second, during the first years of Jacksonian Democracy.

As for the position of the judiciary in government, those two staunch Republicans John Bacon and Barnabas Bidwell quite naturally adopted Jefferson's own view that the judiciary—in which the Federalists had become well entrenched

54. Pittsfield *Sun,* Dec. 26, 1821.

—was guilty of usurping legislative functions. In an eloquent
speech before Congress in 1801 Bacon urged the repeal of the
Judiciary Act and resorted to a syllogism. Setting up new
courts and tearing down old ones, as in the Judiciary Act of
1801, must be, he maintained, either constitutional or unconstitutional. If the former, then abolition of the act must be
equally constitutional; if the latter, then the act ought to
be repealed without delay.[55]

Regardless of the fate of this Judiciary Act, however, the
question as to the extent of judicial powers remained; and
here no more thoughtful opinion ever came out of Berkshire
than that contained in William Jarvis' *The Republican,* published in 1820. Although fundamentally a Jeffersonian, Jarvis also espoused a certain rural conservatism and opposed
change merely for the sake of experiment: "old and familiar
customs and laws ought not to be wantonly changed, with a
view to some small, but speculative advantage. . . . age cre-
ates a respect for laws and ancient customs and usages are
cheerfully observed from habit . . . The house which has
sheltered us for a series of years from the storms of winter,
though low and humble, seems yet our home, although the
favors of fortune have advanced us to a fairer mansion." [56]

To this slightly sentimental preference for the tried and
true, Jarvis added a respect for the bench and indeed for the
whole judicial process which amounted almost to reverence;
and the result was an attitude toward the problem of judicial
powers hardly to have been expected from so prominent a
Republican. The judicial process, he asserted, could as easily
be corrupted from below by overweening democratic pretensions among the people as from above by executive usurpation. If real justice were to come out of the legal process, the

55. John Bacon, *On the Repeal of the Judiciary Act* (Boston, 1802),
p. 5.
56. William C. Jarvis, *Oration before the Washington Benevolent
Society, Pittsfield, Massachusetts, July 4, 1812* (Stockbridge, 1812), p. 15.

judges must be not only learned and upright but independent.

> . . . departure from the true intent and meaning of the laws . . . will necessarily occur, in every country, where the judges are dependent upon the sovereign, or people; and no guard can be interposed against their recurrence, so effectual, as the complete independence of judges during good behaviour.
>
> It is not however necessary to fall into one difficulty, in order to avoid another. It is not consonant to reason, that judges should hold their offices, after the infirmities of old age, have disqualified them for the execution of them; nor that they should be placed beyond the reach of impeachment, for corrupt conduct. It is only requisite, that so long as they continue to discharge their duty, with ability and integrity, they should be beyond the reach of party. Party ought to have nothing to do with them, in the course of their official duty, or they with party; they ought to stand as consecrated men around the altars of justice, to whom the injured may fly for redress, and the oppressed for relief.[57]

Convinced that judicial independence provided the best possible safeguard of the Constitution, Jarvis defended judicial review in words that sounded more like John Marshall than like a loyal Jeffersonian:

> . . . the importance of the Judicial authority, established by our constitutions . . . is as a check upon any unconstitutional exercise of power, by any other branches of the government.
>
> Fundamental laws would be useless, and worse than useless, if they might be disregarded or neglected, in the administration of the government: it is therefore within

57. Jarvis, *The Republican,* pp. 148–49.

the authority, delegated to our judicial tribunals, to
refuse to give effect to any unconstitutional laws or or-
dinances. The judicial authority, thus constituted, oper-
ates continually, to keep the administration of government true to its fundamental laws, and original principles.[58]

Jarvis' book elicited a letter of decided protest from Jefferson, who felt, quite understandably, that he was implying a
superiority of the judiciary to the other branches of government:

You seem . . . to consider the judges as the ultimate
arbiters of all constitutional questions; a very dangerous doctrine indeed, and one which would place us
under the despotism of an oligarchy. Our judges are as
honest as other men, and not more so. They have, with
others, the same passions for party, for power, and the
privilege of their corps. Their maxim is *"boni judicis est
ampliare jurisdictionem,"* and their power the more
dangerous as they are in office for life, and not responsible, as the other functionaries are, to the elective control. The constitution has erected no such single tri-
bunal, knowing that to whatever hands confided, with
the corruptions of time and party, its members would
become despots.[59]

Ultimate sovereignty, Jefferson insisted, must not be allowed
to reside in any one of the three branches of the government
but must be reserved to the people alone—a people educated
to meet their responsibilities. "When the legislative or executive functionaries act unconstitutionally, they are responsi-

58. Ibid., p. 84.
59. Jefferson to W. C. Jarvis, Sept. 28, 1820, *The Works of Thomas
Jefferson,* ed. Paul L. Ford (12 vols. New York, 1905), *12,* 162.

ble to the people in their elective capacity. The exemption of the judges from that is quite dangerous enough. I know no safe depository of the ultimate powers of the society but the people themselves; and if we think them not enlightened enough to exercise their control with a wholesome discretion, the remedy is not to take it from them, but to inform their discretion by education. This is the true corrective of abuses of constitutional power." [60]

Jarvis quickly disavowed any intention of preaching judicial supremacy, and while continuing to defend quietly the right of review, he went on to enunciate the doctrine of judicial restraint. In the exercise of control by the judiciary, he conceded, "great candour is necessary on the part of the judges; they never ought to be rash in questioning the doings of the legislative and executive branches of the government." [61]

Earlier, that other voluble Jeffersonian in Berkshire, John Leland, had gone on record with a far more radical Republican view. In a pamphlet entitled *An Elective Judiciary* (1805), he proclaimed emphatically that if the voters were to be regarded as too ignorant to choose their own judges, they must also be considered too ignorant to choose their own lawmakers and their own executive, and democracy itself must be merely a delusion. Once elected, the judge should, in Leland's opinion, enjoy life tenure as a means of guaranteeing impartiality. Still, he argued, the judges are only human, and even if the judiciary is supposed to serve as a check to save the people from a usurping legislature, "what check have they [*the people*] against the usurpation of the judiciary?" [62]

60. Ibid., p. 163.
61. To Thomas Jefferson, October 16, 1820, *Collections of the Massachusetts Historical Society*, 7th ser. *1*, 299–300.
62. Leland, *Writings*, p. 290.

At the same time that Leland was making his sweeping judgments of the situation, another Berkshire layman, Asa Greene, was beginning to publish in his *Berkshire American* equally inclusive and far more acid condemnations of the legal abuses going on around him. A deep desire to better the lot of the downtrodden and unfortunate prompted him to begin a series of editorials in 1827 in which he lashed out at the system of writs, delays of trials, debtors' prisons, public executions, and legal extortion. His peculiar contribution lay not in any originality of ideas—ideas in which many reformers had anticipated him—but in his bitingly sarcastic method of attack:

> 'Twas motion'd, and carried *nom. con.*
> That all these intentions
> And De'ilish inventions
> Should be skillfully mingled in one;
> And the ills, thus combin'd,
> From the bottomless pit
> Be sent up to mankind
> In the form of a WRIT! [63]

With all the fault-finding in the law then going on in Berkshire, however, it still remained for the lawyer members of the Sedgwick family to present the specific and constructive suggestions necessary to promote the actual reform of legal procedure. For sheer legal brilliance, no mind in that illustrious family ever equaled that of the eccentric and emotionally unstable Henry Dwight Sedgwick, second son of the old judge. Born in Stockbridge in 1785, he graduated from Williams in 1806 and was admitted to the Berkshire bar two years later. Then he moved on to New York to set up a law office with his brother Robert and never again returned to Stockbridge except for vacations and during periods of ill-

63. *Berkshire American*, Jan. 23, 1828.

ness. Unlike his father, he had never been an admirer of the English common law, and he was soon to become one of the sharpest critics of common law practices. Having grown up in Berkshire on the borderline between the legal practice of New York and that of Massachusetts, he had early developed a keen eye for their differences, but he could still be shocked by the greater intricacies of the New York practice over the relatively simple system with which he had dealt in Boston.

Eventually, his observations led him to write his most important pamphlet on law reform: *The English Practice.* Thoroughly convinced that lawyers had failed in the past and were destined always to fail in working for reformation from within, Sedgwick went over the heads of the gentlemen of the bar and appealed his case to the people. "I have," he explained, "long been deeply impressed with the opinion, that the practice of the common law of England as adopted . . . in the United States is not compatible with the spirit or character of the age . . . [*and that*] a remedy for the evil is not to be sought exclusively from the members of the legal profession, but that that subject is level to the comprehension of every intelligent man." Once the common man had understood the problem, Sedgwick believed that he could urge his representatives to take action and that "the ordinary powers of the legislature are competent to the regulation of the practice of the law." Quite well aware of the opposition his proposed reforms would encounter in legal circles with a vested interest in the intricacies of the law, he took the precaution of pointing out that a failure to produce reforms now would simply encourage already simmering resentments and that soon an exasperated faction harboring bitter feelings against all lawyers would force the enactment of reforms. What better reason, then, for an immediate extension throughout the United States of "the simple, direct system . . . which by way of distinction, I shall call the American

practice. . . . I have never heard any accusation preferred
against it, except the vague and general one, that it was loose,
and informal." [64]

Sedgwick's legal associates soon began to realize that this
young upstart colleague of theirs was advocating not an easy
and gradual modification of English practice but its complete
abolition. A comparatively inexperienced attorney was actually daring to assert that only superstitious veneration for useless past forms was keeping English practice alive in America.
Sedgwick took particular exception to a system in which
three out of the twelve days of Supreme Court sessions in
New York must be reserved for decisions on points of practice. Under the much-to-be-preferred American practice, he
said, "the rules and forms which respect the mere conduct of
suits are so few and so simple, that it may almost be said that
there is no practice; there is no such thing as a separate study
of practice. . . . A stranger might attend the whole of a
law term of the highest court of many states and very possibly
he would not once be reminded that there was any such thing
as a practice of law." [65]

Upon the publication of his treatise, Sedgwick found the
mail filled with letters of comment, many of them by no
means so unfavorable as he might have expected. Jared
Sparks considered it an agreeable expression of his own sentiments, but felt obliged to defer to the opinion of his lawyer
friends who feared that it might be fraught with dangerous
principles.[66] Thomas Cooper of South Carolina went much
further and gave his wholehearted approval to the proposed
reform—a reform which he felt would let the public "see that

64. Henry D. Sedgwick, *The English Practice. A Statement Showing
Some of the Evils and Absurdities of the Practice of the English Common Law, as Adopted in Several of the United States and Particularly
in the State of New York* (New York, 1822), pp. 3, 4, 34.

65. Ibid., p. 35.

66. Jared Sparks to Henry D. Sedgwick, Nov. 18, 1824; SP.

the law may be reduced to an intelligible science, which common sense need not be ashamed of." [67] The shrewdest comment, however, came from Sedgwick's brother-in-law, William Minot of Boston. While he was in complete sympathy with Sedgwick's aims, he warned prophetically that he must not expect too much and that "the history of almost every remedial statute proves that the minds of the learned judges are almost as inconstant as the popular will." [68]

Sedgwick's mental breakdown and early death came before he had realized his ambitious plans, but he had at least succeeded in planting the seeds of reform enthusiasm in two other forward-looking Berkshire lawyers. One of these was his energetic young clerk, David Dudley Field; the other was his own brother, Theodore Sedgwick, Jr. After listening to Henry's arguments, both had become actively aware of the many imperfections in current law practice. Although Theodore Sedgwick, Jr., never brought about or even instituted any concrete legal reforms, he made his contribution by transmitting both his reform enthusiasm and his knowledge of existent shortcomings to his many friends among the leading Democrats and to his son, Theodore Sedgwick, II. When failing health forced him to abandon his Albany law practice in 1822, he retired to the Sedgwick manse in Stockbridge and devoted his energies to the problems of economic, agricultural, and legal reform. Endowed with an enthusiastic, romantic temperament, he felt an extreme distaste for the petty routines of the law—a feeling which lay at the root of many of his reform ideas:

> Here I am [*He wrote to Henry in 1806*] . . . going through the daily drudgery of an office, without a thought and hardly a wish *"ultra crepidam"*— Truly a shoemaking business— . . . there is no true dignity of

67. Thomas Cooper to Henry D. Sedgwick (no date); SP.
68. William Minot to Henry D. Sedgwick, Feb. 5, 1822; MC.

mind or human greatness in it. In the presence of the
august Roman upon the rostrum, with grateful clients
at his feet, and a countless multitude of spectators hang-
ing upon his lips, how would these modern attornies
shrink. —Indeed the profession seems to have fallen
from its high estate. —From our best pleaders you hear
nothing but the monotonous cuckoo note of the conven-
ticle. —No man seems to dare to step out of the track of
his predecessors lest he should be laughed at by the dull
admirers of old form.[69]

Sedgwick's letters to his son reveal him not only as the reform lawyer but as the aristocrat, motivated by an almost pas-
sionate eagerness that the family tradition of distinguished
public service be perpetuated. In 1833, only a year after
Theodore the second's admission to the bar, he received from
his father a series of earnest letters concerned as much with
the prospective fame of the reformer as with the reforms
themselves. The gentlemen of the bar may revile a reformer,
admitted the senior Sedgwick, but a grateful populace will be
quick to elect him to high public office.

Actually, Theodore Sedgwick II, though an eminent
scholar of jurisprudence, carried the tradition of legal reform less noticeably forward than did his friend and contemporary David Dudley Field, Jr., who was to draw on similar
sources in becoming a major figure in nineteenth-century
American legal history.[70] Inspired in part by his Stockbridge
experiences and in part by the guidance of his unofficial legal
mentor, Theodore Sedgwick, Jr. (a Stockbridge resident from
1822 to 1839), Field undertook the Herculean task of codify-
ing the laws of New York State and thus of reducing somewhat the uncertainties of jurisprudence and bringing justice

69. Theodore Sedgwick, Jr. to Henry D. Sedgwick, Oct. 6, 1806; SP.
70. His work as counsel for Jim Fisk and Boss Tweed obviously de-
tracted a bit from his reputation as a reformer.

"within the reach of all men." He and Theodore Sedgwick, II, marked the end of a line of Berkshire lawyers who had, in the era of Thomas Allen, begun to make Berkshire a center of enthusiasm for legal reform.[71] All of them had felt a deep concern for increasing within, and later outside, the County the amount of substantial justice rendered by legal institutions; and their efforts to improve and simplify legal machinery reflected both the long-standing impatience of Berkshirites with legal technicalities and the Calvinist's concern for social justice.

Later, however, the Calvinistic strain was to reveal itself quite differently in the judicial career of Stephen, younger brother of David D. Field, Jr. Certainly when Stephen J. Field was sitting on the United States Supreme Court, one of the main sources of his power as a conservative lay in his tendency to equate law and morality.[72] Reared by a Stockbridge minister of sternly Calvinistic beliefs, he came quite logically to his conclusion that any legislative attack on laissez-faire was not only illegal and unconstitutional but also immoral. From the Slaughter House Cases in the 1870's to the Income Tax Case of the 1890's, he remained unswervingly a doctrinaire believer in the sanctity of property rights, and in many of the crucial cases he carried the majority of the court with him. As a rigid and forceful scion of rural Calvinism he could, in short, muster a strength which few liberals were able to match.

Perhaps it was this same quality of absolute certainty which had inspired all of Berkshire's outspoken criticism and commentary on the law for the hundred years past. From Thomas

71. Arthur Schlesinger, Jr., in his *The Age of Jackson,* sees Stockbridge as a center of reform, producing as it did an outstanding group of progressive minds in the persons of the Sedgwick brothers and David D. Field, Jr.—men of liberal tendency who helped give meaning to Jacksonian Democracy in legal affairs.

72. Carl B. Swisher, *Stephen J. Field, Craftsman of the Law* (New York, 1930), pp. 1–24.

Allen to Stephen J. Field, nearly every contributor to the
county's legal tradition had, after all, seen his analysis of
statute law as an accurate reflection of God's fundamental
law and thus had spoken from an incontrovertible sense of
righteousness. Committed to a religion that reduced all men
to sinners before the Great Judge and that acquitted or saved,
condemned or damned the whole race of men, the Berkshire
lawyer was understandably preoccupied with a legalistic approach to earthly life. The result was a tradition not necessarily remarkable for its innovations but very decidedly remarkable for its force.

## Chapter 9. NEW ENGLAND CHARACTER

WHEN Catharine Maria Sedgwick, at twenty-three, wrote to her brother from Boston to confess that "my heart clings to that interchange of domestic kindness which gives life and permanence to our affections," she was, in effect, expressing a cautious conservatism shared by a good many Berkshirites. Still somewhat cut off from Massachusetts even after sixty years, Berkshire had bred into its second generation of inhabitants an attachment to traditional cultural values as profound as that felt by their fathers, and the writing they did between 1810 and 1830 continually reflected their conservative outlook. The result was a regional literature strikingly original by comparison with the unimaginative Augustan phrases being composed to the east; and paradoxically, its authors came to be regarded as radicals because they were innovators. In the larger perspective, however, satirists like David Hitchcock and Asa Greene and regional novelists like Catharine Sedgwick—all drawing their inspiration from the grass roots—were declaring not only their faith in past values but their suspicion of cultural change; and if they appeared radical and even revolutionary, it was simply because Boston had long since sold out to a cosmopolitan, Europeanized literature. Within Berkshire this period of literary productivity actually marked the high point of cultural provincialism and led directly into the climactic Jubilee of 1844.

At first Berkshire showed little promise of fostering a respectable literary history outside the realm of theology. As in most other parts of the country in the late eighteenth century, the verses produced were at best mediocre, the essays sterile, and fiction virtually nonexistent. Nowhere in the County could the newspapers discover any verses more orig-

inal than the affected and colorless offerings of "Emily" or
any prose more inspired than the dry and mannered style of
the "Berkshire Sentimentalist." Loring Andrews might find
such productions "tolerable," but he must have recognized
with keen disappointment their essentially ephemeral and
derivative character. Berkshire writers remained for many
years enamored of the library shelf and of a long-dead English
tradition. A few of them, like the anonymous author of the
*Poem on the Wolf Hunt in Stockbridge,* caught glimpses of a
native imaginative literature, but most of them ignored the
promising literary materials close at hand—the realities of
nature and social life in the County. Then, in the early nineteenth century David Hitchcock, William Cullen Bryant,
Asa Greene, and Catharine Sedgwick began to write, and a
vigorous literary tradition gave promise of flourishing in
Berkshire.

As for those Berkshire poets of the early nineteenth century whose works never reached the printed page—Emanuel
Hodget of Great Barrington, who, Homer-like, sang his poetry in the streets, and Nathan Dillingham of Lee—almost
nothing remains of their work. Nathan Torrey, the peasant-
bard of Hinsdale, did, however, leave a few scattered hints
of his genius, and he must surely have been one of the most
intriguing of the oral poets. Combining an authentic folk-
song style with a natural and irreverent sense of humor, he
expanded upon religious themes with a levity which only
confirmed the orthodox in their tendency to regard poetry as
frivolous. When, in 1812, Reverend Ebenezer Jennings requested a verse for the dedication of the new Dalton meetinghouse (a structure with an unusually flat roof), Torrey
promptly obliged:

> Flat roof, tall steeple,
> Blind guide, ignorant people.[1]

1. Smith, *History of Berkshire, 1,* 650.

The sentiment would doubtless have been readily seconded by any Boston Unitarian. But Torrey's claim to immortality lay actually in his being credited with writing the *Elegy on the Young Man Bitten by a Rattlesnake*.[2] One of the most celebrated folk songs in all New England history and somewhat reminiscent in its rhythm and language of many of the folk songs of the southern Appalachians, its general tone is set in the first three stanzas:

> On Springfield mountains there did dwell
> A likely youth who was knowne full well
> Lieutenant Mirick onley sone
> A likely youth nigh twenty one
>
> One Friday morning he did go
> In to the medow and did moe
> A round or two then he did feal
> A pisin sarpent at his heal
>
> When he received his dedly wond
> he dropt his sithe a pon the ground
> And strate for home wase his intent
> Calling aloude stil as he went [3]

2. Although Torrey's authorship cannot be clearly established, one authority does say that "Nathan Torrey . . . has the honor of authorship, if any reliance can be placed upon the most direct and authentic tradition on the subject." Cf. Rufus P. Stebbins, *An Historical Address Delivered at the Centennial Celebration . . . of Wilbraham* (Boston, 1864), p. 206.

3. Ibid. The ballad was sung first to the stately tune of "Old Hundred" and then in 1840, provided with a rather gay tune, it was performed on the stage as a comic song: "The Pesky Sarpint that bit the Youth's Heel on Springfield Mountain." J. G. Holland could report in 1855 that "the versions of it are numberless." For a fine discussion of the evolution of the song from an elegy to a comic stage song, see Donald Davidson, "The Tradition of Irreverence," *Still Rebels, Still Yankees, and Other Essays* (Louisiana State University Press, 1957), pp. 105–27.

Sounding a more pious note than Nathan Torrey was
John Leland of Cheshire, whose numerous hymns revealed
a reverent simplicity assuring them widespread popularity. A
century later, when many churches found quite attractive
his neglect of theological doctrine and his emphasis on piety,
two of the best-known hymns were still sung, one of them
beginning "Through grace I am determined to conquer
though I die," [4] and the other the still more famous "Evening
Hymn":

> The day is past and gone
> The evening shades appear:
> O may we all remember well,
> The night of death draws near [5]

Whatever the views of the writers who came later—
whether with Leland they joined the pious majority or with
Torrey the impious minority; whether they chose the popular road of Jeffersonianism or the narrower path of Federalism—they wrote always with a practical purpose. Sometimes
they fixed their attentions exclusively on religion, sometimes
on politics, sometimes on social reform, but they were never
purely romancers, never solely entertainers. Indeed, a brief
acquaintance with Stockbridge citizens led the perceptive
Englishman, Basil Hall, to characterize all Americans as
"woefully ignorant of the difficult art of being gracefully
idle." [6] Still, they were not devoid of a sense of humor; in
fact, some of the Berkshire writers were born satirists. But
the members of their audience were almost all Calvinists and
Yankee farmers soberly intent on redeeming their time, and
any humor, they felt, must have a serious point.

It was partly because Great Barrington's cobbler-poet

4. W. Rowene Edgerton, *Favorite Hymns and Their Authors* (Pittsfield, 1907), p. 213.

5. Leland, *Writings*, p. 322.

6. Hall, *Travels in North America*, 2, 78.

David Hitchcock was trying so hard to appeal to this serious-minded side of the Berkshire outlook that he almost failed to realize his own poetic potentialities. Certainly his first ambitious venture into poetry revealed very little of the humorous, colloquial style he was later to develop. Too much impressed by his own wide range of reading—admittedly remarkable in a cobbler who had left school at the age of thirteen—and inclined to take himself rather seriously, he launched himself upon his literary career in 1805 with a ninety-seven page philosophical monologue grandiosely entitled *The Shade of Plato: or a Defence of Religion, Morality and Government,*[7] a title meant to impress even Bostonians.

Unfortunately, Hitchcock could never feel at home in abstract thought, and as a result, his diction rarely manages to be anything but stilted and unimaginative. *The Shade of Plato* reflects not a cobbler's earthy vision, but the mannered preachings of a would-be philosopher. Like many another amateur poet of his time, he chose Pope as his model for literary form. Though expressed in borrowed meters, his poem at times breathed a tone of urgency. His poverty and his struggle to support his family and to pay his debts bred in him both a deep concern over social and religious problems and a rankling resentment of college-trained men with their genteel learning and condescending airs. His Calvinist conscience was urging him to produce a serious philosophical exposition, and his yeoman's pride was prompting him to display to the snobbish intellectuals his knowledge and his talent. He was a Federalist and a Calvinist, not because the library shelves had directed him but because a chaotic ado-

7. David Hitchcock, *The Shade of Plato,* Hudson, N.Y., 1805. His later works were to include: *The Knight and the Quack,* Hudson, 1805; *A Poetical Dictionary,* Lenox, 1808; *The Social Monitor,* Stockbridge, 1812; *The Bond of Friendship* (address to Washington Benevolent Society), Stockbridge, 1812; *Christ Not the Minister of Sin,* Hartford, 1832.

lescence in Bethlehem, Connecticut, and a tragically insecure
young manhood in West Stockbridge and Great Barrington
had permanently convinced him that:

> All human beings, at the best,
> Of selfish motives are possest.[8]

Pope might complacently conclude that "Whatever is, is
right," but Hitchcock, with staunch "peasant conservatism"
and a firm spirit of Christian stoicism, which residence in
Berkshire did nothing to discourage, categorically rejected
such easy optimism. A pessimist through and through, he
despised the Utopianism of Rousseau and remained a true
son of Berkshire—clinging stubbornly to the orthodox theology of Edwards. With overtones of bitterness reminiscent
of *Piers Plowman* rather than of the smugness of Fisher
Ames, Hitchcock presented one of the most coherent and
forceful statements of a cynical conservatism to be made in
nineteenth-century Massachusetts.

The next six years were to bring a startling revolution in
his poetic method. He was to discover the artistic wisdom of
being himself and of writing in that easy conversational style
in which he felt so completely at home:

> We're harass'd both by day and night
>     With an insatiable *itch* to write;
> Which by the by if *critics* please,
>     Is quite a popular disease,
> And one which tasks their whole discretion
> To bound its dangerous progression
>
>         .    .    .    .    .
>
> And Masters of the learned school
> After they've spent their ridicule,
> And vainly lavish'd all their skill
> To keep us, *"hobbling authors"* still,

8. Hitchcock, *The Shade of Plato*, p. 101.

> As well may bear to hear us chatter
> On this, as any other matter.[9]

Here was the volume of poems which revealed Hitchcock at his best, writing with ill-concealed personal resentment alternating with periods of humorous detachment. He could never forget his innate dislike of the literati, but instead of defying their superiority by imitating their intellectuality, he could try to dismiss them in four derisively tolerant lines:

> . . . that dear *distinguish'd* few
> Who claim, as their inherent due,
> All merit, ministry, and money,
> Like *drones* that smuggle all the honey.[10]

Probably few beyond the Berkshire boundaries ever considered Hitchcock a good poet. His framework was too derivative and his vision far too limited. Yet he managed, nonetheless, to make a significant contribution to Berkshire's literary tradition and to demonstrate that American poets need not look back to England and to the eighteenth century for their inspiration—that they had more to gain poetically by talking in familiar language about familiar things. He was a poet of the common people and was not easily to be eclipsed in popular affection even by his eminent fellow townsman William Cullen Bryant.

Actually, Bryant remained always somewhat aloof from Berkshire social life. A lonely and detached figure in a Bostonian blue cloth suit, he plied his legal trade in Great Barrington with irreproachable efficiency but without enthusiasm and without warmth. Only two things about Berkshire met his wholehearted approval—the scenery and the Sedgwicks—and both were to influence him profoundly. Looking back later to the October day in 1816 when he first traveled down the Housatonic Valley to Great Barrington, he wrote:

9. Hitchcock, *The Social Monitor,* pp. 17–18.
10. Ibid., p. 58.

The woods were in all the glory of autumn, and I well remember, as I passed through Stockbridge, how much I was struck by the beauty of the smooth, green meadows, on the banks of that lovely river, which winds near the Sedgwick family mansion, the Housatonic, and whose gently-flowing waters seemed tinged with the gold and crimson of the trees that overhung them. I admired no less the contrast between this soft scene and the steep, craggy hills that overlooked it, clothed with their many-colored forests. I had never before seen the southern part of Berkshire and congratulated myself on becoming an inhabitant of so picturesque a region.[11]

Bryant had come to Berkshire that fall not so much from choice as from necessity. He would rather have settled in Boston and did not hesitate to say so, but he lacked the financial means for setting up a practice there, and George Ives' suggestion of a partnership in Great Barrington offered too much promise to be ignored. Probably predisposed to dislike the town, he drew his negative conclusions quickly. "This place is like most other villages in this country," he wrote impatiently to his father, "—there are not many who suffer an excessive passion for books to interfere with other employments or amusements, and they encumber their houses with no overgrown collections. This scarcity of books, indeed, occasions me much inconvenience after having been accustomed all my life to have access to very respectable libraries."[12] In reality, his quarrel was never with the physical aspects of Great Barrington. "The village," he recalled, "was then a quiet little place—two rows of scattered dwellings under the shadow of the great elms which almost met over the road."[13] But among the townspeople he missed the pres-

11. W. C. Bryant, "Reminiscences of Miss Sedgwick," *Life and Letters of Sedgwick*, p. 437.

12. Parke Godwin, *The Life and Works of William Cullen Bryant* (6 vols. New York, 1883), *I*, 153–54.

13. Bryant, "Reminiscences," pp. 439–40.

ence of kindred spirits, and he referred rather wistfully to a letter from Edward Channing as a "distant voice of kindness that cheers me in the pursuit of those studies which I have nobody here to share with me." [14]

Not until May 1820 and his meeting with Catharine Sedgwick did he find relief from his intellectual loneliness. Thirty years later he would have found Hawthorne and Melville, Longfellow and Holmes, but it was his fate to have come early to Berkshire as to American poetry—something of an anachronism in both. Yet, uneasy though he might be in his inadvertent role of pioneer, perhaps the fates were kinder than he thought. The Berkshire hills, after all, still possessed an isolation which Boston could not offer—and correspondingly an insulation from those British literary and philosophical influences which had so often engulfed the poets as well as the theologians of the seaboard. Just as Berkshire had led Boston in the development of the peculiarly American Edwardsean theology, so she was to lead in the creation of an American literature. Once there, Bryant was not to remain impervious to outside influences, and his response to the diverse beckonings of various Sedgwicks was soon to indicate that he could, on occasion, be influenced and led by people whom he liked and respected.

As for the citizens of Great Barrington, they influenced him virtually not at all. Annoyed by their interminable legal bickerings and exasperated by their provinciality, he came to dislike them almost as thoroughly as he disliked his chosen profession:

> my dislike for my profession was augmenting daily, [*he confessed to Dana after leaving Berkshire in 1825*] and my residence in Great Barrington, in consequence of innumerable quarrels and factions which were springing up every day among an extremely excitable and not very enlightened population, had become quite disagreeable

14. Godwin, *Life and Works, I,* 159.

to me. It cost me more pain and perplexity than it was worth to live on friendly terms with my neighbors; and, not having, as I flatter myself, any great taste for contention, I made up my mind to get out of it as soon as I could and come to this great city, where, if it was my lot to starve, I might starve peaceably and quietly.[15]

Not even the beautiful and literate Miss Frances Fairchild, whom he met and married in Great Barrington, could make either the people or the cultural milieu any more acceptable to him. He felt trapped in the town and in his profession by the force of economic necessity and ruefully recognized the truth of his old teacher William Baylies' remark that "Poetry is a commodity . . . not suited to the American market." [16]

On their side, the people of Great Barrington, who had done so much to encourage the poetic output of their own David Hitchcock, hardly even thought of Bryant as a poet. Until the publication of his first volume of poems in 1821, they regarded him simply as their competent but not very sympathetic legal mentor—an entertaining speaker at public gatherings and now and then a passable versifier, when the occasion demanded. Actually, they had no reason to dislike him. Knowing nothing of his dissatisfactions and frustrations, they could only judge him by his legal success and by his participation in local affairs. It was to his credit that he never

15. Letter of Bryant to Dana, May 25, 1825, ibid., p. 216.
16. Ibid., pp. 147–48. To this same William Baylies, his friend and law teacher he wrote in 1817: "Alas! sir, the Muse was my first love, and the remains of that passion, which is not *rooted out* nor chilled into extinction, will always, I fear, cause me to look coldly on the severe beauties of Themis. Yet I tame myself to its labors as well as I can, and have endeavored to discharge with punctuality and attention such of the duties of my profession as I am capable of performing. When I wrote you last I had a partner in business. He has relinquished it to me. I bought him out a few days ago for a mere trifle. The business of the office has hitherto been worth about ten or twelve hundred dollars a year." On the average, Bryant earned only two dollars apiece for his poems.

sulked or withdrew into an uncommunicative shell as he might have done and consequently never inspired either resentment or awe. Emanuel Hodget's jaunty remarks to him are proof enough of that. "Well, Squire Bryant," he observed airily, "they say you are a poet like me; is that so? I've never heerd any of your varses; would you like one of mine? Here goes!

> Squire Bryant is a man so bold
> He scorns to be controlled;
> And keeps his books under his arm,
> For fear they might be sold." [17]

Still, there were some of his fellow townsmen, even as early in the century as 1816, who were aware of the praise which "Thanatopsis" had gained from the Boston and New York critics; and these few joined with a larger number who respected his integrity as a lawyer to elect him tithing man in 1819 and town clerk a year later.[18] Bryant, in his turn, contributed with considerable generosity to Berkshire cultural life. The Great Barrington Bible Society heard him deliver an address on the political and social influences of the Bible in the world in 1818,[19] and so tactful was he that they scarcely had any awareness of his antagonistic Unitarian beliefs. Two years later the task of composing a Fourth of July speech, which almost always devolved upon a local lawyer, fell to him, and he complied with a refreshingly lucid and rational oration—one whose antislavery overtones were reminiscent of the sharpness of his early satires, "The Embargo" and "Gurgliolmes." [20] By this time, he was, according to Pitts-

17. Godwin, *Life and Works, 1,* 204.
18. In this same year he was also appointed to the respected post of justice of the peace.
19. *Berkshire Star,* Jan. 29, 1818.
20. *The Embargo,* written in 1809, was a satire on Jefferson's administration and his morality; "Gurgliolmes" (corruption of "Gulielmus"), never published, was an attack on Williams College, of whose alumni association he was later to become a devoted member.

field's minor rhymster, William Pitt Palmer, "already looked upon as a person of unusual literary attainments—one of the first botanists [21] of Berkshire, one of the best classical scholars in all Massachusetts, and a poet *facile princeps* on this side of the Atlantic." [22]

Only rarely, however, did Berkshirites ever catch a glimpse of the Bryant whom the rest of America was hailing as the country's first truly native poet. One of these brief glimpses came with his ode for the Agricultural Society Fair—a poem published in the Pittsfield *Sun* and unaccountably omitted from later collections:

> Since last our vales these rites admir'd,
>     Another year has come and flown,
> But, where her rosy steps retir'd,
>     Has left her gifts profusely strown.
>
> No killing frost on germ and flower,
>     To blast the hopes of spring, was nigh;
> No wrath condens'd the ceaseless shower,
>     Or seal'd the fountains of the sky.
>
> But kindly suns and gentle rains,
>     And liberal dews and airs of health,
> Rear'd the large harvest of the plains,
>     And nurs'd the meadow's fragrant wealth.
>
> As if the indulgent Power, who laid
>     On man the great command to toil,
> Well-pleased to see that law obey'd,
>     Had touch'd, in love, the teeming soil.

21. At least great opportunities were offered him in this field during his year at Williams, since he found there Professor Chester Dewey, one of the leading botanists of New England.

22. Godwin, *Life and Works, 1, 165.*

And here, while autumn wanders pale
    Beneath the fading forest shade,
Gather'd from many a height and vale,
    The bounties of the year are laid.

Here toil, whom oft the setting sun
    Has seen at his protracted task,
Demands the palm his patience won,
    And art has come his wreaths to ask.

Well may the hymn of victory flow,
    And mingle with the voice of mirth,
While here are spread the spoils that show.
    Our triumphs o'er reluctant earth.[23]

The more celebrated ode, "Far back in the ages," written for another agricultural fair five years later, nowhere so truly reveals either Bryant's genius or his characteristic view of God as a benevolent Being reflected in nature and at the same time far transcending it.

For Bryant the poet the everyday world of Great Barrington scarcely existed at all, and what seemed to Berkshirites a strange sort of detachment in his manner was actually a tendency to withdraw from the local scene and from the humdrum atmosphere of litigations. As an artist, only two worlds held permanent meaning for him: the world of the Boston literati who freely gave him the encouragement he needed and his own personal world of ethical and spiritual values. Had he found the human frailties and eccentricities which he encountered daily in the civil courts either deeply disturbing or highly diverting, he might have become a different kind of poet. Instead, he found them always dull and often deplorable and retreated from them into himself and into a

23. Pittsfield *Sun,* Oct. 14, 1818. Reprinted in Smith's *History of Pittsfield,* 2, 350–51.

contemplation of those natural beauties which the smallness of men could only accentuate.

From the moment of Richard Henry Dana's first surprised and jubilant reaction to "Thanatopsis," the literary world of Boston never ceased to urge Bryant on to further accomplishment. Willard-Philips, Channing, Allston, and Sparks soon joined their voices with Dana's, and through their various influences, the young poet eventually saw his works published in such eminently respectable periodicals as the *North American Review,* the *Idle Man,* and the *United States Literary Gazette.* By the end of 1821 he could already reflect pleasantly on the warm reception accorded his delivery of "The Ages" before the Phi Beta Kappas of Harvard, and he could hold in his hands his first published volume—a forty-four page collection of eight poems. Easily the most distinguished volume of poetry yet to appear in America, it included, besides "Thanatopsis" and "To a Waterfowl," two poems written after his coming to Berkshire: "Green River" and "The Ages."

The Berkshirites who read and admired Bryant's poetry may conceivably have felt moved to compliment themselves on having produced so accomplished an artist. Yet their direct influence on him was never anything but negative and seldom even that. The intrinsic quality of his work came from the quality of those inner resources which he had brought with him from Cummington and was to carry away with him to New York. Neither any individual in Berkshire nor any experience there seriously altered his fundamental beliefs in the beauties of nature and its power to heal, in God's unfailing benevolence, and in the mystery and kindliness of death. If Great Barrington had any artistic hold on Bryant, it was merely the fact of having produced in him a persistent and poetically fruitful tension between the fear of damnation by writs and briefs and the counteracting hope of salvation through communion with nature:

> Though forced to drudge for the dregs of men,
> And scrawl strange words with the barbarous pen,
> And mingle among the jostling crowd,
> Where the sons of strife are subtle and loud.—
> I often come to this quiet place,
> To breathe the airs that ruffle thy face,
> And gaze upon thee in silent dream,
> For in thy lonely and lovely stream
> An image of that calm life appears
> That won my heart in my greener years.[24]

Only rarely did Bryant ever allude so specifically to the legal calling which he had come to despise. Few of his other poems reflected this almost pathetic longing to escape the responsibilities and necessities which were binding him to Great Barrington and to the law:

> Yet, fair as thou art, thou shunnest to glide,
> Beautiful stream! by the village side;
> But windest away from the haunts of men,
> To quiet valley and shaded glen;
> And forest, and meadow, and slope of hill,
> Around thee, are lonely, lovely, and still.
>
> .    .    .    .    .
>
> And I envy thy stream, as it glides along
> Through its beautiful banks in a trance of song.[25]

Clearly localized though Bryant's references often were, however, he never altered the underlying convictions with which he had arrived in Berkshire. Both his life in Great Barrington and his strolls among the Berkshire hills simply served to reinforce an attachment to nature and a belief in its moral values already apparent in "To a Waterfowl." Po-

24. Bryant, "Green River," *Poetical Works of William Cullen Bryant,* ed. P. Godwin (2 vols. New York, 1883), *1*, 33.
25. Ibid., p. 32.

etry itself, he was convinced, derived its justification from the poet's perception of these values:

> Among the most remarkable of the influences of poetry is the exhibition of those analogies and correspondences which it beholds between the things of the moral and of the natural world. I refer to its adorning and illustrating each by the other—infusing a moral sentiment into natural objects, and bringing images of visible beauty and majesty to heighten the effect of moral sentiment. Thus it binds into one all the passages of human life and connects all the varieties of human feeling with the works of creation. Any one who will make the experiment for himself will see how exceedingly difficult it is to pervert this process into an excitement of the bad passions of the soul. There are a purity and innocence in the appearances of Nature that make them refuse to be allied to the suggestions of guilty emotion. We discern no sin in her grander operations and vicissitudes, and no lessons of immorality are to be learned from them, as there are from the examples of the world. They cannot be studied without inducing the love, if they fail of giving the habit, of virtue.[26]

Certainly Bryant never drew such ideas as these from the stern Calvinist atmosphere in Berkshire; but most probably that rigid spiritual tradition bolstered him in his refusal to go to the extreme of romantic pantheism. Intellectually he was only in part a Berkshirite. Yet, though he rejected the Calvinistic doctrines and the legalistic preoccupations that he found among the hills, he could never reject the hills themselves. To them he belonged wholeheartedly and would

26. Bryant, "On the Value and Uses of Poetry," in Godwin, *Life and Works, 5,* 19.

always turn instinctively for his poetry as long as he remained
in Great Barrington. In this sense, at least, he was a true son
of the Berkshire area, if not specifically of Berkshire County.
Born in Cummington, only four miles away from its eastern
boundary, he had grown up with New England beauty, and
the best, the freshest, the most American of his poems belong
to Berkshire. Although only twenty-nine when he left the
County behind, he was never to surpass the work he had already done.

To the Berkshire literary tradition he contributed with a
lavish generosity. His Berkshire poems are full of the beauties
that he felt and saw—from the evanescent light and color
captured in the lines of his "Autumn Woods" to the Byzantine splendor reflected in the hot and dazzling August world
of "Summer Wind." And from the fullness of his poetic
powers came "Monument Mountain":

> Thou who wouldst see the lovely and the wild
> Mingled in harmony on Nature's face,
> Ascend our rocky mountains. Let thy foot
> Fail not with weariness, for on their tops
> The beauty and majesty of earth,
> Spread wide beneath, shall make thee to forget
> The steep and toilsome way. There, as thou stand'st,
> The haunts of men below thee, and around
> The mountain-summits, thy expanding heart
> Shall feel a kindred with that loftier world
> To which thou art translated, and partake
> The enlargement of thy vision. Thou shalt look
> Upon the green and rolling forest-tops,
> And down into the secrets of the glens,
> And streams that with their bordering thickets strive
> To hide their windings. Thou shalt gaze, at once,
> Here on white villages, and tilth, and herds,

> And swarming roads, and there on solitudes
> That only hear the torrent, and the wind,
> And eagle's shriek.[27]

Occasionally, his Berkshire poems dealt with legendary Indian history, for Bryant, like Thoreau, saw in the Indians the nearest human approximation to the life of nature. Legends which the newspaper littérateurs of twenty years later were to treat with superficiality and bathos, he handled with a restraint, a sympathy, and a delicacy which no future travesties could obscure:

> Thus Maquon sings as he lightly walks
>     To the hunting-ground on the hills;
> 'Tis a song of his maid of the woods and rocks,
>     With her bright black eyes and long black locks,
>     And voice like the music of rills.
>
> He goes to the chase—but evil eyes
>     Are at watch in the thicker shades;
> For she was lovely that smiled on his sighs,
> And he bore, from a hundred lovers, his prize,
>     The flower of the forest maids.
>
> The boughs in the morning wind are stirred,
>     And the woods their song renew,
> With the early carol of many a bird,
> And the quickened tune of the streamlet heard
>     Where the hazels trickle with dew.[28]

Yet even during the years when he was writing the best of his poetry, his personal frustrations and his indecision as to

27. Bryant would have approved of Timothy Dwight's energetic Berkshire tour, which included an expedition to the top of Mount Greylock, but Dwight was able to find only five men in Williamstown who had climbed it.

28. Bryant, "An Indian Story." *Life and Works, 1,* 87–88.

the future were becoming increasingly evident. Without the sympathetic understanding of his wife and the friendly concern of the Sedgwicks, he must have lost his characteristic serenity. He was to recall later that the Sedgwicks "from the first, seemed to take a pleasure in being kind to me." [29] He might well have added that they were kind each in his own way. Either the Sedgwicks could not or did not try to come to any agreement as to what Bryant's future course should be, and the indecision within their ranks at first only seemed to add complexity to Bryant's own uncertainties. Catharine, of course, knew a genius when she met one and was convinced that whatever else he might choose to do, his poetry must come first. Charles, with less conviction, gently suggested that he continue his law practice; and Henry and Robert were determined that he should seek a more remunerative and practical literary career in New York. As for Theodore, he was content simply to guide Bryant to a study of politics and economics and to leave him to his own devices regarding the future.

Of the five Sedgwicks, Charles was the first to meet Bryant and to show him kindness, but it was the stronger-willed Catharine who first attempted to influence the artistic course of his life. "I remember very well," wrote Bryant, "the appearance of Miss Sedgwick at that period of her life. She was well-formed, slightly inclining to plumpness, with regular features, eyes beaming with benevolence, a pleasing smile, a soft voice, and gentle and captivating manners." [30] Miss Sedgwick's manner evidently captivated Bryant from the beginning of their acquaintance, and at her behest he obligingly wrote several hymns for the Unitarian hymnal shortly to be published in New York.[31] Thereafter, he was always to enjoy

29. Bryant, "Reminiscences," p. 438.
30. Ibid., p. 438.
31. These included: "Deem not that they are blest alone" and "When he who from the scourge of wrong."

her unfailing esteem—an esteem which she indicated un-
equivocally by dedicating to him her second novel, *Redwood.*
Eight years older than the youthful poet, she exhibited toward him the same benevolence and sincere delight in his
successes which she was to direct toward so many young writers in the years to come.

By 1823 she knew him well enough to sense his growing
indecision and to recognize his exasperation at his own inability to make a living by his pen; and thinking to find a
solution to his difficulties, she urged him to experiment in
the more economically profitable field of farce. Probably
Bryant suspected the outcome of such an unfamiliar undertaking, but snatching eagerly at any promise of escape from
the law, he set to work to produce his only satirical farce, "The
Heroes." [32] For a practical opinion as to its theatrical possibilities, he turned to Charles, whose knowledge of such matters he perhaps considered superior to Catharine's:

> the decision of this question must depend very much on
> the merits of the production. If it is not likely to suc-
> ceed on the stage my advice is to do nothing with it. I am
> really so doubtful of my abilities in the department.
> . . . I should be neither disappointed nor mortified in
> the least, therefore, I entreat you to lay aside all respect
> for the vanity of authorship, in making your decision—
> and all apprehensions of offending a sensitiveness in
> regard to their own works which afflicts most writers,
> and which I myself have my full share of in other in-
> stances but which in the present, I can assure you has
> no place. . . . But if, not merely from the intrinsic
> merit of the production but from other circumstances
> there is a good prospect—not a probable one merely but

32. A satire on the famous duel of the two southerners, Cumming
and McDuffie. G. M. Sedgwick to Henry D. Sedgwick, Feb. 15, 1823;
SP.

a pretty certain one that it will succeed on the stage—
then I would offer it to the manager of some theatre and
get it printed at the same time. If not likely to succeed
on the stage, it is not likely to succeed at all—for who
ever heard of such a thing as a closet farce.[33]

Both Charles and his brother Henry, reluctant as they must
have felt to disappoint their friend, decided that the play
could never become a stage success; and even Catharine had
to admit that "the author's forte is not in this way . . ."
But she added hopefully, "the last act is pretty good and it
may go down." [34]

A year later, with his unsuccessful comedy behind him,
Bryant had arrived at a more highly developed sense of his
own limitations and at last brought himself to reject once
and for all Dana's often-repeated request that he write a
long poem.

> As for setting myself about the great work you mention,
> [*he wrote to Dana in July*] I know you make the sug-
> gestion in great personal kindness toward myself, and I
> cannot sufficiently express my sense of that unwearied
> good-will which has more than once called my attention
> to this subject. But I feel reluctant to undertake such a
> thing for several reasons. In the first place, a project of
> that sort on my hands would be apt to make me ab-
> stracted, impatient of business, and forgetful of my pro-
> fessional engagements, and my literary experience has
> taught me that it is to my profession alone that I can
> look for the steady means of supplying the wants of the
> day. In the second place, I am lazy. In the third place, I
> am deterred by the difficulty of finding a proper sub-
> ject.[35]

33. W. C. Bryant to Charles Sedgwick, Feb. 12, 1823; SP.
34. To H. D. Sedgwick, Feb. 15, 1823; SP.
35. Godwin, *Life and Works, 1*, 195.

By 1825 Bryant could no longer postpone a decision; he must, he now knew, either reconcile himself for good to his legal drudgery in Great Barrington or turn resolutely in some other direction. Henry and Robert Sedgwick were urging him to come to New York as a magazine editor; Catharine was silent and uncertain; and Charles had just written one last wavering defense of the legal profession:

> My Dear Sir: I have thought a great deal of your project since court. The law is a hag, I know, wearing the wrinkled visage of antiquity, toward which you can feel no complacency. Though it comes to us fraught with the pretended wisdom of ages, it wears an ugly drapery of forms, and the principles of virtue and the simple perceptions of truth are so involved in clouds of mystical learning and nonsense that the finest mind must needs grope in obscurity and be clogged with difficulties. Besides, there are tricks in practice which perpetually provoke disgust. The end, indeed, may be good, and success certain, and eminence, too, but the process is perplexing, and the way not pleasant. I can not bear, however, to have you quit the profession, for many weighty personal reasons; and I feel a great interest that you should prove that your genius which delights the world can surmount the barriers of the least inviting and most laborious profession. Still I do not know how you ought to decide. If I had your mind and a very prevailing desire for literary occupations, I should run the hazard of indulging it.[36]

In January, describing himself as a "literary adventurer," Bryant traveled to New York for a visit, and there, at the homes of the Sedgwicks, met Cooper (who seemed "a little giddy with the great success his works have met with"),[37]

36. Ibid., p. 200.
37. Ibid., p. 189.

Gulian Verplanck (the first of the New York critics to echo Bostonian praise of Bryant's poetry), Robert C. Sands, Fitzgreene Halleck, and James Hillhouse. Here was the cultural atmosphere for which he had been longing ever since his arrival in Great Barrington eight years before; and when, largely through Henry Sedgwick's efforts, he was offered the position of co-editor on the New York *Review and Athenaeum Magazine* at a salary of $1,000, he hesitated only briefly.[38] In the spring of 1825 he put both the law and the Berkshire hills behind him for good and journeyed to the city. Berkshire had lost her finest poet, and New York was about to gain an editor of integrity whose future connection with the *Evening Post* was to prove one of the most fruitful in the annals of American journalism.

Meanwhile, in the early years of the nineteenth century, Berkshirites scarcely recognized the existence of any such genre as imaginative prose. The writers to whom they granted their attention and their approval were practical men like John Bacon, John Leland, William Jarvis, and Theodore Sedgwick, Jr.—writers with limited artistic and imaginative horizons but eminently equipped for straightforward expository composition and for a faithful reflection of the Berkshire mind. And Berkshirites asked for nothing more. They might expect a certain amount of frivolous preoccupation in their poets, but from their prose writers they expected and they accepted only serious and unadorned essays. Fiction, of course, they rejected categorically as a hopeless extravagance, and until Asa Greene and Catharine Sedgwick began to write in the 1820's, they found themselves left with little which even deserved the name of literature.

Not that Bacon or any of his ablest successors wrote without inspiration, but it was an inspiration stemming from intellectual convictions and not from imaginative enthusiasm.

38. Ibid., p. 215–16.

In their avid Republicanism, for example, both Bacon and
later Jarvis included far more than the sterile anti-Federalism
and the fruitless opposition to the rule of the "rich, the well-
born, and the able" which seems to have dominated some
of the Republican minds of Boston. They wrote with a
positive and lively belief stemming in part from their
thorough acceptance of physiocratic ideas and in part from
the belligerently sectional feeling of the frontier. Yet Bacon's
book, *Conjectures on Prophecies,* which he wrote in 1799,
merely proved to be an ingenious performance of that exercise so dear to back-country Calvinists—the elucidation of
the prophecies of Daniel and Ezekiel in the Old Testament.
A masterful interlocking of Jeffersonian politics and Calvinist religion, it was everything the Berkshire reading public
could have desired, and recorded much of their current
thinking. And if Leland's writing proved to be more popular,
it was certainly not because it was any less instructive. In
fact, he was conscientiously warning his countrymen of the
threat by monarchy men in the United States government
seeking to subvert the principles of the American Revolution.
Leland, however, could write with an easygoing, humorous,
philosophical flare which Bacon never possessed, and Berkshirites, in spite of themselves, liked to be entertained.[39]

With William Jarvis' *The Republican* came a return to
the expository style of Bacon. A treatise on the principles,
institutions, and policies of American Republican government, the book was truly a product of the Berkshire scene. It
reflected both the continuing demand for emphasis on things
religious and the economic beliefs then dominant in most
Berkshire minds. Not intending to be branded an infidel
by the conservative clergy, Jarvis laid aside his obvious political and economic preoccupations long enough to devote an

39. Apparently other farmers were revealing this same tendency,
since soon after their publication, the "Jack Nips" pamphlets were reprinted in Canandaigua, N.Y., and in Windsor and Brattleboro, Vt.

entire section to the necessity he recognized for the public worship of God, and he carefully balanced his citations of Pufendorf, Locke, and Burlemaqui with approving quotations from Paley and Timothy Dwight. Even more important, he gave explicit expression to the view popular among back-country farmers that the pursuit of agriculture must inevitably prove to be particularly favorable "to the freedom and independence of the human mind [*with*] . . . *a strong claim to preeminence over every other kind of industry*." [40] The book's literary significance, however, quite apart from its mirroring of the local mind, lies in Jarvis' brief allusion to the peril threatening American culture. Stating his fear that English literature might at once warp American patriotism and dominate native culture, he implied a hope that Americans might be quick to produce a cultural heritage of their own—a hope which two of his fellow-Berkshirites, Bryant and Catharine Sedgwick, were to be among the first to fulfill.

Meanwhile, Catharine's brother Theodore, Jr., was beginning to formulate his own ideas on the social implications of democracy and was soon to establish himself as the most distinguished of the Berkshire writers on practical affairs. In his *Hints to My Countrymen,* published in 1826, he set out not so much to reflect as to direct the thinking of the common man in Berkshire. Dedicating his book to the "good people of his native hills," he tried to write with simplicity but without condescension, and "as much of the book is intended for the plainer class of readers . . . I have taken the liberty to italicize many words." [41] The working man and the small farmer, he felt, must learn to hold up their heads, and to abandon all feelings of awe and inferiority—a conviction which he presented through the lively and discursive con-

40. Jarvis, *The Republican*, p. 196.
41. Theodore Sedgwick, Jr., *Hints to My Countrymen* (New York, 1826), p. v.

versations of a traveling bookseller. Again, in his more celebrated *Public and Private Economy,* he attempted "a popular work . . . written expressly for the people." Original in
method if not in thought, Sedgwick passed on to Americans
the ideas of the classical economists in the guise of stories and
case studies which quite successfully enlivened a science
which could easily become too abstract.[42]

Nearly ten years before Sedgwick published his second
book, however, another far more imaginative pen had begun to write in Berkshire. By this time, the center of literary
endeavor in the county had already begun to move north-
ward from Great Barrington to the central area of Stockbridge and Pittsfield, and now, with the appearance of Dr.
Asa Greene, northern Berkshire too could boast for a time a
literary son. Like Catharine Sedgwick, Dr. Greene longed to
expose the cant and the shams of men and institutions and to
show the way to improvements in education, in manners,
in the professions, and in literature. But not attracted by Miss
Sedgwick's moralistic tracts and often rather sentimental
novels, he confined himself, at least in his Berkshire period,
to satirical newspaper editorials and thus served a rigorous
apprenticeship for the novels he was to write after moving

42. Theodore Sedgwick, Jr., *Public and Private Economy,* New York,
1836–39. His brother-in-law, the conservative William Minot, called
it "a fine illustration of the nonsense of teaching science to the common
people by stories" (Theodore Sedgwick, Jr., *Dictionary of American
Biography*); Mark Hopkins wrote Sedgwick from Williamstown after
the appearance of the first volume congratulating him and expressing
the hope that he would treat monopoly carefully in the next volume
(M. Hopkins to T. Sedgwick, March 2, 1836, SP). Sedgwick had mentioned the feasibility of such a book in 1826; his debt to Harriet Martineau, whose *Illustrations of Political Economy* appeared 1832–34 and
was in some respects similar to his book, would be difficult to ascertain.
From the records of her visits to Stockbridge in 1834 and 1836 it would
appear that most of her contacts with the Sedgwick family were limited
to Catharine.

to New York City in 1830.[43] In his essays for the *Berkshire American* he anticipated the basic themes for both his fine satirical novel on foreign travelers in the United States and his later novel on quack doctors. Certainly his thorough knowledge of his subject and his deep but controlled feelings toward it gave him all the equipment he needed to become a shrewd and competent satirist of the Berkshire scene.

One other Berkshire author had long since anticipated Greene, and that was David Hitchcock. Very probably, however, those two masters of acid social commentary never met. Hitchcock had plied his poet's trade in southern Berkshire more than ten years before Dr. Greene began publication of his *Berkshire American,* and after *The Social Monitor* in 1812 he produced almost nothing. And although both men fixed a keenly critical gaze on many aspects of the daily life going on around them and both chose satire to express their dissatisfactions, their meeting might well have resulted only in a clash of personalities. Dr. Greene was to write with the clear and objective, if not always unemotional, outlook of the reformer motivated by principle; Hitchcock had written with the often clouded and egocentric vision of the yeoman motivated by a strong sense of personal grievance. They frequently found fault with the same men and the same institutions, but their reactions invariably reflected the difference in their viewpoints.

Fresh from a thorough medical training at the Berkshire Medical Institution, Greene approached the ailments of Berkshire with the clinical attitude of a conscientious physician. He was the sympathetic but clear-sighted country doc-

43. Works of Asa Greene: *The Life and Adventures of Dr. Dodimus Duckworth A.N.Q.,* 1833; *Perils of Pearl Street,* 1834; *A Yankee among the Nullifiers,* 1835; *Travels in America by George Fibbleton, Exbarber to His Majesty the King of Great Britain,* 1835; *A Glance at New York,* 1837; *Debtor's Prison,* 1837.

tor, disturbed by contemporary symptoms of stupidity, hypocrisy, and decay and determined at least to discover the cause if he could not always provide the cure. Because he belonged wholeheartedly to the life of the County, he often wrote more acidly and felt more deeply than did that other physician-littérateur, Dr. Oliver Wendell Holmes, who followed him to Berkshire. As compared with Holmes' hearty manner, Greene's satire seemed heavier, less genial, and notably freer of sentimentality, and he wrote with a more obvious intention of effecting reforms.

No one, not even Catharine Sedgwick, ever took a more encyclopedic view of Berkshire society. Public executions, the militia, quack doctors, local idiosyncrasies of speech, schools, theatricals, stage coach facilities—all these and more appeared in the columns of the *Berkshire American,* where their faults were reduced to absurdity or subjected to relentless and unsmiling castigation. Never a man to be easily intimidated by public opinion, he dared to poke fun even at the sacred subject of politics:

> "Hurra for Jackson . . . he's the man for me; I'll vote for him through thick and thin." "Vote for him!" said another, "what that tarnal ragamuffin, that fout thirteen duels, and hanged Packenham and Gibson! Why, I'd sooner vote for my old hoss. I'm for John Squincy Adams and the 'merican system of infernal improvements.[44]

Nor did the school system escape any more easily. Although subjected to criticism from many sources, it probably suffered the most under Greene's humiliatingly humorous picture of a typical teacher examining board:

> Rev. Mr. Longwind. Mr. Teacher, what portion of mankind are foredained to be saved?

44. *Berkshire American,* Mar. 19, 1828.

Teacher. All who conduct themselves in a Christian manner.

Deacon Pitchpipe. How *many* mollases will it take to keep thanksgiving in the whole *state* of New England?

Teacher. That depends on the number of pumpkin-heads.

'Squire Round. Which is the most properest way of speaking—to say, "I *in*spect," or "I *ex*pect?"

Teacher. That depends on whether it be a matter of inspection or expectation.

Dr. Liver. Which of the *Western* States is *Feladelfa* in?

Teacher. It is in one of the Middle States.[45]

Behind nearly all of Greene's satirical thrusts lay a sincere desire either to raise the standards of professional men and expose imposters or to encourage a realistic view of those local institutions too often accepted as sacrosanct. Scorning genteel traditions and the pretensions to aristocracy so prevalent among the well-to-do, he published a scathing commentary on the would-be village Chesterfields:

*Etiquette* is the daughter of *Folly,* who gave her in marriage to *Wealth,* with whom she has lived in a pretty tolerable degree of harmony for several hundred years. . . . She is not only to be found at the seat of government, and in the large cities of our country, but she presides in our small towns and villages, and takes special pleasure in making her *country* subjects as ridiculous as possible. She delights in turning them into monkeys, that she may see them ape the empty ceremonies and vexatious formalities of the most empty-headed of her citizen subjects. . . . If she finds a man, who like a mushroom, has suddenly grown high from his native dunghill, she causes him to put on a variety of ridiculous airs; one of which is, to hold up his chin as high as

45. Ibid., Nov. 21, 1827.

the tops of his neighbors' heads; another is, to deal out his attentions to his fellow-mortals in the direct proportion to the number of dollars they happen to have in their pockets. . . . Etiquette has been for a long time at war with *Nature,* and with various success. But wherever she has carried the day, she takes pleasure in making her tributaries uncomfortable. She lays a perpetual embargo on the enjoyments of *social life,* and causes the intercourse of friends and neighbors to evaporate in cold form and empty ceremony.[46]

Then, abruptly abandoning his comic style, Greene addressed the common man with a straightforward earnestness closely akin to that of his enthusiastic colleague, Theodore Sedgwick, Jr.:

If the dignity of things may be measured by their importance to mankind, there is nothing, perhaps, which can rank above the mechanic arts. In fact, they may be called the lever, the fulcrum, and the power which move the world. They do not want the *"whereon to stand"* of Archimedes; they have a sufficient foundation in themselves. What gives to civilized nations their superiority over the savage? It is, chiefly, mechanic arts. By them the beautiful and convenient mansion is substituted for the rude and uncomfortable wigwam; and scarlet and fine twined linen supply the wardrobe, in place of the skins of wild animals. They are the foundation of nearly all the improvements and the comforts of life— and further, we may say, of the glory and the grandeur of the world. . . . There is a philosophy in mechanic arts— The mechanic who brings to his occupation an inventive, enlightened and inquiring mind, who is master of his craft in theory as well as practice, has more of real philosophy in him than twenty of those "minute

46. Ibid., Apr. 27, 1826.

philosophers," who spend their lives in puzzling the
world with empty metaphysical speculations . . .[47]

On such rare occasions as this the satirist in Greene gave
way to the earnest reformer. An artist of integrity and
taste, he could never bring himself to treat with humor the
issues about which he felt most deeply. When he became
angry, he wrote angrily, without regard for his own popularity, and no spectacle ever aroused in him such disgust as
a public execution. "If life must be taken," he wrote, "there
could not in our opinion, be a worse mode devised than that
of public execution . . . it tends to harden the heart and
render the spectator himself more likely to commit murder." [48] And again, a year later: "It is a vile taste that leads
people to such shocking sights; it is evidence of a low degraded state of feeling—or rather we should say, of a lamenta-
ble want of feeling." [49] That the hypocritical people of
Berkshire could shamelessly attend such spectacles and then,
in the name of morals and religion, could conduct demonstrations against innocent theatricals like the one staged in
North Adams in 1827, Greene found hard either to explain
or to excuse.[50]

By the year 1828 Berkshire's doctor-editor had emerged
as the most articulate custodian of local tastes and mores. In
an age deeply committed to sentiment and romance, he was
daring to experiment even more boldly than had Hitchcock
with realistic subject matter, with a breezy colloquial style,
and with ironical conversational sketches sharply alive to
the hypocrisies, the absurdities, and the humor of contemporary American life. For his novel, *The Life and Adventures of Dr. Doddimus Duckworth,* which he was to write
five years after leaving Berkshire, he had already planted the

47. Ibid., Oct. 24, 1827.
48. Ibid., Nov. 16, 1826.
49. Ibid., Aug. 29, 1827.
50. Ibid., Aug. 8, 1827.

seed in his merciless Dr. Coppernose sketches for the *American:*

### Doctor Coppernose.

Scene—a country tavern—enter Doctor Coppernose, with his face bloated, and his nose looking blue.

Q. Good morning, Doctor? How is Mrs. Asthmatic?

Doct. Much better since I had the management of her —her cough has decided, her appetite has retrograded, and she is fast progressing to—

Q. The other world, I dare say—was the man much hurt that fell from his horse yesterday?

Doct. O most destructively! The knuckle-bone of the whirl-joint was dislocked, the cap of the shoulder was onslipped, the ankle-bone discharged on both sides, and the esophagus broke and much comminated. . . .[51]

Himself a determined realist, Dr. Greene could find little sympathy for the current sentimentality then dominating the writing of so many American novelists. With tongue in cheek, he offered his own recipe for a successful novel: "Wreck a ship, or overturn a coach. Let there be an interesting young woman with a child in her arms, saved from the perils . . . [*the child grows up as the*] beautiful Julietta, or Amoretta, or Heavenlietta, or whatever name you have selected for her . . . and the nobleman Lord Tenderheart falls in love with her. . . . Mix in a considerable quantity of honey and sugar . . . and garnish with Zephyr's wings and cupid's darts." [52] If the sometimes uncharitable Dr. Greene was thinking of Catharine Sedgwick as he wrote this invective against rampant romanticism,[53] then certainly his critical insight this time partially failed him. Perhaps Miss

51. Ibid., Dec. 21, 1826.
52. Ibid., Oct. 26, 1826.
53. Greene's plot does run parallel to Miss Sedgwick's *Redwood* at several points.

Sedgwick did, at her worst, succumb to the faults of romanticism and sentimentality, but at her best she had already surpassed Greene himself in a realistic portrayal of Berkshire life, and even as he was acknowledging the failure of his journalistic career, she was enjoying both the acclaim of Berkshirites and the applause of Bostonians and New Yorkers.

In fact, the youthful Asa Greene had just begun his medical studies when, in 1822, Catharine Sedgwick self-consciously presented to the literary world her first and, in point of originality, her best novel, *A New England Tale,* and thus gave promise of becoming the most famous member of a distinguished generation of Sedgwicks. Much to her own surprise, she found herself suddenly sharing with the already eminent Bryant an enviable position among the true pioneers in the creation of a native American literature— a position which she had achieved, as Bryant generously pointed out, "without asking . . . permission from the critics of Great Britain." [54] And until 1863, when the sophistications of New York at last drew her away from Berkshire forever, she spent more than half of every year in residence there and reigned with enthusiasm and warmth over the lively literary culture of the county.

Unlike Bryant, Miss Sedgwick was to come to literature more through the accident of circumstances than through any unquiet voice of genius within herself. Had she accepted the "noble" Mr. B.'s proposal of marriage in 1819, she might well have been content to retire into a complacent and literarily unproductive life of domestic felicity. Instead, she chose to remain single,[55] perhaps fearing that no husband could ever replace her incomparable brothers and that no family life could approach that domestic golden age of her own girlhood in Stockbridge. Born in 1789, the third child

54. Bryant, "Reminiscences," p. 443.
55. *Life and Letters of Sedgwick,* p. 108.

in a family of four boys and four girls, Catharine had shared
in an atmosphere of pure joy which reminiscences made increasingly idyllic with every passing year:

> I was reared in an atmosphere of high intelligence. My
> father had uncommon mental vigor. So had my brothers.
> Their daily habits, and pursuits, and pleasures were
> intellectual, and I naturally imbibed from them a kin-
> dred taste. Their "talk was *not* of beeves," nor of mak-
> ing money; that now universal passion had not entered
> into men and possessed them as it does now, or, if it had,
> it was not in the sanctuary of our home—there the
> money-changers did not come. My father was richer
> than his neighbors. His income supplied abundantly
> the wants of a very careless family and an unmeasured
> hospitality, but nothing was ever given to mere style,
> and nothing was wasted on vices.[56]

Her father, whom she idolized, died in 1813, and then one
by one she watched her sisters and brothers marry and leave
Stockbridge. The last to go was Robert, and it was perhaps
no coincidence that the year of his marriage was also the
year of *A New England Tale*.[57] Having already anticipated
Robert's future plans, Catharine was fortifying herself against
her prospective loneliness. Although she was to make her
home with one or another of her brothers as long as they
lived, the loneliness was already beginning. "Charles is constantly at Lenox," she wrote to Robert in the summer of
1821, "and seldom comes home at night. . . . this place is
dreadfully changed without him. I have never felt so oppressed by the changes in our family. The house is so still and
solitary. My imagination is continually filled with those

56. Ibid., pp. 46–47.
57. Ibid., p. 95.

looks and voices that animated every part of the house—that beamed with love and rung with joy." [58]

Earlier in that same year Catharine had at last arrived at a long-considered decision to leave the Congregational Church for Unitarianism and thus to bring voluntarily upon herself a spiritual solitude in the midst of Berkshire orthodoxy. Her own happy family life had long since prompted her to categorize the main doctrines of the orthodox clerics with "the misanthropic sayings of all the old bachelors and cynics," [59] and her father's deathbed confession to Dr. Channing of his firm if unpublicized preference for liberal Christianity had undoubtedly affected her profoundly. The final impulse toward open rebellion, however, came not from the Stockbridge clerics West and Field but from the narrow and aggressive Calvinistic preachings of her New York pastor, Dr. Mason. A voluminous correspondence ensued, some of it addressed to Dr. Channing and Mrs. Frank Channing and some to brothers Henry and Theodore; and later, out of her new-found spiritual release from the severities of Calvinism and more specifically from Theodore's suggestion that she take up writing, came *A New England Tale*.

First conceived as a short story to be used as a tract by the Unitarian Society, the novel grew from Henry's insistence that Catharine expand her original manuscript into a more ambitious undertaking. Eager for a time-consuming occupation and always ready to accept the counselings of any of her brothers, Catharine willingly took up her pen once more, this time not only to serve the cause of "human virtue and improvement" but "to add something to the scanty stock of

58. Ibid., p. 121. And for some Calvinists the loneliness of the Unitarian Catharine would extend to the next world. One of her aunts said, "Come and see me as often as you can, dear, for you know, after this world, we shall never meet again" (p. 157).

59. Ibid., p. 90.

native American literature. . . . [*by rendering*] some
sketches of the character and manners of our own country." [60] This secondary purpose she made clear in the sub-
title of her work: *A New England Tale, or Sketches of New
England Character and Manners*. She dedicated her book to
the English writer Maria Edgeworth, in recognition of "her
eminent services in the great cause of Human Virtue and
Improvement," and, like her English model, she was destined
to begin as a novelist of local color and to end as a moralist.

*A New England Tale* was a novel which Berkshirites and
puritanical New Englanders everywhere could read with a
clear conscience—a novel whose moralistic purpose shone
through on nearly every page. People who had never read
any novel before found Catharine Sedgwick's instructive
paragraphs thoroughly worth while, and the ranks of the
novel-reading public swelled noticeably. No heroine capable
of uttering such unimpeachable sentiments as did Jane Elton
could have offended even the sternest conscience:

> When I first heard you trifle with the obligations of re-
> ligion, and express a distrust of its truths, I felt my heart
> chill. I reproached myself bitterly for having looked on
> your insensibility on this subject as the common care-
> lessness of a gay young man, to be expected, and for-
> given, and easily cured. These few short months have
> taught me much; have taught me, Erskine, not that
> religion is the only sure foundation of virtue—that I
> knew before—but they have taught me, that religion
> alone can produce unity of spirit; alone can resist the
> cares, the disappointments, the tempests of life; that it
> is the only indissoluble bond—for when the silver cord
> is loosed, this bond becomes immortal.[61]

60. Sedgwick, *A New England Tale*, introduction.
61. Ibid., p. 222.

This is not to imply that Catharine Sedgwick's moral emphasis offered anything new to the novel. Nor had Maria Edgworth ever ranked as an innovator. The eighteenth century had seen discussions of virtue even as far back as Defoe and Richardson, and if Miss Sedgwick found the early nineteenth-century American public unusually receptive to her novel, it was probably because she had spared no pains to point up the moral. Without the liberal theological teachings, the novel itself would disappear; anti-Calvinism was the very core of the book. Jane Elton, in fact, never became anything more than a rather uninteresting symbol of Miss Sedgwick's liberal theology. She was completely good and Mr. Lloyd was completely good; Mrs. Wilson and Elvira were completely bad. The tale, in Miss Sedgwick's unpracticed hands, proceeded jerkily and virtually without drama. No reader could have experienced any great surprise when Jane Elton and the middle-aged Mr. Lloyd at last found their happiness together, and when Aunt Wilson's hypocritical Calvinism drove her to misery and to the edge of insanity. A caricature of Calvinism, Mrs. Wilson was the villain of the piece, self-righteously denying the necessity for good works and herself pursuing a line of conduct worldly in the extreme.

None of the critical reviews of *A New England Tale* found anything to praise in Miss Sedgwick's handling of her theological theme. Indeed, even the Unitarian periodical *The Christian Disciple* reprimanded her for having gone too far in her anti-Calvinist crusade and for having sacrificed philosophy to pamphleteering. Dismayed by such a reaction to her moralizings, Catharine hastened to her own defense. Had she not, after all, kept sectarian spirit to a minimum in her book by making the hero not a Unitarian but a Quaker? In fact, as she wrote to Theodore, "except for a single slap at *total depravity*, there is no condemnation of doctrines, but only of their abuse in individuals. There is no Unitarianism, not a pint of it. . . . My principal male character is a quaker. My heroine a simple Bibleist—the founder perhaps of a new sect for there is no mention of her creed—unless by inference you might get at her faith from her works." [62]

Perhaps the real credit for Catharine's early success should go to Henry, whose suggestion it was that the original Unitarian tract be expanded into a novel. Admittedly, that suggestion may have led Catharine into many novelistic clichés. But it may very probably have led her, too, toward that realistic handling of the natural and the social setting from which the book derives its strength. There are evidences of uncharacteristic sentimentality; there is a welter of unrelated and unjustified subplot; and there is one entirely gratuitous scene of Gothic horror—all of which must indicate Catharine's abortive effort to dignify her short story with appropriate novelistic trimmings. Yet none of these labored departures ever obscures her ability to convey the feeling of solidarity and to imply the essential worth of the Berkshire villagers of "Greenwood"—and, by implication, of New England civilization as a whole. Indeed, her incidental social sketches still ring with charm and authenticity. Of the militia drill she wrote with a humorous appreciation of omnipresent New England thrift:

> The village tavern was in full view, and within a short distance, and the company was performing some marching evolutions a little beyond. An election of captain had just taken place; and the suffrages of the citizen soldiers had fallen upon a popular favorite, who had taken his station as commanding officer, and was showing his familiarity with the marches and counter-marches of Eaton's Manual. He had been just promoted from the

62. To Theodore Sedgwick, Jr., Mar. 29, 1822; SP.

rank of first lieutenant; and previous to the dismissal
of his men, which was about to take place, he drew them
up in front of the village store, when, according to custom, and with due regard to economy, which made the
store a more eligible place for his purposes than the
tavern, he testified his gratitude for the honour which
had been done him by copious libations of cherry rum,
and of St. Croix, which was diluted or not, according to
the taste of each individual. The men soon began to
grow merry . . .[63]

With customary brotherly solicitude, Henry handled the
details of publication, and by May he could report with satisfaction: "Bliss White has increased orders from booksellers.
. . . Bliss says the only difficulty with the book is the unfavorable representation of the New England character, and
that the writer must bring out something of the same kind
in which this mistake is corrected. I think he is right. . . .
The title (though taking) is certainly unlucky; that's my
fault. The orthodox do all they can to put it down." [64]

Taking such criticisms to heart but secure in the knowledge of her literary success, Miss Sedgwick wrote her second
novel, *Redwood,* with less regard for moral lessons and
more attention to a loving study of New England character.
With *A New England Tale* safely tucked away on the select
shelf once reserved for Cooper and Irving, Catharine at
thirty-four was feeling quite competent to formulate her
own theory of fiction, the peculiar province of which, she
had decided, must be "to denote the passing character and
manners of the present time and place. . . . We live in a

63. Sedgwick, *A New England Tale,* pp. 243–44.
64. H. D. Sedgwick to C. M. Sedgwick, May 25, 1822. *Life and Letters
of Sedgwick,* pp. 152–53. The transplanted Berkshirite Ezekiel Bacon
wrote Henry requesting twenty-five copies for sale in Utica, New York,
in 1822, and the demand for the book was sufficient to make the publishers print a new edition as late as 1852.

country which is, beyond parallel, free, happy, and abundant. As such we would describe it—but as no Arcadia, for we have found none. We have indeed little sympathy with that narrow-minded patriotism which claims honors that are not yet merited." [65]

Actually, the title of Catharine's first novel, to which orthodox New Englanders so indignantly took exception, might have been better applied to her second. In *Redwood* the meanness and hypocrisy of latter-day Puritanism found no place; the aggressive anti-Calvinism was abandoned. Catharine could not resist a mild reference to the obscurantism of the Shakers and the restlessness of infidels, but so minor a position did she assign such topics that they hardly interfered at all with the mellow portrait of New England she was drawing.

Those who had taken the anti-Calvinism of her first book to be a wholesale condemnation of New England civilization could get no such impression from *Redwood*. Still critical of abuses, she nevertheless allowed her deep veneration for New England to shine through more clearly; and if the vestiges of romance and sentimentality remained to plague her, she reached far beyond them in her inspired creation of Miss Debby Lenox, one of New England's most admirable fictional spinsters. Blunt to the point of rudeness, scorning the niceties of toilette, and speaking always with a humor born of complete independence of mind, Miss Debby was in some respects reminiscent of Emerson's Aunt Mary Moody and was beyond a doubt the most memorable of all Catharine's characters.

Many of her critics, Bryant among them, could readily forgive the shortcomings of the plot. A poor frame could not spoil a good picture; and scarcely anyone denied that Catharine's picture of New England was a good one. Bryant, in fact, considered her portrayal both noble and humorous—

65. C. M. Sedgwick, *Redwood* (New York, 1824), p. ix.

and in both ways a welcome relief from spread-eagled nationalism and the romanticizing of the noble yeoman.

Probably Catharine never realized the debt she owed
Bryant. Requested by Jared Sparks to review *Redwood* for
the *North American Review,* he had at first demurred. Miss
Sedgwick, after all, had dedicated her book to him, and he
could scarcely repay her kindness with an unkind critique.
Determined, however, that the book should be noticed in
this the most respected literary journal of the day,[66] he finally
agreed, on condition that the review remain anonymous.
Then, with characteristic restraint and without ever sac-
rificing his integrity, he wrote:

> The peculiarities in the manners and character of our
> countrymen, have too long been connected with ideas
> merely low and ludicrous. We complain of our English
> neighbors for holding them up as objects simply ridicu-
> lous and laughable, but it is by no means certain that
> we have not encouraged them by our example. It is
> time, however, that they were redeemed from these gross
> and degrading associations. It is time that they should be
> mentioned, as they deserve to be, with something else
> than a sneer, and that a feeling of respect should mingle
> with the smile they occasion. We are happy to see the
> author of this work connecting them, as we find them
> connected in real life, with much that is ennobling and
> elevated, with traits of sagacity, benevolence, moral cour-
> age and magnanimity. These are qualities, which by no
> means impair any comic effect those peculiarities may
> have; they rather relieve and heighten it. They trans-
> form it from mere buffoonery to the finest humor. When
> this is done, something is done to exalt our national

66. W. C. Bryant to Jared Sparks, Oct. 23, 1824, Sparks Collection,
Harvard. *A New England Tale,* because of its controversial theology,
had been skipped over by all the reviews.

reputation abroad, and to improve our national character at home. It is also a sort of public benefit, to show
what copious and valuable materials the private lives
and daily habits of our countrymen offer to the writer
of genius. It is as if one were to discover to us rich ores
and gems lying in the common earth about us.[67]

The American public shared Bryant's appreciation of the
genuine local color in Catharine Sedgwick's novels, but their
enthusiasm may well have been equally aroused by the tone
of uplift for which they felt a personal attraction. "How
noble a trait," wrote Emerson, "does Miss Sedgwick draw in
her Mrs. Hyde, when Lucy Lee says, 'It makes people civil to
speak to her.' How we glow over these novels! How we drivel
and calculate and shuffle and lie and skulk in real life!" [68]

By late summer of 1824 Catharine Sedgwick's name had
risen nearly to the height of Bryant's on the contemporary
roster of fame; and like Bryant, although much less consciously, she had ended her first and best period of literary
creativity. In August brother Harry wrote to reassure her
of the satisfactory sales of *Redwood* in New York.[69] The book
was already being reprinted in England and translated into
Italian, Swedish, German, and French, and some readers
of the anonymous Paris version were even attributing its
authorship to Cooper. Cooper can hardly have been pleased
by such gratuitous recognition, but Catharine still remained
modest enough to feel flattered. Actually, the flattery was
only beginning, and she was soon to find herself sought out
by a number of visiting Europeans. Begun by Basil Hall in
1827, these pilgrimages to Stockbridge were to continue as

67. Review of *Redwood,* in the *North American Review, 20* (1825),
271–72. The book was reviewed rather less favorably by Professor
Everett in the Boston press.

68. Emerson, *Journals, 4,* 458.

69. *Life and Letters of Sedgwick,* p. 168.

long as Catharine chose to make her summer residence there and were destined to raise Berkshire almost to the level of Concord in its reputation as a center of American culture. "Mrs. [*Charles*] Sedgwick said," Emerson recalled later, "that it was well enough to go to New York or to London, but she did not think it needful. She had found that by sitting still in Lenox, year after year, all the people she had heard of and wished to see came by, sooner or later." [70]

Captain Hall, who delighted in making rather sweeping judgments on everything he saw, unhesitatingly pronounced Stockbridge the most beautiful place in America. Indeed, he added, he could recall only one vale in England to compare with it.[71] Not accustomed to remaining long a stranger anywhere, he soon made himself a welcome dinner guest of the Sedgwicks, and marched like a native in the procession to the annual Berkshire Fair. Noticing that only one in ten of the farmers touched his hat in respect to the clergy, he was later to evaluate this observation charitably as not intentional rudeness but merely "the rather clumsy compromise which arises from wealth and station and the nominal rights and privileges of that much talked about equality that belongs to democracy." [72]

Four years later, two famous Frenchmen, recently arrived in New York, prevailed upon Henry Sedgwick to write for them a letter of introduction to his sister. Henry obliged, and on September 7, 1831, Beaumont and Tocqueville came to Stockbridge. Keenly disappointed to find Catharine away, Beaumont was to recall afterward: "Her brothers and sisters received us *à merveille,* but this did not satisfy our purpose, which was to see a lady whose works have rendered her famous. Of course, we could have seen her by staying a day longer

70. Emerson, *Journals, 9,* 450.
71. Elizabeth Sedgwick to Robert Sedgwick, Oct. 1827; SP.
72. Hall, *Travels in North America, 2,* 81.

in Stockbridge; but we were too impatient to arrive at Boston." [73] Evidently the village charms of Stockbridge could not captivate Beaumont quite as they had captivated Captain Hall, even though he did feel moved to comment:

> The country through which we passed is remarkably picturesque, the great number of mountains there encountered . . . a striking contrast to Western New York. . . . We were struck by the appearance of riches and prosperity reigning in Massachusetts; everything there proclaims a happy population; it is no longer that wild nature that one meets with everywhere in the states of the west; the virgin forest has long since disappeared and you no longer find a single trace of it. Massachusetts, which as you know once bore the name of New England, is evidently a vieux pays . . .[74]

As for Tocqueville himself, he recorded no impressions, but perhaps his encounter there with brother Theodore and nephew Theodore, II, more than compensated for Catharine's absence. Not many years later, as attaché to the American legation in Paris, young Theodore, II, was to prove of immense assistance to Tocqueville in the composition of his great book on America and was thereafter to remain his lifelong friend.

Other celebrities were to follow Beaumont and Tocqueville to Berkshire in the years to come, and Miss Sedgwick was to make her summer home there until 1863. Yet spiritually and intellectually she had weakened her ties to Berkshire and the country long before. In fact, as early as 1827 the excitement of sudden fame and the sophistications of life in New York had begun to obscure from her both the literary goals toward which she had once worked and her own artistic limitation, of which she had once displayed such acute

73. G. W. Pierson, *Tocqueville*, p. 350.
74. Ibid., p. 350.

consciousness. Stockbridge and Lenox might still enjoy her presence, but they were too soon to lose her literary loyalty. Abandoning her earlier intention of sketching the character and manners of her native hills, she turned to the broader and more conventional field of the romantic historical novel —"better adapted," she explained, "to the general taste of the novel-readers . . . because it has romantic faults." [75] She could admit the faults, but she could no longer feel so careless of success as to want to escape them.

In her assessment of the novel-reading public she knew whereof she spoke. *Hope Leslie,* published in 1827 and heavily indebted for romantic inspiration to Sir Walter Scott, was to prove her most popular book. A historical novel detailing the romantic adventures which befell a group of New England colonists captured by the Indians, it retained only a modicum of the moralistic concern of her earlier works,[76] and the charm of intimate New England village life was gone. Miss Sedgwick was beginning to write like a professional story-teller, with an eye fixed on the prospects for immediate popularity and with less of her former concern for the development of a native literature. And by 1830, with the publication of *Clarence,* she had so completely lost her faculty for accurate self-assessment that she could speak to Charles of this novel of contemporary New York as having "a great deal more in it that anything else I have written. . . ." [77] Five winters spent among the awe-inspiring literati of New York had converted her, temporarily at least,

75. *Life and Letters of Sedgwick,* p. 205.
76. Ibid., p. 192. Carrying her Unitarianism back a century, Miss Sedgwick presented such a critical view of the puritan fathers—"Their bigotry, their superstition, and, above all, their intolerance"—that she provoked a letter of mild protest from the famous Swiss historian, Sismondi. She admitted applying nineteenth-century standards in her judgment; and thus began a long and fruitful correspondence between the historian and the novelist.
77. Ibid., p. 205.

to a city cosmopolitanism compared with which the Berkshirites of whom she had recently written with such sympathy seemed only quaintly picturesque, a little awkward,
and decidedly insignificant. "New York [*she wrote to Jane
Sedgwick in 1829*] is as usual full of strangers—from all
quarters and of all degrees—you may think what the con-
course is when you reflect on the representatives from Stockbridge— When Charles Wells can overcome his repugnance
to expense—and old Caldwell can be lured from his perch at
the turnpike gate on West Stockbridge Mountain— Aunt
Dwight is here—Catherine Russell and Heaven only knows
who all." [78]

Five more winters in New York produced *The Linwoods*
and with it the end of Catharine's second novelistic phase.
Another historical novel, this time set in Revolutionary
New York, the book reflected the same unashamed debt to
Scott as had *Hope Leslie,* but was more suggestive of the
writer's maturing technical powers. It was the irony of Catharine's literary lifetime that she should have lost her artistic
vision just as she was about to gain some technical mastery
of her medium. Had *Redwood* and not *The Linwoods* appeared in 1835, she might have deserved the comparison with
Cooper which some critics had been making ten years earlier.

But whatever shortcomings posterity was to find in Miss
Sedgwick's novels, the world of the 1830's found little to
criticize, and the difficult road over the hills to Berkshire
continued to be much traveled. Perhaps the European ladies
of the era possessed qualities of endurance in an unusual degree, for two of them, Harriet Martineau and Fanny Kemble,
made the trip several times before the railroad of 1842 had
come to remove the challenge of the hills. Certainly, their
qualities of perception surpassed the slower faculties of most
Americans, and they were spending long months in Berkshire
many years before it became a vacation spot of fashion. A
few celebrated Americans, Washington Irving and Daniel

78. May 14, 1829; SP.

Webster among them, did stop for one-day visits with the famous Miss Sedgwick, and President Van Buren once ventured to travel from Washington for a conference with that leading Democratic light, Theodore Sedgwick, Jr., but none remained to extol the scenery and the charms of rural solitude, and probably none viewed it with Fanny Kemble's happy appreciativeness. "I have been riding sixteen miles over these charming hills," she wrote exuberantly from Lenox in 1839. "The day is bright and breezy, and full of shifting lights and shadows, playing over a landscape that combines every variety of beauty. . . . I have good friends, and my precious children, an easy, cheerful cultivated society, my capital horse, and, in short, most good things that I call mine." [79]

Another famous Englishwoman, Mrs. Jameson, had spent the difficult fall of 1837 in the understanding and stimulating company of Catharine Sedgwick and had found the trying months of divorce arrangements made easier by life amidst quiet Berkshire scenery.[80] Many years later Fanny Kemble was to express to Catharine's sister some sense of this exhilarating combination of Sedgwick and Berkshire charm:

> Of the society which gathered summer after summer to the pleasant hill region, the seat of her family home, attracted thither even more by the delightful intercourse of its various gifted members than by the pure air and fine scenery of Berkshire, Miss Sedgwick was the centre and soul, dispensing the most graceful hospitality, and doing the honors of her beautiful hills and valleys to her visitors with an unwearied kindliness and courtesy that must forever have combined in their memories the most delightful social intercourse with the most charming natural scenery.[81]

79. Kemble, *Records of Later Life,* p. 158.
80. Anna Jameson, *Memoirs and Essays* (New York, 1846), p. 133.
81. *Life and Letters of Sedgwick,* p. 417.

Catharine, in her turn, once confided to her sister that to
"the enchantress, Fanny Kemble, I owe . . . some delightful
hours when I have felt something approaching to the en-
raptured feeling of youth." [82]

With the soberer and more disciplined Harriet Martineau
—a formidable woman of Intellect and Purpose—Catharine
apparently felt considerably less at ease. "What are we to
do for mankind?" she wrote desperately to sister Louisa in
anticipation of Miss Martineau's prospective arrival in the
fall of 1834. "Women guests are hard to entertain without
their aid— The major [*Theodore Sedgwick, Jr.*] distrusts her
profundity in political economy and Mr. A[*shburner*] her
soundness in radicalism and both I think are a little shy of
a confederate or rival . . . in petticoats.[83] Eventually, Catharine Sedgwick and the aggressive Miss Martineau split
openly over the issue of slavery, and Miss Martineau was
later to recall with a kind of grim satisfaction: "I remember
Miss Sedgwick starting back in the path, one day when she
and I were walking beside the sweet Housatonic, and snatching her arm from mine when I said, in answer to her inquiry,
what I thought the issue of the controversy must be. 'The
dissolution of the Union!' she cried. 'The Union is sacred,
and must be preserved at all cost.' My answer was that the
will of God was sacred too." [84] Catharine, who could not
regard the disagreement in quite such a sternly humorless
light, afterwards commented with some amusement on Har-

82. Ibid., p. 231.

83. To Louisa Minot, Stockbridge, Sept. 24, 1834; SP. Mr. Ashburner,
a retired Englishman who had made his fortune in India, being an
ardent Benthamite and atheist, found the atmosphere of England oppressive and came to America because of her free institutions. The
Reverend D. D. Field often made innuendos at his atheism from the
Stockbridge pulpit. A close friend of the Sedgwicks, his daughter married Theodore Sedgwick, II.

84. *Harriet Martineau's Autobiography*, ed. Maria Chapman (2 vols.
Boston, 1877), *1*, 376.

riet Martineau's "martyrology"—referring to her firm belief that she might be lynched in Louisiana for her brave
stand on slavery.[85]

During those eventful and productive years, Miss Sedgwick was spending perhaps a third of her time in New York
and the rest in Berkshire, thus enjoying the best of both
worlds. New York never ceased to fascinate her, and the in-
termittent stimulation of the city led her to adopt a classic
viewpoint toward the values of rural Berkshire reminiscent
of Mark Hopkins—the superiority of character to intellect,
the beauty of honest mediocrity. "The city," she wrote, "is
the theatre for great men. The energy of one powerful mind
is diffused through a great number; the magic touch of eloquence awakens them to life and action; the dry bones are
shaken; a living soul is breathed into them, and they are
thus quickened in the paths of pleasantness and peace." But
with the clearer insight of these middle years, she could observe with complete conviction that the country, although
"condemned to the ministrations of inferior men . . . presents every facility for moral refinement and religious improvement." [86] And this conviction was soon to lead her
away from that facile romantic writing which had brought
her so large a measure of worldly success.

Although Catharine always remained deeply interested
in improving society, she could never be classified with Lydia
Maria Child as primarily a reformer, and she never chose
to ally herself with any of the radical reform movements of
her time. If amused by the more fatuous reformers, she was
too kind to be satirical toward them, and her sincere concern
for the downtrodden became evident in her active partici-

85. C. M. Sedgwick to Louisa Minot, Mar. 16, 1836; MC. Later, Miss
Martineau was to state that the real cause of their split lay in Miss
Sedgwick's possession of that general American weakness of flattery—
of praising people to their faces.

86. *Life and Letters of Sedgwick,* p. 101.

pation in the New York Women's Prison Association. On the other hand, when Catherine Beecher asked her to join a philanthropic committee for "saving the country," she wrote to Horace Mann for advice concerning anything *practical* she might do in this cause. "There are obvious difficulties in acting in concert with Miss Beecher . . ." she explained, "and besides I do not understand what responsibilities are incurred by becoming one of Miss B's collaborateurs." [87] Indeed, her somewhat sentimental idea of the country as a sort of retreat removed from the oppressions and tragedies of life, together with her concern for the sane, law-abiding majority of society, stood uppermost in her thoughts; and on one occasion such preoccupations combined with her loyalty to Berkshire to arouse in her a rare indignation against Dr. Pomeroy's proposal to establish a home for discharged convicts in Stockbridge:

My dear Doctor, —I am seldom bold enough to doubt the wisdom of your decisions, but it seems to me that your better judgment has been led captive by your humanity toward a portion of the community who, from having been the objects of desertion and despair, have suddenly become the chief subjects of effort, hope, and Christian love. I am not surprised at Louis's zeal, but that you and other judicious, and thinking, and patriotic members of our village society should have banded together to introduce into our still pastures and by our sweet water-courses, amid our flocks of defenseless sheep and lambs, these state-prison wolves, is, I confess, a mystery to me. I entreat you to reconsider the matter —to think how great a portion of our peace and happiness results from the safe character of our people, from the security with which we can go out and come in, and lay our heads on our pillows at night. If the effort must

87. Jan. 31, 1848; Mann Collection, MHS.

be made, there are places thinly inhabited, remote from villages, that would be more suitable. Has a colony ever been thought of in some part of our fine unoccupied territory? In the name of Heaven, let some other portion of this habitable globe be selected than our village.[88]

It was, nevertheless, Catharine's sincere concern over problems of social welfare which prompted her, only three years later, to turn away impatiently from historical romance. Even as she was completing *The Linwoods* her dissatisfaction was growing, and in March 1835 she was writing to brother Theodore: "Where is your book? [*'Public and Private Economy'*] I thought you would have begun the publication before now. Are you afraid of a Sedgwick 'glut'— I assure you my labor will no more come into competition with yours than ladies plumes and artificial flowers do with blankets and bread stuffs. You know there are people who live on pâté de foie gras, omelette soufflé and such flummery, they are not perhaps worth keeping alive, but they *pay* for their living and therefore are worth something to their feeders." [89]

Before 1840 she had already more than compensated for the "flummery" of *The Linwoods* by producing no less than four sketches on manners and morals—*Home* in 1835, *The Poor Rich Man and the Rich Poor Man* in 1836, *Live and Let Live* in 1837, and *Means and Ends* in 1839. She was never to return to the idle pursuit of historical romance or even to attempt any more complete fulfillment of her first heartening promise to native American literature. Instead, she was to formulate in these later and sadder years of her life a far narrower theory of the writer's task—a theory which went back even beyond *A New England Tale* to that original

88. *Life and Letters of Sedgwick,* pp. 225–26.
89. To Theodore Sedgwick, Jr., Mar. 29, 1835; SP.

moralistic tract intended to further the cause of Unitarianism. "I thank Heaven," she wrote to Channing in 1837,
"that I am not now working for the poor and perishing re-
wards of literary ambition. . . . I think the time has gone
by, or perhaps, has not come to our country, when they are
legitimate objects. With the great physical world to be sub-
dued here to the wants of the human family, there is an
immense moral field opening, demanding laborers of every
class, and of every kind and degree of talent. . . . There is
much sin from mere ignorance. . . ." [90]

Grief-stricken by the deaths of brothers Harry and Theodore and shocked by the depression of 1837 into a horrified
realization of how many had put their faith in material
things, she suddenly saw her raw and chaotic country being
threatened by untold dangers and could find no promise
of salvation for the Republic but in a revival of domestic
virtue. From her friend, the Reverend Henry Ware of Harvard, had come the first suggestion of her future literary
course. Early in 1834 he had written to request "a series of
narratives, between a formal tale and a common tract, so as
to present to view an image, a portrait of the Christian religion according to our understanding of it, and at once en-
lighten readers by a familiar exposition of principles, and improve them by a display of their modes of operation. In a
word, I fancy that a succession of *Illustrations of Christianity*
might be made to do as much for religion as *Illustrations of
Political Economy* for that science . . ." [91]

The result was *Home,* for which Miss Sedgwick's literary
reputation ensured a wide audience. Dedicated to farmers
and mechanics, the book reflected something of brother
Theodore's somewhat calculating Republican conviction. "I
have labored to convince my boys," explains the worthy Reverend Barclay, "that there is nothing vulgar in the mechanic

90. To William Ellery Channing, Aug. 24, 1837; SP.
91. *Life and Letters of Sedgwick,* p. 239.

professions,—no particular reason for envying the lawyer or the doctor. . . . It is certainly a false notion in a democratic republic, that a lawyer has any higher claim to respectability, —gentility, if you please,—than a tanner, a goldsmith, a printer, or a builder. . . . the mechanic is of the *lower orders,* only when he is self-degraded by ignorance and coarse manners . . ." [92] Such eminent leaders of reform as Horace Mann, Harriet Martineau, and William E. Channing found Miss Sedgwick's renewed moralistic pursuits admirable,[93] and thus encouraged she hurried on in the next year to *The Poor Rich Man and the Rich Poor Man.* An almost unconscious effort to interpret reform in terms of ethics rather than economics, this new book assigned its author to a position more closely akin to Channing's than to that of the thoroughly Jacksonian Theodore. The rich, she affirmed none too subtly, are far more subject to selfishness and to harassing worries than those workers who lead simple, happy lives. Even so elementary an observation found a ready audience in the discontented 1830's, and by November Catharine was able to write to Louisa: "My last little book has been received with far more favor than I expected. Nothing that I have written has seemed so well to suit the *country* market— the *good* people praise it and talk of it for their Sunday libraries— This is an honor I did not expect this side the grave—if I am ever well enough again to write anything more than a letter it will be books of this description which suit the mass of readers. In this country we must do everything for the majority." [94]

In her almost medieval acceptance of the hierarchical social order, Catharine was far more outdated than she knew and far more indebted to her aristocratic Berkshire background

92. C. M. Sedgwick, *Home* (New York, 1835), p. 38.
93. Horace Mann to his sister Lydia, Nov. 20, 1835; Mann Collection. *Martineau's Autobiography, 1,* 378.
94. Mar. 20, 1837; MC.

than she might have been willing to admit. She seemed unconsciously determined to cling to the village social system
to which two or three generations had lent their sanction but
which both Charles and Theodore had outwardly rejected.
Unable to condone the social restlessness she had seen in New
York, she hastily retreated—even during the economic upheavals of 1837—to the static social philosophy of *Live and
Let Live,* the title of which was ironically expressive of her
conservative reform theories. The book immediately elicited
from Channing a letter of high praise. It was, he felt, a real
contribution to social stability: "Thousands will be the better
and happier for it; thousands as they read it, will feel their
deficiencies, and resolve to do better. No relation is so little
understood among us as that of head of family and domestic.
The false notions of it which prevail in England . . . exist
here, in defiance of the spirit of our institutions and of Christianity . . . Instead of feeling the dignity of their vocation,
that they are contributing essentially to the happiness of the
family, and may render services for which wages are a poor
equivalent, they connect ideas of degradation with their
work . . ." [95]

With *Means and Ends: or Self Training,* Catharine closed
a peculiarly contradictory decade in her life. Having begun
it in 1830 with the romantic *Clarence,* she was now ending it
with a realistic attack on rampant feminism. "If women
would attain their proper moral and intellectual might," she
wrote, "their rights would follow. Women should not enter
courts, politics, or vote. Woman's duty is to form character
in children—be these her sons or pupils—to occupy high
places in the country." [96]

95. *Life and Letters of Sedgwick,* p. 270.
96. C. M. Sedgwick, *Means and Ends* (New York, 1839), p. 269.
Catharine herself was a feminist, at least to the extent that she used her
influence in the Massachusetts legislature in an effort to get a bill
passed which would give married women more property rights.

Whether she recognized it or not, Catharine Sedgwick's basic purpose in all of her later moralistic tracts seems to have been simply to civilize that majority for whom "we must do everything"—to smooth the corners of the rough individual, to bowdlerize the bawdy element in lower-class humor, to regularize conduct by idealizing such institutions as the home, the school, the church, etiquette, the law courts. She would satisfy every American's desire to conform by giving him a definite code to conform to; she would bring the oaf and the yokel *unter den Pantöffel,* bent on making them presentable and at the same time harmless. It was the special irony of Miss Sedgwick's life that, having won her considerable literary reputation by her appreciation of New England peculiarities, she ended by losing sight of their attractiveness and by lending her pen to the cause of wiping many of them out.

Indeed, all the instruments of political control had proved less effective to the aristocracy in their efforts to quell the high spirits of the masses than those subtler methods like Miss Sedgwick's which aimed at bringing about demoralization by an appeal to vanity, and which were devastatingly effective. Midcentury Berkshirites showed little relation to those sturdy people of earlier decades who had gloried in a sort of backwoods individualism. In those years Berkshire had produced notable leaders of the great popular tradition of the American lowbrow—men who would have delighted in eating from their knives in Miss Sedgwick's stuffy presence or in keeping their hats on when talking to her father. The movement had been authentic and natural in the early years, and its dominant proponents had been John Leland and David Hitchcock. Leland—once derisively dubbed "the ignorant cheese-monger" by the Federalist Yale graduate Manassah Cutler—had been a radical protestant who hated all institutions and who took gleeful pleasure in embarrassing the proper, college-educated clergy with his witty questions

and pithy epigrams. David Hitchcock had reveled in his role
of cobbler poet and along with Leland had subscribed wholeheartedly to the Jacksonian insistence that, given a chance,
the common man could do anything. In fact he had seen no
reason to doubt that the man possessed of a sharp native wit
and educated in the school of hard knocks could not generally
go the self-styled aristocracy one better.

By the 1850's men of the Hitchcock-Leland stamp had virtually disappeared, soon to be replaced by men like Josh
Billings, who chose to use the rural pose as a stage effect.
Even with a good deal of contrivance, such men managed to
become only shadowy suggestions of what Leland had been
with full-blooded naturalness. The backwoods wit was transformed into a self-conscious "character," and the victory for
the forces of civilization and institutionalism was unmistakable. The Catharine Sedgwicks had won out over the John
Lelands; and not only newspapers, pulpits, and presses but
the entire army of educators activated by Horace Mann and
the whole movement from village to town and from town to
city and from poverty to economic security were firmly
aligned on the side of refinement and civilization.

But along with the growth of refinement the years saw the
emergence of unpredictable social forces; forces which had
proved irresistible enough to call Catharine Sedgwick down
to earth from her comfortable clouds of romance. She could
only eye such changes with suspicion and could, in her own
limited way, fervently echo the sentiments of that great conservative John C. Calhoun when he said in 1817, "We are
great, and rapidly—I was about to say fearfully—growing!"
Wherever she looked, whether to the feminist movement, to
the chaotic social scene of Jacksonian democracy, or to the
insistent slavery question which she would have preferred to
ignore, she saw the sands shifting under the old institutions.
Even in Berkshire, once so pleasantly insulated from the
world, she saw the railroad, the new industrialism, and a

sizable Irish immigration becoming solvents of the old order.

The sense of foreboding which most old-time Berkshirites
shared had become so acute by 1844 that the idea for a Berkshire Jubilee seemed to issue almost as a spontaneous phenomenon. Within a few months after the day on which the
Reverend R. S. Cook made the first mild suggestion, two
planning committees were at work. William Cullen Bryant,
David Dudley Field, and the Reverend Orville Dewey were
the most notable representatives of the New York City emigrés; Charles Sedgwick, the Reverend John Todd, and the
Massachusetts governor, George Briggs of Lanesboro, formed
part of the local committee. The outcome of their delibera-
tions was a gathering of 4,000 Berkshirites in Pittsfield on
August 22, some of them still county residents, some having
come from Boston, from New York, and from as far west as
St. Louis. With Johnson's Band playing a lively march, they
proceeded up Jubilee Hill by the hundreds.[97]

The anthem, the prayer, the psalm singing were as traditional as they could have wished. But as soon as Mark Hopkins mounted the wooden speaker's platform to begin his sermon—certainly the "keynote address" of the occasion—the
more perceptive participants must have sensed that here was
a new kind of provincialism. The old provincial spirit in
Berkshire, the sometimes subtle but often stubborn consciousness of being different, was giving way to that somewhat
artificial glorification of Berkshire that marked the second
provincialism. In the midcentury search for values and for
a lost sense of security, the Berkshire way of life seemed to
promise a framework extensive enough to circumscribe all
of the three environments of man: spiritual, physical, and
social. As a spiritual bulwark, there was, of course, latter-day
Puritanism, stripped of Edwardsean doctrinal content but
offering as compensation the confidence of a faith in eternal

97. *The Berkshire Jubilee, Celebrated at Pittsfield, Massachusetts,
August 22 and 23, 1844* (Pittsfield, 1845), pp. 7–25.

verities and in ethical restraint. As a physical reassurance, there were the hills and the Pittsfield Elm. As a testament to social stability there were the rural villages where three or even four generations of a single family often remained together to provide a continuity through time and where social and economic coherence assured a meaningful relationship between individuals. "There are," wrote Catharine Sedgwick, "no barriers between you and your neighbors. . . . The highest and lowest meet in their joys and their sorrows, at weddings and funerals, in sicknesses and distresses of all sorts. Not merely as alms-bearers, but the richest and highest go to the poorest to "watch" with them in sickness, and perform the most menial offices for them; and though your occupations, your mode of life may be very different from the artisan's, your neighbor, you meet him on an apparent equality, and talk with him as members of one family." [98]

In 1844 no one could have stood as a more representative scion of that Berkshire family than did Mark Hopkins. Born in Stockbridge, he could count among his ancestors the missionary John Sergeant, the theologian Samuel Hopkins, and the leading lawyer of colonial Berkshire, Colonel Mark Hopkins. He had gone from the Stockbridge schools to Williams College and the Berkshire Medical Institution and later to Lenox for law training with Charles Sedgwick; and as president of Williams College he had become one of the most powerful guardians of the old New England virtues—the man who, "standing on Plymouth Rock," was to confute the heresies of Hume, Kant, Darwin, and Huxley without even reading their books.[99] To his students he seemed the greatest mind in New England; to the disciples of Berkshire present at the Jubilee, he was the Berkshire spirit incarnate.

As soon as he took his place on the platform and began to speak, the Jubilee became transformed. No longer merely a

98. *Life and Letters of Sedgwick,* p. 49.
99. Rudolph, *Mark Hopkins and the Log,* pp. 27–28.

"great tea party with talk ad libitum," it became instead
something of a religious rite, important in the annals of the
shaping of the Berkshire (and even the New England) mythology. The earlier provincialism had emphasized the independence of the Berkshire spirit from Boston domination;
but the second provincialism was unfolding as a preoccupation with the "New England spirit" and the dangers of its
being submerged in the nation. Why were the sons of Berkshire, once so proud of their separateness from New England,
suddenly so eager to call themselves New Englanders? Why
the sentimental references to the "old Bay State," the repeated paeans in praise of "New England character"? Not too
long before, Berkshirites had balked obstinately when Horace
Mann had ventured to suggest that their schools might do
well to conform to state standards; the Berkshire Medical
Society had threatened to turn its collective back on Boston
in favor of the less dictatorial associations offered by upper
New York State; and for a century Berkshire's economic life
had been linked to New York City in preference to any New
England port. Yet now, in the summer of 1844, some strange
diminution in self-assurance, which Mark Hopkins was articulating, compelled these apostates to close ranks.

For most of the Jubilee speakers, or at least for those
thoughtful enough not to become totally involved in mean-
derings about "the banks of the winding stream" and the
"old school house," [100] a look at the Berkshire past seemed
inevitably to point up the need for a re-examination of the
New England spirit. The ancestral world of pure religion
and able political leaders had seemed to possess a timeless
validity, and now that world was undeniably crumbling.
While it would be difficult to say how many midcentury
Berkshirites could conscientiously bemoan the decline of
clerical influence and the rise of the businessman to pre-

100. *The Berkshire Jubilee*, p. 158, introductory speech by Governor
George Briggs.

eminence, still some could not but recognize that such a thoroughgoing social revolution must be muddying the basic precepts of the New England character in too many minds.

Sensing the necessity for a redefinition of that character, Mark Hopkins proposed to capture its essence in terms of purity. The acme of civilization had been achieved, he felt, "when a pervading reverence, and the principles and affections necessarily connected with that, are called into action by spiritual objects and their relations, with the least possible appeal to the senses." In the New England experience he saw a major factor in the "cultivation of reverence towards God and State, without a nobility in the State, and without forms in religion." Joshua Spencer, in his oration on the morning of the second day, rather less profoundly bade the *"religious* man to be aroused to his Duty," that he might "send forth deeper and broader streams of the Bible's softening, peaceful influences." Probably both of these men would have agreed with chairman R. S. Cook's peremptory dictum: "It is time that the world should know what is the influence of the Puritan stock and Puritan Institutions." [101]

Neither man, however, seemed able to shake off the fear of future uncertainties which characterized so much of the Jubilee. "Whatever the future course of events may be," Mark Hopkins intoned comfortingly, "the past is secure; and God has dealt bountifully with us in permitting us to live to the extent we have, under the influence of such a past." This same past-mindedness, this clinging to stability, threaded its way through the entire Jubilee program. No one ventured—probably because no one either could or dared try—to redefine New England in current, mid-nineteenth century terms. Poets and orators alike praised at length "the bright meadow, the lofty mountain and the deep glen" and took courage from such stanzas as William Allen's:

101. Ibid., pp. 23, 49–51, 130.

> Not Tempe's boasted vale e'er shone so bright,
>   With trees so broad, with grassy turf so green:
> Each Mountain form, uptowering in his might,
>   Stands as the giant-guardian of the scene.[102]

Indeed, the very names of the speakers themselves revived confidence: Mark Hopkins; Catharine Sedgwick and Theodore Sedgwick, II, offspring of old Judge Theodore; William Allen, son of that Thomas Allen who had inspired the Berkshire Constitutionalists in the Revolution and had led the town in politics and religion from his Pittsfield pulpit for five years; Oliver Wendell Holmes, descended from the one-time owner of most of Pittsfield, Jacob Wendell; Ezekiel Bacon, son of Berkshire's congressman and champion of religious freedom John Bacon. In the presence of such personages, Berkshirites seemed to find reassurance—living evidence that the past, which they were so reluctant to leave behind, was not dead after all.

The essential irony of the Jubilee, in fact, lay in this past-mindedness and in the consequent omission by every speaker of a critical consideration of the impact of nationalism and industrialism on New England culture. Instead, even the most perceptive kept insisting that the impact must be the other way around. The national and industrial scene must stand indebted to New England for whatever moral stamina it possessed. "Where upon the face of the earth," asked Joshua Spencer, "if not in New England, in the 'old Bay State,' in our own dear 'Berkshire' amidst these hills, peopled as they are by a homogeneous race of men, can the great principles on which the stability and perpetuity of our government rest, be at the same time garnered up and diffused throughout the land?" Yet even as he spoke the "homogeneous race of men" was dissolving into unreality. The Irish

102. *Ibid.*, pp. 52–53, 74, 192.

were coming in by the hundreds and long-time Berkshirites were departing in appalling numbers, bound for New York or for the West.

Where the national scene was concerned, Spencer could be analytical enough. "We live," he had said earlier, "in an eventful age. . . . It is obvious to the most superficial observer that physical and intellectual man in their career, have in this our day far outrun religious man. . . . With these developments of physical and intellectual power our people are absorbed, and have become impatient of restraint." But somehow New England, in Spencer's mind, seemed to represent the saving remnant, and the nation could be saved simply "by a careful study of the elements of New England character, and by the maintenance and preservation of their combined whole in all its symmetrical proportions." The mass exodus from Berkshire to the West could thus be neatly turned to good account. John Mills might counsel those seated before him to "be happy and contented *where you are*. . . . Dream not of removing to the west . . ." But if Berkshirites and New Englanders generally were yielding to the lure of distant prosperities, were they not, after all, carrying with them a rich moral inheritance?

> Over lands and oceans,
> Peddling Yankee notions,
> Morals, law, and lotions,
>     Of our ancient Berkshire home.[103]

The same sense of insecurity which was leading Jubilee orators into ponderous self-examination was thus leading them too into a rather ambivalent self-justification. They could hardly ignore the deplorable emigration, when half the jubilant assembly were emigrant sons. But they could and did, in effect, make a virtue of necessity. They haled with

103. Ibid., pp. 125–31, 169, 180, part of a song written anonymously for the local choir.

Mark Hopkins the conception of New England as a vast character factory exerting an unparalleled seminal influence on the country: "history furnishes no example of a people possessing a soil more fertile and a climate more bland than ours, who have not degenerated and become luxurious and effeminate. No doubt the landing of the Pilgrim Fathers where they did, was ordered of God. If they had landed at New Orleans, the result would have been widely different." [104] Later on the same day they reveled in self-congratulation over William Allen's poetic announcement that "No foot of slave e'er treads our sacred soil," and near the conclusion of the celebration they applauded with Theodore Sedgwick, II, "that more than royal progress which the sons of New England are making now towards the Pacific."

Even as Sedgwick spoke, the strident wail of the still-infant railroad was sounding through the hills—at once symptom and symbol of all the mounting subconscious fears. With the railroad had come industrialism and with industrialism, Jacksonian democracy. Sedgwick, himself a "conservative" Jacksonian, extolled "the stock of New England" as "the stock of Old England, their virtue, their intelligence, with equality added." [105] More critically, Sedgwick's nephew was to recall in the 1890's the character of the new aristocracy which had moved to Berkshire:

> . . . we may observe that the men and women who used to form the cultivated elements of society were outwardly distinguished from its humbler members only by the quiet and kindly dignity of their deportment, and by their never forgetting that *noblesse oblige*. The liveries, the dress, the drags, the formal receptions, the Anglicanism, all the diversified phases of wealth which have changed the surface of society, have not always

104. Ibid., p. 40.
105. Ibid., pp. 170–72.

stifled the sweetness and virtue of the past, but have
often hidden them under a load of formal self-conse-
quence which makes them hard to find . . .[106]

Even in 1844 Mark Hopkins sensed that economic individualism working with human pride might deprive men of the
meaningful social context which their nature required. "It is,
indeed, the fundamental question of the present day," he
declared, "whether the principle and the reverence that are
necessary to the greatest strength and beauty of society, can
be preserved in connexion with the simplicity of our civil
and religious institutions. Men will not be trampled upon,
nor will they have their sensibilities and their taste outraged.
If there is not a general state of things that will secure them
against this, they will retire behind a standing army, and
behind forms." [107]

The Jubilee orators, of course, did not manage in two days
of declaiming to close down the factories or turn back the
railroad on its tracks. Whatever they said betrayed the beginning of the second provincialism and the death of the
older, more genuine provincial spirit. Yet the same motives
which had prompted Berkshire emigrés to return to the
county—the search for a quiet, unspoiled rural area and for
traditional values—were soon to bring a group of famous
outsiders over the Barrier and thus were to perpetuate Berkshire's identity as a meaningful cultural unit for a few years
more.

106. Henry D. Sedgwick, "Reminiscences of Literary Berkshire,"
*Century Magazine, 50* (1895), 568.
107. *The Berkshire Jubilee,* p. 52.

# Chapter 10. THE AMERICAN LAKE DISTRICT

AFTER a year on his sizable farm in Lenox, young Samuel Gray Ward was writing his father with enthusiastic satisfaction: "I have harvested a hundred bushels of excellent potatoes . . . [and] am thinking of translating Goethe's autobiography this winter." [1] Within the twenty years to come, many another celebrated man of letters was to discover in Berkshire a similar opportunity for cultural and agricultural accomplishment, and the land was to prove undeniably good for both activities. The irrepressible Dr. Holmes would one day take considerable pride in having planted 700 trees on the rolling expanses of Canoe Meadows; Hawthorne would spend serene hours with his dearly loved chickens behind the little red cottage near Stockbridge Bowl; and Melville—the only one to depend heavily on the land for sustenance— would trudge home many nights exhausted from his work in the fields at Arrowhead. And from Canoe Meadows would come some of Holmes' finest odes; from the Rose Cottage, *The House of the Seven Gables;* and from Arrowhead, *Moby Dick.*

Impelled by his frail health and by his "unsatisfied passion for the country and the land," [2] Samuel Gray Ward had led the way to Berkshire, and living there from 1844 to 1850 he remained the most loyal Berkshire supporter among the host of distinguished visitors in the county. Indeed, so quickly did he become a part of Berkshire life that he himself never seemed a visitor at all, and his closest Berkshire friend,

1. To Thomas Wren Ward, Oct. 20, 1845; TWW.
2. Samuel Gray Ward, "A Long Letter to My Grandchildren," *Ward Family Papers, Collected and Written by Samuel Gray Ward* (Boston, privately printed in an edition of twelve copies, Norwood Press, 1900), p. 88.

Charles Sedgwick, could describe him, only three months after his arrival, as "very popular and more beloved than some old settler." [3] Later he was to serve as the common denominator between Fanny Kemble and Charles Sumner and between Longfellow and the Sedgwicks, but even then he never sacrificed his place in the affections of the Lenox townspeople.

Ward's regard for Lenox went back to the boyish recollection of a carriage tour he had made with his mother through western Massachusetts to the Lebanon Springs. Four years at Harvard and two years in Europe had not dimmed the memory, and he at first regarded his second trip across the Barrier as a romanticist's return to nature. Once settled, however, he looked at his surroundings more realistically and soon wrote to his father: "We seem to have made a happy selection in this part of the country, for we find simple and economical habits united with an excellent society." [4] Because he enjoyed a generous allowance from his family, his own habits never were and never needed to be economical, but his approach to his new life was nonetheless sincere and practical. "City-bred people," he had realized from the outset, "never understand country-bred people, and are not admitted to the 'freedom' of the country. This barrier I wanted to break down, and succeeded so effectually that I was accepted as one of themselves." [5] In retrospect he was to write further:

Although I was not robust enough for hard labour, farming, under such circumstances, I had a great delight in. I could do anything that was to be done with horses, ploughing, harrowing, etc.; ploughing particularly, and driving at the same time, required just enough attention and skill to help and not to interrupt the flow of medita-

3. To Kate Minot, Sept. 2, 1844; MC.
4. S. G. Ward to T. W. Ward, June 3, 1844; TWW.
5. Ward, *Ward Family Papers*, p. 180.

tion, and my friends the farmers were greatly edified and amused at my beginnings. I got up a farmers' club to meet at each other's houses at stated times in the evenings, and to measure and compare crops etc. which brought me quite near to them. Then there was shooting enough to afford an excuse for long rambles with dog and gun.[6]

When his father's plan of retirement in 1850 obliged him to abandon the pleasant environs of Lenox for the practical business world of New York City, the North Stockbridge Farmers' Club saw him go with sincere regret and voted: "Resolved that the farmers' club deplore his loss as a member of the club, as a citizen and resident of Berkshire as a public misfortune." [7]

Neither Dr. Holmes nor Melville was ever to become so completely a part of the rural scene as Ward was becoming during these years of bucolic retreat. "I love farming," he wrote to his father with candor. "There is such a variety and simplicity, such an adaption of means to ends, such room for the exercise of ingenuity and contrivance, as well as for the cultivation of perseverance and patience that I find an endless interest in it." [8] Less than two weeks later he was writing still another letter filled with the enjoyment of country life: "We have mid-winter weather and the most perfect sleighing. . . . Yesterday morning being a bright morning we went over to Lebanon, Anna and I in an open sleigh. We started after breakfast, and when we returned at noon the thermometer stood no higher than 7° and considerable wind; yet we did not suffer and had a charming drive of twenty-two miles. Think of that! Cold weather here is more bracing and less chilling I think than on the coast." [9]

6. Ibid., p. 181.
7. C. M. Sedgwick to Samuel G. Ward, Mar. 5, 1850; SGW.
8. S. G. Ward to T. W. Ward, Dec. 1, 1845; TWW.
9. Idem, Dec. 12, 1845; TWW.

The very civilized Emerson never tired of commenting with wry humor on his friend's strange attachment to the comparatively rustic rural life, and on the occasion of Ward's first winter trip to Boston, he wrote playfully:

> I hope the city looks friendly and domestic to her one-time son, and not reproachful and too mindful of his wanderings. Tis a good goblin, and the most devout lovers of nature will find the Exchange, the Tremont House and the Concert Room tolerable in February. The woods of Berkshire (a week ago all cased in diamond) the frozen lakes and skies a little too pure must reckon themselves happy if a fortnight hence they preserve the least charm for your imagination. Indeed what a maceration and self-immolation in these children of art and civility to have lent their grace to those rocks and wilderness so long! I praise and admire you, though would never see the Saddleback mountains again. Well I long to hear the tale of your horrible sufferings in savage life, and shall hurry to town before the charm of your escape is worn off.[10]

Actually Ward's years in Berkshire were perhaps not so "savage" as Emerson liked to think of them. The demands on the time of a gentleman farmer never proved unreasonable, and he could find ample leisure, especially in the winter months, not only for an extensive correspondence with Emerson but for his proposed translation of Goethe and later for those remarkable essays of literary criticism one day to be published in the *Aesthetic Papers* and the *Massachusetts Quarterly Review*.

10. R. W. Emerson to S. G. Ward, Jan. 31, 1845; SGW. Though the bulk of the letters of Emerson to Ward appear in either Emerson's *Letters to a Friend*, ed. Charles Eliot Norton (Boston, 1899) or Ralph L. Rusk, *The Letters of Ralph Waldo Emerson* (6 vols. New York, 1939), I have worked from the manuscripts in order to avoid the necessity of collation.

Whatever Emerson might think of Berkshire isolation, the fact remained that Lenox in the 1840's harbored a small but growing corps of literati whose knowledge owed apologies to no one and whose sophistication could rival any to be found in America. And if Ward's peculiar genius drew virtually nothing from the Berkshire tradition, still he discovered among the isolated hills an unsurpassed workshop in which to experiment upon and expand that genius. With adequate time for reading in his "warm and bright" winter library; with welcome occasions for thinking as he jogged easily along behind his plow in springtime; with pleasant opportunities for conversations with Fanny Kemble, the Reverend Henry Neill, the Sedgwicks, and his sometime guests, Charles Sumner, Longfellow, and Judge Lemuel Shaw; and with the prospering business of his father to assure him a comfortable subsistence, young Samuel Ward could hardly have asked for more. Even the dubious Emerson could not resist a wistful inquiry. "Do the muses speak in these sharp whistling winds?" he asked. "Are your Berkshire torrents chained up? I have always wished to know how hill countries look in winter but I doubt I shall never have vigor enough to go and see them." [11]

Two years in Lenox saw the completion of the Goethe translation and the end of an intellectual phase in Ward's life which went back to Margaret Fuller's dominating influence during his Cambridge years. Neither Berkshire nor America played an active role in this ambitious undertaking, and certainly it could scarcely have stood further from those indigenous portraits of rural life which Catharine Sedgwick had created only a few miles away. Yet impelled by a determination to educate Americans in an appreciation of the masterworks of western culture, Ward had made a significant contribution of which both Berkshire and America might well be proud. After such a performance, Emerson perhaps

11. To S. G. Ward, Dec. 17, 1844; SGW.

felt that Ward might be profitably encouraged in his agricultural pursuits, and in April of 1845 he wrote without whimsy:
"Yesterday I was in town and saw at Munroe's the last proof
sheet of 'Goethe.' It seemed a good time to greet you on your
mountains, as you are regaining your freedom again, if with
regrets like Gibbon's. The reluctant spring has yielded us
some golden days and I do not know any idleness so delicious
as dilettantism in fruit trees. Grafting and pruning turn a
day into pure dream . . ." [12]

For three more years Ward continued to enjoy an existence
nicely balanced between culture and agriculture, and his essay on criticism in the *Aesthetic Papers* [13] unmistakably established him in his enviable role as Berkshire's literary gentle-
man-farmer supreme. The sanity of Ward's views on the
problems facing the American critic is evident:

> Our first misfortune is, that there is a reference to a
> standard from without, viz., from England. As the spirit
> that dictates this is, from many causes, unfair and de-
> preciating, a natural consequence has been to cause all
> our own criticism to take the opposite ground, to over-
> praise that which we felt to be undervalued or invidi-
> ously regarded. . . . although all original literature
> comes from and refers to the heart of the people, it can-
> not, except in a rude age, address itself to that people,
> except through a class capable of receiving it. If great
> works do not find such a class in their own age, they wait
> till time and their own influence create it. . . . We be-
> lieve a conscious greatness inseparable from a critical
> literature; and such, therefore, we look for in this coun-
> try:—a literature and art based on thorough criticism,

12. Idem, Apr. 30, 1845; SGW.
13. This journal was edited by Elizabeth Peabody, but ceased publication after the first issue. As a contributor, Ward was in the company of
Emerson, Thoreau, and Hawthorne.

and thorough knowledge of what already exists in the world.[14]

Ward's idea of a "creative criticism" that would always supply a regenerating force in a nation's literature found sympathetic response in the Lenox pastor Henry Neill:

> . . . your sketch of the history of literature among the nations beautifully and directly led to the announcement that there might be such a thing as *creative* criticism, ever new and advancing until every point of view was exhausted and on until there were no more forms in which the facts could arrange themselves, which might never be, and thus criticism be endless and ever-increasing. . . . I believe you might on this hint point out some of the lines and forms which criticism will take after the German phase is exhausted, just as you have . . . philosophically and satisfactorily pointed out and remarked on the forms which it does take and has taken. You have assigned in your article many new causes for existing facts not generally recognized as entering into them.[15]

Berkshire's once stern and uncompromising orthodoxy must indeed have been undergoing a radical change when a Congregational cleric could speak with such perception on literary criticism, and Ward himself did much to introduce cosmopolitan currents of thought into the county. Yet during these same six years the genial glow of his personal charm was perhaps contributing even more to "literary Berkshire" than was his critical work. For Ward, the isolation which Emerson so often mentioned never had anything more than geographical validity. He possessed a rare genius for dispensing warm hospitality and drew upon that genius freely during his Berkshire years.

14. S. G. Ward, "Essay on Criticism," *Aesthetic Papers* (1849), p. 24.
15. Henry Neill to S. G. Ward, June 26, 1849; SGW.

Hardly had he settled in Lenox before he issued an invitation to Charles Sumner and Dr. Samuel Gridley Howe—an invitation which both men accepted with alacrity. Sumner, who was then in Pittsfield with the Appletons recuperating from an illness, traveled the seven miles to Lenox in September and there encountered again the beautiful Fanny Kemble Butler,[16] with whom he had been so much impressed in Boston. With Ward, he watched while "in a field not far off, the girls and others engaged in the sport of archery. Mrs. Butler hit the target in the golden middle." [17] If Mrs. Butler did not, as later romanticists would have liked to think, hit the heart of this austere and handsome Boston bachelor "in the golden middle," at least she inspired in him a sincere admiration and friendship, and probably Berkshire never again could be separable in his mind from her "peculiar, bold, masculine, and unaccommodating" personality.[18] "Your presence," he wrote to George Hillard from Lenox, "would help me bear the weight of Fanny Kemble's conversation; for, much as I admire her, I confess to a certain awe and a sense of her superiority." [19]

During her many summers in Berkshire, Fanny Kemble was to inspire in many this same awe she had inspired in Sumner, in some an even greater admiration, and in a few a reaction of shocked surprise. Living sometimes with the Charles Sedgwicks and sometimes at the Curtis Hotel, she

16. Fanny Kemble had married the Philadelphia socialite Pierce Butler in 1834 and they had two daughters. By 1844, however, she and Butler had separated—partly over the slavery issue and partly over a hopeless difference of opinion regarding wifely obedience—and in 1848 they were formally divorced.

17. Charles Sumner to George Hillard, Sept. 10, 1844, in Edward L. Pierce, *Memoir and Letters of Charles Sumner* (3 vols. Boston, 1877), 2, 317.

18. C. Sumner to Dr. Samuel G. Howe, Pittsfield, Sept. 11, 1844, ibid., 2, 319.

19. Ibid., 2, 319.

was always to make a profound impression on everyone she encountered among the hills. With no thought for the proprieties of polite society, she lived with an unconsciousness of self and with an unlimited self-confidence which were to add to the already diversified literary society of the County something of the flavor of the Elizabethan era which she intuitively experienced in her study of Shakespeare.

In fact, Berkshire itself, at least in the minds of outsiders, eventually came to share with the unpredictable Mrs. Butler her reputation for freedom and for an open disregard of convention; and Puritanical Berkshirites were sometimes scandalized by this emancipated new society prospering in their very midst. Thus when, one fine autumn, Fanny Kemble joined Mary Channing, Fanny Wright, the Pomeroys, and a group of Mrs. Sedgwick's girls for an omnibus outing to Bash Bish Falls, such a demonstration of "eating, drinking, dancing, singing, tearing, climbing, and screaming" ensued as had never before been seen in southern Berkshire, and popular indignation ran so high that the spirited ladies soon found themselves the target of a liberal deluge of rotten eggs.[20]

Berkshire literary circles could chuckle to themselves over such an indication of prim disapproval, but they could not and would not tolerate any serious expression of critical censure from outsiders. To the vicious and widespread rumor that Fanny Kemble posted over the Berkshire hillsides seated *astride* her capital horse—a rumor to which *Scott's Weekly Paper* of Philadelphia lent its sanction in an article disrespectfully entitled "Unwomanly Freaks"—Charles Sedgwick took instant and angry exception. The story, he wrote curtly to the editor of *Scott's Weekly,* "is utterly false. No one in Lenox has seen Mrs. Butler ride astride." [21]

Perhaps unaware of her gallant defenders, Fanny Kemble blithely continued to neglect whatever proprieties did not

20. Fanny Kemble to Kate Sedgwick, Oct. 2, 1839; SP.
21. To W. Scott, no date; MC.

please her, and on occasion she managed to shock Berkshire's polite society just as thoroughly as she shocked the townspeople. That eager celebrity-hunter Maunsell Field was to recall with delight, in his reminiscences, a certain evening at the Sedgwick house when:

> Seated in this window, with her back to the river, was Fanny Kemble, and sitting on either side of her were the Rev. Dr. Parker and the Rev. Justin Field, both clergymen of the Protestant Episcopal Church. Thereupon I drew up a chair, and, facing the lady, completed the partie carrée. She was doing the talking just then, and her subject was horses, for which animals she had a passionate fondness. From horses in general, she soon passed to war or cavalry horses. "By the bye," she went on to say, "this reminds me that the last time I was in England I met Sir Harry Smith. He told me that he was a captain of horse at Waterloo, but that his command was not called into action during the day. In the afternoon the Duke of Wellington, at the head of his staff, rode up to where he was, and called to him, 'Come, sir, get your troop in motion—get your troop in motion!' Now Sir Harry did not yet know any thing about the fortunes of the day; so, saluting his commander, he hesitatingly asked, 'Which way, sir?' " As she gave the Duke's reply, she rose to her feet like a tragedy queen, and, with clenched hand, shouted, "Forward, sir, by God!" At this her immediate auditors started as if electrified; but she calmly resumed her chair, and went on with the conversation as if unconscious that she had violated any of the proprieties.[22]

Perhaps it was this very unconsciousness which saved both Fanny Kemble and the Berkshire literary society of the 1840's

22. Maunsell B. Field, *Memories of Many Men and of Some Women* (New York, 1875), pp. 201–2.

and 50's from degenerating into sheer bohemianism for its own sake and which allowed them instead to develop a healthy perspective toward the fine points of etiquette and a refreshingly relaxed attitude toward the bourgeois niceties. "You know the sort of life that is lived here," wrote Mrs. Kemble approvingly to Mrs. Jameson: "the absence of all form, ceremony, or inconvenient conventionality whatever. We laugh, and we talk, sing, play, dance, and discuss; we ride, drive, walk, run, scramble, and saunter, and amuse ourselves extremely with little materials (as the generality of people would suppose) wherewith to do so . . ." [23]

It might well have surprised and disappointed her to know that the Berkshire hostelers and shopkeepers in whose sturdy independence and homely wisdom she so often delighted at first found her formidable and terrifying.[24] Even had she known, however, she could hardly have changed in herself that blunt outspokenness which had become so much a part of her personality, and in time the common people of the County with whom her active life brought her into contact learned to be themselves with her and to meet her on her own terms. She was probably seldom more thoroughly pleased than when the little man in the lobby of the Curtis Hotel whom she had abruptly reprimanded, "You should remove your hat. Gentlemen always do so in my presence," quietly and firmly replied, "But I'm not a gentleman, ma'am, I'm a butcher." [25]

She was to encounter this same faculty for proud independence many times during her stay in Berkshire, especially in the years after she had settled into "the Perch," her little cottage on the edge of Stockbridge Bowl; and it would never fail to impress and delight her. Many years after she had left Berkshire, she was to remember one summer afternoon when,

23. Kemble, *Records of Later Life,* p. 165.
24. Pittsfield *Sun,* Oct. 29, 1885.
25. *The Berkshire Hills,* Federal Writers Project, p. 126.

having ordered a barrel of beer for the group of yeomen
mowing her meadow, she heard herself sharply rebuked for
trying to introduce such a deleterious habit; [26] and even as
an old lady she could still recall a particular afternoon fishing
trip with the son of the village baker. "Now Mrs. Kemble,"
he had asked, "I want to know what would be the difference
between all that we see here now if we were in England instead of America." "Well, William," she had answered, "in
England, all that we see here now would probably be the
property of one man." To which his only reply had been,
"Oh, My! That's bad!" "This fellow," commented Mrs.
Kemble, "was as ignorant as it is possible for a Massachusetts
man to be; but think of the intelligence evinced by both his
question and answer." [27]

Probably the Berkshire hills never played host to a guest
more appreciative of both their natives and their natural
charms. Fanny Kemble filled her letters with highly colored
descriptions of the beauties she had come to know and love,
and no prospect ever became more precious to her than the
one visible from her little cottage on a Lenox hilltop:

> Immediately sloping before me, the green hillside, on
> the summit of which stands the house I am inhabiting,
> sinks softly down to a small valley, filled with thick, rich
> wood, in the centre of which a little jewel-like lake lies
> gleaming. Beyond this valley the hills rise one above
> another to the horizon, where they scoop the sky with a
> broken, irregular outline that the eye dwells on with
> ever new delight as its colors glow and vary with the as-
> cending or descending sunlight, and all the shadowy
> procession of the clouds. In one direction this undu-

26. Kemble, *Records of Later Life,* pp. 11–12.

27. Kemble, *Further Records,* pp. 192–93. Near the end of her life
Fanny Kemble wrote a very readable novel of Berkshire life, *Far Away
and Long Ago,* London, 1889.

lating line of distance is overtopped by a considerable mountain with a fine jugged crest, and ever since early morning, troops of clouds and wandering showers of rain and the all-prevailing sunbeams have chased each other over the wooded slopes, and down into the dark hollow where the lake lies sleeping, making a pageant far finer than the one Prospero raised for Ferdinand and Miranda on his desert island. . . .[28]

Like Bryant before her, she never tired of wandering over the hills, and like him, although far more wholeheartedly, she contributed her own talents with tireless generosity to the cultural life of the County. She could hold any Berkshire audience, whether in the Lenox Court House or in Pittsfield's Burbank Hall, spellbound with her unequaled Shakespearean deliveries, and no Sedgwick soirée, either in Lenox or in Stockbridge, was ever considered complete until she had read a scene from *Macbeth* or had sung a Scotch or German ballad to her own piano accompaniment. A born entertainer, she could feel equally at home acting on a New York stage or delivering a poem for the Lenox Academy commencement.

Fanny Kemble was in short the personification of all that was brightest and most alive in Berkshire cultural life, and in 1848 she enjoyed the rare distinction of emerging in Longfellow's slow-moving diary as one of the few aspects of the Berkshire summer that never lulled him to sleep. Longfellow recorded a multitude of impressions of the County during his two extended summers there—comments on the rivers and the factories, on the hillsides, on the Sedgwicks, on the mountains and the woods—and he found inspiration there for a famous poem and for his only novel; but every entry seemed wrenched from a drowsy mind and even the Housatonic, which Melville thought "sparkling," appeared to him as nothing but a "shallow brown stream, not very clear." He

28. Kemble, *Records of Later Life,* p. 164.

might, in fact, have been thus describing his own benumbed
brain during those dreamy summer days in Pittsfield and
Lenox, and try as he might to "be up and doing" in accord
with his own cheerful philosophy, he could not conquer las-
situde.

His wedding trip over the hills to Pittsfield had given him
no warning of his own inherent unsuitability for country
life. He had remained at Elm Knoll with the Appletons for
a few happy weeks in 1843, had seen there on the staircase the
soon-to-be-immortalized old clock, and had returned, full of
inspiration, to Cambridge to write:

> Somewhat back from the village street
> Stands the old-fashioned country-seat.
> Across its antique portico
> Tall poplar trees their shadows throw;
> And from its station in the hall
> An ancient timepiece says to all—
>     "Forever—never! Never—forever!"

And in the golden moments of dalliance at Cambridge in
1846, with his last classes over and the prospect of a long
summer vacation stretching before him, he could still reflect:
"I have a longing for Berkshire or the seaside. Both Nahant
and Stockbridge beckon . . . let me see if I cannot bring
my mind into more poetic mood by the sweet influences of
sun and air and open fields." [29]

In reality the mood he at last settled into was to be neither
poetic nor inspired, and by 1848 he could only conclude: "I
find it quite impossible to write in the country. The influences are soothing and slumberous. In coming here, I hoped
to work successfully on Kavanagh; and as yet I have written
scarcely a page. . . . The capacity of the human frame for

29. *Life of Henry Wadsworth Longfellow,* ed. Samuel Longfellow
(2 vols. Boston, 1886), 2, 49.

sleep in summer is very great." [30] He never, in fact, managed to finish *Kavanagh* during that summer in Berkshire and was compelled at last to postpone the conclusion until he was back in the more invigorating air of Cambridge. Still, most of the writing and much of the limited stimulus came from Berkshire; and if the resulting novel never rose above mediocrity, perhaps it was because, as Longfellow's Mr. Churchill remarked, scenery cannot "create genius. At best it can only develop it." [31]

Longfellow himself admitted feeling "perplexed about Kavanagh," and certainly it is a perplexing book. Hardly a novel at all, it reflects in its strangely confused and episodic progress the sluggish inattention of a sleepy brain driving itself on to the unwelcome task of composition. The shallow and conventional romanticism of the plot and the unimaginative descriptions of the countryside proved nothing but a thin excuse for a series of notebook epigrams painstakingly strung together with numerous obiter dicta on everything from national literature [32] to theological liberalism. The little New England village of Fairmeadow was unmistakably patterned after Lenox, although so hopelessly romanticized as scarcely to retain any shreds of individuality; but the hero—"tall, very pale, with beautiful black eyes and hair"—was merely a brother to dozens of identical Byronic heroes of the early nineteenth century. Stripped of his attractive poetic façade,

30. Ibid., 2, 120.

31. H. W. Longfellow, *Kavanagh*, pp. 114–15.

32. In a conversation between the schoolteacher Mr. Churchill and the editor Hathaway, Longfellow sets forth his view of national literature: "In a word," says Hathaway, "we want a national literature altogether shaggy and unshorn, that shall shake the earth, like a herd of buffaloes thundering over the prairies! . . . Let us have our literature national. If it is not national, it is nothing." To which Churchill (speaking for Longfellow) replies: "on the contrary, it may be a great deal. Nationality is a good thing to a certain extent, but universality is better." *Kavanagh*, pp. 114–15.

Longfellow became surprisingly empty, with only an occasional authentic touch to enliven his pedestrian efforts:

> Moreover, the Grand Junction Railroad was opened through the town, running in one direction to the city, and in the other into unknown northern regions, stringing the white villages like pearls upon its black thread. By this, the town lost much of its rural quiet and seclusion. The inhabitants became restless and ambitious. They were in constant excitement and alarm, like children in story-books hidden away somewhere by an ogre, who visits them regularly every day and night, and occasionally devours one of them for a meal.
>
> Nevertheless, most of the inhabitants considered the railroad a great advantage to the village. Several ladies were heard to say that Fairmeadow had grown quite metropolitan; and Mrs. Wilmerdings, who suffered under a chronic suspension of the mental faculties, had a vague notion, probably connected with the profession of her son, that it was soon to become a seaport.[33]

Not entirely unaware of the book's shortcomings, Longfellow had realized shortly before its publication that "The title is better than the book, and suggests a different kind of book. One more long, spiritual chapter must be written for it. . . . It must go into the book as the keystone into the arch. An idea so very obvious, and yet coming so late!" [34] In Berkshire, Longfellow discovered, as Catharine Sedgwick had found before him and as Holmes would find later, the fullest and strongest expression of Calvinism; [35] and by adding the contemplated "spiritual chapter" to *Kavanagh,* he placed it

33. Longfellow, *Kavanagh,* pp. 100.
34. *Life of Longfellow,* 2, 136.
35. Ibid., 2, 54. In his diary for Aug. 16, 1846, Longfellow recorded: "Dr. Todd preached. Among other things he said of the hard-hearted. 'Nay, they may go up Calvary so far that they can hear the blood dropping from the Saviour's side upon the stones below, and yet they will not be moved.' The parish consider it a great sermon."

in the tradition of Berkshire novels which had begun with *A New England Tale* and would end with *Elsie Venner.* Young Kavanagh, Longfellow decided, must come to Fairmeadow to succeed the "painful preacher of the word," who had, for fifty years, been hardening the hearts of his parishioners with Calvinist hellfire.[36] In happy contrast, Kavanagh himself "did not so much denounce vice as inculcate virtue; he did not deny but affirm; he did not lacerate the hearts of his hearers with doubt and disbelief, but consoled and comforted and healed them with faith. . . . His words were always kindly; he brought no railing accusations against any man." [37] Here was the keystone which Longfellow would add to his plot, and if not wholly effectual, it at least provided one of the few unifying themes of the novel.

Even late in the summer of 1848 *Kavanagh* remained unfinished, and Longfellow was still uttering lethargic complaints. "It is impossible to do anything here in the way of writing," he grumbled in his diary. "Such an empty house one's head becomes in this 'land of drowsy-head.' " Yet, in spite of himself, he was at last learning to enjoy the languid Berkshire summer and could go on to recount: "We drove to Stockbridge to dine with Mrs. Sedgwick; a pleasant dinner. Mr. Theodore from town. After dinner a drive along the Lee road by the meadow and the river. . . . The evening we passed at Sam Ward's. Rackmann played Chopin and Mendelssohn and Schubert. Mrs. Butler sang a ballad. ——— said that everything seemed to be Sedgwick in this region; the very grasshoppers in the fields chirp, 'Sedgwick! Sedgwick!' " [38] Less than two weeks later Longfellow "left Pittsfield for Cambridge. Farewell to Melvill Hall, the lake, the piny mountain, the breezy orchard! Farewell Fayaway; and the

36. In 1845 the Calvinist Reverend Samuel Shepard of Lenox died after a fifty-year pastorate and was replaced by the liberal Reverend Henry Neill.

37. Longfellow, *Kavanagh,* p. 101.

38. *Life of Longfellow,* 2, 121.

playful Major! Farewell the sleepy summer, and the long drives!" [39]

The Berkshire hills were never again to welcome Longfellow for any extended stay, but only a year later they were to welcome a second and rather more adaptable Bostonian. Dr. Oliver Wendell Holmes traveled to Pittsfield in 1849, and there he built, on what remained of the old Wendell estate, the impressive "Holmesdale," where he was to spend seven delightful summers. Unlike Longfellow, he had felt drawn to Berkshire from the first, and is credited with having remarked: "The best of all tonics is the Housatonic." Certainly the poems which Holmes composed during his summers at Canoe Meadows drew much from rural life in Berkshire—so much, in fact, that they prompted Longfellow to observe: "Do you know, I see the Pittsfield farm in your book,—not exactly 'hay in your hair,' but buckwheat in your laurels, which I much delight to see. These blossoms from the roadside and odor of pennyroyal give a freshness to poems which nothing else will. I hope one day to turn a portion of the Housatonic—what runs over your dam above —on to my mill wheels." [40]

But Longfellow was never to carry out his intention of returning, and Holmes remained the reigning summer poet of the Berkshire hills. "If you would be happy in Berkshire," he once wrote, "you must carry mountains in your brain," [41] and he loved the mountains as he knew the sea-drawn Longfellow never could. With the characteristic enthusiasm of the

39. Ibid., 2, 122. The Longfellows spent the summer of 1848 at Major Thomas Melvill's spacious summer resort Melvill Hall. It was later renamed Broadhall and purchased by the Morewoods. Today the building serves as the nucleus of the clubhouse of the Pittsfield Country Club.

40. Longfellow to Holmes, October 28, 1850, *Final Memorials of Henry Wadsworth Longfellow,* ed. Samuel Longfellow (Boston, 1887), p. 389.

41. Oliver Wendell Holmes, *The Autocrat of the Breakfast Table* (Boston, 1895, 1st ed. 1858), p. 265.

born extrovert he plunged at once into the midst of County activities, and by the end of his first Pittsfield summer he was already serving conscientiously on the judging commit-tee for the ploughing contest of the annual Berkshire Fair and was mounting to the church pulpit to deliver an ode composed especially for the occasion.

The Ploughman [42]

Clear the brown path, to meet his coulter's gleam!
Lo! on he comes, behind his smoking team,
With toil's bright dew-drops on his sunburnt brow,
The lord of earth, the hero of the plough! . . .

Still, where he treads, the stubborn clods divide,
The smooth, fresh furrow opens deep and wide;
Matted and dense the tangled turf upheaves,
Mellow and dark the ridgy cornfield cleaves . . .

If her chained bandogs Faction shall unbind,
These stately forms, that bending even now
Bowed their strong manhood to the humble plough,
Shall rise erect, the guardians of the land,
The same stern iron in the same right hand,
Till o'er their hills the shouts of triumph run,
The sword has rescued what the ploughshare won!

More homely and local than Bryant's contributions, it proved the best-loved of all the odes written for the Fair; and from that summer forward, neither Great Barrington's Samuel B. Sumner [43] nor Pittsfield's William Pitt Palmer

42. *The Poetical Works of Oliver Wendell Holmes* (Boston, 1900, 1st ed. 1858), pp. 97–98. The inspiration for the ode appears to have been Herman Melville's uncle, Thomas Melvill.
43. During the 1850's Sumner delivered his poems on seven public occasions in Berkshire, the most famous one being that composed for the Stockbridge celebration to honor Cyrus Field in Aug. 1858. Sam-

was ever to challenge Holmes' position as Berkshire's occasional poet par excellence. With a generosity flowing from his boundless energy, he was to compose two poems for the ladies of St. Stephen's Episcopal church, another for the 1850 dedication of the Pittsfield cemetery, and odes for the Commencement of the Pittsfield Young Ladies' Institute and for the Berkshire Horticultural Society [44]—all this even while his *Autocrat* and *Elsie Venner* [45] were in process of composition and while he was indulging his scientific faculties by working on electrical experiments. "I did not tell you," he wrote to his mother in 1854, "that I had been at work with electricity as a part of my summer plan of instructive amusements. The old machine is mounted on its ancient footing, or rather, with new splendor, and gives sparks an inch long. . . . I find that many of my old tastes return upon me whenever they get a chance; chemistry will have its turn by and by, perhaps mineralogy and the rest of them." [46]

uel B. and Charles A. Sumner, *Poems by Samuel B. and Charles A. Sumner* (New York, 1877), pp. 132, 134.

### Atlantic Cable Poem

Huzza! the magic cable's laid; and now, across the main,
Britannia hails her daughter fair, who answers back again:
With lightning flash, through watery depths that roll and surge between,
Columbia's President responds to Britain's smiling Queen . . .

44. This latter ode, entitled "The New Eden," was first printed by Henry Marsh in the Pittsfield newspaper—a concession granted by Holmes on condition that he be allowed corrections and be given one hundred copies printed on note paper. After sixteen proofs had been corrected, the poem finally appeared in the *Berkshire County Eagle.* Cf. J. E. A. Smith, *The Poet among the Hills* (Pittsfield, 1895), p. 146.

45. The final contribution of the Holmes family to Berkshire culture was to come many years later when Oliver Wendell Holmes, Jr., donated 1,000 volumes from his father's library to the Berkshire Athenaeum.

46. John T. Morse, *Life and Letters of Oliver Wendell Holmes* (2 vols. Boston, 1896), 2, 280–81.

For Holmes nearly every activity eventually had its turn during those unparalleled Berkshire summers. He rode his "little horse" on long pilgrimages through the hills, most often perhaps to Lenox to visit Dr. Neill or the Sedgwicks and to admire Fanny Kemble—"the tragedy queen herself" —and then he would return "once more up among those other hills that shut in the amber-flowing Housatonic—dark stream, but clear, like the lucid orbs that shine beneath the lids of auburn-haired, sherry-wine-eyed demi-blondes . . ." This contemplation of Holmesdale and Canoe Meadows almost invariably stiffled all restraint, and he could write only in superlatives of:

> the home overlooking the winding stream and the smooth, flat meadow; looked down upon by wild hills, where the tracks of bears and catamounts may yet sometimes be seen upon the winter snow; facing the twin summits which rise in the far north, the highest waves of the great land-storm in all this billowy region,—suggestive to mad fancies of the breasts of a half-buried Titaness, stretched out by a stray thunderbolt, and hastily hidden away beneath the leaves of the forest . . . that home where seven blessed summers were passed, which stand in memory like the seven golden candlesticks in the beatific vision of the holy dreamer . . .[47]

Against this idyllic background Dr. Holmes was to draw his dark, unhappy portrait of Elsie Venner—a portrait strangely in contrast with his own cheerful disposition and with the sun-drenched hillsides which he loved.[48] *Elsie Venner*,[49] in fact, came essentially from a grimly sober strain

47. Holmes, *Autocrat*, pp. 244–45.
48. The town of Pigwacket Center in the novel would appear in several respects to be a fictionalized Pittsfield.
49. *Elsie Venner* appeared serially in the *Atlantic Monthly* from Dec. 1859 through Apr. 1861.

in his nature which hated Calvinism with an instinctive passion; and not entirely by coincidence did it fall directly into
the main liberal theological stream of Berkshire fiction.
"You see exactly what I wish to do," Holmes later wrote to
Mrs. Stowe; "to write a story with enough of interest in its
characters and incidents to attract a certain amount of popular attention. Under cover of this to *stir* that mighty question
of automatic agency in its relation to self-determination." [50]
*Elsie Venner,* as its author was the first to admit, was a novel
with a purpose. Dr. Holmes was proposing to slay once and
for all the despised dragon John Calvin and all his vestiges
in nineteenth-century America. Profoundly convinced that
orthodox theology presented a hopelessly false view of the
relations of man to God, he set himself the task of probing
with clinical matter-of-factness [51] into the unsympathetic
doctrine of original sin. "Any decent person ought to go
mad," maintained the Autocrat, "if he really holds such
. . . opinions." [52]

Even in the 1850's the spiritual atmosphere of Berkshire
could still do much to nourish in Holmes that strong anti-
Calvinism he had brought with him from Boston. Among the
Berkshire hills he discovered a Calvinism which was far
from dead; and whether or not it actually provided the motivation for *Elsie Venner,* it must, at least, have kept taut in
him that inborn indignation which was to be the mainspring
of his novel. Certainly Berkshire's religious atmosphere presented a dramatic contrast to the enlightened theology of
Cambridge which he knew. In Berkshire, too, he of course
encountered the highly sympathetic Sedgwicks, who, like

50. Sept. 13, 1860, in Morse, *Life and Letters of Holmes, I,* 263.

51. Throughout one of the summers in which he was working on the
book, Holmes kept in his home a caged rattlesnake; finding it fascinat-
ing, he made a careful study of its eyes, strikes, and habits, and spared
no pains in the writing to make the reptile vivid to the reader. Cf.
Morse, *Life and Letters of Holmes, I,* 258.

52. Holmes, *Autocrat,* p. 42.

Holmes himself, clung in their anti-Calvinism to a solid common sense and totally rejected such rampant enthusiasms as transcendentalism.[53] "I am so tired," Catharine had written to Holmes in 1846, "of the little kernel of the transcendentalists involved in a mass of elaborate shellwork—of the glimmering of a few stars thro' a tangled thicket, of the exaggeration of involvement, like wrapping a very small holiday gift in a series of hyeroglyphic papers, that it is a relief as well as a delight to have sound sense in sound plain English and graceful and poetic in the form in which it springs from the poet's head." [54]

Yet there was at least one writer in Berkshire in the early 1850's whom the local Calvinistic theology neither depressed nor worried—a writer whose novels not only owed nothing to Calvinism but who probably never recognized the existence of theological questions. This was the astoundingly prolific historical romancer George Payne Rainsford James, that gregarious and slightly eccentric Englishman who lighted briefly in Stockbridge in 1851, wrote a few more of his best-selling novels there, and quite unconsciously contributed to the Berkshire cultural tradition a little of the flamboyant romanticism of his indefatigable personality. He had first come to America in 1850, seeking a speedy re-

53. Like the Sedgwicks, the mass of Berkshirites opposed Emerson's flight from orthodoxy. "They [*the transcendentalists*]," wrote Catharine, "seem to me a sort of darkling flight over earth, heaven and hell and a way off into space. . . . It is not the first time a turbid stream has been mistaken for a deep one" (C. Sedgwick to Jane Sedgwick, Mar. 6, 1842; Miscellaneous SP, Harvard). And Charles Sedgwick, who was generally a good barometer of the Berkshire mind, and who was not at all unhappy in 1846 when the Fourieristic community Brook Farm was destroyed by fire, wrote to Sam Ward in March: "it is right that the Lord should not smile on such an ill-devised Harem as that in the land of the Pilgrims—that a house where men are 'to toil for heirs they know not who' should be burnt down" (Charles Sedgwick to Samuel G. Ward, Lenox, Mar. 16, 1846; SGW).

54. Nov. 14, 1846; Holmes Collection, Harvard Library.

covery from recent financial reverses through the expedient
of a whirlwind lecture tour and intending at the same time
to fasten a wary eye on his American publisher. In June of
1851 he abruptly decided to rent the Ashburner house in
Stockbridge, and after a year of healthy, outdoor life among
the hills, Evert Duyckinck could observe that "the American
sun has much improved his countenance but he is still baggy
and English in figure." [55]

Duyckinck might have remarked also that he was still in-
curably English in his way of life; and with his box of snuff
and his indispensable red bandanna he presented a strangely
incongruous appearance in the quiet village of Stockbridge.
Insisting upon open grates and log fires in his sitting rooms,
he cultivated that peculiarly English talent for highly productive activity concealed behind a façade of gentlemanly
idleness. He would, according to his onetime friend and
collaborator, Maunsell B. Field, spend every evening and
morning "industriously pegging away at book-making, although to the casual observer he appeared to be the least
occupied man in the place. He never did any literary work
after eleven a.m. until evening. He was not accustomed to
put his own hand to paper, when composing, but always employed an amanuensis. At this time he had in his service in
that capacity the brother of an Irish baronet, who spoke and
wrote English, French, German, and Italian, and whom I
had procured for him at the modest stipend of five dollars a
week." [56] And, recalled a later amanuensis, "He would walk
up and down in his library and dictate by sentences . . .
he always kept a paper of snuff upon the table. . . . He had
a sketch of the plan and plot of the book in outline prepared
before, and a very brief analysis of what each chapter would

55. Luther S. Mansfield, "Glimpses of Melville's Life in Pittsfield,"
*American Literature, 9* (1937–38), 38. Letter of Evert Duycinck to his
wife, Aug. 7, 1851.
56. Field, *Memories,* p. 203.

contain. He had a large library of reference and other works." [57]

Hawthorne once loyally insisted that James' novels were "admirable stories; admirably told," [58] and certainly Harper and Brothers had good reason to treat their endlessly productive novelist with anxious and kindly concern. During his lifetime he produced ninety-one works,[59] many of them three-volume historical romances and many destined for an immediate ascent to high rank in the midcentury best-seller list. "He turns out a novel every six months," observed James Harper to Thackeray, "and the success is always the same and tremendous. . . . The main reason is that his romances can always be safely placed upon the family table, with the certainty that no page will sully, or call the blush to, the cheek of any member of the household." [60]

Among Berkshirites, James might provoke amusement but he never inspired either awe or withdrawal. They liked him and accepted him with little hesitation, and he providentially arrived in Stockbridge just in time to fill the serious vacancy created by Sam Ward's departure. Like Ward he was a cheerful, social, outgoing man, possessed of a heartily convivial personality and bubbling over with anecdotes and recollections; and like Ward, he could effortlessly draw out writers of shy or chilly natures—notably the reticent Haw-

57. Ibid., pp. 203–4.

58. James T. Fields, *Yesterdays with Authors* (Boston, 1859), p. 63.

59. Of these, seven were written in Berkshire in the year and a half James was there: #75: *Henry Smeaton, A Jacobite Story of the Reign of George I*, 3 vols. London, 1851; #76: *The Fate*, 3 vols. London, 1851; #77: in *Graham's American Monthly Magazine* (1851), *Christian Lacy, Justian and Theodora, A Sonnet to Jenny Lind*; #78: *Revenge*, London, 1852; #79 (with Mauncell B. Field): *Adrian, or The Clouds of the Mind*, 3 vols. London, 1852; #80: *Pequinillo*, 3 vols. London, 1852; #81: in *Harpers'*, June to Nov. 1852, *The Bride of Landeck*.

60. Stewart M. Ellis, *The Solitary Horseman; or, The Life and Adventures of G. P. R. James* (Kensington, 1927), p. 134 n.

thorne, who so much needed and appreciated the healthy association of uncomplicated, sunny dispositions. In the gentlemanly pursuit of agriculture, he never quite equaled Ward's vigorous activity, and his friend Maunsell Field had to admit that "notwithstanding his long India rubber boots and affectation of rustic attire, he was not a success as a farmer." [61] Still, he never tired of swamping on his damp little plot of land just to the north of Monument Mountain.[62]

Sam Ward, Fanny Kemble, and Catharine and Charles Sedgwick, and James imparted to the midcentury villages of Lenox and Stockbridge an air of quiet distinction and a brilliant if largely imported cultural life which set them off even from the rest of Berkshire. The people of Lenox, commented Lenox Academy's principal Mathew Buckham, were "elevated by education and refinement far above the rusticity so characteristic of too much of our New England yeomanry, yet they do not aspire to the pomp of gay life, or the pageantry of fashion." [63] Most of them, in fact, aspired only to being themselves; and if the prospect of Fanny Kemble dancing with Kossuth in the parlor of the Curtis Hotel [64] or

61. Field, *Memories,* p. 203.

62. "Swamping" was a term applied to lumbering in swampy areas—a practice then becoming widespread in those parts of New England being subjected to increased population pressure. This was probably the origin of the term "swamp Yankee"—hardly applicable to the aristocratic James.

63. Mathew Buckham, "Lenox as a Jungle for Literary Lions," Chapter XI of Godfrey Greylock [J. E. A. Smith], *Taghconic* (Boston, 1852), p. 95.

64. J. T. Cutler, "The Literary Associations of Berkshire," *New England Magazine,* new ser. 9 (1893), 3–22. Kossuth came to Berkshire in 1850 and caused a considerable stir, but a few Berkshirites, among them Orville Dewey, feared that the new nationalism would eventually cause general war. Dewey wrote to his enthusiastic daughter at Lenox his belief that the United States must give Kossuth nothing more than favorable opinions: "Moral influence gradually changing the world, is what *I* want. But Kossuth and the Liberals of Europe want to bring

of the young Harriet Hosmer "in very tight yellow breeches" [65] delivering a comic lecture did seem a little bizarre, such events were readily offset by the eminently respectable presences of the "dear little Swedish spinster" Frederika Bremer summering with the Sedgwicks,[66] of Henry Ward Beecher in Lenox for his annual pursuit of "cloud culture," and of Jenny Jerome, Ellen Emerson, Charlotte Cushman, and Lydia Saltonstall at Mrs. Sedgwick's school.

Not unaware of this atmosphere of refinement and gentility, the rest of Berkshire was sometimes resentful and sometimes only amused. Orville Dewey once extended to his daughter a mildly satiric invitation to "descend upon us from the heights of Lenox—from the schools of wisdom, from fiction and fine writing, from tragedy and comedy, from mountain-mirrors reflecting all surrounding beauty, down to plain, prosaic still-life in Sheffield." [67] And ten years afterward a correspondent in the Pittsfield *Sun* reported sardonically that "the quagmire called *Nigger Pond* formerly in Great Barrington, has, according to the last survey, crossed the line north into Stockbridge. It is now called *Agawam Lake*." [68] Catharine Sedgwick had managed a few years earlier to antagonize the citizenry of Pittsfield by untactfully remarking in an article for *Graham's Magazine* that "Pittsfield is the metropolitan village of Berkshire and the whole County must yield to it in working day prosperities . . . [*but*] in refinement and rural beauty Pittsfield is inferior we think to some of our more secluded and unambitious villages." [69] Thereafter, residents of Stockbridge and Lenox

on that great war of opinion, which, I fear, will come only too soon" (Dewey, *Autobiography*, pp. 226–27).

65. Fanny Kemble to William Minot, Lenox, Dec. 22 (no year); MC.

66. H. D. Sedgwick, "Literary Berkshire," p. 566.

67. Dewey, *Autobiography*, p. 203.

68. Pittsfield *Sun*, Aug. 18, 1859.

69. Reprinted in Pittsfield *Sun*, June 20, 1844.

learned to keep their feeling of conscious superiority to themselves, and Charles Sedgwick wisely restricted to his own correspondence his pride in Lenox. "Please set it down to the credit of Lenox," he boasted privately "that it is the only town in the county, and almost in the State, where a 'Know-Nothing' representative was not elected; almost the only town in the State, where a 'Know-Nothing' lodge has not been formed." [70]

Perhaps, in reality, even the convivial Charles did not find the new refinement and busy cosmopolitanism of Lenox quite so pleasantly restful as the old uninterrupted quiet before the fame of Catharine and the conveniences of the railroad had brought on the "press of population." "I have become sadly hardened to the decencies of life," he confessed to Sam Ward, "and have done little but dodge strangers when I could and breast myself to the shock when discerned in some lurking place . . ." [71] Yet when Fanny Kemble returned from New York in 1858, she felt none of Charles' reservations and rejoiced to "find both villages in a perfect glory of dissipation—masquerades, private theatricals,—balls at the town hall and tea drinkings at the ———— . . ." [72] And Catharine thought Lenox "at its culminating point of gaiety. Henry Ward Beecher begins the programme on Sunday with brilliant sermons and Rackemann closes the week with a 'successful soirée' . . ." [73]

No county ever found more enthusiastic publicists than did Berkshire in Henry Ward Beecher and in those two other distinguished clergymen Charles Parkhurst and Washington Gladden, who so generously reported the charms of Berkshire to the outside world. Even after settling in New York to launch his famous crusade against Tammany, Dr.

70. *Letters of Charles Sedgwick* (New York, 1863), p. 147.
71. Sept. 6, 1853; SGW.
72. To Kate Minot, 1858; MC.
73. To Anna Barker Ward, Aug. 14, 1854; SGW.

Parkhurst was never to forget his six-year pastorate in Lenox
and the beauties of the Berkshire hills; and Gladden, after
a year in Williamstown, was to take precious time from his
preaching to write *From the Hub to the Hudson*—"an attempt to show people how and where they may cheaply and
pleasantly spend their few days of summer vacation. . . .
A book that helps anybody to see and enjoy the Connecticut
Valley or the Berkshire Hills, will be likely to do less harm
than a book about the Mode of Baptism or the Origin of
Evil." [74]

Pre-eminent among the rusticating clerics, however, was
Beecher himself, who had come to Lenox in 1853, had
bought John Hotchkin's farm there,[75] and had settled down
comfortably for summers of leisurely contemplation. "The
chief use of a farm, if it be well selected, and of a proper
soil," he wrote, "is, to lie down upon. Mine is an excellent
farm for such uses, and I thus cultivate it every day. Large
crops are the consequence, of great delight and fancies more
than the brain can hold. My industry is exemplary. Though
but a week here, I have lain down more hours and in more
places than that hard-working brother of mine in the whole
year that he has dwelt here. Strange that industrious lying
down should come so naturally to me, and standing up and
lazing about after the plow or behind his scythe, so naturally
to him! My eyes against his feet!" [76] Like Parkhurst and

74. Washington Gladden, *From the Hub to the Hudson* (Boston,
1869), p. iv. Berkshire's own cleric, Orville Dewey, also did his part
as a publicist for the county by urging Bryant to "turn your poetical
genius to account by describing the beautiful ride up the valley of
the Housatonic and this our beautiful Berkshire" and to "request the
[*Twenty-One*] Club to meet at my house some day in the coming summer" (Dewey, *Autobiography*, pp. 215–16).

75. The $4,000 purchase price of the farm had been raised for Beecher
by his Brooklyn parishioners. Lenox Church Records, Sept. 1, 1853;
typescript, p. 383.

76. Beecher, "Dream-Culture," *Star Papers*, p. 268.

Gladden, Beecher felt moved to spread his doctrine of the good life in Berkshire as far beyond the mountain barriers as he could, and it was with this thought in mind that he first began work on his *Star Papers*. He intended, he said, "to urge those who can command leisure in September or October, avoiding all beaten paths of pleasure, to make a tour through the mountain country of western Connecticut and Massachusetts. If you are young, and not abundant in means, and can get a friend to accompany you, go afoot. If you are able, go on horseback. If you wish to take your wife, your mother, or a sister, then a light, four-wheeled, covered buggy is to be elected." [77]

Yet Beecher knew enough of the New England mind to realize that a mere prescription for summer loafing and day dreaming was not enough unless it be justified for the Puritan conscience, and to that conscience he spoke next. Rusticating, he wrote in words reminiscent of Bryant's appreciation of nature, "if it gives great delight, if it keeps the soul awake, sweet thoughts alive, and sordid thoughts dead . . . if it be like a bath to the soul, in which it washes away the grime of human contacts . . . it will have answered a purpose which is in vain sought among stupid conventionalities." [78] Even the thought of death became more endurable in Lenox with the comforting prospect of burial in the graveyard on the hill. "No dark and sickly fogs ever gather at evening about it. It lies nearer heaven than any place about. It is good to have our mortal remains go upward for their burial, and catch the earliest sounds of that trumpet which shall raise the dead!" [79]

Three years before Beecher's arrival in Lenox, another very different visitor had sojourned there—a visitor in whom

77. Idem, "A Country Ride," *Star Papers,* p. 175.
78. Idem, *Star Papers,* p. 269.
79. Ibid., p. 180.

Berkshire graveyards inspired not triumphant contempt but a grim fascination with death and decay. On his first trip to Berkshire in 1838 Nathaniel Hawthorne had prowled curiously into the tomb of the Thomas Allen family in the Pittsfield cemetery and had noted with morbid interest the white mold on the coffins, and twelve years later he was to discover a strange preoccupation with the sight of an old decaying wood pile near his cottage. Much of what he saw, along with whatever reflections those sights inspired during his eighteen months in Lenox, eventually found its way into his notebooks, there to await a possible resurrection and transformation in the pages of some future story or romance.

Always a restless wanderer, Hawthorne had brought his family to Berkshire in June of 1850, partly because he knew nowhere else to go. He had lost his job in Salem as Surveyor of the Port; Mrs. Caroline Tappan had kindly offered him the use of her little red cottage in Lenox [80] at a nominal rate; and perhaps he felt he owed to Sophia and to Una and Julian this temporary security. "We give only three cents a quart for best of milk . . ." Sophia soon wrote happily of household economics, "Butter is fourteen cents a pound, and . . . the most superb buckwheat at half the price we gave at the East." [81]

Hawthorne himself found relative happiness in Lenox, at least for the first few months. The Salem Customs House had left him physically tired, *The Scarlet Letter* had enervated his spiritual resources, and he needed the relaxation and the vigorous outdoor life which Berkshire could give him. With Una and Julian he cultivated his fruit trees and his corn patch and observed the chickens in his "sumptuous" hennery —especially the "laughably womanish" ways and the "self-

80. The cottage actually stood two hundred yards inside the Stockbridge border, but mail always came to Lenox.

81. Sophia to her mother, June 23, 1850, in Julian Hawthorne, *Nathaniel Hawthorne and His Wife* (2 vols. Boston, 1885), *1*, 371.

important gait" of his favorite speckled hen.[82] "We are getting along very well," he wrote contentedly to his friend
Bridge at summer's end. "Una and Julian grow apace, and
so do our chickens, of which we have two broods. . . . We
have become so intimately acquainted with every individual
of them, that it really seems like cannibalism to think of eating them. What is to be done?" [83]

The problem, however, did not weigh heavily on his mind,
and he gave himself over to the delights of outdoor life with
rare openheartedness and abandon. He climbed one of Berkshire's miniature mountains with Sophia in "mellow autumnal sunshine"; he fished and boated with Julian in a
leaky punt; he went sledding with the children on crisp
winter afternoons. And nearby "Tanglewood" glen lured
him out to muse and ramble in every season—in midsum-
mer a dense, shadowy obscurity, in October "absolutely full
of sunshine." "The trees are sunshine, and many of their
golden leaves being freshly fallen, the glen is strewn with
sunshine, amid which winds and gurgles the bright, dark
little brook." [84] No wonder Hawthorne could suddenly find
his soul so full of sunlight that he composed the *Wonder-
Book*—admittedly not a major work but certainly among
the most relaxed and cheerful sketches he ever wrote.

Whatever the weather, he would never miss the short
daily trip to Luther Butler's for milk, and in Butler he
discovered, as Sam Ward had earlier, a man of striking integrity and earthly wisdom—in short, the embodiment of
the noble Berkshire yeoman.[85] And during those same

82. Hawthorne, *American Notebooks,* p. 130.
83. Hawthorne to Bridge, Aug. 7, 1850, in Horatio Bridge, *Personal
Recollections of Nathaniel Hawthorne* (London, 1893), p. 138.
84. Hawthorne, *American Notebooks,* p. 133.
85. Both of the Hawthornes appreciated, though with a slight air
of condescension, Luther Butler. Sophia wrote Anna Ward: "I had
a good talk with Luther Butler today. What a noble nature he has. It
is delightful to hear him speak of you and Mr. Ward. He really seems

months he almost never failed to walk every day to the Lenox post office and thus to make an acquaintance with the countryside nearly as intimate as Bryant's and Ward's. His notebooks for 1850 and 1851 are full of those walks on the Lenox roads. Among the finest testaments ever written to the beauty of the Berkshire hills, they rank with Bryant's poems and with Melville's prose idylls. Yet for Hawthorne, the feeling toward Berkshire was one of admiration rather than of that deep attachment felt by Ward and Holmes, and it was the majesty of the distant scene—of Monument Mountain, Taconic Dome, and Rattlesnake Hill—which most often caught and held his eye. He might write occasionally in his notebook of a wasp or a chickadee or a clump of violets, but these were phenomena he could find quite as readily in Salem or in Concord, and they could never excite in his wondering mind the same interest as the variations and seasonal changes of the distant hills.

Melville was to swear fealty to Greylock; Hawthorne, to Monument Mountain. From the second-floor study of his red cottage he could look across his lake in every season to that remarkable expanse of greenery and crumbling marble rising 1,400 feet into the air—in August "in the early sunshine; its base enveloped in mist," looking like an island in the sky; [86] in October "the foliage having its autumn hues . . . like a headless sphinx, wrapt in a rich Persian shawl"; in February "black and shaggy"; and in May responding "with livelier effect to the shine and shade of the sky." [87]

Yet most of these observations were destined to remain buried in his notebooks—never to be resurrected anywhere in his creative works—and the atmosphere of Berkshire was to prove, at last, not so much an inspiration as a relaxation.

capable of appreciating you and him from a native honor and tone of high feeling born with him" (Lenox, Mar. 23, 1851; SGW).

86. Hawthorne, *American Notebooks*, p. 131.

87. Ibid., pp. 132, 134, 138.

The long walks and the happy hours of leisure did bring a genuine re-creation of his artistic powers; but unlike the young and still uncertain Melville, Hawthorne had achieved his ultimate creative potentiality before he came to Lenox, and he was no longer groping for any answers that the Berkshire surroundings could provide. The idea for *The House of the Seven Gables* had its roots, of course, in his native Salem, and he carried it with him to Lenox nearly formed. The first summer there gave him leisure for planning, but in September, although he had begun to write, he felt obliged to warn publisher Fields: "I shan't have the new story ready by November, for I am never good for anything in the literary way till after the first autumnal frost, which has somewhat such an effect on my imagination that it does on the foliage here about me,—multiplying and brightening its hues; though they are likely to be sober and shabby enough after all." [88] The autumnal frost of 1850 must have been a particularly salutary one, for on January 26, 1851, he carried the final pages of his manuscript to the Lenox post office.

By the following summer he was beginning to tire, and perhaps Berkshire had already begun to lose something of its original fascination. "The truth is," he wrote to sister Louisa, "the pen is so constantly in my fingers that I abominate the sight of it." [89] Still, he had almost completed in a little over a month "a book of two or three hundred pages for children, and I think it stands a chance of a wide circulation . . ." [90] This was the *Wonder-Book* and brought an end to his Berkshire productivity. It also brought to an end, at least temporarily, his depression of a few days earlier, and by July 15 he was writing contentedly to Fields: "Mrs. Kemble writes very good accounts from London of the reception my

88. James T. Fields, *Hawthorne* (Boston, 1871), p. 28.
89. Julian Hawthorne, *Hawthorne and His Wife*, *1*, 408.
90. Horatio Bridge, *Recollections of Hawthorne*, p. 141.

two romances have met with there. She says they have made a greater sensation than any book since 'Jane Eyre'; but probably she is a little or a good deal too emphatic in her representation of the matter. . . . I am going to begin to enjoy the summer now, and to read foolish novels, if I can get any, and smoke cigars, and think of nothing at all; which is equivalent to thinking of all manner of things." [91] Among other things during that summer and fall he was to think about *The Blithedale Romance*—and to "seize the skirts of ideas and pin them down for further investigation," [92] as was his wont in summertime.

By fall the feeling of depression was again descending on him—a feeling brought on partly by a climate he found increasingly oppressive and partly by the growing difficulty of securing solitude at the red cottage. He was not, by nature, a thoroughgoing recluse, but at Lenox, as at Salem and at Concord, he discovered only a few people whom he sincerely enjoyed and multitudes who thrust themselves upon him against his will. All too soon the Lenox cottage became a kind of shrine to which "secret criminals" and "spiritual invalids" [93] came in search of soul-massaging at the hands of the now famous author of *The Scarlet Letter* and on which a few intruded merely to catch a glimpse of the great man's face.

Occasionally, too, Hawthorne's inherent reticence deprived him of associations which he might well have come to enjoy. The Charles Sedgwicks made every effort to be kind during the first summer; and Sophia, at least, felt a deep gratitude for their generosity. "The truest friendliness is the great characteristic of the Sedgwick family in all its branches," she had written her mother in August. "They

91. Fields, *Hawthorne,* p. 34.

92. Rose Hawthorne Lathrop, *Memories of Hawthorne* (Boston, 1897), p. 130.

93. Hawthorne, *Hawthorne and His Wife, 1,* 358.

seem to delight to make happy, and they are as happy as summer days themselves. They really take the *responsibility* of my being comfortable." [94] But even four months later Charles Sedgwick was writing to Sam Ward: "Of the Hawthornes we know nothing, I have made three or four calls there, five or six— Hawthorne has never been here but once when he was specially invited to spend the day. But my wife is indefatigible." [95]

Hawthorne, in fact, opened the door of the red cottage willingly to only a very few. The James Russell Lowells and the biographer, Joel T. Headley, stopped to see him in September; Fanny Kemble would ride up whenever she was in Berkshire to converse "in heroic phrases with the inmates of the red house" or to snatch up young Julian "the Apostate" and gallop away with him on her large black horse; and G. P. R. James [96]—"an excellent man and his wife a plain, good . . . kind-hearted woman"—could offer just the kind of cheerful, undemanding, uncomplicated friendship that Hawthorne most desired. But even with the jovial James he could not always conquer diffidence, and once even hid like a "frightened schoolboy" when James and Maunsell Field presented themselves at the front door.[97] Yet, like many another shy man, he could become bolder on paper than he ever dared to be in reality, and he left it to Eustace Bright of the *Wonder-Book* to pay his tribute to Berkshire writers:

> I wish I had Pegasus here. . . . I would mount him forthwith, and gallop about the country, within a circumference of a few miles, making literary calls on my brother-authors. Dr. Dewey would be within my reach, at the foot of Taconic. In Stockbridge, yonder, is Mr. James, conspicuous to all the world on his mountain-

94. Lathrop, *Memories of Hawthorne*, pp. 130–31.
95. Charles Sedgwick to S. G. Ward, Dec. 29, 1850; SGW.
96. Hawthorne, *American Notebooks*, p. 232.
97. Field, *Memories*, p. 205.

pile of history and romance. Longfellow, I believe, is not yet at the Ox-bow, else the winged horse would neigh at the sight of him. But, here in Lenox, I should find our most truthful novelist, who has made the scenery and life of Berkshire all her own. On the hither side of Pittsfield sits Herman Melville, shaping out the gigantic conception of his 'White Whale,' while the gigantic shape of Greylock looms upon him from his study-window. Another bound of my flying steed would bring me to the door of Holmes, whom I mention last, because Pegasus would certainly unseat me, the next minute, and claim the poet as his rider.[98]

Whatever the uncertainties in Hawthorne's feeling toward Melville, there is no reason to think his tribute to him any less sincere. The two men had met on August 5, 1850—perhaps the most fruitful and significant meeting in the history of American letters. In a railroad car rumbling up the Housatonic from New York City, the distinguished attorney David Dudley Field, en route to his summer home in Stockbridge, encountered editor Evert Duyckinck, on his way to visit Melville at Pittsfield, and together they arranged a rendezvous. Duyckinck, a friend of both Melville and Hawthorne, agreed to bring Melville to Stockbridge on August 5 for an all-day outing at Monument Mountain, and Field promised to take care of the rest. Invitations were quickly

98. Nathaniel Hawthorne, *A Wonder-Book for Girls and Boys* (Boston and New York, 1883, 1st ed. 1851), p. 196. Pittsfield's poet, William Pitt Palmer, called the Berkshire of the 1850's an idyllic era in Berkshire—in an interlude between the ruggedness of the "Stump Age" and the bustle of the urban. In 1885, Holmes wrote a Pittsfield friend lamenting the urbanization of the town: "such a beautiful, healthful, central situation could not resist its destiny, and you must have a mayor, I suppose, by and by, and a common council, and a lot of aldermen. But you cannot lose the sight of Greylock, nor turn the course of the Housatonic" (J. T. Morse, *Holmes, I*, 201).

issued—to Hawthorne and Dr. Holmes, to Cornelius
Mathews and Joel T. Headley, to editor J. T. Fields and
his bride, and to Field's daughter Jenny and her enthusiastic
young escort Henry D. Sedgwick, Jr. Hawthorne was at his
best—nearly every trace of shyness and moodiness gone—
and Duyckinck reported delightedly to his wife on the outcome of the plotted meeting:

> As we scrambled over the rocks at the summit a black
> thunder cloud from the south dragged its ragged edges
> toward us—the thunder rolling in the distance. They
> talked of shelter and shelter there proved to be though
> it looked unpromising; but these difficulties, like others,
> vanish on trials and a few feet of rock with a damp un-
> derground of mosses and decay actually sheltered pub-
> lisher Fields curled whiskers, his patent leathers and his
> bride's delicate blue silk. Dr. Holmes cut three branches
> for an umbrella and uncorked the champagne which
> was drunk from a silver mug. The rain did not do its
> worst and we scattered over the cliffs, Herman Melville
> to seat himself, the boldest of all astride a projecting
> low stick of rock while Dr. Holmes peeped about the
> cliffs and protested it affected him like ipecac. Haw-
> thorne looked wildly about for the great carbuncle.
> Mathews read Bryant's poem. The exercise was glori-
> ous.[99]

Mathews was later to catch the "glorious" mood even better. "Higher, higher up we go," he exclaimed in retrospect,
"stealing glances through the trees at the country under-
neath; rambling, scrambling, climbing, rhyming,—puns flying off in every direction like sparks among the bushes." [100]
At the top, they paused for a rest and for a reading of Bry-

99. Aug. 6, 1850, in Mansfield, "Glimpses of Melville's Life," p. 30.
100. Cornelius Mathews, "Several Days in Berkshire," *Literary World*,
Aug. 24, 1850.

ant's *Monument Mountain* and a toast to "the dear old poet"; and then Hawthorne, in rare high spirits, was off again, lurking behind the dark edges of the Ice-Glen and shouting threats of certain destruction on the whole party.[101]

Two days later, still full of enthusiasm, he was writing to Bridge: "Duyckinck, of the *Literary World,* and Herman Melville are in Berkshire, and I expect them to call here this morning. I met Melville the other day, and liked him so much that I have asked him to spend a few days with me before leaving these parts." [102] They came the next morning and found Hawthorne's little corner of Lenox "one of the most purely beautiful spots in the region. . . . Hawthorne gave us some Heidsieck which a literary friend had presented to him, popping the corks in his nervous way . . ." [103] Thereafter, Melville came often to the red cottage, and Hawthorne opened his door hospitably to him as he had done to few others among his Berkshire neighbors. Una and Julian adored "Mr. Omoo," rode on his big Newfoundland dog, and listened wide-eyed to his fabulous stories of the South Sea Islands; and Sophia, with keen penetration, recognized in him "A man with a true, warm heart, and a soul and an intellect,—with life to his finger-tips . . . and I am not sure that he is not a very great man." [104]

Sophia was to think still more highly of Melville when she discovered him to be that anonymous critic—"so fearless, so rich in heart, of such fine intuition"—who had written in the *Literary World* high praise of *Mosses from an Old Manse.*[105] Hawthorne, meanwhile, was just beginning to read Mel-

101. Fields, *Yesterdays with Authors,* p. 53.

102. Hawthorne to Bridge, Aug. 7, 1850, in Bridge, *Recollections of Hawthorne,* p. 137.

103. Duyckinck to his wife, Aug. 9, 1850, in Mansfield, "Glimpses of Melville's Life," p. 34.

104. Sophia to her mother, Sept. 4, 1850, in Lathrop, *Memories of Hawthorne,* p. 135.

105. Sophia Hawthorne to E. Duyckinck, Aug. 29, 1850, in Jay Leyda, *The Melville Log* (2 vols. New York, 1951), *1,* 391.

ville's works "with a progressive appreciation of the author. No writer ever put the reality before his reader more un-flinchingly than he does in 'Redburn,' and 'White Jacket.' 'Mardi' is a rich book with depths here and there that compel a reader to swim for his life. It is so good that one scarcely pardons the writer for not having brooded long over it, so as to make it a great deal better." [106] Probably the relation-ship between Hawthorne and Melville represented the most complete meeting of minds that either experienced during his lifetime—a meeting leading not merely to philosophical dialogue but to deep friendship and mutual understanding. Perhaps the main basis for this profound rapport between the two lay in their common concern for the darker human depths—depths which Melville had quickly recognized in Hawthorne and had thus unconsciously revealed also in him-self:

> There is a certain tragic phase of humanity [*he wrote*] which, in our opinion, was never more powerfully em-bodied than by Hawthorne. We mean the tragicalness of human thought in its own unbiassed, native, and pro-founder workings. We think that into no recorded mind has the intense feeling of the visible truth ever en-tered more deeply than into this man's. By visible truth, we mean the apprehension of the absolute con-dition of present things as they strike the eye of the man who fears them not, though they do their worst to him. . . . There is the grand truth about Nathaniel Hawthorne. He says No! in thunder; but the Devil himself cannot make him say *yes*. For all men who say *yes*, lie; and all men who say *no*,—why, they are in the happy condition of judicious, unincumbered travellers in Europe; they cross the frontiers into Eternity with nothing but a carpet-bag,—that is to say, the Ego.[107]

106. To E. Duyckinck, Aug. 29, 1850, in Leyda, *1*, 391.
107. Ibid., *1*, 410.

Melville continued to haunt the red cottage, and in March, Hawthorne, who rarely visited anyone else in Berkshire, brought Una with him for two days at Arrowhead. The two men sought out the barn both for seclusion and as a refuge from the weather, and there they smoked and talked metaphysics by the hour, Hawthorne seated on a carpenter's bench and Melville sprawled in the hay. They must be sure, remarked Hawthorne, to commemorate the occasion by publishing "A Week on a Work-Bench in a Barn." The same carefree spirit evidently continued throughout the spring, and in June Melville was insisting that "we—that is, you and I—must hit upon some little bit of vagabondism before autumn comes. Greylock—we must go and vagabondize there." [108] Instead, they settled in August for a trip to Lebanon with Evert and George Duyckinck to see the Shakers.

In that same month, Hawthorne, still tolerably cheerful, was recording in his notebook: "a cavalier on horseback [came along the road, and] saluted me in Spanish; to which I replied by touching my hat, and went on with the newspaper. But the cavalier renewing his salutation, I regarded him more attentively, and saw that it was Herman Melville! . . . After supper . . . Melville and I had a talk about time and eternity, things of this world and of the next, and books, and publishers, and all possible and impossible matters, that lasted pretty deep into the night . . ." [109] It was such lengthy talks as these with Hawthorne that gave to Melville the spiritual reinforcement he so much needed for *Moby Dick*. "If ever, my dear Hawthorne," he wrote in June, "in the eternal times that are to come, you and I shall sit down in Paradise, in some little shady corner by ourselves . . . then, O my dear fellow mortal, how shall we pleasantly discourse of all the things manifold which now so

108. To Hawthorne, June 22, 1851, in Mansfield, "Glimpses of Melville's Life," p. 46.
109. Hawthorne, *American Notebooks*, p. 220.

distress us,—when all the earth shall be but a reminiscence, yea, its final dissolution an antiquity." [110]

Yet by the fall, Hawthorne's feeling of depression had extended even to his relations with Melville. The powerful intellect and the penetrating eyes suddenly only wearied and oppressed him, and the easy-going companionship of James came to seem infinitely preferable. Even in the late spring, he had begun to show signs of restlessness, and under the seemingly inevitable monotony of too much rustication had written to Longfellow: "I mean to come to Boston in a month or two. I need to smell the sea-breeze and dock mud, and to tread pavements. I am comfortable here, and as happy as mortal can be; but sometimes my soul gets into a ferment, as it were, and becomes troublous and bubblous with too much peace and rest." [111] By July his growing discontent was bubbling over unrestrainedly, at least in the privacy of his notebook: "This is a horrible, horrible, most hor-ri-ble climate; one knows not, for ten minutes together whether he is too cool or too warm; but he is always one or the other; and the constant result is a miserable disturbance of the system. I detest it! I detest it!! I detest it!!! I hate Berkshire with my whole soul, and would joyfully see its mountains laid flat . . . here, where I hoped for perfect health, I have for the first time been made sensible that I cannot with impunity encounter nature in all her moods." [112]

In November, unable to live with his own dissatisfactions any longer, Hawthorne abandoned the little red cottage for good, and Melville was left spiritually alone. He was to remain in Berkshire ten years longer and was never again to find so intimate and sympathetic a companion as he had found in Hawthorne. For a brooding and restless

110. Eleanore Melville Metcalf, *Herman Melville, Cycle and Epicycle* (Cambridge, 1953), p. 108.

111. May 18, 1851, in *Life of Longfellow*, 2, 208.

112. Hawthorne, *American Notebooks*, p. 215.

mind like Melville's such companionship could come only rarely, and in his eagerness to realize it fully, it seemed inevitable that he should ask too much. Himself willing to give everything to the relationship, his demands on the man he idealized could only be excessive. He wanted both friend and father-confessor, and Hawthorne, by nature a reserved and solitary figure, had already given all he could—more, perhaps, than he had ever given to another man.

In respect to length of residence, Melville was to be more truly a Berkshirite than Ward or Holmes; yet each of them, within the space of a few months, had managed to become a more intimate part of the local scene than Melville ever managed to become in all the years he lived there. The failure to integrate, however, came not so much from deliberate choice, as it had with Hawthorne, as from an eccentricity in his personal outlook which grew more pronounced with every year of spiritual solitude. At first, that "promoter of universal happiness," Mrs. Sarah Morewood, had welcomed him delightedly into her social orbit. In the one-time Melvill Hall adjoining Arrowhead she and her husband gathered around them as many of the local literary élite as they could muster—a perfect "maelstrom of hospitality" [113]—and Melville played the part of bon vivant with a flourish. He loved the picnics on Constitution Hill or at the edge of Lake Pontoosuc, the overnight outings on Greylock, the frequent musicales; and he would spend long afternoons and evenings in the excellent Morewood library.

But the Melville who firmly refused to "believe in a Temperance Heaven," [114] who cheerily bade Hawthorne "have ready a bottle of brandy," [115] and who blatantly accused the local clerics of peddling round "indulgences from divine or-

113. E. Duyckinck to his wife, Aug. 13, 1851, in Leyda, *1*, 425.

114. Melville to Hawthorne, June 1, 1851, in Hawthorne, *Hawthorne and His Wife*, p. 403.

115. Idem, June 29, 1851, ibid., p. 400.

dinations," [116] was not destined for lasting social success in puritanical Pittsfield. John Morewood would not tolerate impieties, and even as early as the fall of 1851 Mrs. Morewood was writing to George Duyckinck: "It is a pity that Mr. Melville so often in conversation uses irreverent language—he will not be popular in society here on that very account—but this will not trouble him— I think he cares very little as to what others may think of him or his books so long as they sell well . . . I laughed at him somewhat and told him that the recluse life he was leading made his city friends think that he was slightly insane—he replied that long ago he came to the same conclusion himself but if he left home to look after Hungary the cause in hunger would suffer." [117]

In reality, Melville was not quite the hopeless recluse that Mrs. Morewood thought him. Dr. Holmes at least neither regarded him as insane nor was shocked by his heterodox theology, and once engaged him in a discussion of East Indian religions and mythologies which, according to the omnipresent Maunsell Field, "lasted for hours. . . . I never heard better talking in my life . . . we took no note of time, and the Doctor lost his dinner as we lost ours." [118] Nor was Holmes the only Pittsfield resident whom Melville's theological eccentricities could not alienate. Both the engineer and part-time littérateur John E. Hoadley [119] and the poet-historian Joseph E. A. Smith [120] remained steadfast friends,

116. Herman Melville, "The Lightning Rod Man," *The Complete Stories of Herman Melville,* ed. Jay Leyda (New York, 1949), p. 221.

117. Dec. 28, 1851, in Mansfield, "Glimpses of Melville's Life," p. 48.

118. Field, *Memories,* p. 202.

119. Hoadley was to marry Melville's sister, Catherine, in 1853.

120. Smith arranged concerts for Burbank Hall, was editor of the *Berkshire County Eagle* for a time, and under the pseudonym "Godfrey Greylock" wrote several books on Berkshire legends and Berkshire literary society, and with his excellent *History of Pittsfield* emerged as one of the leading local historians of his time.

and with Smith, Melville took long cross-country tramps —to the Hopper, to Balanced Rock in Lanesboro, and to tiny Ashley Pond high on Hoosac Mountain. Himself a man of limited literary talents, Smith functioned admirably as the common denominator between local and imported culture, and through his untiring intercessions Melville's works were assured ample publicity in the Berkshire press.

Still, Mrs. Morewood was right in assuming that Melville cared little for the opinions of the world; and eventually, he came to feel an attachment for the land in Berkshire surpassing any personal attachment there, excepting only that with Hawthorne. Paradoxically enough, neither Longfellow nor Hawthorne—both born and bred on the land—could ever feel so deep a love for inland Berkshire as did Melville, the seaman who had sailed so many months before the mast. Both of them went hurrying back to the smell of the sea and left it to Melville to discern with a sailor's eye the fundamental unity of nature and her moods.[121] "I have a sort of sea-feeling here in the country," he wrote to Duyckinck, "now that the ground is covered with snow. I look out of my window in the morning when I rise as I would out of a porthole of a ship in the Atlantic. My room seems a ship's cabin, and at nights when I wake up and hear the wind shrieking, I almost fancy there is too much sail on the house, and I had better go on the roof and rig in the chimney." [122] And in summertime, he could imagine his piazza a quarterdeck:

> sitting here, one is often reminded of the sea. For not only do long ground-swells roll the slanting grain, and little wavelets of the grass ripple over upon the low piazza, as their beach, and the blown down of dandelions

121. Melville did escape from Berkshire for two long sea voyages, but both times he returned to Arrowhead.

122. Melville to Duyckinck, Dec. 12, 1850, in Meade Minnigerode, *Some Personal Letters of Herman Melville and a Bibliography* (New Haven, 1922), p. 71.

is wafted like the spray, and the purple of the mountains is just the purple of the billows, and a still August noon broods upon the deep meadows, as a calm upon the Line; but the vastness and the lonesomeness are so oceanic, and the silence and the sameness, too, that the first peep of a strange house, rising beyond the trees, is for all the world like spying, on the Barbary coast, an unknown sail.[123]

Farming, however, he would readily admit possessed its unromantic aspects, and "no man by that means accumulates a fortune from this thin and rocky soil." [124] Indeed, in June of 1851 he was already complaining to Hawthorne: "but see my hand! four blisters on this palm, made by hoes and hammers within the last few days." [125] Yet he felt stifled by the city and probably more than once during his time in New York "mounted [*his*] green jacket and strolled down to the Battery to study the stars"; [126] and bitterly though he might complain of hardships and of persistent duns, he evidently found the regularity of his farm routine preferable to the uncertainties of the city life from which he had come:

> I rise at eight—thereabouts—and go to my barn—say good morning to the horse and give him his breakfast. (It goes to my heart to give him a cold one, but it can't be helped.) Then, pay a visit to my cow—cut up a pumpkin or two for her, and stand by to see her eat it—for it's a pleasant sight to see a cow move her jaws—she does it so mildly and with such a sanctity.
>
> My own breakfast over, I go to my workroom and light

123. Melville, "The Piazza," *Complete Short Stories of Melville*, p. 440.

124. Melville, *Israel Potter, His Fifty Years of Exile* (New York, 1855), p. 10.

125. Melville to Hawthorne, June 1851, in Leyda, *1*, 412.

126. Melville to E. Duyckinck, Mar. 7, 1850; Duyckinck Collection, NYPL.

my fire—then spread my MSS. on the table—take one
business squint at it, and fall to with a will. At 2-½ P. M.
I hear a preconcerted knock at my door, which (by request) continues till I rise and go to the door, which
seems to wean me effectively from my writing, however
interested I may be.

My friends the horse and cow demand their dinner—and
I go and give it them. My own dinner over, I rig my
sleigh and with my mittens and rubbers start off for the
village—and if it be a "Literary World" day, great is the
satisfaction thereof.[127]

Neither Catharine Sedgwick nor Dr. Holmes nor Sam
Ward ever knew the Berkshire countryside so intimately or
expressed that knowledge so eloquently as did Melville.
Within a fortnight of his arrival in Pittsfield, he had purchased Field's *History of Berkshire* [128] for use as a guidebook
and, with his brother Robert,[129] had embarked on a three-
day wagon tour through southern Berkshire. Thereafter, he
never grew tired of taking long hikes into the hilly country
of the north or of admiring the autumn brilliance of the
foliage, and he was to fill his letters to Duyckinck and later
his stories with sensitive descriptions of the countryside. "It
has been a most glowing and Byzantine day—" he wrote to
Duyckinck that first fall, "the heavens reflecting the hues of
the October apples in the orchard—nay, the heavens themselves looking so ripe and ruddy, that it must be harvest-home
with the angels, and Charles' Wain be heaped high as Saddle-

127. Idem, Dec. 12, 1850, in Minnigerode, *Some Personal Letters,*
pp. 70–71.

128. It was in Chester Dewey's section on Berkshire Natural History
that Melville found inspiration for his short story *The Apple Tree
Table or Original Spiritual Manifestations.*

129. Robert was chairman of the Viewing Committee of the Berkshire
Agricultural Society, and Herman was later to be the ghost writer of
his report in the *Berkshire Culturist and Gazette.*

back with Autumn's sheaves. You should see the maples—
you should see the young perennial pines—the red blazings
of the one contrasting with the painted green of the others,
and the wide flushings of the autumn are harmonizing [both].
I tell you that sunrises and sunsets grow side by side in these
woods, and momentarily moult in the falling leaves." [130]
Three years later he was to christen the rounded hill two
miles southwest of Arrowhead October Mountain "on account of its bannered aspect in that month." [131]

But deep though Melville's attachment to Berkshire was
destined always to remain, his life among the hills hardly
touched *Moby Dick* at all. The hints of a rural existence were
later to reveal themselves at least superficially in *Pierre* and
more than superficially in many of his stories, but *Moby Dick*
had progressed beyond the reach of passive external influences before Melville reached his decision to settle in Pittsfield. As Hawthorne had brought with him to Lenox the
blueprint for *The House of the Seven Gables,* so Melville
had brought the skeleton of *Moby Dick,* and neither book
ever really belonged to Berkshire.[132] At Arrowhead he did
find a quietness and a regularity of routine highly favorable
for that delicate operation of "taking the book off his brain,"
but the even tenor of life in Berkshire—"The calm, the cool-

130. Melville to Duyckinck, Oct. 6, 1850, in Minnigerode, *Some Personal Letters,* pp. 68–69.

131. Melville, "Cock-A-Doodle-Doo!" *Complete Stories of Melville,*
p. 138.

132. Melville did owe one of his symbols to Berkshire, and that was
Ahab's scar—inspired almost beyond a doubt, by the great Pittsfield
elm. Cf. *Moby Dick* (Modern Library, New York, 1926), p. 121: "Thread-
ing its way out from among his gray hairs, and continuing straight
down on either side his face . . . you saw a slender . . . mark, lividly
whitish. It resembled that perpendicular seam sometimes made in the
straight, lofty trunk of a great tree, when the upper lightning tearingly
darts down it, and without wrenching a single twig, pulls and grooves
out the bark, from top to bottom, ere running off into the soil, leaving
the tree still greenly alive, but branded."

ness, the silent grass-growing mood in which a man *ought* always to compose" [133]—imparted no placid contentment to the feverish brain creating Captain Ahab. On the contrary, the book proceeded from a mind possessed; it was, as Melville said to Hawthorne, "broiled in hellfire."

Of those Berkshirites who read *Moby Dick,* many no doubt agreed with critics who pronounced it either incomprehensible or impossible. From Lenox, however—from the one man for whose opinion Melville really cared—came a letter of warm appreciation. "A sense of unspeakable security is in me at this moment," he wrote gratefully to Hawthorne, "on account of your having understood the book. . . . I would sit down and dine with you and all the Gods in old Rome's Pantheon." Had the meeting between Melville and Hawthorne in Berkshire never occurred, *Moby Dick* would probably have been a different and less powerful book. On the trips through the Berkshire hills and the long afternoons in the barn at Arrowhead, Melville had discovered in the author of *The Scarlet Letter* that "infinite fraternity of feeling" [134] which gave dignity to his own tumultuous uncertainties. Hawthorne's heart, Sophia once remarked, "opens the bosoms of men," and certainly a sympathetic audience—even a one-man audience, did much to encourage the creation of *Moby Dick.*

Once the inmates of the red cottage had left Berkshire behind, Melville turned to the only other creative inspiration he could readily discover. "My Dear Lady," he assured Sophia early in 1852, "I shall not again send you a bowl of salt water. The next chalice I shall commend, will be a rural bowl of milk." [135] The salt water had been dedicated to Hawthorne; the milk was to be dedicated to "Greylock's Most Excellent Majesty":

133. Hawthorne, *Hawthorne and His Wife,* p. 402.
134. Metcalf, *Herman Melville,* pp. 128–29.
135. To Sophia Hawthorne, Jan. 8, 1852, ibid., p. 131.

In old times authors were proud of the privilege of dedicating their works to Majesty. A right noble custom, which we of Berkshire must revive. For whether we will or no, Majesty is all around us here in Berkshire, sitting as in a grand Congress of Vienna of majestical hilltops, and eternally challenging our homage.

But since the majestic mountain, Greylock—my own more immediate sovereign lord and king—hath now, for innumerable ages, been that one grand dedicatee of the earliest rays of all the Berkshire mornings, I know not how his Imperial Purple Majesty (royal-born: Porphyrogenitus) will receive the dedication of my own poor solitary ray.

Nevertheless, forasmuch as I, dwelling with my loyal neighbors, the Maples and the Beeches, in the amphitheater over which his central majesty presides, have received his most bounteous and unstinted fertilization, it is but meet, that I here devoutly kneel, and render up my gratitude, whether, thereto, The Most Excellent Purple Majesty of Greylock, benignantly incline his hoary crown or no.

In its final conception *Pierre* proved to be not quite so "rural" a book as Melville might like to have thought it. The setting is in part Berkshire—intermixed with certain aspects of Lansingburgh, New York—but it is a Berkshire so romanticized and encumbered with unorthodox prose as scarcely to be recognizable. The Balanced Rock of Lanesboro is there, but it is there for symbolic and not at all for realistic effect. On one level it represents Melville striking out angrily at those people, not only in Berkshire but everywhere, who failed to understand his books—who, "in their hoodwinked unappreciativeness," saw this wondrous "Memnon Stone" as no Memnon Stone at all, but as "nothing but a huge stumbling block, deeply to be regretted as a vast prospective obstacle in the way of running a handy little cross-road through that wild part of the manor." [136] On a more philosophical level, it represents Melville's growing conviction of the precariousness of human life and sanity:

> Pierre had called it the Terror Stone. Few could be bribed to climb its giddy height, and crawl out upon its more hovering end. It seemed as if the dropping of one seed from the beak of the smallest flying bird would topple the immense mass over, crashing against the trees.
>
> It was a very familiar thing to Pierre; he had often climbed it, by placing long poles against it, and so creeping up to where it sloped in little crumbling stepping-places; or by climbing high up the neighboring beeches, and then lowering himself down upon the forehead-like summit by the elastic branches. But never had he been fearless enough—or rather foolhardy enough, it may be, —to crawl on the ground beneath the vacancy of the higher end; that spot first menaced by the Terror Stone should it ever really topple. [137]

*Pierre,* wrote one Boston reviewer, "might be supposed to emanate from a lunatic hospital rather than from the quiet retreats of Berkshire." [138] Most probably, however, those very "quiet retreats" had proved Melville's artistic undoing. Pittsfield society had apparently ceased to interest him, the novel-reading public had at best offered his masterpiece an indifferent reception, and Hawthorne had deserted Berkshire for good. With no one left except his "loyal neighbors the Maples and the Beeches," Melville was losing his perspective on himself and was exclaiming with the disillusioned Pierre: "This day I will forsake the censuses of men, and seek the

136. Melville, *Pierre, or The Ambiguities,* ed. R. Forsythe (New York, 1930), p. 148.
137. Ibid., p. 149.
138. Review in the Boston *Post,* July 1852, in Leyda, *1,* 456.

suffrages of the god-like population of the trees, which now seems to me a nobler race than man. Their high foliage shall drop heavenliness upon me; my feet in contact with their mighty roots, immortal vigor shall so steal into me." [139] His objectivity with regard to his own philosophy was gone; he could not recognize his own excesses; and living in a self-imposed spiritual solitude at Arrowhead, he had no one to tell him that he had gone too far.[140]

After *Pierre*, however, economic necessity forced Melville to write more reasonably, and he set himself doggedly to the task of composing short novels and stories which might please the undiscriminating public. In these, he often turned to daily life in Berkshire, perhaps for lack of any more acceptable inspiration, and he found there ample materials for both realism and symbolism. And if his outlook remained often morose and almost always negative, at least he was again writing about the familiar scenes and normal people that the reading public could readily accept. Among his Berkshire stories there was only a single exception—the morbid "Tartarus of Maids," in which he transmuted a winter trip to Carson's paper mill in Dalton into a darkly symbolic narrative. Borrowing a page from Poe and another from Hawthorne, he turned the mill into a dungeon of ghastly females and the quiet Housatonic into the weird Blood River.

Yet, for the most part, he contented himself either with embittered social commentary or half-humorous thrusts at

139. Melville, *Pierre*, p. 120.

140. In *Pierre*, Melville makes an interesting inversion of Edwardsean theology. Like Edwards, Melville was passionately concerned with finding absolute and eternal foundations, but unlike the theologian, Melville failed. Speaking from this tortured doubt rather than Edwards' faith, but agreeing with Edwards fully that the distance between earth and heaven was very great, and that man's ways were not God's ways, Melville proceeded to advise men (through the philosopher, Plotinus Plinlimmon) to scale down their conduct to the relative morality which will not lead them to destruction in this world.

the clergy, at times combined with highly descriptive scenic passages which were reminiscent of his earlier gay letters to Evert Duyckinck. On another level many of these stories—notably "Cock-A-Doodle-Doo!" "Poor Man's Pudding," and "The Lightning-Rod Man"—were personal expressions of his own determination to adopt an attitude of resignation to his disappointments and failures, to assure the triumph of cheerfulness over disillusionment, to cling to optimism. In "The Lightning-Rod Man," he was rejecting both the narrow Calvinism of which he heard so much in Berkshire—"the Deity will not of purpose, make war on man's earth"—and the fearful sense of defeatism which he saw threatening his own sanity: "I seized it; I snapped it; I dashed it; I trod it . . ." In that same year he had published "Poor Man's Pudding" and a year earlier "Cock-A-Doodle-Doo!"—two grimly realistic portrayals of the poor but courageous farmers he discovered in the countryside around him. The first of these went still farther and presented a savage satire on the complacent attitudes of such books as Catharine Sedgwick's *The Poor Rich Man and the Rich Poor Man.* "Of all the preposterous assumptions of humanity over humanity," he wrote angrily, "nothing exceeds most of the criticisms made on the habits of the poor by the well-housed, well-warmed, and well-fed." [141]

Two years later came "I and My Chimney" and "The Piazza" and with them further indication that Melville was regaining objectivity. "I and My Chimney" still suggested bitterness and resentment and "The Piazza," unhappy resignation (illusions and aspirations, he concluded, must neces-

---

141. Melville, "Poor Man's Pudding," *Complete Stories of Melville,* p. 177. In his copy of *The History of Berkshire County,* Melville entered a marginal note beside the author's reassurance that there was no danger of society's becoming impoverished by charitable efforts and Bible societies. "The danger," wrote Melville sardonically, "is not very imminent."

sarily collapse upon close scrutiny), but both gave unmistakable hints of a new humor and geniality. He could chuckle, not heartily perhaps but not mirthlessly either, at the doubts his family harbored as to his sanity and he could poke good-natured fun at the grimly tolerant spirit with which his Berkshire neighbors regarded any eccentric so foolhardy as to build a piazza on the north side of his house. He knew he had sound reasons, whether they chose to sympathize or not:

> Well, the south side. Apple-trees are there. Pleasant, of a balmy morning, in the month of May, to sit and see that orchard, white-budded, as for a bridal; and, in October, one green arsenal yard; such piles of ruddy shot. Very fine, I grant; but to the north is Charlemagne.
>
> The west side, look. An upland pasture, alleying away into a maple wood at top. Sweet, in opening spring, to trace upon the hill-side, otherwise gray and bare—to trace, I say, the oldest paths by their streaks of earliest green. Sweet, indeed, I can't deny; but, to the north is Charlemagne.
>
> So, Charlemagne, he carried it. It was not long after 1848; and, somehow, about that time, all round the world, these kings, they had the casting vote, and voted for themselves.[142]

"The Piazza" was, in fact, at least on this surface level, a superb prose idyll in praise of the Berkshire hills.

During the intervals between short stories in these early years of the 1850's, Melville had found time for *Israel Potter,* a novel neither so ambitious nor so original as *Pierre,* but "saner" and far more acceptable to the public. He adapted it, as he was to do with so many of his later and less imaginative works, from a known legend—in this case, from a short biography of a Revolutionary exile—and skillfully transferred

142. Melville, "The Piazza," *Complete Stories of Melville,* p. 439.

the scene of the hero's birthplace to Berkshire. Himself a spiritual exile in the world, Melville discovered in Potter a lonely figure toward whom he could feel a kind of embittered sympathy. Potter's Berkshire is the Berkshire hill country which Melville knew, altered only to agree with historical fact, but it is a countryside seen more often through old and disillusioned eyes and not with the wholehearted appreciativeness that Melville usually reserved for his hills. The final description indeed sounds rather like Hawthorne:

> Ere long, on the mountain side, he passed into an ancient natural wood, which seemed some way familiar, and midway in it, paused to contemplate a strange, moldy pile, resting at one end against a sturdy beech. Though wherever touched by his staff, however lightly, this pile would crumble, yet here and there, even in powder, it preserved the exact look, each irregularly defined line, of what it had originally been—namely, a half-cord of stout hemlock (one of the woods least affected by exposure to the air), in a foregoing generation chopped and stacked up on the spot, against sledging-time, but, as sometimes happens in such cases, by subsequent oversight, abandoned to oblivious decay—type now, as it stood there, of forever arrested intentions, and a long life still rotting in early mishap.[143]

Except for his two lengthy sea voyages and a series of unhappy lecture tours, Melville was to remain in Pittsfield until 1863, becoming increasingly ingrown with the passing years. The gay conversationalist and excursionist of 1850 and 1851 had disappeared, and in his place was a meditative hermit whom one Williams College student, Titus Coan, making a pilgrimage to Arrowhead, found somewhat disappointing:

> In vain I sought to hear of Typee and those Paradise islands, but he preferred to pour forth his philosophy

143. Melville, *Israel Potter,* p. 274.

and his theories of life. The shade of Aristotle arose like
a cold mist between myself and Fayaway. We have quite
enough of Greek philosophy at Williams College, and I
confess I was disappointed in this trend of the talk. But
what a talk it was! Melville is transformed from a Mar-
quesan to a gypsy student, the gypsy element still remaining strong in him. And this contradiction gives him
the air of one who has suffered from opposition, both
literary and social. With his liberal views he is apparently considered by the good people of Pittsfield as little
better than a cannibal or a "beach-comber." His attitude
seemed to me something like that of an Ishmael; but perhaps I judged hastily. I managed to draw him out very
freely on everything but the Marquesas Islands, and
when I left him he was in full tide of discourse on all
things sacred and profane. But he seems to put away the
objective side of life and to shut himself up in this cold
North as a cloistered thinker.[144]

During these later years in Berkshire, as Melville dissociated
himself from society, he retreated into a ceaseless pursuit of
those frustrating metaphysical reflections which brought no
final answers. Preoccupied by doubts and always searching
desperately for the certainties and absolutes which his spirit
demanded, he had eventually come to care little for companionship and nothing for public opinion. In 1856 Hawthorne
saw and talked to him for the last time and exhibited his customary sympathy and understanding:

Melville, as he always does, began to reason of Providence and futurity, and of everything that lies beyond
human ken, and informed me that he had "pretty much
made up his mind to be annihilated;" but still he does
not seem to rest in that anticipation; and, I think, will

144. Quoted in Raymond Weaver, *Herman Melville: Mariner and
Mystic* (New York, 1921), p. 351.

never rest until he gets hold of a definite belief. It is strange how he persists—and has persisted ever since I knew him, and probably long before—in wandering to and fro over these deserts, as dismal and monotonous as the sand hills amid which we were sitting. He can neither believe, nor be comfortable in his unbelief; and he is too honest and courageous not to try to do one or the other. If he were a religious man, he would be one of the most truly religious and reverential; he has a very high and noble nature, and better worth immortality than most of us.[145]

In October of 1863 Melville sold Arrowhead to his brother Allan and went back once more to New York City. He was, in his own words, returning to "my native town, after a twelve years' visit in Berkshire." [146] In that same year, Catharine Sedgwick left her native Berkshire for good and journeyed down the Hudson to New York to live out the remaining four years of a long and productive lifetime; and the 1860's thus saw Berkshire's existence as a meaningful cultural unit dissolving. The Berkshire Medical Institution expired; a wealthy summer resident from New York endowed the Lenox Library; a Gothic edifice replaced the old Bulfinch church; and the century-old Pittsfield elm, symbol of Berkshire tradition, was cut down. No longer a state of mind, Berkshire had become by the end of the decade merely a geographical location.

145. Leyda, 2, 529.
146. Melville to Miss Sophie Van Matre, Dec. 16, 1863, ibid., p. 664.

# SOURCES

ANY HISTORIAN who has chosen to concentrate his researches on a circumscribed region must concede a certain validity to Emerson's offhand definition of genius as "the ability to generalize from a single instance." All too often, the writer of local history will find himself obliged to depend entirely on single bits of revealing information—momentary insights recorded either in family diaries, letters, and memoirs or, less frequently, in newspapers or formal histories. Yet if he indulges his generalizing instinct too far, if he fails to approach his minimal evidences with some spirit of finesse, he may produce conclusions which amount to little more than opinionated essays. In view of the inevitable gaps he will encounter in the evidence, he would seem well advised not to reach for conclusions which lie, in fact, beyond the end of the rather short tether allowed him by his materials. The special solidity of local history—its peculiar verisimilitude as compared to the higher level of generalization noticeable in national histories—depends upon restraint.

If, however, the local historian must exercise restraint in theorizing, he must certainly set himself no limit in his survey of available source materials. Even though hours of research may produce only a single usable insight, thoroughness is essential; and it is this fact which makes his final task of compiling a bibliographical essay so difficult. He may well have found fragments of useful information in a tremendous number of sources, yet space permits him to mention only a fraction of them. He must, therefore, decide at the outset which can best be omitted and must then try to impose some sort of order on the remaining materials, however overlapping or divergent they may be.

Perhaps the local historian as bibliographer will do best to distinguish, as does Charles Beard, between history as record (the documents a society leaves behind it) and history as it is written by the historian trying to reconstruct the past. With specific reference to Berkshire in the years between 1761 and 1861, certain sources in each of these historical categories will cast light on many different phases of the county's growth. Others will be pertinent to only one or two particular aspects.

In an over-all survey of the primary materials for Berkshire history (history as record), the Sedgwick Papers stand pre-eminent in both quantity and quality. They include not only several thousand manuscript items in the Massachusetts Historical Society, but also two published volumes of inestimable value: *The Life and Letters of Catharine M. Sedgwick,* ed. Mary E. Dewey, New York, 1871; and *Letters of Charles Sedgwick,* no editor, New York, 1863. Because all history must depend finally on available records, Berkshire history will probably always be written with a more predominant Sedgwick tint than would be entirely justified by its history as actuality. The flavor of any historical study must necessarily be partially dictated by those people of the past who— motivated partly by vanity and partly by their fear of time and mortality (or perhaps some intimation of sainthood)— felt prompted to save every relic.

Of all Berkshire families, the Sedgwicks had this instinct for conservation best developed. Indeed, their manuscript papers are reminiscent of the two boxes of string in a New England attic, one marked "string—save" and the other marked "string—too short to save." Letters written by Catharine at the age of twelve, countless executions by Theodore Sedgwick against debtors (helping to explain his having been one of the most hated targets of Shays' men in 1787), detailed specifications drawn up for the builder of the family mansion in Stockbridge, letters from Congressman Sedgwick to his wife, letters received by Charles from William Cullen Bryant —the Sedgwicks saved everything.

The papers, both manuscript and printed, convey a living sense of the physical, economic, and social changes going on in Berkshire: the final achievement of safety from the Indians in the 1760's; the latent radicalism of the American Revolution; the emigrations to the west of the 1790's. Until the old Judge's death in 1813, the papers concentrate on legal and political affairs. Thereafter, the subject matter diverges in accordance with the varied interests of the second generation —Theodore, Jr., commenting largely on agriculture and economics; Charles throwing some light on legal matters of his day, and Catharine voluminously concerned about religion, education, and literature. Because Catharine was a Unitarian and hence something of an "outsider" in religious affairs, her comments on religion provide a useful critical source on the subject of Berkshire orthodoxy. Because she was Horace Mann's most faithful Berkshire ally, her papers provide real insight into the problems involved in trying to spearhead on the local level the movement for public-school reform. And because she was herself a novelist, her critical judgments on men and movements in the arts are numerous and occasionally quite perceptive.

Other than the Sedgwick materials, the most useful sources for Berkshire history are probably the various newspapers published in the county. Although they are less helpful than one might at first have hoped and do not provide answers to many specific questions, they do create a general sense of the tenor of Berkshire life. Of some thirty newspapers published at one time or another before the Civil War, four are of particular interest: the Pittsfield *Sun* (complete file, 1800–1906, at the Berkshire Athenaeum); the *Western Star,* later *Massachusetts Eagle* (most nearly complete file at the American Antiquarian Society); the Great Barrington *Berkshire Courier* (best file at the Great Barrington Public Library); and the North Adams *Weekly Transcript* (best file at the North Adams Public Library). In all of these publications the editorials, letters to the editor, and advertisements reflect a number of Berkshire phenomena: the evolution of the area from an agricultural hinterland into a reasonably diversified economy; the impact of the railroad and of the Irish immigration in the 1840's; and the color and heat of the various political campaigns.

Aside from local and national politics, however, many of the real issues and interests of Berkshirites failed to reach the newspaper page. The age was disappointingly reticent, and by and large all the newspapers must be open to criticism from the local historian's point of view for their neglect of nonpolitical matters. The *Western Star,* for example, offers editorial advice to Washington with regard to the Jay Treaty but makes no mention of the current local debate on school appropriations. And the Pittsfield *Sun* goes to some lengths in describing Napoleon's relations with his marshals and yet neglects entirely the scandalous accusations of intemperance leveled by the Reverend Ephraim Swift against the Stockbridge pastor Dr. Stephen West and his wife. Editors apparently hesitated to waste newsprint on items of information already widely known by word of mouth. Even in the second quarter of the nineteenth century, when the four major newspapers were beginning to assign an increasing amount of space to local news, such news is too often a mere chronicle recorded without comment and must be used in conjunction with other sources before it becomes meaningful.

Only slightly less important than the newspapers as a general source for Berkshire cultural life is David Dudley Field's *A History of the County of Berkshire, Massachusetts,* Pittsfield, 1829. The first and more valuable of the two parts into which the work is divided amounts to a survey history of the county. Written by the Berkshire educator and scientist Chester Dewey, it treats such topics as geography, flora and fauna, education, and religion and is highly revealing as to the light in which an intelligent member of the orthodox church viewed county affairs in 1828. The second part of the work simply supplies a brief historical sketch of each Berkshire town written by the local pastor and characterized by a maximum of facts and a minimum of interpretation.

Especially helpful also among the primary sources for Berkshire history are the records of Mark Hopkins and his family, the manuscript portions of which are on deposit at the Williams College Library and the Massachusetts Historical Society. Among the printed volumes, those most deserving of mention are *Early Letters of Mark Hopkins,* ed. Susan Hopkins, New York, 1929; Mark Hopkins, *Miscellaneous Essays and Discourses,* Boston, 1847; and *Lectures on the Evidences of Christianity before the Lowell Institute, January, 1844,* Boston, 1846. Both the *Early Letters* and the *Miscellaneous Essays* are particularly notable for their illumination of education and religion in Berkshire. Indeed the letters supply the best single first-hand account to be found anywhere of a poor boy's struggle for an education in the county. And the essays have an added significance in that they contain at points a superb expression of Berkshire's dominant provincial feeling.

Finally, a considerable group of books exists which provides brief but penetrating comments on the Berkshire scene as a whole: Timothy Dwight, *Travels in New-England and New-York,* 4 vols. New Haven, 1821–22; Rochefoucault-Liancourt, *Travels through the United States . . . ,* 2 vols. London, 1799; Frances Anne Kemble, *Records of Later Life,* London, 1882; Henry Ward Beecher, *Star Papers,* New York, 1855; J. E. A. Smith, *Taghconic, by Godfrey Greylock,* Boston, 1852.

Among the many available manuscripts and printed works dealing with particular aspects of Berkshire's cultural development, those concerned with religious affairs are decidedly the most numerous. The church records of most Berkshire towns have been compiled into several typescript volumes by Rollin H. Cooke, all of which are on file in the Berkshire Athenaeum, and in them the researcher can find both detailed accounts of religious revivals and extensive information on cases of church discipline. For sketches of orthodox clergymen, three books are outstandingly good: *Memoirs of the Rev. Alvan Hyde,* Boston, 1835; Alvan Hyde's *Sketches of the Life, Ministry, and Writings of the Reverend Stephen West,* Stockbridge, 1819; and Stephen West's *Sketches of the Life of the Late Reverend Samuel Hopkins,* Hartford, 1805. Indispensable for gaining an over-all picture of the Berkshire Congregational churches are the *Proceedings at the Centennial Commemoration of the Organization of the Berkshire Association,* Boston, 1864; and for providing expressions of the orthodox doctrines there are the sermons of Stephen West, Thomas Allen, and Jacob Catlin at the American Antiquarian Society.

In a list of existing critiques of Berkshire orthodoxy by the Baptists, none can quite compare with *The Writings of the Late Elder John Leland,* ed. L. F. Greene, New York, 1845. Hard-bitten and witty, the volume gives effective expression to that grass roots resentment of the wealthy, respectable Congregational Church which was felt by the poor and often embittered hill-town Baptists. A second outspoken critic from this same minority was Clark Rogers in *The Husbandman's Aim to Confute the Clergy,* New London, 1801. One of the best Unitarian critiques of orthodoxy is contained in the *Autobiography and Letters of Orville Dewey,* ed. Mary E. Dewey, Boston, 1883. Finally, in tracing the trend of orthodoxy away from doctrine to activism the best sources are Heman Humphrey's *On Doing Good to the Poor,* Pittsfield, 1818; and John Todd's *Hints to Young Men,* Pittsfield, 1843.

On the subject of educational institutions, a number of useful manuscript collections exist, including the Bernhard Hoffman Collection (the manuscript records of the Stockbridge Public Library, which are now on file at the New York Public Library); the Ballard Collection at the Berkshire Athenaeum (largely concerned with the Berkshire Academies); and the Jonathan Tenney Papers at the American Antiquarian Society (containing a commentary on the Pittsfield High School in its early years). For understanding the status of the primary schools, Ezekiel Bacon's *Recollections of Fifty Years Since* (Utica, 1843) can hardly be equaled, and for a knowledge of the aims and accomplishments of the Berkshire Agricultural Society, no researcher can afford to ignore either Elkanah Watson's *History of the Rise, Progress, and Existing Condition of Modern Agricultural Societies on the Berkshire System* (Albany, 1820) or the annual presidential addresses delivered at the Berkshire Cattle Fairs (the best collection of which are on file at the American Antiquarian Society).

Among the sources for legal affairs, the Court Records are far and away the most voluminous. Both Probate Court records and those for the Court of Common Pleas remain on file in the Berkshire County Court House in Pittsfield, but they are too numerous to be dealt with extensively without the use of statistical methods. An occasional glimpse behind the façade of the law courts can be found in the Taft Collection of the Massachusetts Historical Society, the Dwight Collection (now in the possession of Mr. Henry W. Dwight of Stockbridge), and the Rockwell Collection at the New-York Historical Society. Other than these, no legal sources seem to merit special attention with the significant exception of William Jarvis' *The Republican,* Pittsfield, 1820. As a Pittsfield lawyer, Jarvis' views on the proper position of government *vis-a-vis* the judiciary are of particular interest, as well as his definition of government's role in such other areas as education and economic life.

In considering, finally, the primary sources having to do specifically with Berkshire's literary flowering, perhaps creative works of fiction and poetry should be mentioned first. Those actually written in and inspired by Berkshire would include Catharine Sedgwick's *A New England Tale,* New York, 1822; and *Redwood,* New York, 1824; most of Byrant's poems composed between 1817 and 1825; H. W. Longfellow's *Kavanagh,* Boston, 1849; Oliver Wendell Holmes' *Elsie Venner* (Boston, 1865) and four or five of his poems; Herman Melville's *The Piazza Tales,* New York, 1856; and David Hitchcock's *The Shade of Plato,* Hudson, 1805; *Poetical Dictionary,* Lenox, 1808; and *The Social Monitor,* Stockbridge, 1812.

More enlightening than these works, however, in studying the Berkshire area are the letters and diaries which emanated from the literary circle. A considerable list of such often invaluable source materials can readily be compiled: letters exchanged by Melville and Evert Duyckinck (the Duyckinck Collection, New York Public Library); Hawthorne's *American Notebook,* ed. Randall Stewart, New Haven, Yale Press, 1932; Julian Hawthorne's *Nathaniel Hawthorne and his Wife,* 2 vols. Boston, 1885; Samuel Gray Ward's *Ward Family Papers,* Boston, 1900; the Samuel Gray Ward Collection at the Harvard Library; and the Thomas Wren Ward Papers at the Massachusetts Historical Society. A more general treatment of Berkshire's literary society is to be found in such books as Maunsell B. Field's *Memories of Many Men and Some Women,* New York, 1874; John T. Morse's *Life and Letters of Oliver Wendell Holmes,* 2 vols. Boston, 1896; Samuel Longfellow's *Life of Henry Wadsworth Longfellow,* 2 vols. Boston, 1886; and Parke Godwin's *Life of William Cullen Bryant,* 2 vols. New York, 1883.

In turning to secondary works of general interest for a study of Berkshire County, the researcher will discover not only a variety of histories ranging in subject matter from a single town to all of western Massachusetts but also several guidebooks and gazeteers and a few works which combine history with nature study. By all odds the most useful of the town histories is Joseph E. A. Smith's *History of Pittsfield*, 2 vols. Boston, 1869–76—a work which stands as convincing proof that catholicity of material need not preclude a coherent narrative and that local history need not be so parochial as to ignore the main stream. Several other town histories are also helpful, although all of them are far more sharply limited in their range than is Smith's Pittsfield study and provide no such comprehensive view of the county as a whole. A selective list should include Electa F. Jones, *Stockbridge, Past and Present*, Springfield, 1854; Sarah C. Sedgwick and Christina Marquand, *Stockbridge 1739–1939: A Chronicle*, Great Barrington, 1939; Charles J. Taylor, *A History of Great Barrington, Massachusetts*, Great Barrington, 1882; Arthur L. Perry, *Williamstown and Williams College*, Norwood, Mass., 1899; C. M. and Alexander Hyde, *Lee, A Centennial and a Century*, Springfield, 1878; DeWitt R. Mallory, *Lenox and the Berkshire Highlands*, New York, 1902; and Charles J. Palmer, *History of Lenox and Richmond*, Pittsfield, 1904.

Of the more general county histories, Josiah G. Holland's *History of Western Massachusetts* (2 vols. Springfield, 1855) would certainly rank as the best. Written by a Springfield newspaperman and minor poet and novelist, the work excels particularly in its treatment of railroads, schools, and newspapers and in the historical sketches of individual towns. It is, however, strangely silent on the subject of literary Berkshire. A second general history of the county also deserves mention if only for its sheer magnitude. The *History of Berkshire County, Massachusetts*, edited by J. E. A. Smith and published by the J. B. Beers Company (2 vols. New York, 1885), although notable for its survey of the legal and medical professions in Berkshire, fails for the most part to offer anything more than an uninspired rewriting of earlier histories.

With its many full-page pictures of leading citizens (very likely the highest-paying patrons of the J. B. Beers historical project), the work typifies certain late nineteenth-century county histories in which business combines with the pleasure of self-advertisement to eliminate that disinterested intellectual curiosity so essential to good historical writing.

Among guidebooks and gazetteers, the best of the nineteenth century are Hamilton Child's *Gazeteer of Berkshire County 1725–1885,* Syracuse, 1885—an especially useful source for statistics on economic growth; John Hayward's *Gazetteer of Massachusetts,* Boston, 1849; and *A New Book of Berkshire,* ed. Clark Bryan, Springfield, 1890. None of these, however, compares in over-all relevance to a twentieth-century guidebook entitled *The Berkshire Hills* (New York, Funk & Wagnalls, 1939), written under the auspices of the Federal Writers Project of the WPA. Symptomatic of the burst of regional enthusiasm then becoming apparent, the book emphasizes points of scenic and historic interest as they might be encountered in a looping automobile trip of Berkshire towns and achieves a pervasive sense of regional color by including here and there an anecdote or a brief character sketch. Yet in spite of its general accuracy, its effectiveness is somewhat marred by a certain overdrawn folksiness—probably the result of the city dwellers' slightly condescending, slightly nostalgic conception of rural life.

By the 1940's the interest in regional studies had become marked. Roderick Peattie edited a book of essays entitled *The Berkshires* (New York, 1948) in which he included a number of discussions of plant and animal life in western Massachusetts and also the best short essay on Berkshire history yet to be printed (the work of Walter Pritchard Eaton). And in the same decade, Chard Powers Smith published *The Housatonic* (New York, 1946), a highly readable volume tracing the history of all the major towns on the Housatonic River. Smith's book is an eloquent lament for the decline of

Puritanism. The new values of an acquisitive society are, he feels, a poor substitute for the nobility of the old single-mindedness. He ends by presenting an extreme statement of the twentieth-century's re-estimation of Puritanism—perhaps a needed corrective to the rather narrow critique provided by Brooks Adams, James Truslow Adams, and Parrington et al. As a result, the book becomes not so much a critical study as a contribution to that powerful mythology of the "New England character."

Two recent books of formal history remain to be mentioned, both of them dealing with Berkshire in the Revolutionary period. Robert J. Taylor's *Western Massachusetts in the Revolution* (Providence, Brown University Press, 1954) is outstanding for its thorough research and clear writing and includes an especially interesting chapter on the legal system. Both this chapter and certain other chapters in his book confirm the idea that the Revolutionary years witnessed an internal social revolution of considerable proportions. (The other side of the case is argued—less convincingly, I think—by Robert Brown in his *Middle-Class Democracy and the Revotion in Massachusetts, 1691–1780,* Ithaca, Cornell University Press, 1955. A less detailed account of a slightly larger area is contained in Lee N. Newcomer's *The Embattled Farmers,* New York, Columbia University Press, 1953. Like Taylor, Newcomer buttresses his political narrative with social and economic history and asks the kind of questions which suggest the influence of James Franklin Jameson's *The American Revolution Considered as a Social Movement.*

Of the numerous volumes which supply detailed data or general background information on just one or two areas of Berkshire culture, only a fraction can be discussed here. Three books dealing with the changing theological structure of New England come to mind immediately as essential to an understanding of Berkshire's neo-Calvinism: Frank H. Foster, *A Genetic History of the New England Theology,* Chicago, 1907; Herbert W. Schneider, *The Puritan Mind,* New York, 1930; and Joseph Haroutunian, *Piety versus Moralism: The Passing of the New England Theology,* New York, 1932. Three other books concerned with related matters of church and state are also of significant value: Jacob C. Meyer, *Church and State in Massachusetts 1740–1833,* Cleveland, 1930; Anson Phelps Stokes, *Church and State in the United States,* 3 vols. New York, Harpers, 1950; and Edward Buck, *Massachusetts Ecclesiastical Law,* Boston, 1866. And finally with reference to Berkshire's religious history, Joseph S. Clarke's survey of the relative strength of the Unitarians and the orthodox in *A Historical Sketch of the Congregational Churches in Massachusetts from 1620 to 1858* (Boston, 1858) is quite helpful.

In the area of Berkshire educational institutions, Williams College has received by far the best historical coverage. In his *Mark Hopkins and the Log* (New Haven, Yale University Press, 1956), Frederick Rudolph has written an excellent study both of the college and of Hopkins' ideas, and his awareness of the problem of intellect and character in education is commendable even though he may at times view them too exclusively in an opposing relationship. An adequate survey of the college from its beginning is to be found in Leverett W. Spring's *History of Williams College,* Boston, 1917.

For a general knowledge of nineteenth-century primary and secondary education, the well-known books by Dexter and by Butts and Cremin are useful, but on Berkshire's particular problems of public education the only worthwhile work is Joseph E. A. Smith's *The Public School System of the Town of Pittsfield 1761–1880,* Pittsfield, 1880. Unfortunately, competent historical treatment is also lacking on the subject of rural newspapers, and even the bench and bar have received very little historical attention. The two published articles by Frank Grinnell come at once to mind as relevant to legal developments in Berkshire: one "The Constitutional History of the Supreme Judicial Court of Massachusetts from the Revolution to 1813," *Massachusetts Law Quarterly*, 2 (1917), 359–550; the other "The Influence of Thomas Allen and the 'Berkshire Constitutionalists' on the Constitutional History of the United States," *American Bar Association Journal*, 22 (1936), 168–74, 210–11.

A listing of secondary works pertinent to Berkshire's literary world would include the standard works on American literary history as well as a number of articles having to do with Berkshire's literary society. Among the latter, probably Henry D. Sedgwick's "Reminiscences of Literary Berkshire," *Century Magazine*, 26 (1895), 552–68, stands first in both accuracy and usefulness. Several sound insights are also to be found, however, in J. T. Cutler's "The Literary Associations of Berkshire," *New England Magazine*, new ser. 9 (1893), 3–22. Finally, added to these should be a long-defunct journal which is useful both in literary and in other areas— *Papers and Collections of the Berkshire Historical and Scientific Society*, 3 vols. Pittsfield, 1883–1900.

# INDEX

Academies, 116–32; subject to clerical influence, 119; textbooks, 123–4; Calvinism and moral science, 125; pre-eminent position of Lenox Academy, 15, 127–31. *See also* Hotchkin, John; Buckham, Mathew

Adams, John: letter to Berkshire Agricultural Society, 179; influence on Massachusetts Constitution of *1780*, 225

Allen, Phineas, 15, 171, 188–94; arrival in Berkshire, 188; master of political invective, 190

Allen, Thomas, 26, 43, 49, 353; leading Berkshire liberal, 7; at the Battle of Bennington, 57; cause of schism in the Pittsfield Church, 89–91; political authority in Berkshire in the Revolution, 222–25; report to the General Court, 223

Allen, William: records Berkshire economic growth, 32; succeeds father in Pittsfield Church, 91; poet of Berkshire Jubilee, 318–19; boasts of freedom in Berkshire, 321

American Home Mission Society, 67

American Revolution: effect on County administration, 1; a blow to aristocracy, 26, 214; interregnum in Berkshire, *1774–80*, 222–26

Andrews, Loring, 33, 51, 79, 106, 260; editor of the *Western Star*, 185–94

Arminianism, 4; opposed by Edwards and Hopkins, 43, 45–47, 64; compared with democracy, 191

Arrowhead, 363

Atlantic Cable, 340 n.

Bacon, Ezekiel, 15, 91; critic of common schools, 107; opposes Federalism at Williams College, 138

Bacon, John, 22, 26, 41; proponent of religious freedom, 88; on the Berkshire Bench, 236; critic of Judiciary Act of *1801*, 247–48; *Conjectures on Prophecies*, 282

Baptists, 22, 43, 50, 70, 81, 92

Baylies, William, 268

Beard, Charles, 381

Beaumont, Gustav de, 31, 301–2

Becket, Congregational Church Society of, 76–77

Beecher, Catherine, heads committee for "saving the country," 308

Beecher, Henry Ward, 11, 14, 164, 171; *Star Papers*, value of rural vacations, 350–52

Bellamy, Joseph, 44 n.

Bench and Bar, 214–47; aristocracy and the legal profession, 215–16; professional attorneys and pettifoggers, 216–17; intricacy of common law procedure, 218–19; Bar rules, 231–33; popular feeling against lawyers, 235; Berkshire Law Library, 163–64, 232–33; forced closing of courts, *1774*, 221–22; increasing complexity of cases, 233; trend to centralization of court system, 239

Berkshire Agricultural Society, 173 ff.; aims, 173; connection with Merino sheep, 174; as an information center, 175; annual fair, 175–76, 203,

Berkshire Agricultural Society (*cont.*) 270–71; premiums and finances, 178

Berkshire Association of Congregational Ministers, 53; evidence of presbyterianizing tendency, 54–56; declining power of, 62, 63 n., 65

Berkshire Constitutionalists, 222–25; aid from churches, 223; opposition to anarchy, 225

Berkshire County School Society, 108–10; first County Convention, 108

Berkshire Education Society, 69, 141

Berkshire Gymnasium, 15, 117

Berkshire Jubilee, 315–22; planning committees, 315; Mark Hopkins' sermon, 315–18; strengthening the New England myth, 317–20; essential conservatism of, 322

Berkshire Medical Institution, 15, 145–51; Boston opposition to charter of, 145–46; faculty, 146–47; relations to Massachusetts Medical Society, 148; first professorship of pathology, 149; financial problems of, 150–51

Berkshire provincialism, 6, 9, 12, 14; geographical basis of, vii, 1, 3, 19, 21; Berkshire Barrier, 2 f., 17; economic aspects, 26–28; in education, 113–14, 151; in local press, 208–11; in literature, 259, 313–14; the "second provincialism," 315–22

Berkshire Republican Library, 154–61; rules for usage, 157; auction of books at Lenox, 160

Berkshire Sabbath School Union, 69

Berkshire Society for Promoting Good Morals, 68

Bernard, Gov. Francis, 1, 135

Bidwell, Barnabas, 26, 154–55; description of reactions to Shays' Rebellion, 180

Bishop, Nathaniel, 236

Bradley, Jesse, excommunication of, 61–62

Bryant, William Cullen, 15, 128, 176, 246, 260, 265–81; first impressions of Berkshire, 266; critique of Great Barrington, 266–67; dislike of legal career, 267, 271–73; speech to Bible Society, 269; poem for Berkshire Fair, 270–71; *Green River*, 273; moral analogies in nature, 274; *Monument Mountain*, 275, 361; *An Indian Story*, 276; friendship with Catharine Sedgwick, 277–78; removal to New York City, 280–81

Buckham, Mathew, 120, 348

Bush, Samuel, 200

Butler, Luther, 354 n.

Calvinism, 2, 6, 12, 44; Berkshire isolated from rationalistic temper of Boston, 41, 42; Calvinistic ethic and farming, 42–44; Jonathan Edwards a true Calvinist, 46–47; degradation of Edwards' ideas by followers, 48–51; native critics, 49–52; and the law, 258; attacked by novelists in Berkshire: Catharine Sedgwick, 291–96; Longfellow, 339; Holmes, 343–45. *See also* Congregational Church; Religion

Camp, John, 63

Catlin, Jacob, 48; vulgarizer of Edwardsean theology, 49, 55, 61

Channing, Edward, 267

Channing, William Ellery, 51; approval of Catharine Sedgwick's books, 311

Chickering, Henry, 200, 203–5

Child, Lydia Maria, 307

Childs, Henry Halsey: spokesman for religious freedom, 75, 98; founder of Berkshire Medical Institution, 148–49

Childs, Timothy, 91; leader of opposition to courts in *1774*, 221

Civil War, vii; slavery question, 321–22

Collins, Daniel, 57

Colman, Benjamin, 36

Colt, James D., 231

Commissioners for Indian Affairs, 39, 43

Common School Controversy, 111–14, 127

Congregational Church: the orthodox tradition in theology, 38–49; ecclesiastical organization, 53–56; privileged position under the Massachusetts Constitution, 80–83; gradual decline of the parish system, 85–102. *See also* Calvinism; Berkshire Association; Religion

Congregational Missionary Society of Berkshire and Columbia, 66–67

Cook, R. S., originator of Berkshire Jubilee, 315

Cooper, James Fenimore, 300

Cooper, Thomas, 254

Connecticut, influences on Berkshire, 2, 21

Connecticut River Valley, 2, 17–22, 46

Court of Common Pleas: established, 214–15; Republican bias, 236; criticism of its ignorance of law, 237–39

Court of General Sessions, 214–15

Crane, Zenas, 30–31

Crown Point Campaign, 20

Curtis Hotel, 348

Cushing, J. D., 201

Dana, Richard Henry, 267–68, 272

Davidson, Donald, 261 n.

Dawes, Henry C.: editor of the Adams *Weekly Transcript,* 203; criticism of New York weeklies, 207–8; author of the Dawes Act, 208 n.

Dewey, Chester, 15, 18 n.; in revival

at Williams College, 64; head of Berkshire Gymnasium, 120, 122 n.; notes decline in quality of popular literature, 161

Dewey, Israel, 51 f.

Dewey, Orville, Lectures on Human Destiny, 71; appreciation of Sheffield library, 151; aids Berkshire Jubilee, 315

Dillingham, Nathan, 260

Dissenting sects: Baptists, 22, 43, 50, 70, 81, 92; Episcopalians, 50, 76, 78 f.; Methodists, 78; Quakers, 22; Unitarians, 5, 42, 52–53, 98; Roman Catholics, 25; Shakers, 50, 78, 81 n., 363

Dow, Lorenzo, 78

Drury, Nathan, donor of Drury Academy in Adams, 117

Durant, Will, viii, 17

Dutch fur traders, 17; corrupting Indians, 37

Duyckinck, Evert: notes on G. P. R. James, 346; arranges Monument Mountain party, 359; visit to Shakers, 363; friend of Melville, 367

Duyckinck, George, 363

Dwight, Henry, 140

Dwight, Joseph, 39, 215

Dwight, Timothy, 3, 5

Economic life, 20–32; population, 20–23; fertility of soil in intervales, 23–24; general prosperity and diversity of economic life, 24; emigration to the west, 25; revolutionary inflation and social structure, 27; Pittsfield a typical town, 28–31; small-scale manufacturing, 30–32

Education. PRIMARY: state requirements and Berkshire failings, 105–7; beginnings of reform, 106–9; Common School Controversy, 110–14. SECONDARY: pre-eminence of

Education *(continued)*
Sheffield, 115; the academy movement, 116–32. HIGHER: Williams College, 133 ff., similarity to Yale, 136–37; Federalism and Calvinism, 137–38; question of removal of the college, 139–41; study of science, 142–44. *See also* Dewey, Chester; Hopkins, Mark; Sedgwick, Catharine

Edwards, Jonathan, 4 f., 15; interest in founding of Stockbridge Mission, 35, 39–51; elements of his theology, 46–48; collected works popular at Williams College, 137 n. *See also* Calvinism

Edwards, Timothy, 29; founder of Berkshire Republican Library, 154

Emerson, Ralph Waldo, 171; praises Catharine Sedgwick, 300; notes the isolation of Berkshire, 326; definition of genius, 380. *See also* Ward, S. G.

Episcopal Church, 50, 76

Fairchild, Frances, 268

Federalism: relation to orthodox Congregational Church, 51, 84; support of parish system, 87; at Williams College, 138; in Berkshire press, 180–91. *See also* Sedgwick, Theodore; Andrews, Loring; Little, Woodbridge

Field, Cyrus W., 340 n.

Field, Rev. David Dudley, 18 n., 53, 359, 383

Field, David Dudley, Jr., 232, 255–57

Field, Maunsell B., 332, 346

Field, Stephen J., 232, 255–58; Calvinism and the Supreme Court, 257

Fisk, Mrs. John, 59

Fitch, Ebenezer, 137–38

Fort Massachusetts, 34

Franklin, Benjamin, 153

Geography of Berkshire, 2–4, 17, 20–24

Gladden, Washington, 350–51

Glezen, Levi, 120

Great Awakening, 45, 50

Great Barrington, Bryant's criticism of, 266–67

Greeley, Horace, 171, 207

Greene, Asa: as editor, 204, 210–11; as satirist, 259, 266; effect of his medical background, 285; attacks politics and rural pretensions, 286–88; defense of mechanic arts, 289

Guignebert, Charles, relation of rural living to ethics, 44

Hall, Basil, Americans are too busy, 262

Hastings, Thomas, composer of music for Bryant's ode, 176

Hawthorne, Julian, 354

Hawthorne, Nathaniel, 353–64; description of Berkshire scenery, 4, 14, 355; effect of seasons on literary labors, 357; visitors to the Red Cottage, 357–58; his shyness, 358; friendship with Melville, 360–64. *See also* Ward, S. G.; Melville, Herman

Hawthorne, Sophia: low cost of living in Berkshire, 353; estimate of Melville, 361

Haystack Meeting, 68

Headley, Joel T., 359–60

High schools, 132–34; problem of finances and public support, 132–33; Tenney's leadership at Pittsfield, 134

Hitchcock, David, 15, 51, 259–60, 263–65, 268; early poverty, 263; *The Shade of Plato*, 263–64; satire in *The Social Monitor*, 264–65; a writer of genuine rural character, 313–14

Hoadley, John F., 366

Hodget, Emanuel, 260; verse on Bryant, 269

Holbrook, Josiah, 166

Holland, Josiah G., 171; criticism of Asa Greene, 212; as historian, 388

Holmes, Oliver Wendell: description of rural virtue, 8; pride in Canoe Meadows, 323, 325, 340 ff.; seven summers in Pittsfield, 340; *The Ploughman,* 341; scientific experiments, 342; the Autocrat's Berkshire idyll, 343; *Elsie Venner* and the anti-Calvinist tradition, 343–45; discusses eastern religions with Melville, 366

Hoosac Mountain, 2

Hoosic River, 4

Hopkins, Mark, as prophet of Berkshire provincialism, 2, 6, 12, 316–21; enters Berkshire Association of Congregational Ministers, 62; theological views, 72–74; approval of religious freedom, 101; thoughts on secondary education and democracy, 131; lyceum lecturer, 171

Hopkins, Col. Mark, 56; as teacher of lawyers, 217

Hopkins, Samuel, 15, 34, 40 ff.; the Hopkinsian Theology, 44–47; nicknamed Old Benevolence, 47; troubles with Israel Dewey and the Episcopalians, 73–75

Hotchkin, John, 67; emphasizes classics at Lenox Academy, 120; founder of Lenox Library Association, 164; lyceum lecturer, 169–70

Housatonic River Valley, 2, 4, 17, 19, 21

Howe, Samuel, his law school at Northampton, 231

Hubbard, Henry, 109–10

Humphrey, Heman, 141, 165; as Pittsfield pastor, 91

Huntington, Joseph, defends Mrs. Fisk, 59–61

Hutchinson, Governor Thomas, 40

Hyde, Alvan, 61, 64, 65; typical orthodox cleric, 55–57; fears decline of parish system, 101

Hyde, Caleb, radical spokesman for religious freedom, 99

Irish immigrants, 5, 319

Jacksonian Democracy, 13, 314, 321

James, George P. R.: settles in Stockbridge, 345; methods of writing, 346–48; healthful effects of Berkshire, 348

Jarvis, William C., 7 f.; favors religious freedom, 99–101; opposed to removal of Williams College, 140; *The Republican,* discussion of role of judiciary, 248–49; answer to Jefferson's criticism, 250–51; his agrarian philosophy, 282–83

Jeffersonian party, 85, 137–38; relation to religion, 86. *See also* Allen, Thomas; Bacon, John; Leland, John; Politics

Jennings, Ebenezer, 260; danger of mixing politics and religion, 85

Judson, Ephraim, 41

Kemble, Frances Anne (Mrs. Pierce Butler), 164, 304–5, 324; describes Lenox in *1839,* 10, 12; poem for Lenox Academy commencement, 130; appreciation of Catharine Sedgwick, 305–6; relations with Charles Sumner, 330; gaiety and strong language, 331–32; love of rural folk, 333–34

Konkapot, Chief, 18, 36

Kossuth, Louis, 348

La Rochefoucauld-Liancourt, Duc Français de, 23–24

Laurel Hill Society, 11

Lee, Ann, 50, 78

Leland, John, 8, 43; opposition to religious activism, 70; favors religious freedom, 92 ff.; admiration for Jefferson, 94; dangers of mixing politics and religion, 96; critique of academies, 126; hatred of lawyers, 235; *An Elective Judiciary*, 251; as hymn-writer, 262; exponent of genuine local color, 313. *See also* Baptists

Lenox: as a literary shrine, 301; air of refinement, 303

Lenox Convention of *1786*, criticism of courts and government in, 227–28

Libraries: society organization, 153; first public libraries, 153–54; Berkshire Republican Library, 154–61; Lenox Library Association, 164–65; Charles Sedgwick Reading Room, 165; Pittsfield Library Association, 165

Litchfield Law School, 231

Literature, native Berkshire writers: anonymous newspaper writers, 193–95; Catharine Sedgwick, 291–314; William Cullen Bryant, 265–81; David Hitchcock, 263–65, 313; Asa Greene, 210–11, 286–88; John Leland, 262, 313; writers vacationing in Berkshire: S. G. Ward, 323–28; H. W. Longfellow, 336–69; O. W. Holmes, 340–45; G. P. R. James, 346–48; H. W. Beecher, 350–52; Hawthorne, 353–64; Melville, 364–79

Little, Woodbridge, leader of opposition to Thomas Allen, 89–91

Longfellow, Henry Wadsworth, 335, 364; vacation in Pittsfield, 324; inspired by the Appleton's clock, 336; soporific effect of Berkshire, 337; anti-Calvinism of *Kavanagh*, 338–39

Lyceums: at Berkshire Medical Institution, 167; advocated in Lenox

*Journal*, 167; lecture of Edwin Dwight on purpose, 168–69; Abolition Lecture of H. D. Sedgwick, 170–71

Mann, Horace: disgust with Berkshire Schools, 103; opposed to districting, 105–6; controversy with Edward Newton, 110–14, 127; attacks lyceums, 172

Martineau, Harriet, 304; argument over slavery with Catharine Sedgwick, 306–7

Massachusetts Association of Congregational Ministers, 54

Massachusetts Constitutional Convention of *1820*, 75

*Massachusetts Eagle* (Pittsfield): conservatism, 200; appeal to women, 201

Massachusetts General Court, 18, 20; establishment of Berkshire Court System, 214

Massachusetts Supreme Judicial Court, 82, 241–43

Mathews, Cornelius, 360

Melvill, Thomas, 5, 178; Melvill Hall, 340 n.

Melville, Herman, 14, 323; school teacher in Pittsfield, 109–10, 359 ff.; meets Hawthorne on Monument Mountain party, 360; society of the Morewoods, 365; his irreverence, 366; farm work, 368; appreciation of nature, 369–70; *Moby Dick*, 370–71; dedicates *Pierre* to Mt. Greylock, 372; symbolic use of Balanced Rock, 372–73; "Tartarus of Maids," 374; "Poor Man's Pudding," 375; "The Piazza," 375–76; *Israel Potter*, 377; visits Hawthorne in England, 378–79; return to New York City, 379

Methodists, 78

Mills, Samuel J., 68
Minot, William, 255
Mohican Indians, 17
Monson, Samuel, 63
Monument Mountain, 4, 11; Hawthorne's interest in, 355; literary party on, 359–61
Morewood, Mrs. John, 365, 367
Morse, Jedidiah, 67 n.
"Mountain gods," 21, 26

Nash, Thomas, 18
Neill, Henry, 71; as literary critic, 329
Neo-Calvinist orthodoxy, 2, 15, 44, 47, 50; compatability with farming, 42; expression in missionary endeavor, 66
New York, 10, 13, 14, 21, **223**
Newspapers: period of the rivalry of Pittsfield *Sun*, and Stockbridge *Western Star*, 180–97; proliferation of the press, 197–213; crusading journals, 198–99; newspapers as a vehicle of local spirit, 205–7
Newton, Edward A., 32, 111–14
Noble, Matthew, 18
North Adams Patriotic and Economical Society, 246–47

October Mountain, 4, 370
Orthodox clergy: unworldliness of, 42; unity and discipline of, 54–61

Palmer, William Pitt, estimate of Bryant, 270
Parish system, 75, 79–84; emergence of a poll parish in Pittsfield, 91
Parker, Simon, 82
Parkhurt, Charles, 350–51
Parsons, Joseph, 18
Parsons, Theophilus, 241, 242 n.
Pittsfield, economic life of, 28–31
Pittsfield Congregational Church, controversy over tax for new building, 77–79; schism in the parish, 15, 89–91
Pittsfield *Sun*, 7; founding, 182; circulation, 184; news gathering, 185; Republican bias, 188–89
Plunkett, Charles, 31, 166
Politics: Berkshire radicalism, 8–9; an essential purpose of early newspapers, 180–97; deleterious effect on religion, 82–84, 89–91; complicates legal affairs, 237–39, 243
Pomeroy, Lemuel, 117
Pomeroy, Theodore, 31

Quakers, **22**

Rathbun, Valentine, 78 f.
Raymond, Henry, 207
Regionalism, vii, 9
Religion, period of dominance, 15; peculiar significance in Berkshire, 33 f.; position in schools, 71, 112–14; impact on all areas of culture, 6, 33, 315–20. *See also* Calvinism; Dissenting sects
Revivals, 64–66
Rhode Island, 21 f.
Rogers, Clark, 51
Roman Catholic Church, 25
Rosseter, David, 67

Sabbath-breaking, 58
St. James' Church, 76
Scholfield, Arthur, 30–31
Sears, Edmund H., 162–63
Sedgwick, Catharine, 15, 16, 26, 52, 53, 161; ally of Horace Mann, 113–14; description of Shays' Rebellion, 226; love of domesticity, 259, 292; meets Bryant, 267; dedication of *Redwood*, 278; *New England Tale*, 291–96; leaves Congregational Church, 293; anti-Calvinist tone of her books, 297–98; *Redwood*, reviewed by Bryant, 299; Emerson's

Sedgwick, Catharine (*continued*)
    appreciation of her work, 300;
    turns to more romantic fiction, 304;
    opposition to building home for
    ex-convicts in Stockbridge, 308–9;
    returns to moralistic writing, 309–
    13; *Poor Rich Man*, 311; *Live and
    Let Live*, 312; refinement versus
    vulgarity, 313–14; her fundamental
    conservatism, 314; organic social
    life of the village, 316
Sedgwick, Charles, sublimity of liti-
    gation, 244–45; criticism of Bryant's
    farce, 278–79; defense of legal pro-
    fession, 280; a sponsor of Berkshire
    Jubilee, 315; befriends S. G. Ward,
    324; relations with Hawthorne, 358
Sedgwick, Mrs. Charles, runs a girls'
    school, 117, 170
Sedgwick, Henry D., 26, 52, 214;
    criticizes common law in *The Eng-
    lish Practice*, 252–54; aids Bryant,
    280–81
Sedgwick, Robert, friend of literary
    men, 280
Sedgwick, Theodore, 26, 51, 84; op-
    poses parish system, 79; large law
    library, 163; hatred of Berkshire
    radicals in Revolution, 224; efforts
    to improve Massachusetts Court
    System, 239–42
Sedgwick, Theodore, Jr., 152; descrip-
    tion of Berkshire Fair, 177; the
    democratic gentleman farmer,
    *Hints to My Countrymen Public
    and Private Economy*, 283–84
Sedgwick, Theodore, II: efforts at re-
    form of legal procedure, 255–57;
    speech at Berkshire Jubilee, 321
Sergeant, John, 35, 37; his theology,
    38; plans for educating Indians, 39,
    41
Shakers, 50, 78, 81 n.; visited by Mel-
    ville and Hawthorne, 363
Shays' Rebellion, 8, 105; reaction of

clergy to, 57–58, 180; opposition to
    taxes and courts, 226–28; suppres-
    sion of, 229, 235
Shepard, Samuel, 56, 64
Sigourney, Lydia H., 210
Skinner, Thompson, presiding justice,
    Court of Common Pleas, 236
Smith, Chard P., 389–90
Smith, Jonathan, speech for federal
    Constitution, 229–30
Smith, Joseph E. A., friend of Mel-
    ville, 366–67
Society for the Propagation of the
    Gospel, 38 n.
Sparks, Jared, 254
Spencer, Joshua, on national influ-
    ence of New England, 319–20
Stockbridge, remoteness of, 3; as a
    literary shrine, 301; Tocqueville's
    visit, 302
Stockbridge Indians, 38 f.
Stockbridge Mission, 4, 34, 35
Stoddard, Col. John, 37
Stoddard, Solomon, 46
Stone, Ethan, 236–37
Storrs, Roger, 180
Strong, John, 221
Sumner, Charles, 324; visits Berk-
    shire, 330–31

Taconic Mountains, 3
Taft, Henry W., as editor, 200; as
    clerk of courts, 243
Tanglewood, 354
Tappan, Mrs. Caroline, 353
Tenney, Jonathan, 133–34
Tocqueville, Alexis de, 31, 301–2
Todd, John, writer on religious edu-
    cation, 71; pastor and chairman of
    Pittsfield School Board, 132–33
Tories, 57, 224
Torrey, Nathan, 260; *Elegy on the
    Young Man . . .*, 261–62
Trollope, Mrs. Anthony, 33
Turner, Frederick Jackson, 4

Tyler, William, 147 n.
Tyringham: *frontispiece*, 20; church controversy, 86–87; in Shays' Rebellion, 180

Unitarianism, 5; latent in Berkshire, 52, 53 n.; favors parish system, 98

Van Schaack, Henry: leads attack on parish system in Pittsfield, 79–84; laments admission of Republicans to the Bar, 234

Wadsworth, Benjamin, 17
Walker, William, 67
Ward, Samuel Gray, 3, 164; passion for the land, 323–24; organizes farmers club, 325; vacations in Boston, 326; reflections on life of a Berkshire gentleman farmer, 326–28; influence of Margaret Fuller on, 327; "Essay on Criticism," 328–29; leader of Berkshire literary society, 330
Ware, Henry, suggests book topic for Catharine Sedgwick, 310
Washington Benevolent Society, 191
Watson, Elkanah, 5, 30; founding of Berkshire Agricultural Society, 173 ff.
Webster, Charles, 200
*Weekly Transcript* (Adams), editorial concern for railroads and temperance, 203–4
Werden, Peter, 22

West, Stephen, 15, 160; theological views, 40–51; acts as prosecutor in the Fisk Case, 59–61; recommends that clergy not preach politics, 84–85; accused of intemperance, 91
West Stockbridge Congregational Society, 80–81
Western Railroad, 3, 321
*Western Star* (Stockbridge), 30, 182 ff.; circulation, 184; news agents, 185; as center of Berkshire Federalism, 186; book publishing, 186; relationship of editor to Theodore Sedgwick, 187–88; use of space, 189 n.; rivalry with the *Sun*, 190–91; literature fastidious and homespun, 193–95
Westminster Catechism, 12, 33, 55 n.
Whigs, 57, 222 ff.
Williams, Ephraim, 37, 39
Williams, John C., 90
Williams, William, 18
Williams College, 133 ff; opposition of Harvard to the charter, 135; Ephraim Williams, the founder, 135–36; similarity to Yale, 136–37; Federalism of President Fitch, 137–38; debate over removal, 139–41; financial aid to students, 141; study of science, 142–44
Woodbridge, Timothy, 38

Yale College, 21, 136
Yeomans, John, 71, 101

# Date Due